Advance Praise for
The Suitcase

"Taussig-Boehner has meticulously sorted through a treasure trove of her late father's letters, photographs, diaries and other memorabilia and has produced, with Housman, a historically enlightening and literarily entertaining glimpse into the privileged community of European expats, businessmen, socialites and diplomats in pre-World War II and wartime Shanghai. A must read for anyone curious about some of the more subtle, less pronounced sources of present Sino-Western relations." — **Valdis O. Lumans**, Distinguished Professor Emeritus of History, University of South Carolina

"Combining historical research and constructive imagination, Taussig-Boehner and Housman have replicated from a suitcase full of paper ephemera the eventful life of a Czech adventurer. The central narrative takes the reader across the globe, from Prague to Shanghai to London and New York during the pivotal 1930s and 40s. An engrossing novelization of one man's remarkable life, *The Suitcase* offers a rewarding read." — **Dr. Tom Mack**, USC Distinguished Professor Emeritus, Author of *Circling the Savannah*

"This informative and entertaining true story, spanning two decades and several countries, is an exceptional read. Thorough research married with autobiographical findings in family archives immerse the reader in one man's struggles and successes during the turbulent 1930s and '40s." — **Dacre Stoker**, International Bestselling Author and Great Grandnephew of Bram Stoker, Author of *Dracula*

"*The Suitcase* is utterly compelling ... a superb intertwining of unflinching truth and informed imagination. Remarkably, it is a true story—with additional context and conjecture supplied from meticulous research. Focused primarily on China between the World Wars, this is a fascinating story told through an intriguingly personal perspective, during a time when the world came to terms with its conscience and changed its soul—along with that of one man: a Czech, a Jew, a father's son. This first-person experiential narrative goes clubbing in pre-WWII Shanghai, steps over the rubble of war-ravaged cities, is witness to Nazi death camps, fights lonely battles, and writes letters home. This is an authentic scrapbook of human history leading up to and through WWII—like it was never taught in any classroom." —**Marti Healy**, author of *Blinding the Moon, The Secret Child*, and others

"*The Suitcase* is an epic story with two focal points: the colorful and eventful life of Vladimir George Taussig, and the tumultuous events he lived through. Taussig comes unforgettably alive as a bon vivant and a dashing ladies' man who also exemplified an old-fashioned sense of duty and patriotism. The research that Deborah Taussig-Boehner and Lauren Housman have done is meticulous and exemplary: they have succeeded in bringing Vladimir Taussig to life on the page. The book reads like a novel. But at the same time it is an important historical work, charmingly recreating the sporting life of the wealthy expatriate community in Shanghai between the wars, and detailing the horrifying reality of life and death of the Jewish community in Nazi concentration camps, where members of Taussig's Czech family perished." —**Richard Tillinghast**, author of *Journeys into the Mind of the World: A Book of Places*

THE SUITCASE
THE LIFE AND TIMES OF CAPTAIN X

DEBORAH TAUSSIG-BOEHNER & LAUREN HOUSMAN

The Suitcase

By Deborah Taussig-Boehner and Lauren Housman

ISBN-13: 978-988-8769-58-2

© 2023 Deborah Taussig-Boehner and Lauren Housman

Photo credit: Chloe Giancola

Cover design: YuYu

BIOGRAPHY

EB151

All rights reserved. No part of this book may be reproduced in material form, by any means, whether graphic, electronic, mechanical or other, including photocopying or information storage, in whole or in part. May not be used to prepare other publications without written permission from the publisher except in the case of brief quotations embodied in critical articles or reviews. For information contact info@earnshawbooks.com

Published by Earnshaw Books Ltd. (Hong Kong)

Dedicated to courage, decency, honesty, and tolerance.

Authors' Note

THE SUITCASE is the life story of Vladimír George Taussig (1899-1966), also known as Captain X, among other pseudonyms. Taussig retained numerous letters, reports, memoirs, and other primary documents which influenced the narrative structure to form organically around his voice. Therefore, we have told his story in the first-person point of view, and believe that he would have written it in the same voice. The stories of his family members are written in third person because Vladimír did not personally witness their experiences.

Very little has been fabricated. The story has been meticulously reconstructed from physical evidence: hundreds of documents, dozens of letters, hundreds of photographs, scrapbooks, military reports, newspaper clippings, posters, tickets, matchbooks, programs, menus, itineraries, business cards, and more. All have been contextualized and verified with the use of other primary sources, which have also helped the authors discover and detail certain parts of the story. This work is not meant to be an academic thesis, but an accounting of one man's experiences that is as accurate as possible. We intentionally did not annotate the text, but the selected bibliography contains all major works that contributed to the facts presented.

Names, places, and events are real. Liberties have been taken with dialogue, within reason. Any scenes or conversations, while created for the flow of the story, are based on documented events and outcomes.

THE SUITCASE

We used British spellings because much of the story takes place in Shanghai and in Great Britain, where Taussig was surrounded by the British and their language.

Passages in quotations that are not part of a dialogue come from outside research. In these instances, the authors felt it more powerful not to paraphrase.

It was also important not to italicize foreign words in dialogue and exposition, as is traditional. This practice promotes the othering of non-English languages, when Vladimír lived, as we all do, in a very multi-national, multi-cultural world. He felt very strongly that a common humanity superseded any national, religious, or linguistic lines that mankind might have drawn in the past, and the authors agree.

We thank you for allowing us to share this slice of history, and this unique individual, with you. We feel that this is an important and timely work, and hope that our readers will see parallels and find meanings that resonate in many ways.

To view select contents of *The Suitcase*, visit www.readthesuitcase.com.

Deborah Taussig-Boehner and Lauren Housman, 2022

PREFACE
by Deborah Taussig-Boehner

WHEN I TURNED fifteen in February 1970, I received a dozen scarlet carnations, as I did every year, purchased by my mother in fulfilment of my father's request. However, this year was different, and my mother also handed me an envelope containing a letter written by my father, who had died four years earlier. The letter discussed his views on religion, character, and other worries that a father might have for his maturing daughter, and advice on the important facets of a good life. My sister, four years my junior, received the same letter on her own fifteenth birthday.

When he died, my father, Vladimír George Taussig, left a meagre estate, providing no financial security for my widowed mother who was just thirty-nine years old. There was no life insurance, nor money for a funeral, and besides, he didn't want one. He specifically stated in his will that he wanted no service nor mention of religion. His remains were donated to New York University's medical school. Though he died at home, my mother didn't allow my sister and me to see our father's body being removed. She was afraid our final memory of him would be of that lifeless state.

The man revealed by the possessions my father left behind were anything but lifeless. There were a few random items, including a collapsible opera hat, a set of brass knuckles, a wooden tennis racket, a pair of tall riding boots, a necktie embroidered with monkeys giving the middle finger, Danish cufflinks, a sterling silver cigarette case—and a suitcase. It contained an assortment of letters and written reports, matchbooks, scrapbooks, photo albums, loose photos, and a family tree dating back to the mid-1700s. It was the jumbled collection of a lifetime, and much of it was in Czech.

Eventually my sister and I grew up, moved away, married, and established our own families. Over the years, my father's suitcase traveled all over the eastern coast of the United States, harbored by whoever had space to store it.

Despite several attempts to understand its contents, including the translation of dozens of family letters into English in the 1970s, the suitcase sat largely unexplored for nearly fifty years.

In 2012, after my retirement, I was able to follow up on decades of curiosity. It was time for the suitcase to reveal its secrets. The stitching that held the suitcase's sides to the frame had deteriorated to dust. The suitcase could no longer hold its contents.

It took months to translate the remaining documents and organize the letters and photographs in chronological order. The contents of the suitcase revealed a life story spanning conflicts and continents, shaped by historic events, and filled with colorful people and fascinating situations.

Hazy childhood memories came into focus. I remembered my father singing "Land of Hope and Glory" when he tucked me into bed. Also, our 1964 trip to Madison Square Garden to view the Lipizzaner Stallions, where he admired the magnificent steeds while critiquing their riders' equitation. Then there was Betty Wragge, a radio actress who, as a child, I knew as "Aunt Bettywragge," along with "Aunt Eileen" Webster, and others who used to visit my parents. There was Dr. Kulka, the obstetrician who had delivered me and my sister. My mother always referred to him as an "old Jewish doctor," and there he was, captured in

PREFACE

a photo alongside my father as part of a Czech military group in Shanghai. There, too, was "Uncle" Frank Popper. I recalled him and his wife, "Aunt" Hedy, whom my father had taken me to visit in Montreal when I was four years old; I stayed in contact with them even after I was married.

I read all I could about the people and places influential in his life, and traveled to Europe and Asia, enlisting guides, researchers, and translators in the Czech Republic and China, England and the United States.

It was thrilling to converse with somebody who knew my father, or to find his name in other primary sources. As the contents of the suitcase were verified, months became years of researching, writing, and rewriting his story. I needed to tell the story that my father would have told, had he lived long enough. Thankfully, I met a talented young lady who shared my vision and my passion for research and who had just finished her master's degree in creative nonfiction. Our collaboration over eight years has produced *The Suitcase*.

My father's story is even more timely now, fifty-six years after his death, than anyone could have imagined. But then, there are many components to this story that no one could have imagined.

Deborah Taussig-Boehner, 2022

Prologue
Tuxedo Park, New York
June 1964

THE MOVERS are scheduled to arrive in the morning. The girls are with my in-laws. Joan is in the kitchen, packing. It is our final night in the Tuxedo Park apartment.

We moved to Tuxedo Park to escape the chaos of the Bronx. It is an idyllic setting, reminiscent of the sort of place in which I had been raised. The surroundings remind me of my home in Czechoslovakia.

Situated near the Ramapo Mountains, near the Sterling Forest and Harriman Park, Tuxedo Park was established as a utopian community in the late-1800s, when it became a luxurious retreat for elites to visit, and to hunt and fish. Its heyday was from the Gilded Age to the 'twenties. It is where the American "tuxedo" dinner jacket originated. It is the place from whence Emily Post's *Blue Book of Etiquette* emerged.

Tuxedo Park is one of the oldest gated communities in the United States. A massive stone gate and guard tower separate the citizens of the town of Tuxedo from the Blue-Blooded elite families that once resided in Tuxedo Park—men like J. P. Morgan, William Waldorf Astor, and Augustus Julliard. Such renowned and illustrious former inhabitants as these were another reason why I felt I would be at home in Tuxedo Park.

The ornate mansions inside the Park had been embellished by Italian artisans who were imported specifically to sculpt plaster,

PROLOGUE - TUXEDO PARK, NEW YORK - JUNE 1964

carve wood, and create stained glass and mosaic masterpieces. These immigrants then took up their own humble residences in the "Italian Village," located quite literally on the other side of the tracks. Those tracks, of the Erie Lackawanna commuter train, now carry Joan and me to our jobs in New York City each day. Joan is the executive secretary to a powerful attorney; I am a broker with Pickard & Company.

Since Tuxedo Park's zenith, some mansions have been carved into apartments, and it is in one of these apartments that Joan and I have made our home, thinking that Tuxedo Park would afford our girls the best opportunity to grow up free from the financial and social strife of the previous few decades.

Instead, my school-aged daughter faces the same sort of quarrels that I once experienced myself. Half a century ago, in what was then the Austro-Hungarian Empire, different nationalities, different religions, and different economic classes often clashed. Sadly, some things have not changed, and children are still latching on to one another's differences, and modelling their playground interactions on the ignorant and divisive rhetoric of their elders.

More times than I care to remember, my daughter returned home from school in tears because the other first-graders told her she didn't belong in public school and should be attending the private Tuxedo Park School, like others who lived in the gated community. Eventually, unkind words escalated to physical altercations. I realised that the environment in Tuxedo is no different than that which had caused so many complications in the world years before.

After four years in Tuxedo Park, four years of scrimping and saving, it is time to leave. In the morning, we will be moving to a split-level home in Blooming Grove, New York. Owning this home is "the American dream." At sixty-five years of age, it is the first house that I have ever owned, but it is also further away from the city, extending our daily commute.

I move through the apartment, inspecting each room to ensure all is in order, pausing to look at the stacked boxes that hold my girls' belongings. I have always worried about providing for my family, yet the contents of these boxes are proof that I have given them all of what they need, and some of what they want.

After ascending the stairs to our bedroom, I reach up to the top shelf of the closet, and my hand finds its target. My old suitcase. The leather handle is no longer attached to the case and I gently lift it to bring it downstairs. This, I am not trusting to the care of the moving company. I set it on the dining room table along with several other precious items that we will carry in our car.

In the light, I see how the once-fine leather veneer is dull and scratched. The cardboard beneath the leather is softened and frayed. I smile at the familiar logos of exotic hotels, and of the steamships that carried me to those locales. My initials, V. G. T., are printed in white in the middle of the case. I trace these letters with a reverent finger, then carefully pry open the snap locks that lost their spring action long ago. I open the suitcase. Stitched on the blue ticked lining of the lid is the label of the manufacturer, *Cathay Trunk Co. Shanghai, China.*

Inside are artefacts from my lives in Prague, in Shanghai, in New York City, and in London, with stops along the way.

A stack of letters, marked by postmen and censors on four continents, occupy most of one side. I remove a letter and read the words of my oldest friend, written two decades previously. One passage in particular draws my attention:

> *...If I were you, I should write your memoirs. After all, everybody does these days, and if you put little bits in dealing with your juicy experiences at Farren's, Casanova, and Ella's Bar, I am sure it would be a paying proposition...*

PROLOGUE - TUXEDO PARK, NEW YORK - JUNE 1964

I laugh. Anyone familiar with Shanghai would know what went on in the establishments my friend named. But the charismatic bachelor I had been when I met my friend on the voyage to Shanghai had changed. Age has smoothed me out, like a good whiskey.

If I were to write my memoir, it would be a story not of conquest, but of redemption.

One day, when I retire — if I can ever afford to retire — perhaps I will take my old friend's advice. The story is all there, in the suitcase, waiting to be pieced together.

I rifle lightly through the relics of my past, contents I have not examined in years, yet which I still knew like my own shoes — a Czech saying. Here are photographs of my conscription during the Great War, my mother's heart-wrenchingly familiar Czech script on fragile onionskin paper, my typewritten military reports from Shanghai during the Second Sino-Japanese and Second World wars, clippings from the society and sporting pages of the *North-China Daily News*, portraits of young starlets, theatre tickets, steamship tickets, posters from my speaking tour in England, the letter from my family's former housekeeper confirming my most horrible fears...

Yes, someday I should like to tell my life's story.

But not now. The movers are scheduled to arrive in the morning.

PART ONE

Estate Nový Berštejn, Dubá, Czechoslovakia
Thursday, 15 January 1931

> *Dobré jméno, nejlepší dědictví.*
> *[A good name is the best of all treasures.]*
> — Czech Proverb

My men stood in pairs and small groups, shuffling their feet and blowing steam in the cold morning air as I addressed them from horseback. "I should like to use this week's meeting time to give a speech," I said, shifting my gaze between the sub-managers and managers of the various farms and departments. "It has now been two years since my arrival at the estate. There have been many changes, and I thank you for your continued efforts. It takes time to steer a large ship towards a new horizon. It has only been possible for Nový Berštejn to reach these new waters owing to the expertise, and the patience, of the ship's crew."

I looked at the small crowd, locking eyes with a man here and there. I had come to value and respect the experience of these men who had dedicated their lives to the success of this estate. While they may have resented my relative youth when I first arrived at the age of twenty-nine, we soon established a mutually supportive relationship.

I resisted the urge to add a remark about the proverbial ship's captain, the owner of estate Nový Berštejn, Tomáš Maglič. The ship was not in good hands and, unbeknownst to its crew, the estate had been in some financial difficulty for at least the past year, often at the expense of my pay, and in spite of many profitable improvements I had made. I planned to confront Maglič, who happened to be my father-in-law, next time he showed his face.

I continued addressing the men: "When I arrived two years ago, there was no communication between departments. Since we have instituted these regular meetings, the estate has been more productive than ever. Communication is vital. No department stands alone here."

Under Maglič's management, the men never comingled with workers from other divisions. Few men had understood their role in the larger framework of the estate as a whole.

Nový Berštejn was a massive enterprise. It consisted of three agricultural farms, totalling 9,000 acres. These acres contained field products, vegetable gardens, fruit orchards and nurseries, and a cannery. We also raised dairy cows, meat cattle, pigs, and poultry, and bred Czech Warmblood horses. The estate owned 18,000 acres of forests. The forestry division practised pro-rationing cutting. One of the estate's three lakes was home to a sawmill. The additional 40 acres of lakes contained fish hatcheries for trout and carp. Nový Berštejn's brewery turned the estate's hops and barley into bottled lager. A brick works and small quarry were used for road improvements in the nearby town of Dubá.

"Because of your hard work," I continued, "every department is thriving. Take the small pond we have added at the edge of the sawmill. Below the water, we are growing edible fish, while up top we are using the water to transport lumber to the cutters. When the wood has been sawed, the shavings, once burned as waste, are now fuelling wood-burning generators. Gentlemen, we are using 'waste' to power the estate's brewery and farms, and, with the new high-tension wires," I gestured at nearby

ESTATE NOVÝ BERŠTEJN, DUBÁ, CZECHOSLOVAKIA
15 JANUARY 1931

posts and cables, "we are even supplying power to the town of Dubá." Owing to our success in the sawmill, I had been able to install two more American speed cutters and expand the lumber sales department.

"Let us consider the brewery. Two short years ago, we were selling our hops and barley to wholesalers, who then sold to exporters, who then sold to foreign breweries. Now we have established sales agencies in England and Switzerland and sell directly to breweries, at thirty- to fifty-percent more profit. Add to that, two short years ago, we were selling our milk to the big dairy industry firms. We have three hundred dairy cows and the latest pasteurizing equipment, but somehow we were not profitable. Our butterfat measurements never tallied with the big firms' figures, did they?"

The dairy industry paid the minimum price for milk containing a certain percentage of butterfat, and, for every half-percent of butterfat over and above the minimum, the combine had agreed to pay extra.

"The estate was the constant loser," I said. "Well, no more! Now we sell locally. I convinced the choicest establishments in the region that our milk is superior to any product they have used in the past." Once they began buying milk directly from the estate, I took the liberty of visiting the blacksmith and having butter moulds made that featured the big Prague hotels' and cafes' names: *Imperial Café, Palace Hotel, Café Slavia, Café Savoy.* How could they not buy our butter when they saw their business so cleverly promoted right there on the butter pat?

"Prague's best establishments began buying our whipping cream. So did patisserie bakeries. Delicatessens purchased the cheese we make from our skim milk. We obtained cooled lorries to ensure that we were conveying these products safely to the city," I said, gesturing towards Prague.

THE SUITCASE

"As we traveled into the city, we also delivered our poultry, fish, and vegetables," I continued.

All the products were sold at prices between thirty- and one hundred percent higher than we had once gotten from the cooperatives and big combines.

"Once the lorries were emptied, we collected kitchen waste from those high-end establishments, and mixed it with water to create swill for the piggery." All we had to do was return any cutlery we found in the waste, a simple enough task when the establishments' names were engraved. "That free swill enabled us to add four hundred mother pigs to our stock," I said.

Many of the men were smiling and nodding.

"As you are all aware, our region is famous for its poppy seeds, which retain their silver-blue hue even after being baked."

This was also met with agreement.

"Each year, we plant hundreds of acres of poppies and, in the past, we have had to burn the poppy seed shells to prevent the flowers from germinating amidst the other crops."

Men nodded.

"But no more. Now we sell the poppy seed shells to a pharmaceutical company, and we make almost as much from the shells as we do from the seeds themselves. We have now doubled the size of our poppy fields!"

I continued, "The estate has always sold the forest's undergrowth and protective trees as firewood. But, our head groom," I gestured to the man, "who was a coal miner in his youth, suggested that they could have value as timber supports in mine shafts. Now the coal mine has agreed to buy all of our undergrowth and malformed trees for the next five years, and they are paying prices close to what we see for commercial timber woods. The mine has even paid a year in advance," I said with a smile.

ESTATE NOVÝ BERŠTEJN, DUBÁ, CZECHOSLOVAKIA
15 JANUARY 1931

It was a shame—all of those improvements, and no profits to show for them.

"And finally," I said, "I think back to my first winter here, when we had the severe freeze. Our forest master told me about a large forest fire he had witnessed in his youth. After the fire had already begun, temperatures dropped below zero. Nurseries were in danger of suffering major losses—but not the trees in the path of the warm smoke. Those trees survived. Every tree outside of the smoke's path was frozen and ruined."

The forest master gave a nod.

"With his words in mind," I said, "we burned piles of wet straw continuously, all around the estate's orchards, didn't we?"

Men were smiling. Most all had played a role in the effort.

"Did we not save our fruit tree nurseries, and also many of our older trees? Other orchards in the area, who attempted to imitate our technique, undertook their efforts after the cold had already struck. They failed to save their trees. But not our estate," I said with pride. "All of the other orchards in the region suffered such heavy losses that, when spring came, the demand for saplings was so high, we were able to sell ours for five times the normal price. We have had so many successes, gentlemen," I said. "Especially in instances when we have turned waste into profit—the wood shavings, the restaurant scraps, the poppy seed shells, the forest undergrowth. Continue to listen to, and learn from, one another. Your roles, your successes, are all connected, as are your failures. If your department takes on too much water, the entire ship will sink."

I made eye contact with a few more men.

"I shall see you all at our next meeting. Thank you for your time, gentlemen." I turned my horse and trotted away.

As we crossed the frosty grass leading to the back entrance, I heard Tomáš Maglič's Škoda 422 rumbling in the front drive. So he had chosen to grace the estate with his presence. Good, now I would have a chance to speak with him. The muffled barking of my spaniels, Barry and Eda, came from inside the house and carried across the lawn.

In the harsh mid-morning winter sun, Nový Berštejn's plaster façade appeared muddy-yellow. Dormers peered like eyes from the roofline. A copper clock tower and cupola, blackened in some places and verdigris in others, extended the building by another storey. Even in the morning light, the clock tower looked ancient and sinister.

The estate dated back to the 1500s and had survived many important eras. In the early 1600s, the Bohemian Revolt led to the Thirty Years' War. During the Battle of White Mountain outside of Prague, Czech nobility were annihilated, and their lands and estates were handed to Catholic Germans. Estate Nový Berštejn was turned over to Albrecht von Wallenstein, Generalissimo of the Imperial Troops. When Wallenstein was murdered during the Thirty Years' War, the estate was awarded to one of his killers. The war ended in 1648. Bohemia became a German-ruled Catholic nation. For centuries, various owners had expanded the manor house and had made improvements. Maglič, having purchased the estate during the agrarian reforms that redistributed the lands after the Great War, had improved nothing, save the installation of a clay tennis court. His presence on the grounds only made the old manor house's atmosphere more oppressive.

Nový Berštejn was just like Maglič. What had once enticed me as a castle was, in actuality, a draughty manor house.

At the stables, I brushed my horse and gave him a carrot, then turned towards the house. I remembered my arrival at Nový Berštejn. I had come down the drive expecting to see lights glowing warmly in the windows and the servants lined up

ESTATE NOVÝ BERŠTEJN, DUBÁ, CZECHOSLOVAKIA
15 JANUARY 1931

outside to greet me. Instead, the house had been dark and cold, with no one to receive me, forcing me to carry my own luggage and build my own fire.

I sighed and walked to the house, opening the heavy iron gate that safeguarded the main door of thick walnut planks studded with wrought iron. At the far end of the hall, a similar door, but made of glass, was shielded by another gate. Nový Berštejn's windows were covered by iron bars, which once protected inhabitants from raiders.

I stepped over the stone threshold, tall enough to keep vermin out, and into the grand foyer. My spaniels greeted me with excitement. Their happy sounds echoed in the entrance hall's vaulted ceiling. "Ke mně," I said. Come.

It was cold inside. The thick plaster that kept the rooms cool in the summer also kept them cool in the winter, and, on an estate with hundreds of acres of trees, Maglič was sparing with lighting fires.

The entrance hall split the house into two wings. One held the formal dining room, parlour, kitchen, and servants' quarters; the other held the Maglič family's private apartments and rooms.

I hardly ever ventured into the reception wing. When I first arrived at the estate, I had envisioned holding parties in the enormous dining room. The long tables would be filled with acquaintances from Prague and beyond. A band would be hired for dancing; food would pour from the kitchen; drinks would flow. No such parties had ever materialised. I had actually only eaten in the dining room a handful of times. Everyone tended to take their meals in their quarters.

The main wing held a total of four private apartments as well as several single rooms, like Tomáš Maglič's office. I entered the wing with my spaniels in tow and stopped before Maglič's door. I could hear him inside. At my signal, Barry and Eda sat obediently. Then I opened the door, prepared to pat the snake with bare feet — a Czech saying.

I could see my breath in the chilly air between me and Maglič, who sat at his desk, looking down at his ledger. White smoke curled from a crystal ashtray where a dying cigarette lay half-smashed in the ashes.

"Taussig," he said, without looking up. "How long have we known one another?"

I paused and thought. "Twenty years, perhaps?" I said, as I began walking towards his desk. "Since before the war, when my sisters were in finishing school with your eldest daughters. Then you started doing business with my father ten or eleven years ago, when you bought the estate. Four years ago, when my parents designed their villa in Prague near your own, is when I suppose I really came to know you and your family." Maglič was writing something. "Why do you ask?"

"Then two years ago you agreed to move here and marry Ann and manage the estate."

"Yes," I said, stopping a short distance from him. "What are you getting at?"

"I am just sorting the facts out before I speak to my attorney this afternoon," Maglič said. "I plan to tell him how you have stolen from the estate's accounts."

I scoffed. "I have not stolen! I have simply taken portions of what I am owed." I took a step towards him. "Payments for my work as manager have been late. Beyond that, you have borrowed funds from me. Meanwhile, you have yet to fulfil the arrangements made in lieu of a dowry."

Instead of a wedding dowry and monthly support, like the 3,000 koruna allowance Ann's married sisters received, we had agreed that our "dowry" would consist of Maglič refurnishing our Nový Berštejn apartment, which ran the length of one

ESTATE NOVÝ BERŠTEJN, DUBÁ, CZECHOSLOVAKIA
15 JANUARY 1931

wing and featured a main hall with a large living space and six separate rooms. Our food and servants would be provided. Ann would have a small allowance for toiletries, seamstresses, trips to and from Prague, and other incidentals.

I continued, "Because my role at the estate involves collecting payments, I have been depositing a portion of those funds into my own accounts, to recoup some fragment of what I am truly owed. I actually came to ask how you are unable to pay me in spite of all of the improvements I have made. I have produced a profit, even during an economic depression. Beyond this, you are a manager at Škoda Auto. You have the sawmill in Litoměřice. Where is all of your money? Why borrow from me? I demand my regular pay, and my bonuses, and I deserve to have the arrangements of the dowry fulfilled."

Maglič gave a short laugh and continued busying himself with his ledger.

"When you hired me," I said, "you agreed to pay me 5,000 korunas monthly, plus ten percent of earnings from the farm business, plus five percent from the lumber business, and three percent from the estate's sawmill. You also promised me 30,000 korunas from the new sawmill in Litoměřice. And you also agreed to furnish the apartments Ann and I share. Nothing you have promised has come to fruition. And, though I enjoy working with the men, frankly, I have been searching for alternate employment."

I had only agreed to manage Nový Berštejn and marry Ann Magličová because no other options had presented themselves. I remained unable to find suitable employment—especially not anything with a salary anywhere near what Maglič was supposed to have been paying me.

"So you are stealing from me and searching for other work behind my back?"

THE SUITCASE

I took another step towards his desk. "I have done nothing wrong," I said. "Every transaction has been made in full view of your accountant and your bookkeeper."

"You have done nothing wrong?" Maglič asked, his eyebrows raised. Taking offense to his tone, one of my dogs gave a warning bark from the other side of the office door.

"I have worked tirelessly to make improvements. I know how profitable Nový Berštejn has become, yet you withhold the money I am rightfully owed. I should not need to remind you that I am not only the manager of this estate, but also your son-in-law and the future inheritor—"

"Future inheritor?" he interrupted. His voice was shrill with anger. "You have stolen from me!" he exclaimed. "You are lucky I have only notified my lawyer, and not the police. But, since you are not remorseful in the slightest, I suppose you leave me no choice." He reached for the telephone on his desk.

I took another step forward. "I have brought this estate back from several years of your neglectful management. You made the most minimal investments possible into this place and its equipment and employees. I have done more in two years than you could have done in twenty!"

Maglič scoffed. "All you do is ride around on your horse in the forest with your dogs and your gun, shooting rabbits and pheasants, and talking to the men and distracting them with tales from your latest trips to Prague, or wherever you go and spend your money."

I laughed heartily. "Is that what you think I do all day? Well, I suppose I shall loaf in the forest and talk to the men more often. It seems to be the recipe for success! Look, you hired me to manage. Let me manage! You discount my experience leading men and teaching in the Army; my studies at the business academy in Graz and at the Roudnická Central Economic School; my father's

ESTATE NOVÝ BERŠTEJN, DUBÁ, CZECHOSLOVAKIA
15 JANUARY 1931

position as the agricultural commissioner in Prague, my —"

He interrupted again: "I hired you because I thought the arrangement would be mutually beneficial, and because you took an interest in my daughter."

I laughed. I took an interest in plenty of peoples' daughters.

Maglič continued, "Now Ann is unhappy, spending days at a time in Prague, and you are stealing from me."

"Please stop saying that," I said calmly. "I have taken only some of what I am owed."

"And just what do you think I owe you, Taussig?" he asked, looking down at the ledger on his desk.

"Including my normal salary, the promised royalties from the new sawmill, and the promised bonuses from the various enterprises, you owe me 129,646.70 korunas." I had been keeping account, in preparation for this discussion.

He asked, "How long have you been funnelling money into your own account?"

"Since last January. It has been a year. And you are so uninvolved in the estate's affairs that you've not noticed."

Maglič gave an incredulous laugh. "Unbelievable. And all the while, living your expensive lifestyle using stolen funds."

"I do not have an expensive lifestyle. I live within the means of what I should rightfully be making. Furthermore, you are the one who is obsessed with seeming wealthy. You surely tricked my family into thinking you had means, when as it turns out, you cannot even afford to pay me. Expensive lifestyle?" I thought out loud. "Perhaps you refer to the one ski trip Ann and I have taken?"

We had visited the Krkonoše Mountains, staying in the skiing chalet Adolfova-Bouda at the Czecho-Polish border. She had also taken a trip, by herself, to visit Mariánské Lázně, a spa town not far from Karlovy Vary, but she had used the allowance provided

THE SUITCASE

by Maglič.

"If I had known ahead of time how miserable things are here, I never would have agreed to it. What a horrid business arrangement, to marry off your dutiful, underage daughter and trap a nineteen-year-old in this place." Even the wedding was a business agreement. Instead of a celebration, we had simply signed documents at the courthouse in Prague.

"A divorce could be arranged just as easily," Maglič sneered.

"Is Ann to have no say in the matter?" I asked.

"Why should she?" Maglič asked. "It is my fault I married her off to a thieving, lying man. Now I am going to get her out of it. But how, I wonder, will the marriage end without ruining her reputation?" he said.

"Ruined," I scoffed. While a divorce would carry some social stigma for Ann, I would not say any young woman's reputation could be "ruined" by divorce. It was the 1930s, not the 1800s!

"So, is that it? Is our little business arrangement really over? Ann and I will divorce? You will terminate my employment?"

"Well I certainly don't want a thief for a manager or for a son-in-law," Maglič said.

I rolled my eyes. "Well," I grinned, and prepared to let loose the ammunition I'd reserved for just such a moment, "then I suppose it is now safe for me to say that I know all about your mistresses, and those other bastard children of yours."

Maglič slammed his hand down onto the ledger and half-stood in his chair. "Choose your next words carefully, Taussig," he said.

I ignored him and continued: "Who should we discuss first? Your secretary?" I asked provocatively. "Your wife begged you to release her from your employ. Begged!" Yet the woman still worked for Maglič.

"Then, let's see," I added. "There was the 'nanny' you brought

ESTATE NOVÝ BERŠTEJN, DUBÁ, CZECHOSLOVAKIA
15 JANUARY 1931

back from that trip to America. The Native woman?" Maglič was positively fuming, but I continued. "They say that when you refashioned the Škoda logo, you made it as a tribute to her. They say she's still in your employ, looking after that bastard of yours in the city."

I had it on good authority from Maglič's former chauffeur that Maglič did indeed have a second family in Prague — in addition to his secretary, the aforementioned 'nanny,' and goodness only knew who else. "And I, for one, can't respect a bad businessman and known philanderer."

"Taussig," he growled through gritted teeth.

"Is that why you can't afford to pay me? Has your wallet gotten a little too thin to be able to keep your second family in style? Is having multiple mistresses too 'expensive' of a 'lifestyle'?" I asked.

"You are digging your own grave."

"Did you know that your wife Adéla has, on multiple occasions, attempted to take her own life? And is it any wonder, with the way you keep her locked in this dark castle while you go gallivanting around the countryside sowing your seeds?"

Without taking his gaze from my own, Maglič reached with one hand and grabbed the heavy crystal ashtray from his desktop, and, in one smooth motion, heaved it at me. I stepped out of the way and avoided it with ease. It shattered into large chunks on the hard floor. Outside in the hall, my spaniels barked and whined.

I turned on my heel, unafraid to show my back to him, even though I knew he kept a pistol in his desk. "I will send for my things," I said as I strode toward the door, stepping gingerly around some of the larger bits of ashtray.

"Go!" Maglič ordered, as if I wasn't already on my way out. "Your employment with estate Nový Berštejn is terminated."

THE SUITCASE

"Good riddance," I said without looking back.

"You will hear from my attorney!" he shouted. I let the door close on his words.

In the hall, Barry and Eda's heads were tilted and their brows furrowed with concern. "Ke mně," I said. "Let's get out of here."

*****

As I drove the sixty kilometres to Prague, I considered ways to break the news to my family—that I was now jobless, and wifeless, and would soon face the wrath of Tomáš Maglič and his attorney. I wondered what my family would be doing on my arrival. I expected my father, Karel, would be finishing the morning's work at his office—he worked as Prague's agricultural commissioner and also for Schicht, an agricultural commodities firm—or perhaps he would be at the nearby Palace Hotel for lunch. My brother Jaromír, or Jara, was probably working. My younger sister Marie, who we called Marietta or Mitcka, and my mother were most likely home. I imagined my mother, Julie, our Mamicka, reading in the sunny sitting room. My elder sister, Františka, or Francy, was then living in Berlin with her husband, Zikmund Kühnreich—Zik to me, Zigi to her—and their six-year-old son Jiří.

My spaniels and I soon arrived at my family's villa.

My mother was startled to see me. "Vlada!" she exclaimed. "And Barry and Eda! What a surprise! Are you well? Are you hungry? I will have the maid fetch lunch for you."

In no time, the simple Czech fare of pork and dumplings had materialized before me, while my dogs were invited into the kitchen for scraps.

"So," my mother asked, "are you in Prague on business?"

"I am afraid not, Mamicka," I said. "Actually, as of this

ESTATE NOVÝ BERŠTEJN, DUBÁ, CZECHOSLOVAKIA
15 JANUARY 1931

morning, Maglič has terminated my employment, and my marriage. Owing to him, Ann and I will be arranging for a divorce."

"What happened?" she asked. "And what a shame! I have already gotten a gift for your wedding anniversary!"

"I will tell you when Father comes," I said. "I would rather tell it only once."

I heard the door open. My father's voice, and that of the chauffeur, trailed through the halls. Barry and Eda's paws could be heard running to greet the men. "Oh!" I heard my father say. "I did see Vlada's car, but I was not expecting to see you fellows."

My parents were soon apprised of the general situation. My father did not comment immediately. He was a man who liked to think before speaking.

After some moments, he said, "This was the first decent opportunity you have had since the war."

I nodded. "It was. But Maglič stopped paying my salary and had started borrowing money. So I confronted him."

"Borrowing money from you?" my father asked.

I nodded. "And so I took matters into my own hands," my father groaned, "and I began paying myself. When I collected large cheques, I diverted some of the funds into my own accounts and some into the estate's. But all was done in full view of the accountant. I hid nothing, because I did nothing wrong. I took only what was owed to me. And as his manager, his son-in-law, and the future inheritor of the estate, what was the harm in ensuring I receive my due salary?"

"Why didn't you tell me sooner? Before you took it upon yourself to misappropriate funds or to confront the man? I will have to speak to my lawyer, and I don't know what he is going to say. Vladimír, surely you know that you are in the wrong."

"Why wasn't he paying you?" my mother asked. "If he

wasn't a man of means, we never would have encouraged the arrangement."

"I don't know," I said. "He wants everyone to think he is wealthy, and the head of a happy family, but it's just a façade. There is no money, and there is no happy family. He engages in extramarital affairs. Adéla, his wife, is absolutely miserable. She has tried to kill herself on multiple occasions. It's no wonder Ann comes here, to Prague, to escape, where she has her sisters, and my sister, and you. Although, I don't suppose she'll be visiting any more, now that I'm moving in…"

"Oh, Vlada, really?" my mother asked. "You and those two dogs? It's so peaceful now, and you are such a… spirited young man, and you keep such impossible hours."

I suppressed a grin. "Where else would I go? I have no funds, and no prospects. I have been seeking work for some time to escape Maglič's yoke. But there is nothing suitable. I suppose now I shall have to find something, even if it means settling for reduced pay. When I find employment, I will rent rooms somewhere."

"Perhaps the Schichts will re-employ you," my father suggested.

"Perhaps," I said.

"Have you spoken with Ann about all this?" my mother asked.

"I have not," I said. "This has all only just happened. I came here directly." I paused to finish my meal and wipe my mouth.

"Her sisters are all happy here in the city with their husbands," my mother said. "Can't you leave the estate but stay married?"

"It isn't as if they are madly in love, dear," my father said to my mother. He sighed, shifting his gaze to me. "I am in disbelief that you have managed to spoil things so thoroughly."

"You are quite certain you can't make amends?" my mother

ESTATE NOVÝ BERŠTEJN, DUBÁ, CZECHOSLOVAKIA
15 JANUARY 1931

asked. "What if your father spoke to Maglič?"

I shook my head. "It wouldn't help."

A maid removed my plate and replaced it with apple strudel and cheese. Barry and Eda gave me patient but longing looks until I gave them each a piece of cheese.

"Well, with all of this happening, I have my own issue to raise with Maglič," my father said.

"What do you mean?" my mother asked. "What issue?"

"I am going to sue for the 290,000 korunas he owes my firm for last spring's seed and grain. He has had plenty of time to pay. And if he is unable to pay his manager, then I dare say he doesn't intend to pay my firm."

My father requested payment from Maglič the very next day. Maglič asked if Karel would forgive a portion of the debt, but my father refused and began court proceedings for the 290,000 korunas. Maglič then intimated that I had made the 290,000-koruna purchase without his authorisation. Had I not so badly mismanaged the estate, he said, he might have been able to pay his debts: "Great losses have come about as a result of the wrongful negotiations made by Vladimír, for the entire duration of his management of the Nový Berštejn estate. I am disappointed that you did not bring to my attention Vladimír's complete disinterest in work," Maglič said.

Maglič continued: "I am sure that if I should present you with expenses illegally charged to my estate by your son, you will, with equal respect, pay me the obligations of your son. In total, including interest, this amounts to 77,838.70 korunas." They were ridiculous expenses, such as food and stabling for my horse, or fuel for my automobile—expenses which had been vital to my role as the estate's manager.

Maglič told my father that if my alleged debts were not paid within five days, he would take me to regional civil court in

Prague. And that is precisely what happened.

The pre-trial testimonies dragged on over a period of months.

Maglič produced an itemized list for the courts detailing all of the expenses I supposedly wrongly incurred on the estate's behalf. Though I no longer had access to the estate's books, I did show the court the amount I had calculated that Maglič owed me, totalling 129,646.70 korunas. I informed the court that even if I were to pay Maglič the 77,838.70 korunas which he claimed I owed, he would still owe me nearly 52,000 korunas.

Meanwhile, the other employees of the estate, and the other members of the Maglič family, provided testimony that certainly did me no favours.

Foreman Ferdinand Bender had been with me in Litoměřice when I visited a warehouse to collect payment from a company. He then saw me cash the cheque at the bank and keep the money. When the time came for him to testify for the courts, he completely deflected their questions. "The best information I can provide," he said, "is that the bookkeeper, Joseph Jorak, and the cashier, Vojtěch Kusina, are still employed at Nový Berštejn estate. [Go ask them.]"

Said cashier, Vojtěch Kusina, testified: There was a debt "owed by the Farmers Union in Czech Lipa to the Nový Berštejn estate" in the amount of 1,500 korunas "for a farm product that had been delivered to them." When Ferdinand Bender attempted to collect payment from the Farmers Union, he was informed that payment had already been collected — by Vladimír Taussig. But the 1,500 korunas had never been deposited into the estate's accounts.

The cashier said: "Vladimír Taussig never delivered this money to me, and I felt that he had kept it. I checked the financial books and this sum of money was never entered. From this, one can see that the accused never delivered the money to the office."

"There was no reason to keep this in the dark," I told the

ESTATE NOVÝ BERŠTEJN, DUBÁ, CZECHOSLOVAKIA
15 JANUARY 1931

courts, "since I had not been paid any salary. Given the same circumstances, I would do the same again."

The situation was maddening.

I argued: "The prosecution overlooks my position at the Nový Berštejn estate. I was not just a director as any other office holder, but as a son-in-law and future owner of the estate, I was in an exceptional position." Maglič had never expressed any interest in directing any activity at the estate, and as his son-in-law and manager, I did not consider it vital to look for an approval of each of my actions. He had hired me because of my experience commanding men. Yes, I had collected his receivable claims, and yes, I had retained portions of payments to the estate, and I had not acted in any secrecy, because I had not participated in any wrongdoing. "Were the court to investigate all the circumstances, the prosecution would arrive at the conclusion that there is no sufficient data to make me guilty. Were my and Maglič's mutual claims to be resolved, we should not be talking about the supposed fraud I committed, but instead only about the calculation of the sums of money Maglič is requesting from me and I from him. Please grant a decision to this request: the accusations are unacceptable, and the case is dismissed."

But the case was far from being dismissed.

When my father insisted that Maglič pay his outstanding debt to his firm of 290,000 korunas, Maglič dragged my relationship with Ann into the matter, in an attempt to "publicly display an unhappy ending of a broken marriage," as he put it. He said that "a deep ravine" had developed in my marriage "due to a heavy unfaithfulness."

I was so lusty, Maglič testified, that "in the absence of... Ann, who was in Prague, Mr. Taussig tried to rape or commit perversion with my servant Irma in his apartment at Nový Berštejn. Due to this event, [it was] my daughter, Ann, [who]

THE SUITCASE

decided to sue for divorce." It was then, Maglič said, that I "was immediately fired" and "left permanently."

It was an infuriating accusation. Maglič clearly had the maid, Irma, in his pocket and had paid for her testimony. And who could blame her for going along with his request? Her livelihood depended on Tomáš Maglič.

As with the entire proceeding, it had become my word against Maglič's.

And before long, the civil case became a criminal accusation of embezzlement.

I responded by providing some testimony that revealed Maglič's own broken marriage, in an attempt to discredit his character and accusations.

My statement shed light on the oppressive atmosphere in the household, and the high tensions that reached a breaking point when Tomáš Maglič was around. I explained that the household's unhappiness was grounded in Maglič's various affairs, and I revealed in detail the three times that I caught his wife Adéla attempting to kill herself.

But Adéla testified to the contrary. "As it is in all marriages, we had our misunderstandings," she said, "but none of them were serious... It was never so serious that I would... be in despair. Contrary, I believe that our family provides a normal living environment... It is definitely not true that there were any great disputes within our family..."

I called upon the former chauffeur. He had been the first one to clue me in to Maglič's extramarital doings. But when the time came, his testimony was as follows:

> I was employed as a driver at castle Nový Berštejn. I know of big problems between Tomáš Maglič and his wife because he had an ongoing love affair with his

ESTATE NOVÝ BERŠTEJN, DUBÁ, CZECHOSLOVAKIA
15 JANUARY 1931

secretary and did not want to lay her off, despite the insistence of his wife. He was courting other women, but I did not know them. When Taussig got married, I was no longer working there and I cannot know what was going on. Specifically, I do not know... that the wife of Tomáš Maglič tried to commit suicide.

While his statement corroborated some facets of my testimony, it was not enough.

My father testified that Ann was constantly visiting my parents' villa: "My daughter-in-law had a problem with her family's behaviour and several times brought up the subject, and often spent the better part of a week in my place in Prague, where she felt 'happy,' by her own statements."

Yet Ann's statements naturally sided with her father: "As to the relationship with my family, it was never as bad as the accused claims..."

None of it mattered. As Maglič had warned, I had dug my own grave, and the proverbial nails had already been hammered into the lid of my coffin.

Prague, Czechoslovakia
Saturday, 24 December 1932

Nevěř slovům, věř skutkům.
[Don't believe words, believe deeds.]
— Czech Proverb

PRAGUE'S BUILDINGS and squares were decorated; the city's shops and holiday markets were bustling. Street corners were dotted with barrels of carp splashing in water and awaiting their eventual transfers to bathtubs, then dinner tables.

It was the second night of Hanukkah, and it was also Christmas Eve. Later that night, Ježíšek, the Baby Jesus, would bring Christmas gifts to the children of Prague.

My own mood was anything but festive. The cold winter sun struck the crystal of my whiskey glass as I took another sip. I sat in the Palace Hotel, brooding over bad news: I had just received notice that my case with Tomáš Maglič would be heard by the courts in May. It was hopeless. Events of the preceding months had made it clear that I would never win in court, even with the aid of an attorney.

The Palace Hotel was a stone's throw from my father's office. I wondered whether I should go and tell him the news. But I also hoped to have some solution worked out, so that when I introduced the problem of the impending court case, I could follow it with a suggestion of what my next steps might be.

All around me, people were reading, talking, laughing. Some were eating lunch, using butter which had likely originated at

PRAGUE, CZECHOSLOVAKIA
24 DECEMBER 1932

Nový Berštejn—big European-style pats with "Palace Hotel" moulded in, as had been my design.

A cheerful table nearby drew my attention. A vivacious brunette and a couple of men talked and laughed as they wagered on a card game. A seed sprouted in my mind: if I could double, or triple, the money in my pocket, then I might be able to offer Maglič a substantial sum to convince him to settle, and thus avoid the impending trial. If that was the case, then I also wouldn't have to reveal the news of the court date to my family.

As I drew my engraved silver cigarette case from my jacket pocket and moved to light a cigarette, the brunette woman excused herself from the nearby table and approached me. She took a cigarette from her beaded handbag and put it to her painted lips. I lifted the crystal lighter from the table and held it up for her use.

She spoke first. "Why are you sitting here all by yourself, looking gloomy? It's a holiday, you know," she smiled and exhaled a little plume of smoke. "Is it a woman?" she asked.

"Not at all," I said. My divorce from Ann had been finalized in September. With my bachelorhood reacquired, I'd had nothing but fun. I grinned. "Isn't it funny? Now that you are here, I can feel the gloom lifting already." I took a drag of my cigarette. "Tell me, what game are your friends playing?"

"Poker," she said. "Would you care to join us?"

"I should like that," I said. I moved to tuck my cigarette case back into my jacket pocket.

"What does that say?" she asked, gesturing to the case's engraved inscription.

I held it out for her examination. "It was an award," I said. "I am a cavalry officer." The inscription etched into the metal read that, as a reserve officer in the Czechoslovak Army, I, Vladimír Taussig, had been awarded the case for my excellent equestrian

THE SUITCASE

work.

"I see," she said, reading the case. "Vladimír Taussig," she said thoughtfully. Then she added, "My beau was also in the army."

"Was he?" I asked. "Is he at the table? I should like very much to meet him."

"He is out of the country," she said. "Are you familiar with the Schwarzenbergs?"

I gave a little start at the mention of the aristocratic name. "I have heard the name, yes, but I have no personal associations with the family," I said.

"So much the better. They disowned him. He is no longer Prince Schwarzenberg; he has become Edmund Černov."

"Disowned? Why ever for?"

She grinned. "He's a gambler. And," she gestured for us to move over to the card table, "he fell in love with a common woman. The family sent him to England, and paid him off to make him forget her, but instead he returned to Praha and married the girl."

"Are you that woman?"

"No, no. His ex-wife."

I took my seat with the others and was dealt into their game. They did not mind that the young woman and I continued our own semi-private conversation. "And where is this former prince now?" I asked.

"He is on his way back from hunting big game in Africa," she said, utterly unaware that Edmund Černov would die the very next day, on Christmas, and be buried at sea.

"Big game hunting in Africa? Like Trader Horn?" I asked. I had read Alfred Aloysius "Trader" Horn's biographical book, published in 1927, and had also seen the 1931 film based on the adventurer's life.

PRAGUE, CZECHOSLOVAKIA
24 DECEMBER 1932

"You know that film?" she asked.

"Of course I do!" It had been the sixth-biggest film in Prague the previous year. "I love the cinema and admire all the stars."

"I am an actress, you know," she said with a grin.

"I don't think I have ever seen your work. I would most definitely have remembered you," I said. Her grin transformed into a full-on smile. "What is your name?"

"Renate Hohnová. I have been doing stage plays, not film, though I would love to act in a movie. I have been working with director Oldřich Stibor. Our next play, *Paní Ňu*, will be premiering in March. You shall have to come see me in it."

"I would love to," I said.

Perhaps I had allowed the young woman to distract me too much, because I lost three hands of cards in a row. It was a higher-stakes game than I had anticipated, and I was bleeding money. I didn't want Renate Hohnová to know I was close to broke, and that I desperately needed to turn my luck around and begin winning, in hopes of reaching a settlement and avoiding court.

When I was dealt a good hand, I wagered all that I had left to my name—and lost.

"Well, I am afraid I must be going," I said. I was in trouble! Broke! "It was lovely to meet you." I reached for a calling card to hand to the young woman as I pushed my chair back and prepared to stand.

"Oh, please stay," she said, placing her hand on my arm. She looked into my eyes.

"I can't stay." I felt my cheeks redden. "I am afraid I can't afford to," I confessed.

"Don't worry," she said. "I will gladly back you. Deal him in," she told our companion with the card deck.

"I simply couldn't," I said. "I fear I should never be able to repay you." It was the truth.

She looked me up and down in a way that made my stomach feel as if it had just received a fresh injection of whiskey. Heat flushed through me. She said, "If that was a concern, I would not have offered."

After a moment's pause, I moved my chair towards the table once more. "If you insist," I said.

"There's gossip that my beau once lost 700,000 korunas in one night. This," she gestured at the table, "is nothing."

"Seven hundred thousand!" I exclaimed.

She nodded. "He was with one of the Kolowrats."

"Heavens," I said, recognizing the noble family's name.

"You shall have to meet him when he returns. You remind me of him," she said, smiling. As the cards were dealt, she continued the conversation. "So, do you have big plans for the holidays?" she asked.

"Dinner with my family. My elder sister and her husband are visiting from Berlin with my nephew, and I have a younger sister and an older brother. It is rare for us all to be together. And you?"

She laughed, "I am actually going to a holiday dinner with Edmund's ex-wife and her daughter. The ex-wife is also an actress." She took a drag of her cigarette. "I would like to think I know everyone worth knowing. I'm surprised I have never met you."

I smiled broadly. "I have been away in the country," I said, "but now that I am back home in Praha, I should hope to be seeing more of you."

Renate Hohnová and I chatted on as we played. I won a few hands but I lost more. At a certain point, I made the decision to wager everything, in hopes of doubling my funds — but as luck would have it, I lost.

The actress further backed me with another promissory note.

PRAGUE, CZECHOSLOVAKIA
24 DECEMBER 1932

"I mean it—I will never be able to repay you," I insisted.

"Don't worry; I would never need, nor want, to collect," she said. "I only write the promissory notes because my Edmund will return soon, and he will wonder where my money has gone." She smiled.

I stayed.

By the time I finally took my leave, I had amassed a substantial debt to her, and I had promised to call after the holiday. She seemed unbothered by the sums I had won and then lost that afternoon, but I disliked being in that enchanting creature's debt. Moreover, I was even further from presenting any sort of settlement offer to Tomáš Maglič.

I left the Palace Hotel, my spirits even lower than they had been before, and took a car. In a few short minutes, it had carried me across the Štefánik Bridge over the Vltava, made its way through the neighbourhood, and deposited me in front of my parents' villa.

Barry and Eda's barking announced my arrival. Inside, the smell of freshly-baked vánočka, or Stollen, sweet Christmas bread baked with dried fruits, trailed throughout the villa.

Like many Jewish families in Prague, we celebrated both Christmas and Hanukkah. Lights glowed on the small tree in the parlour, while in the dining room, a menorah had been placed in one window. I hadn't seen the relic in years; my mother must have resurrected it on account of my nephew Jiří's presence, to make a good showing for her only grandchild.

The servants were bustling; my mother was fussing with dinner preparations; my father sat bent over his desk. I found my brother-in-law Zikmund alone in one of the guest rooms.

"Hello, Zikmund. Where is Francy?" I asked.

"At the shops with Jiří and Mitcka," he said. "They should be back at any moment."

"Good, then there is time to speak with you, privately, before dinner," I said. I stepped into the room and quietly shut the door. Jiří's toy soldiers sat on a table where he had left them, the companies of men grouped into formations I had recently taught the eight year-old boy.

"What is it?" Zikmund asked. I looked at his heavyset, moustachioed face, his dark brown eyes inquisitive beneath his receding dark brown hair.

I cleared my throat, then said, "My father doesn't know it yet, but, I have received notice that Maglič's case against me will be going to court in May."

"Even after all of the statements and depositions you said were made?" he asked.

I shook my head. "I have done my best, but Maglič has access to the estate's ledgers. I do not. Maglič has the ability to pay witnesses who will parrot whatever statements he desires. I do not."

Zikmund scowled. "Paying off witnesses…"

"Yes, they are all in his pocket. Everyone I subpoenaed either changed their tune, or suddenly failed to remember the particulars of the situation. Furthermore," I added, "what was once a civil case, has become a criminal case. He will ruin me." I hung my head.

"Can't some arrangement, some settlement, be reached, before this has to go before a judge?" he asked.

I gave a sad smile. "Well," I said, "I had hoped to have enough money to offer him some sort of settlement, but you see…" I trailed off. I was in no hurry to admit my defeat and helplessness.

"What do I see?"

"I had the thought that I might increase my capital in hopes of getting nearer to a sufficient sum to settle with Maglič,"

"Yes, yes," Zikmund said impatiently.

PRAGUE, CZECHOSLOVAKIA
24 DECEMBER 1932

"But I lost it all. Everything."

"Lost how?" Zikmund asked. Suddenly filled with shame, I didn't respond right away. "Well?"

"Gambling," I said meekly.

"Everything?" he asked.

"I'm broke. Not only broke—I am indebted."

"What do you mean? Indebted to whom?"

I sighed. "An actress."

"Good grief, Taussig, you haven't even been divorced three months and here you are getting entangled with an actress. How much do you owe?" he asked.

"Thousands. I'm not entirely sure, on the whole," I admitted.

"What were you thinking, getting yourself indebted to that sort of woman?"

"She offered. Insisted, really. I agreed, thinking that I would eventually get ahead, or at least break even. We were playing cards, you see..."

He scoffed. "What will the courts say? What will your father say?" He raged on: "Did you really think, given the situation with Maglič, that this gambling was something you should be involved in?" He had grown so excited that he was spitting a little. "Do you want your family's name all over the gossip columns? An embezzlement accusation from Maglič. A rape accusation from one of his maids. A messy divorce from Ann. Now you are gambling with some actress. And all of this at holiday-time, no less."

"It's just the way events unfolded," I said. "If I could have made some money..." I trailed off. Zikmund was fuming and I had yet to arrive at the question I had intended to ask! "I can't let this go to trial," I said calmly. "I simply will not win in court. I am absolutely certain of it. I will end up disgraced, mouldering in Pankrác Prison. I shall never be able to repay what Maglič alleges

THE SUITCASE

I owe, much less repay the actress."

Zikmund barked a single, short laugh. "I suppose I know where this conversation will lead…"

I leaned towards him. "If I could perhaps borrow some money from you…"

"For Maglič or for the actress?" he asked. Then he quickly added, "Either way, I cannot."

I hung my head. "It was my intent to not have to tell Father. About the upcoming court date. About any of it." I let slip a few tears, though whether they were genuine or whether they were shed merely to garner Zikmund's sympathy, even I was not sure.

"My finances are entirely tied up in the move," Zik said.

"What move?" I asked.

"I was going to announce it at dinner. Your sister and nephew and I are moving to Karlovy Vary. We have decided that leaving Berlin will be best for our family, and for my business. We hope to wait until the end of the school term, but we will see."

"Why move?" I asked.

"To put it mildly," he said, "I do not have high hopes for the direction the German government is taking. Since Adolf Hitler demanded the Chancellorship, the anti-Semitic National Socialists have become a substantial political party. We want Jiří to be safe and happy," he said. "And a spa town will be beneficial to your sister's health."

"So everything is invested in the move. I understand," I said. Clearly there would be no bailout from Zikmund. I added, "It will be nice to be closer to Prague, to the family here."

"Yes, but I'll be leaving my own family behind in Berlin," Zikmund replied.

Barry and Eda began barking, heralding the arrival of my sisters and my nephew. Zikmund stood and buttoned his jacket. "It's unfortunate that our announcement about Karlovy Vary

PRAGUE, CZECHOSLOVAKIA
24 DECEMBER 1932

will be overshadowed by your troubling news."

"I don't have to tell them tonight," I said. "Why spoil this happy occasion?"

Zik sighed and gave me a look, then turned and exited the room.

I followed.

Francy, Mitcka, and Jiří were smiling. Their cheeks were flushed with cold. The servants took their packages and coats. I noted with some bitterness that Zikmund had possessed money enough for Francy to go out shopping in Prague, yet he hadn't a koruna to spare for me.

That evening, we gathered in the dining room and watched my mother light the menorah. After lighting the helper candle, she said a prayer in Hebrew: "Blessed are you, Lord, our God, sovereign of the universe, who has sanctified us with His commandments and commanded us to light the lights of Hanukkah. Blessed are you, Lord, our God, sovereign of the universe, who performed miracles for our ancestors in those days at this time."

She then lit two candles on the menorah, as it was the second night of Hanukkah. I caught the gleam of my father's eyes in the candlelight as he rolled them to amuse himself. I grinned. Like him, I felt a great disdain for organised religion. Some combination of upbringing, education, and experience had separately led us to the same conclusions.

Organised religion, we believed, was created by man to control other men. Religion itself, the concept of God, was not something contained in any church or synagogue or its regular gatherings and rote teachings. God, my father and I felt, was everywhere. The best "religion" was to live by the principles of courage, decency, honesty, and tolerance—not to light a prescribed number of candles or say a certain prayer on a particular day. We respected what my mother was doing, and understood that much of it was for Jiří's benefit, but between the two of us, there was secret eye-rolling and private, shared disregard for these ceremonies.

No one else at the table seemed to notice. Mitcka and Jara and I sat along one side, across from Francy and Zikmund and Jiří. Father claimed the head and Mother took the other end. Vánoční rybí polévka, the traditional Christmas carp soup, sat steaming and ready to be served. The customary fried carp and the potato salad were brought in.

I watched my family happily enjoy their meal, while I languished under the burden of my bad news.

In the candlelight, my father looked older than his sixty-five years. Recent stresses surely did not help. My return to Prague, his own battle with Maglič over the seed and grain, and the accusations against me from the maid had all certainly contributed. Then, in July of '31, his brother, my Uncle Julius, and his wife, my Aunt Paula, had died on the same day. Paula died after an operation; Julius died only a few hours afterwards. Their headstone reads: "Unersetzlich. Unvergesslich." In English: "Irreplaceable. Unforgettable."

And to think that I would soon be adding even more to his burden.

A few minutes into the meal, Zikmund decided to make his announcement. The family was delighted to hear that Francy and Jiří and Zik would soon be living nearer to Prague. The mood was light and happy, and even my father was smiling. And so I hesitated.

By the time the serving staff removed the dinner dishes and replaced them with trays of various Christmas cookies and sweets, Zikmund was giving me signals with his piercing stares and emphatic coughing.

PRAGUE, CZECHOSLOVAKIA
24 DECEMBER 1932

The Christmas bell was rung, and Jiří scampered off to the Christmas tree, newly-decorated that evening, as was tradition, to see what gifts Ježíšek had left. It was then that Zikmund said, "I believe there is another announcement to be made," and glared at me. "Vladimír, don't you have something important to share?"

My mother was smiling, excited to hear whatever good news I had to offer. She likely thought I was ready to announce new employment, or that I was moving out of the villa and into a place of my own.

"Well..." I began. I cleared my throat. "I received word that Maglič's case against me will be going to trial in May."

"Oh?" my father asked.

"Good," my mother said. "The courts will find you innocent."

"I'm not so sure that will be the outcome," I said. "Maglič has paid everyone off. No one will take my side. I fear the worst."

My younger sister chimed in: "I thought you didn't do anything wrong?" Mitcka asked provocatively.

"Our brother used his position to his advantage," Francy said. "He took what was not meant for him, from accounts that were not meant for him." She stood from the table. "Excuse me, I'm going to go watch my son open his Christmas gifts."

I sighed. "I do not expect to win in court. It seems like I'll be sitting in prison soon, while Maglič sits high on the profits I have made him. As far as the courts are concerned, I am an embezzler and an accused rapist."

My father had been fairly quiet. "I still think you stand a fighting chance. Yes, you face accusations, but Maglič's reputation is hardly untarnished. Not only was there my suit against him for the unpaid grain, but the architect Jindřich Friedl has also sued Maglič over unpaid commissioned furniture for your apartment at Nový Berštejn. And there is another, similar lawsuit on the books for the non-payment of a clothing order. To say nothing of his adultery."

Zikmund said, "That may be, but you should know that Vladimír's troubles do not end there." He looked at me. "Shall you tell them, or shall I?" he asked. He took a bite of a Christmas cookie. His eyes sparkled in the candlelight.

My mother asked, "What is it, Vlada?"

"It's true," I sighed. "I do have other news."

My sister Mitcka grinned and also reached for a cookie.

"There is a debt I owe," I began. "A gambling debt. I had hoped to win enough money to offer Maglič a sum that would convince him to settle out-of-court and drop the accusations. Instead, I lost everything and am now indebted."

"Who do you owe?" my father asked.

"It's an actress," Zikmund answered.

"An actress? Who?" Marietta asked with excitement. I waved a hand at her. She scowled and returned to her cookie.

"How much?" my father asked.

"He doesn't even know," Zikmund said. "Thousands."

The table was quiet for a moment. My mother was waiting for my father to talk. My siblings looked on wide-eyed, anticipating his reaction. Finally, he spoke.

"You do not appreciate the life you have had," my father said with disappointment. "You were afforded every opportunity. You didn't have to struggle and work your way up the ladder as I did, and as your forefathers did."

I prepared to hear the family history he recounted each time my brother or I elicited his disappointment.

"How easily you forget," he began, "how the Famililiants Laws shaped our world, and how our family was oppressed by the Empire in our choices of marriage, education, and professions. Yet we persevered. I am the fruit of my forefathers' labours: a

PRAGUE, CZECHOSLOVAKIA
24 DECEMBER 1932

businessman, a commissioner—successful beyond any village butcher's wildest imaginings."

I sighed and shifted in my chair, feeling the weight not only of my father's disappointment, but also that of all my ancestors.

He shook his head. "You had tutors. Riding lessons. Music lessons. Tennis. Soccer. The driving club. The military academy. Business school. Skiing trips. I helped arrange a nice job for you at Nový Berštejn, with a young wife, a 'castle,' an estate to inherit when Tomáš Maglič dies, and what did you do? You embarrassed us all. You drove your wife away. You stole from Maglič."

"I did not steal," I said pointedly.

Mitcka interjected. "For what it's worth," she said, "Ann was always miserable. Even at finishing school. Some people are just more melancholy. That part, at least, wasn't Vladimír's doing." I was grateful for this one helpful remark from my generally antagonistic younger sister.

Our father ignored her interruption and continued: "Then you come home to us and flippantly say, at holiday dinner no less, that, on top of everything else, you have lost untold thousands of korunas to an actress at the gambling tables."

I wanted to tell him that, technically, I hadn't lost the money to Renata Hohnová herself, but instead to her companions—but I knew better than to correct him just then. What did it matter, anyway? The end result was the same. I hung my head. Barry sat at my feet; Eda's head rested in my lap. I rubbed the soft fur of his ears. "All I wanted to do," I said quietly, "was to get enough money together so I could solve this on my own, without troubling you with any of it."

Mitcka scoffed. "Clearly that did not pan out." She was back to her old self.

"Clearly not," I said, glaring at her.

Our mother sighed. "You and Maglič both have marks against

your name. But if you were the judge in this case, would you not be inclined to rule in favour of the businessman from Škoda motor works who can produce an endless stream of witnesses and documentary evidence?"

"Paid witnesses. Doctored documents," I said glumly.

"Or," my mother continued, "would you believe a publicly-defamed divorcé who spent his holidays at the card tables with an actress?"

My father frowned. "All of it calls your judgment into question. Your character."

"Yes, yes, I know," I said. "The Taussig character."

"Don't be so dismissive," he said. "Nothing is more important than a man's character. And you continually show that yours is less than admirable and your judgment unsound."

The table was quiet.

I looked to my brother, who had still not said a word. For the longest time, Jara had been considered the family's black sheep because he had run off with some money when he was younger. Now it was my turn to plumb the depths of the family's disappointment.

From the other room, we could hear Jiří exclaim with pleasure at some new gift.

"Have you considered going abroad?" my mother asked. "Just until this settles down? If people inquire, we can simply say that you have gone away, and that we have not heard from you."

Between Bombay, India and Colombo, Ceylon
Tuesday, 24 January 1933

> *When the wind of change blows,*
> *some build walls,*
> *while others build windmills.*
> —Chinese Proverb

I WAS BOUND for Shanghai, the "Paris of the Orient." I would remain abroad until the chaos I had created blew over. Until then, the family would feign ignorance of my whereabouts, and Barry and Eda would remain in their care. All I was asked to do in return was to find temporary employment and write home every fourteen days.

I had been on board the SS *Gange* for nearly a fortnight, having left Prague after my father's and Marietta's birthdays—both on 7 January. Zikmund had escorted me to Italy, to the wharf in Trieste, and had seen me onto the ship. His final advice was to keep my head down, and my ass away from the gambling tables.

The ship had left Trieste on the eleventh. We stopped in Venice the same day and then followed the Adriatic Coast, reaching Brindisi on the twelfth.

After leaving Italy, we had crossed the Ionian and Mediterranean Seas to arrive at British-occupied Port Said in Egypt on 15 January, the day before Jaromír's thirty-seventh birthday. We then spent a week at sea. I had enjoyed the change to warmer weather, and had been golfing on the little green on

THE SUITCASE

the front of the ship, shooting at clay pigeons with my rifle, and chatting to my fellow first-class passengers. After steaming down the Suez Canal into the Red Sea and crossing the Gulf of Aden and the Arabian Sea, the *Gange* arrived at Colonial Bombay.

Now we were bound for the Laccadive Sea and another British territory, Colombo.

As I finished dressing for dinner, I preened in the mirror and straightened my bow tie. I filled my pockets with my silver cigarette case and calling cards — both *Vladimír Taussig* and the more official-sounding *Captain Vladimír George Taussig*.

When I arrived at the first-class dining salon, I stood, stomach growling, scanning the room in search of the maître d'. At one table, I noticed an unaccompanied red-haired beauty in a green evening gown. Had she just boarded in Bombay? Surely I would have noticed her before. She sipped a champagne cocktail with her red-painted lips. I seized the opportunity and approached her with a charming smile.

When I was just steps away, she looked up at me with eyes as green as her dress.

"May I join you?" I asked in English.

The woman glanced behind me, but presented her hand. I bowed slightly to kiss it, my lips a centimetre away from her skin. "Captain Vladimír Taussig," I said. "A pleasure."

I felt a tap on my shoulder. "I am afraid this is not your seat, sir," a voice said behind me. I sighed. The woman giggled as I turned to face the maître d'.

"Should we not allow this enchanting young lady to decide whether she would like my company?" I asked.

"This 'enchanting lady' will soon be joined by her fiancée. If you please, sir," he said, gesturing for me to follow.

"Find me later," I said, winking at the redhead. She wordlessly watched the maître d' lead me away. I walked for a few steps

BETWEEN BOMBAY, INDIA AND COLOMBO, CEYLON
24 JANUARY 1933

before looking back. The woman was smiling.

At my usual table of bachelors and businessmen, the men loosed a volley of comments — "Nice try, Taussig," and that sort of thing.

"She's engaged. Affianced!" I said dramatically, pretending to wipe a tear from my cheek.

I noticed a new face at a nearby table. He caught my attention and grinned. I smiled and gave him a nod.

After dinner, I adjourned to the first-class smoking lounge. It was a beautiful room, with wooden panelling on the walls and a white ceiling accented by dark wooden beams. Wooden armchairs and leather wingbacks were accompanied by standing ashtrays and by small tables with little glowing lamps. I took one of the leather chairs that commanded a view of the room and hoped the Woman in Green would seek me out. Instead, the smiling man from dinner found me there. He introduced himself as Lucien Ovadia.

"Captain Vladimír Taussig," I said. I stood and shook his hand, then returned to my seat. He took the chair next to me.

Ovadia, I learned, had been born in Egypt, educated in France, and trained in England. He was comfortable conversing in a few languages, but I had to admit to him that my English was better than my French.

"I enjoyed your little scene in the dining room," Ovadia said.

I chuckled. "I have spent every meal with bachelors. I would like to demand the creation of a new seating chart, with a full table of unchaperoned young women, and me right at the centre of it." We both laughed. "Are you married, Lucien Ovadia?" I asked. I took a sip of my scotch.

"I am. Almost two years now."

I chose not to divulge that my own wedding anniversary would have just passed.

THE SUITCASE

A member of the serving staff approached.

"Would you care for a drink?" I offered.

"I don't usually partake," he said, "but this is as close to a holiday as I'm going to get, so I suppose I shall join you. Scotch and soda, please," he ordered. "Where are you heading, Captain Vladimír Taussig?" he asked.

"Shanghai," I said. "And you?"

"The same." His drink was delivered. He took a sip, then said, "I work for my cousin, Sir Victor Sassoon, as a risk assessor."

"What does Sassoon do?" I asked.

"He runs the E.D. Sassoon Banking Company. And he owns properties. And racing ponies. Haven't you heard of the Sassoons?"

"I have heard of the poet, Siegfried Sassoon," I said.

Ovadia nodded. "He and Sir Victor share the same great-grandfather."

"I see," I said. "Will this be your first visit to Shanghai?" I asked.

"I have travelled there many times, but this will be my first time living there. My wife and I are relocating. She is already in Shanghai," Ovadia said.

"Then perhaps you are familiar with the 1932 'Incident'?" I asked. The Chinese were engaged in an ongoing conflict with the Japanese, and with one another.

Ovadia said, "Yes, I am familiar. Sir Victor Sassoon has helped the Chinese Nationalists with financial support in the past, and has advised their leader, Chiang Kai-shek, on the formation of labour unions to help the Chinese people. But in spite of the ongoing conflicts, I assure you that you will be perfectly safe in the enclaves the Westerners have created — the International Settlement and French Concession," Ovadia said. "There, you will be protected by Western laws and troops. The Americans

BETWEEN BOMBAY, INDIA AND COLOMBO, CEYLON
24 JANUARY 1933

have their 'China Marines.' The British have the Shanghai Defence Force. There are French and Italian troops. As you know, the Germans are not allowed to station any military there, and neither can the Chinese. There's also the Shanghai Volunteer Corps, a defensive group comprised of a blend of nationalities." Ovadia finished his drink. "I think you'll rather like Shanghai. Once you are settled, you must look me up."

"I will," I said. "Perhaps you can show me all of the best spots." I gestured to the serving staff for another drink.

"The one place I can vouch for is the Cathay Hotel in my cousin's building, the Sassoon House. You must visit the ballroom there during your stay in Shanghai. You can't miss it. It's right on the waterfront, and has an enormous copper pyramid at its apex." Ovadia stood. "Now, if you will allow me to take my leave, I think I'm going to turn in. I have got cables to send when we reach Colombo tomorrow."

I stood and extended my hand. "It was a pleasure to have met you, Lucien Ovadia," I said.

"Likewise, Captain Taussig," he said. "I suppose, if nothing else, I shall see you at our next mealtime. Good luck tonight. I do hope you manage to bump into La Rouquine again—the redhead!"

*****

The following day, Wednesday, 25 January, we stopped in Ceylon and visited Colombo. There, I explored the sprawling seaside Galle Face Hotel. After leaving port, we crossed the Bay of Bengal to Singapore, arriving on Sunday, 29 January. In Singapore, Ovadia and I visited the famous Raffles hotel. We watched people drink gin slings at the Long Bar, mingle in the Palm Court, play billiards, and dance.

"What do you think of the hotel?" Ovadia asked.

I laughed. "I suppose you cannot help but compare, since hotels are part of your business with Sassoon." Ovadia nodded. "The Galle Face was nice. Raffles is nice. They are all nice. What I really want to see is your cousin's hotel in Shanghai."

"We will be there soon enough," Ovadia said. There was just one more stop before Shanghai—Hong Kong.

The *Gange* left Singapore and crossed the South China Sea, moving past French Indo-China and up the Chinese coast. We arrived in Hong Kong on 2 February, where we found the Peninsula Hotel, the legendary "Grande Dame of the Far East," owned by the Kadoorie family.

Ovadia explained, "Silas Kadoorie is the patriarch. His sons Moshi, Elly, and Ellis have all been employed by the Sassoons in China at some point. Sir Ellis has been dead for ten years. Moshi and Elly are still alive and are in their sixties. Elly's sons, Lawrence and Horace, are our age. Businessmen. You will undoubtedly see Elly's mansion in Shanghai. It's called Marble Hall, because they used one hundred fifty tons of Italian marble in its construction. It contains twenty-six rooms and occupies nearly an entire block. It was built as the Jewish country club, but there were not enough Jews to fill the enormous building, so Kadoorie decided to make it his residence. The ballroom is enormous. It has a sixty-five-foot ceiling. Kadoorie opens it to Shanghai for various parties and gatherings, community events and Jewish holidays. Like the Sassoons, the Kadoories are Sephardic Jews."

"So the Kadoories have Marble Hall; where do the Sassoons live?" I asked.

"Sir Victor plans to build a house in the countryside, but, at present, he lives in the pyramid atop the atop the Cathay Hotel," Ovadia said.

"The Cathay Hotel is the same as the Sassoon House?"

BETWEEN BOMBAY, INDIA AND COLOMBO, CEYLON
24 JANUARY 1933

"The Cathay consists of the upper floors of the Sassoon House," Ovadia clarified. "Now, where will you be staying when we reach Shanghai?"

"I have arranged for a long-term contract at the Astor House, which I understand offers a good rate for military officers. I plan to be there until I find a decent position and begin earning a living anyway."

Lucien said, "Oh, I'm sure you will do fine. And you can still live first-rate even if you are temporarily short on funds. You can obtain chits, which will allow you to purchase on credit. At the end of the month businesses will send a Boy — a servant — to collect."

How ironic that, in Shanghai, I would be given credit so unquestioningly, when the very reason for my presence in the city was my alleged mismanagement of funds!

After leaving Hong Kong, the ship travelled up the coast of China, then the deep blue of the Chinese sea became the murky water of the Yangtze River. We were nearing Shanghai, which sat on the Whangpoo River, the last tributary of the Yangtze on its way to the East China Sea. The mud flats we slowly passed became huts; the huts became buildings; the buildings became quite grand.

In Shanghai, the riverfront was crowded with small flat-bottomed junks, larger sailed sampans, warships and steamships. Beyond the water, the impressive buildings looked as if they had been uprooted from all over Europe and replanted on Shanghai's Bund.

One modern-looking building drew my eye immediately. A copper pyramid crowned the building's apex. I knew it at once to be the Sassoon House.

SHANGHAI, CHINA
Thursday Morning, 16 March 1933

> *Kolik jazyků znáš, tolikrát jsi člověkem.*
> *[As many languages you know,*
> *as many times you are a human being.]*
> —Czech Proverb, Goethe trans. by Tomáš Masaryk

CHAPEI WAS a Chinese portion of the city of Shanghai. It had been reduced to rubble and wreckage following 1932's "January 28th Incident." The area had been heavily-populated with working-class Chinese, but Japanese incendiary bombs had laid waste to factories, shops, homes, schools, and temples. Westerners had watched, untouched, from their portion of the city across Soochow Creek.

It was a few kilometres into Chapei, away from the ever-glowing lights of Shanghai's International Settlement, that I found myself walking a recently-broken Mongolian pony through the muddy lanes in the pre-dawn hours.

I had chosen the mud of Chapei to exercise the pony, in hopes that the effort of pulling his hooves from the resistant muck would later result in faster laps around the race track. The pony's owner wanted to qualify for the following week's Sub-Griffin's Derby, a competition between first-year ponies, called griffins. Anyone from any level of society who possessed a bit of money could buy one of the ponies at auction. They were herded from the fields of Mongolia each year and shorn of their shaggy coats, then trained to become racing steeds.

SHANGHAI, CHINA
16 MARCH 1933

Movement in nearby rubble spooked the trudging pony. He stiffened, then bolted down the dark and muddy path. I clung to the saddle for fear of being thrown to the ground and "savaged," as the locals said, by the pony's teeth and hooves. "Snadný," I said through gritted teeth. Easy.

I missed my sturdy, obedient, dignified Czech Warmblood. The prestige of a cavalryman and the deep connection he felt to his noble steed was entirely at odds with my present situation — bouncing around and clinging to a stubborn Mongolian pony.

When we were apparently at a safe remove from whatever had startled the pony, he finally decided to slow. I tried to turn us around to see, but, true to breed, the pony ignored his reins entirely. I was able to squeeze him back on track with my legs, sore from dancing earlier in the night with a woman whose Chinese-style qipao dress had been slit nearly up to her neck, paving the way for other post-dance activities.

What could have startled the pony? I freed my nose from the warm haven of my overcoat and turned my head to examine the darkness from which we had just fled. I was bombarded by the smells that had made many a lesser man lose his lunch: the slimy Soochow Creek, the decaying rubbish, the human excrement awaiting collection by early-morning "honey carts," after which the crap would be sold to local farmers for use as fertiliser. There were no streetlights or moonlight to confirm, but, judging by the smell, I was sure we were treading through shit. Having found no evidence of what has caused the pony's panicked reaction, I swivelled my head forward and tucked my nose back into the warmth of my overcoat.

I imagined a group of ruffians might be lurking in the darkness and wondered if my training from the Great War in close-range hand-to-hand fighting would see me through an altercation. Would I be outnumbered?

THE SUITCASE

If I was killed in the dark in the Chinese city, hardly a soul would have missed me. As I was on the run, neither my consulate nor my hotel was in possession of my family's address. No one would know who to notify or where to forward my effects. I would be buried in a potter's field in the muddy, shitty Shanghai soil. My family would, after some time, assume I had elected not to contact them.

As we trudged further from civilisation, I began seeing the lights of the rebuilt portion of Chapei – the area near the North Railway Station. Businesses had taken advantage of the low-priced land and had sprung up in the midst of the still-present rubble. The appearance of the first streetlights and shop windows were my cue to turn back towards Shanghai proper.

I checked my watch. If the pony cooperated on the return trip, we would be back at the Race Club just before six o'clock, as planned. As we turned around, I caught my full reflection in a nearby window. I looked like any worn-out, well-to-do gentleman in the midst of an early morning's shuffle through the mud might appear – chilly, weary, muck-spattered. Otherwise, I cut a fine figure and looked quite at home atop the saddle.

Below the saddle was a different story. The pony was no more than fourteen hands – at least a foot shorter than my Czech Warmblood. The Mongolian breed's short neck and stocky legs effected an amusing look.

The pony and I turned away from our comical reflection and back towards the stables. With the knowledge that we were bound for the stables, the pony became lively. His steps were eager and sure.

As we passed once more through the war-torn wasteland, the growing grey of sunrise revealed large stretches still filled with rubble, empty lots of land that had been cleared, and blocks crowded with huts made of straw and bamboo. The pony

SHANGHAI, CHINA
16 MARCH 1933

strayed into one of the open lots. We were still travelling in the appropriate direction, so I allowed it. I noticed dark shapes on the ground and stopped the pony to inspect one of the bundles — a heap of newspapers atop a woven straw mat. I leaned over the saddle and used the tip of my crop to nudge the dirty paper aside. I glimpsed a bit of dead, mud-splattered flesh. It was the same sort of tender skin that all infants have.

My stomach lurched. I felt heat in my throat and swallowed, tasting the ghosts of the dinner and cocktails I had purchased on credit with chits that evening before dancing. I swallowed again.

I had seen more than my share of dead boys and men during the war, whether blood-spattered, gas-poisoned, or starved and frozen. I was still new to Shanghai and was not yet accustomed to seeing dead children and infants, their bodies abandoned. It was an awful sight, but the country was in a bad state and many were impoverished, starving, and suffering.

The pony was untroubled by the contents of the bundles on the ground and began moving before I could return the flimsy covering to the infant's corpse. It was left partially exposed. At least the cadaver cart would eventually collect the body — unless wild dogs or other scavengers found it first.

How fortunate to have been born to a commissioner near a bend in Prague's mighty Vltava, and not to a beggar near a bend in Shanghai's putrid Soochow Creek.

As we neared the creek, there were sounds of life. The pony's ears perked up and his plodding quickened once more. On the riverbank, squatters lived packed together. The water itself was no less crammed. Fishermen's sampans scraped against one another while their owners talked and sang, their foreign sounds a comforting affirmation of life.

We crossed the New Lesse Bridge over the Soochow Creek and passed into the International Settlement. We travelled down

THE SUITCASE

Thibet Road, a wide, paved street with power lines, streetlights, parked cars, tramways, sidewalks, trees, sturdy brick rowhouses, and new high-rise buildings outlined in neon lights.

In the distance, I could see the distinctive baroque-inspired central tower of the Great World amusement centre, the top entertainment venue in the Far East. Da Syga, as it was called in Shanghainese, was widely imitated. Beyond the entrance hall of image-distorting magic mirrors, the Great World held countless diversions. Visitors could play mahjongg or fan-tan, try their luck at slot machines, watch acrobats and opera singers, have their hair cut or ear wax extracted, see a peep show or a prostitute, purchase fireworks or incense, and more. All was topped by the iconic multi-storey spire from which, I had heard, people, especially indebted gamblers, sometimes jumped. The spire had no rails or nets. I had been told that management saw no point in making it more difficult for someone to kill themself. A "Great World" indeed!

On the far side of Thibet Road, a red-turbaned British Indian Sikh constable with ironwood staff in hand approached a bedraggled Chinese rickshaw coolie. The Sikhs had a reputation for too-harshly enforcing British law on the coolies, whose rickshaws required monthly inspections to remain licensed. It was a clever move by the British to use the Sikhs as a buffer between their laws and the many thousands who were forced to follow those laws. Many of the Chinese who spent their days pulling better-off Shanghai citizens and visitors around in rickshaws, and their nights in huts and lean-tos or slumped between their rickshaw poles, had once been farmers and landowners but had been driven into the city, and into poverty, by rural injustice and various conflicts throughout China. The pony and I moved on before we witnessed whatever brutalization the coolie, and his rickshaw, probably faced.

SHANGHAI, CHINA
16 MARCH 1933

We continued down the road towards the race track, past advertisements for Coca-Cola, Johnnie Walker, and Ardath Cork-Tipped Virginia cigarettes. A movie poster caught my eye. *The Secret of the Foreign Legionnaire*, which had been retitled for Shanghai audiences as simply *Sergeant X*, would soon be opening at the Strand Theatre on Ningpo Road, one of many cinemas in Shanghai, the "Hollywood of China."

Nearby, my destination, the Shanghai Race Club, was coming to life. Mafoos, or stable boys, along with jockeys and trainers, descended on the grounds. Pony owners who had risen with the chickens were just arriving at their clubhouse to read the news and watch the timing of the ponies 'round the track whilst gorging themselves with full English breakfasts, or breakfast on a fork, as Czechs call a hot breakfast. I did not realise that I was witnessing the final days of the old clubhouse and would soon see the construction of the newest, largest, most modern racing facilities in the world. Also under construction was a massive high rise overlooking the race course, the Park Hotel.

I returned the pony and gave my report to the Chinese mafoo, who would then bathe and feed the animal and prepare him for the day's time trial. I rarely saw the pony's owner, my acquaintance who had hired me, much less his competitors from the big-name racing families — the gentlemen who broke their fast in the Race Club's clubhouse.

Unlike my acquaintance, those men could afford a better pony at auction, keep it in a private stable, and provide top-notch training. The elites' ponies were fed a diet of grains imported from Canada and the finest local vegetables — grown only in American-owned fields, without human excrement for fertiliser. They never would have hired a newcomer in town, a smooth talker who had spent his formative years on horseback. Though my work as an equestrian officer and instructor, and

THE SUITCASE

my participation in the Prague Driving Club, had given me more-than-ample knowledge, I had no practical experience with Mongolian racing ponies.

Having left the pony, I departed the racetrack and climbed into a rickshaw. As I relaxed into the seat, the morning's exercise of what had been probably ten kilometres suddenly felt as if it had been forty. "Astor House," I instructed the coolie. He grabbed his cart's pole handles and leaned me back over the two wheels, then off we went down Nanking Road, me bouncing and swaying along behind him as he ran toward the Whangpoo River, and toward the sunrise.

Nanking Road was a busy shopping fare; banners and signs crowded the street. Signs in English were fairly simple to read — department stores, insurance agencies, photographers, photo supplies, clothing, perfume, tobacco — but many signs that whizzed by were in Chinese, Russian, Hebrew, and Japanese, and were indiscernible.

The rickshaw emerged onto The Bund near a bronze statue of the first English Consul-General in Shanghai, Sir Harry Smith Parkes. Behind the Consul's statue, the wide, brown Whangpoo River was crowded with its usual small wide-sailed junks, little roof-covered sampans, and large steamships and warships. Across the water was Pudong, home to factories, and to warehouses called godowns.

We were near the point on the Bund where my ship had docked only six weeks before. We paused for a moment, waiting to turn onto the Bund. I was able to lean back and admire the mighty edifices that defied the swampy Shanghai riverfront. To my right was the Palace Hotel a six-storey white-and-brick structure.

The Bund continued past the Palace, where the North-China Daily News building was mixed in with several banks, and the

SHANGHAI, CHINA
16 MARCH 1933

Customs House stood with its 110-foot clock tower from which "Big Ching" sang the Westminster Quarters throughout the day. In front of the Customs building sat another bronze British statue, that of Ulsterman Sir Robert Hart, Inspector-General of China Customs for nearly half a century. Beyond Avenue Edward VII, the magnificent buildings continued, becoming the French Bund, the French Concession's waterfront.

The Shanghai Club, located further down the Bund to my right, was, I had recently heard, one of the reasons why the grand building to my immediate left—Sassoon House—had been constructed by Sir Victor Sassoon. The Shanghai Club, with its famous Long Bar, was the most exclusive place in the city, the watering hole of the wealthiest British residents. Local legend held that they had once snubbed Sir Victor because, when Sassoon established his empire in Shanghai, he took advantage of tax incentives offered by British colonial administrators. While other British companies repatriated their profits to the British economy, the profits created by Shanghai's Jewish community remained in Shanghai. Perhaps this was why the British supposedly once excluded them from their exclusive Shanghai Club.

In turn, Sir Victor had built the tallest and most fashionable building on the Bund. Sassoon House was a shockingly tall granite affair with clean lines, capped by its verdigris-green copper pyramid where, nearly eighty metres above the Bund, Sassoon kept his suite. I would be meeting Lucien Ovadia at the Cathay that evening; it would be our first meeting since my arrival in the city, and my first visit to his cousin's establishment.

While Sassoon House towered on our left, the area before us was open, with only parking spaces and little trees between us and the waterfront. The coolie turned left, passing Sassoon House, and continued down the Bund, past Yokohama Specie

THE SUITCASE

Bank, the Yangtze Insurance building, the Jardine Matheson and Glen Line buildings, the French Bank of Indo-China. All were colossal, impressive buildings, but on the Bund, no flag flew higher than the British colours atop Sassoon House.

At the end of the Bund was the British Consulate complex. Beyond the consulate grounds lay the Waibaidu Bridge, called the Garden Bridge owing to the small park nearby. The bridge spanned the Soochow Creek and led into the Japanese-controlled part of the city, Hongkew.

On the far side of the Garden Bridge loomed Sassoon's nineteen-storey Broadway Mansions. It was still under construction, yet it already dwarfed every building nearby, including my own hotel, the six-storey Astor House, the first Western hotel in China, established by a Scottish merchant in the mid-1800s. It had since been updated to feature every modern comfort, like plumbing, electricity, and heated and cooled rooms.

Astor House was part of the Hongkew district's "German Corner." The "Corner" contained a German church, and the German consulate, tucked alongside the Japanese, Russian, and American consulates. I had chosen the site not only because of the Astor's affordable long-term rate, but also because of the German Corner's easy-to-understand signage, familiar food, and nearby Kodak shop. This shop had a special draw, as I had long enjoyed photography.

When the coolie stopped, it was difficult to stand. I was sore and tired, and unaccustomed to stepping out of the little rickshaw carts. While I was still giving him pocket change for the fare, someone exited Astor House and climbed in for a ride. I entered the hotel eager for a hot bath, a stiff drink, and a clean bed.

The lobby always struck me with the comforting feeling of a hotel that might have been located anywhere in the Western

SHANGHAI, CHINA
16 MARCH 1933

world. People sat here and there on the inviting furniture with soft carpets at their feet, reading newspapers or having muffled conversations. Rich wood panelling surrounded them. Arched white ceilings hovered overhead.

At the desk I inquired, "Anything for Captain Vladimír Taussig?" Especially as it afforded me a military rate at the hotel, and a certain esteem with new acquaintances, I had been using my rank again in Shanghai, something I never would have done in my home country, as I was now only in the Reserves. There were no messages.

The lift carried me to my floor, where I instructed one of the "Boys" lining the hall to pay special care to my filthy boots, and to bring a glass of whiskey, neat.

I bathed once for grime, and again for the pleasure of soaking my muscles. As I sipped my whiskey, I calculated that four or five hours of sleep should be possible before it would be time to rise again, dress for the afternoon's business calls, and go downstairs to take the midday meal, "tiffin." Tiffin was the customary two-hour midday break, borrowed from Imperial India, when businessmen dined, relaxed, or engaged in sport. Some visited their racing ponies, especially since the Race Club was so conveniently located to the business district.

I could hear the streets growing busy. I went to the window and looked down at the buses, trams, cars, and wagons, hedged by a slower stream of rickshaws, bicycles, and pedestrians. People moved along the sidewalks in both directions, pooling here and there near buildings and crosswalks before moving along. Between the buildings, patches of the river glinted in the morning sun.

I drew the curtains.

*****

THE SUITCASE

Trumpets blared. Drums pounded. Crowds cheered.

As I had slept, Big Ching had struck noon, and several hundred members of the German community and their friends had gathered at the German consulate grounds, mere yards from my hotel room. They had come to witness an historic event—the hoisting of new flags atop the consulate.

A man named Franz Xaver Hasenöhrl warmed up the crowd with a speech. He was, like myself, a veteran of the Austro-Hungarian Imperial and Royal Army. While I had fought against our former Italian allies, Hasenöhrl had been sent to the Russian lines, where two and a half million Imperial troops were taken prisoner, many of them Czechs. He had escaped from internment and crossed Siberia, entered China, and had become a manager for Siemssen & Company, one of the oldest German trading companies in China.

Hasenöhrl's speech stated that he wanted to "continue to fight with new courage for the soul of the German people, until the last of our fellow citizens has converted to our ideals, and has then converted the National Socialist ideals into deeds."

I was familiar with those National Socialist ideals. It had been several years since the party announced their "Twenty-five Point Program," demanding a redrawing of the allegedly unfair borders dictated by the Treaty of Versailles, insisting on social reform, abolishing peace treaties, and exempting Jews from German citizenship. These were some of the very concerns Zik had shared with me when I asked for his help.

The Acting German Consul, Richard Behrend, backed by a group of brown-shirted Nazis wearing swastika armbands, then read a statement for the cameras and reporters. He announced that Hitler and the New German Parliament—the old Parliament having been destroyed during the Reichstag fire that had occurred about a fortnight previously—had made the decree that

SHANGHAI, CHINA
16 MARCH 1933

the Weimar black-red-gold national and merchant flags would be replaced with the black-white-red of old Imperial Germany, and would be accompanied by the new Nazi swastika flag. And to think, the everyday Chinese citizen passing by might smile upon the swastika as a symbol of luck, as in the Buddhist tradition, when in reality it was anything but.

Voices rose and I recognized the "Horst Wessel Song." Its angry lyrics had been written in reaction to a murder of a stormtrooper. If only their speeches and songs had been foreign to me. Unfortunately, I understood with the fluency of any well-educated Czech, fluent in German.

I staggered to the window, tossing the curtain aside and squinting into the light. The midday sun gleamed off the Whangpoo in blindingly bright spots.

My eyes adjusted on the sight of the flags that would now greet travellers from the world over on their arrival in Shanghai—and which would also now grace my own view each time I looked from my window. To think that, not so long ago, I had insisted on taking that particular room expressly because of its view!

Uniformed Nazis paraded into sight and saluted. The crowd cheered as the soldiers' shiny boots kicked towards the sun, their hands raised in tireless acknowledgment of the new flags.

Every year thereafter, until the end of Shanghai as we knew it, a mid-March edition of the *North-China Daily News* would run a photo of those Nazi flags being hoisted at the German consulate in 1933.

I turned my back on the scene.

The steamer trunk in my room's closet contained many articles I had not needed in the short weeks since my arrival. There was a fair amount of clothing, either because it was unseasonable, or because it had been replaced by new garments when I discovered my ability to purchase bespoke items in the latest fashions using only my chits. I dug past my poker set, a wedding gift from my brother; a couple of guns in their cases, the rifle having recently been used to shoot at targets flung from the deck of the SS *Gange*; my Captain's uniform; spare tennis racquet; photo albums; and so on.

What I sought was in the bottom of my trunk, wrapped around a framed photograph of my family. I unfurled the Czechoslovakian flag. The pre-World War I Bohemian flag had consisted of two stripes, with white on top and red on the bottom. The Czechoslovakian flag of 1920 had introduced a triangle of blue over the left half of the flag — the blue of a democratic nation.

Flag in hand, I phoned down to the reception area. A Boy soon knocked at the door.

He held the flag level on the window while I attached it to the frame with generous amounts of the cello tape he'd brought. My new "curtain" blocked the German consulate from view, provided additional darkening for the benefit of my mid-morning sleeping, and, most importantly, alerted anyone who looked that the Germans weren't the only ones occupying the waterfront in Hongkew.

After I dismissed the Boy, I saluted my flag and, alone in my hotel room in China, I sang the Czechoslovak national anthem, written when the Czechs were just a minority in the vast Austro-Hungarian Empire.

This is our anthem, "*Kde domov můj*":

> Kde domov můj,
> kde domov můj,
> voda hučí po lučinách,
> bory šumí po skalinách,
> v sadě skví se jara květ,
> zemský ráj to na pohled!

SHANGHAI, CHINA
16 MARCH 1933

A to je ta krásná země,
země česká domov můj,
země česká domov můj!

In English, "Where is my Home?":

Where is my home?
Where is my homeland?
Water roars across the meadows,
Pinewoods rustle among crags,
The garden is glorious with spring blossom,
Paradise on earth it is to see.
And this is that beautiful land,
The Czech land, my home,
The Czech land, my home!

Home.

Shanghai had become my home, at least until the situation in Prague cooled down.

Somewhere on the other side of my flag, cheers and applause for the Nazis continued.

*****

The Astor House's dining room ran the length of the hotel's first two floors on its consulate-facing side. A long glass ceiling arched over the room's lower floor and upper balcony, which, combined, could easily have held five hundred.

I was shown to a table and emptied my pockets before I sat. They had been loaded with both sets of my calling cards; my chits, which were smaller than my calling cards and printed with my name; my engraved silver cigarette case and lighter; and

THE SUITCASE

pocket change sufficient for ride fares.

The bubbling voices in Japanese, English, Russian, German, French, and Italian, combined with the constant clinking and clattering of china and metal and glass, joined by the "pleasant" lunch music, was all quite intolerable after such a rude awakening. I hoped coffee would help.

The strong black coffee was as near a Czech brew as the staff could offer. As I drank, I scanned the *North-China Daily News*. The first item on the front page that day was not in the expected English, but was instead in German: an announcement of that day's flag-raising ceremony. I scowled and turned the page.

Looking over the sporting pages, I read briefly about how a racecourse had been established in Nagasaki, in Japan, and that they shortened the track owing to a shortage of flat land. I pored over the Shanghai sub-griffins' lap times. Sub-Derby day would take place the following Saturday. I learned that the Shanghai Recreation Ground on the land in the middle of the Race Course was closed to the winter sports of football and hockey, but that golf holes were now available for play.

I scanned the society page, with its columns devoted to tiffins, teas, and dinners, and to parties, dances, and balls. A formal ball had been given the previous night to honour the soldiers on board the visiting French ship, the *Jenne d'Arc*. Several hundred guests had danced at the French Club, the Cercle Sportif Français, both on the rooftop and in the ballroom, which had been festooned with red, white, and blue streamers.

The following night, Friday 17 March, the French Club would host an Irish Ball, in honour of St. Patrick's Day. I imagined the staff rushing to replace the patriotic French banners and ribbons with ones of Irish green.

I put the paper down and folded it neatly as the first in a long line of food-filled trays arrived. The wait staff presented

SHANGHAI, CHINA
16 MARCH 1933

assortments of cold meats, a tray of cheeses, a selection of relishes and mustards, then baskets of soda crackers and brown bread. Beef tea in a cup followed. Back home I would have been more than satisfied with these offerings and stopped there, but I was enticed by the further selections—veal stew Marengo, curried prawns with rice, fried tomatoes, baked potatoes, and a lentil salad.

After a few more bites, it was time to go. When the staff brought the day's desserts, the bread and butter pudding, the peach compote, and so forth, I had already ducked into a hired car. My newspaper was turned to the crossword puzzle to occupy me during the crawl through midday traffic, to the outskirts of the city where I was to engage in something that came naturally to me, sales calls.

I hoped to impress my boss, an American named Ruthven Nichols, by selling as many life insurance policies as possible. His company, Associated Underwriters, was an umbrella company that sold policies for Sun Life, Crown Life, and West Coast Life insurance companies.

Most importantly, the insurance companies acted as exchange brokers.

A man could exchange a paper dollar for silver pieces, then turn the silver pieces into coppers. He might wait a few hours and, after tiffin, go back and obtain a return on his original investment by exchanging the coppers for paper dollars once more.

There were dozens of currencies in circulation in Shanghai, with ever-changing values: Mexican dollars, American dollars, British pounds, the soon-to-be-abandoned Chinese silver taels, along with Chinese "big money," or paper notes, and "small money," or coppers. Chinese currencies varied by province of origin; there were dozens of types, with differing values.

THE SUITCASE

The ever-shifting currency exchange interested me. This activity was mirrored on a grander scale in commodities exchange.

I knew from my brief time with McKinnon, Smith & Company in Prague, and with the insurance company in Shanghai, that the exchange brokerage business was where I wanted to be. I just needed to find a suitable employer who would hire me without asking too many questions about my past and discovering my alleged misdeeds and my status as a fugitive from the courts.

Thankfully, Shanghai elites were mostly concerned with only two aspects of a man: how he presented himself, and who he knew.

Shanghai, China
Thursday Evening, 16 March 1933

> *He'd glide 'cross the floor*
> *with the girl he adored,*
> *And the band played on.*
> — Palmer & Ward
> "And the Band Played On"

My receding hairline stared back at me in the mirror as I fussed once more with my black bow tie and white pocket square. I wanted to set the perfect appearance not only for Lucien Ovadia and his wife, but also for whatever rich, beautiful, influential women might be present that evening at the Cathay.

Satisfied, for the most part, with my appearance, I donned my black cashmere overcoat, took my hat and gloves in hand, and stepped out for my first evening of many with the Ovadias.

To arrive in proper style, and, considering my fine evening dress and the prowess of the local pickpockets and prostitutes, I took a car despite the short distance.

I soon stood before Sassoon House's ground-floor shop windows and craned my neck to take in the building's height. A few floors above street-level, the lights of a stock exchange firm glowed in the dusk. Above those, other rows of windows were dotted light and dark with hotel inhabitants. Above those floors was my destination. I had never been in a building where I could practically touch the clouds. Prague did not have such high rises, only church and castle spires.

THE SUITCASE

Once inside, I admired my reflection in the brightly lit arcade's shop windows as I passed Rolex watches, leather luggage, silk lingerie, Parisian dresses, Siberian furs, silver tea sets, Chinese jades and ivories, and a thousand other wares.

The lift rose through the building, through the office-filled second and third floors. Floors four through seven comprised the Cathay Hotel. I stepped out of the lift on the eighth floor, which was partially under construction to make way for a new restaurant, the Peking Grill Room. As I walked the hall, I began to see people in evening wear, and to hear music and laughter trailing towards me. The approach to the ballroom was enhanced by soft lighting from Lalique wall sconces.

The ballroom was a massively long hall capable of accommodating several hundred guests. Tables were arranged around the dance floor, each in its own halo of light. A red floral centrepiece graced each white linen tablecloth.

I was shown to one of the best tables, where I found Lucien chatting with a handsome young woman to whom I was immediately attracted. She was tallish, with an athletic figure that would have complemented my own. Her evening gown was of the latest fashion. Her dark hair was short, in the post-flapper style; it framed her face becomingly. The woman's brown eyes glistened as I was introduced to none other than Mrs. Viva Ovadia.

"Viva, I give you Captain Vladimír Taussig," Lucien said.

She allowed me to bow and kiss her hand. Her skin was soft. Her touch, firm.

"Captain Taussig," she said. "So you are the incorrigible bachelor Lucien met on the ship. I have heard your name often in the past weeks. It's nice to finally meet you."

"Pleasure to meet you," I said. "Now I see why Lucien waited so long to introduce us." I gave Lucien a wink.

SHANGHAI, CHINA
16 MARCH 1933

"Come, let's sit," Lucien said. The staff delivered a drink. "I ordered you a whiskey," he added.

"Splendid. Thank you." I took a swig. "So, an 'incorrigible bachelor,' Lucien? Is that how you introduce me?" I laughed.

"Oh, come," he protested. "From the first moment I saw you, you were womanizing." I laughed. Lucien turned his attention to Viva. "So, my dear, what have you been doing this evening since you brought me my tails and tie?"

"Did you really?" I asked Viva. "Have you not left the office all day?" I asked Lucien.

He shook his head. "No. I even took tiffin at my desk."

"I shall begin introducing you as an incorrigible workhorse," I joked. I took another swig and drained my glass.

"Oh, he's always been a hard worker," Viva said as she finished her drink and dropped the cherry garnish into the coupe glass. "I have grown accustomed to it." She signalled to a nearby staff member. "I'd like another Movie Queen, and he'll have another whiskey."

"Scotch. Neat," I told the staff. "What's a Movie Queen?"

"We were just drinking them in the lounge," Viva said. "One of Sir Victor's inventions. Something like a Mary Pickford—fruity, with rum." To Lucien, she said, "Sir Victor invited quite a large group of young women this evening and proposed a photo contest to raise money for a local school. The contest winner will appear at the *Hot Pepper* movie premier at the Nanking Theatre and will win a trip to Hollywood."

Ovadia thought, then said, "Victor did mention something about the Russian Commercial School."

"Yes, that's it. They hope to raise $25,000," Viva said. "Well, Captain," she began as our fresh drinks were delivered, "What do you think of Shanghai so far?"

"There hasn't been a dull moment since my arrival," I said.

THE SUITCASE

"Where are you staying?" Lucien asked.

"Still at the Astor House," I said.

Viva said, "I have heard about the tea dances in the Peacock Hall there, but I haven't attended any. Apparently the orchestra shell is made of glass and coloured like a peacock's tail."

"The ceiling in the dining room is glass too," I said. "Quite impressive."

"So you like it there?" she asked.

"I liked it well enough until this morning, yes," I answered.

"But now?" Lucien asked.

"What happened this morning?" Viva chimed in.

I explained, "I chose to stay at the Astor House because I know the language in that neighbourhood, and requested my room because I had beautiful views of the river and the Bund. Now, after this morning's ceremony at the German consulate, every time I look out the window I will see the Nazi German flags on display. I take no issue with Germans on the whole, only Nazi Germans. Blithering idiots, the lot of them," I concluded.

"Why don't you move?" Lucien asked.

"I may do just that, when my contract at the Astor ends."

"I would suggest that you find a flat near the Czechoslovak consulate," Lucien said, "but then, it's near Shanghai's other German corner, in the French Concession. They may well have hung a flag there too. Have you discovered that area? Near the German school and the Deutscher Garten Klub?"

"Oh yes," Viva said. "It's near the cemetery on Bubbling Well Road. There's an enormous German church there, too. Brand new."

"Yes," I said, "Near the Kadoories' famed Marble Hall," I said.

"That's right," Lucien nodded. He smiled, knowing I had followed through on the conversation we'd had on the *Gange*

SHANGHAI, CHINA
16 MARCH 1933

and had gone to see the mansion.

"It's a thought," I said. Though, given my legal issues at home, I wished to stay as far from the Czechoslovaks as possible.

"Either way, don't worry," Lucien said. "Germans are a minority in Shanghai." The soup course arrived. It was thick and tomato-based. Lucien received it eagerly. That was the last we heard from Ovadia until he had finished his soup.

The dinner show soon began. Whereas Lucien mostly ignored the show in favour of his food, Viva was enraptured by the performers and hardly touched her dishes. When a poached Canadian salmon with hollandaise sauce was delivered, Lucien devoured his filet while Viva gingerly touched chunks of fish to sauce.

"What have you been doing for fun?" Viva asked.

I hadn't had much time for leisure activities. "I would like to get back onto the tennis courts, but the weather, and my schedule, have worked against me. Once I find better employment and have one steady job instead of several odd jobs, I will have time for tennis again."

"Singles? Doubles? Mixed doubles?" she asked with interest.

"All three," I said with a smile.

"Lucien, you should help Captain Taussig secure an improved position post-haste, so that he will have time for tennis this spring. I would so enjoy pairing with a competent partner."

Lucien explained, as he used his fork to tease the last bit of hollandaise sauce from his plate, that since their arrival in the city, Viva had been frustrated that most of the serious tennis players already possessed partners.

"There will be a round of tournaments at the end of summer, I'm told," Viva said. "Perhaps we could be ready by then?"

I laughed. "You are harnessing the carriage in front of the horse," I said. "I would be delighted to play in tournaments, but

I must warn you that I am out of practise."

"Join me at the French Club, whenever you are able, and we'll see," Viva said. "They welcome members of the military."

"Well, you have certainly got your marching orders," Lucien said.

Viva and I would spend many afternoons together at the French Club. Behind its high garden wall were twenty tennis courts. Players had their choice of either grass or hardcourt play. Spectators sat in the shade in wicker chairs while barefooted, loosely-clothed servants provided refreshment.

Ovadia said, "Victor has a residential hotel near the French Club, the Cathay Mansions. If you lived there, you could walk across the street and play tennis. It would certainly suit your needs. Everyone criticised Victor when he bought that land, because the whole area was so underdeveloped, but now it's an incredibly desirable location. It has furnished rooms. There's a roof garden with views all the way to the river," he gestured to the Whangpoo River that flowed just outside the Sassoon House's windows. "Even has its own bakery. He is building another residential building nearby, Grosvenor House. It should be completed by next year. We'll have a flat there."

"It's settled then," Viva said. "When you live at the Cathay Mansions and have plenty of spare time, you can simply walk downstairs and practise tennis with me whenever you like."

I would indeed eventually live at the Cathay Mansions, where the views of the French Club's verdant grounds and tennis courts were infinitely better than those of the Nazi German flag flying over the riverfront.

Point steak with bacon, potatoes, and onions arrived. Lucien resumed his concentrated eating efforts.

"If I am to be honest," I said, "This is the first reputable dancing establishment I have visited. I have been frequenting the

SHANGHAI, CHINA
16 MARCH 1933

dance halls, where you buy tickets to dance."

"Taxi dancers?" Viva asked.

"She's been reading about them," Lucien said in between bites. Upper class women didn't visit places like that.

"They are called 'taxi girls' because you can take them into a taxi and have a go with them," Viva said.

Lucien nearly choked on his dinner. "Viva!" he exclaimed.

"Not all of them," she said coolly, "but I understand that's the origin of the name."

"You are being shocking, darling," Ovadia said.

"Oh, don't worry, my friend. I am not so easily shocked. It's not as if she asked me outright whether I'd ever taken that type of taxi ride," I chuckled and gave Lucien a little wink. I tried to maintain my placid poker face but felt myself turning red as I recalled the after-dancing activities I'd engaged in since my arrival in the city.

Viva said, "I wonder what their lives were like before they became taxi girls. What wars or other hardships sent them into the dance halls and into the taxis of Shanghai... I understand many of those young women came from good families and are well-educated."

"That's what makes them such good companions," Lucien said. "Or so I have heard."

"Imagine if, in order to keep a roof overhead, and food on the table, and clothing on your family's backs, your sister or mother had to dance — or worse — with strange men," Viva pondered.

I had been taking a sip of my drink. I stopped and casually said, over the rim of my glass, "It would never happen."

"And why not?" Viva asked somewhat indignantly.

"First of all, I would never allow it, nor would my father or my brother. Then, considering that my elder sister is married —" I began.

THE SUITCASE

"So are some of the taxi girls," Viva interrupted.

"Fair enough," I assented. "And my younger sister…" I began to laugh. "She's simply too mean! Mitcka would step on customer's toes and spit into their drinks."

"Oh!" Viva began laughing too.

"I imagine she would feign ignorance of their language, to avoid speaking with them," which was ironic, since she had studied languages, music, dancing—everything an upper-class girl needed for a life of entertaining and being entertained.

Lucien said, "I'm sure some of them do behave that way." He placed the final piece of steak on his fork.

"How old is she?" Viva asked. "Your sister."

"Twenty-nine," I said. "She's the youngest of four. I'm second youngest; I'm thirty-three."

"Lucien's your age," Viva said. "I am twenty-five."

Leg of lamb with mint sauce, French flageolet beans, and an endive salad was brought to the table.

"Does your younger sister want to marry?" Viva asked.

"I don't think so," I said.

"I suppose that's not uncommon these days. Especially for a Jewish girl," Lucien said.

"Or for a modern woman," Viva added pointedly.

I laughed. "I don't think either one is the cause. She is simply not a very warm or loving person. I cannot imagine her being in love. I think I received the lion's share of amorous intent in the family."

"When is your birthday?" Viva asked.

Lucien rolled his eyes.

"November the second," I said. "Why do you ask?" I grinned at Lucien and looked back and forth between him and his wife.

With excitement, Viva said, "You are a Scorpio! You are ruled by your genitals."

SHANGHAI, CHINA
16 MARCH 1933

"Viva! Really!" Lucien exclaimed. Viva ignored him.

"She's not wrong," I said with hearty laughter.

"And when is your younger sister's birthday?" she asked.

"The seventh of January. The majority of my family's birthdays fall in January," I said.

"Interesting." Viva began nodding. "Then they are probably all Capricorns. Capricorns tend to be very sober, practical people. They are restrained and disciplined. Rational. Methodical. Capricorns do well with adversity because they are so patient and determined to endure. Your sister might not be cold-hearted—she's just a Capricorn."

Lucien chuckled to himself, as he clearly thought this line of conversation absurd. "As you can see, our Viva is quite interested in horoscopes and astrology."

"I was wondering how she's so knowledgeable about Scorpions and Capricorns," I said.

"Scorpios," she corrected. "You see, Lucien was born in November; I was born in January." She grinned.

Trays were circulated that contained pudding Nesselrode—an old Victorian iced dessert, and gâteux secs—little biscuit cookies. Coffee service accompanied the desserts. I welcomed the dark coffee that came steaming out of the silver pot, and quickly downed the contents of my little cup before opening my cigarette case.

"So, Astrologer Extraordinaire, what sort of women do Scorpios match well with?" I lit my cigarette and took a long drag.

She said, "Virgos, and Cancers, and Pisces. And Capricorns," she finished. We exchanged a glance. Lucien had his head down and was busy eating large scoops of pudding.

"How are you going to manage that?" Lucien asked between mouthfuls.

THE SUITCASE

Anxiety flashed over me. "What's that?" I asked. Maybe he had noticed our glance after all.

He stopped eating for a moment and wiped his mouth. "How are you going to court women according to their astrological associations?" he asked.

"Oh," I laughed. "Well, I suppose I shall have to ask them up front," I said.

Lucien waved a hand, then returned to his pudding. "Once the fashionable season begins, the ballrooms will be so full each night, you won't care about their birthdays."

The other diners began to applaud for the performers, whose adagio dancing and song crooning I had mostly ignored. Viva clapped with genuine enthusiasm. The entertainment band, The Olympic Trio, retired for the evening and the dancing band, Henry Nathan's Cathay Tango Orchestra, set up for the night. Patrons who hadn't come for dinner, but who wanted to dance that evening, were shown into the ballroom.

As the revellers entered, the Ovadias pointed out quite the Who's Who of young Shanghailanders they promised I would soon meet. Most were siblings: brothers Cecil and Denzil Ezra; sisters Kay and Lorna Lucas; brothers David and Edmund Toeg; the Chieri sisters: Itala, called Itsie; Matilda, or Mats; and Laura.

"Well," Lucien said as he clanked his spoon around, fishing for the last bits of pudding, "I really must go downstairs and finish a few things."

"Oh, Lucien, can it not wait until the morning?" Viva asked.

"If you would like to stay for a little while, I'm sure Captain Taussig wouldn't be opposed to taking a few turns. He has never danced on this floor before." To me, he said, "Sir Victor ensured it was made of the highest quality sprung wood." He addressed both of us: "And if you are going to partner in tennis, you'll need to get accustomed to one another sooner or later anyhow."

SHANGHAI, CHINA
16 MARCH 1933

"I would have worn my dancing shoes," I said. I did own thin-soled patent leather dancing shoes made for gliding around the ballroom.

The three of us rose from our table. Lucien kissed Viva on the cheek, gave me a nod, and exited the ballroom. Viva and I were alone in the crowd.

Viva smiled and extended her arm. "Shall we?" she asked. "No, wait," she said. She leaned over the table. The fabric of her gown draped closely to her haunches — was she even wearing undergarments?

She pulled a scarlet carnation from the table's centrepiece and snapped the flower's long stem so she could tuck it into my boutonniere.

"Red is good luck here," she said. She was so close to me, as her hands worked on my lapel, tucking the flower's stem into the little thread latch. I could see every detail of her sparse makeup, every single hair on her head, the very pulsing in her veins. Her perfume smelled smoky-sweet and exotic, like Shalimar. "And," she added, "carnations are January's birth flower. There," she said, stepping back to admire her handiwork. We locked eyes for the briefest moment. Was the warm feeling in the pit of my stomach a result of the whiskey? Or was it a reaction to the handsome, clever, interesting woman with whom I was about to dance?

I took her arm. She led me to the dance floor, where we came face-to-face once more. The deep "v" cut of her dress exposed her strong back; my open palm rested on her bare skin. A single piece of satiny fabric separated me from the front of her. I felt it imperative that I not reveal any excitement to my new friend's wife and thought it best to continue the conversation.

"I have spoken so much about myself this evening," I said. "Tell me more about you."

THE SUITCASE

"Me?" she asked. "I'm from the Fownes family. Fownes gloves?" She searched my face for a spark of recognition but found none. "Well, the name is quite well-known in England. We have been making gloves since the 1700s. My mother is from a jewellery-making family in Birmingham."

The way she moved against me was quite distracting.

"Let's see. I have four sisters. The eldest is your age. One is thirty, one is twenty, and the youngest is eighteen."

"Do these sisters ever visit Shanghai?" I asked with a sly smile.

She laughed. "If they did, I surely wouldn't let a fox like you near their henhouse."

"Do you and Lucien go dancing often?" I asked. "You are a wonderful dancer."

"Perhaps I should start charging a fee, like a real dance hall girl," she joked.

"I do have chits in my pocket," I said, "I shall issue you one for the dances tonight, and at the end of the month you can send a Boy around to collect."

She laughed. "Is that what the proper high-end dancers do? How much should I charge?" she asked. "What's the going rate?"

"Oh, charge whatever you like," I said. "Men would gladly pay it. In fact, the more exorbitant the fee, the better. Keep it exclusive. People want what they can't have."

"People want what they can't have," she repeated. She wore a thoughtful expression. I was sure she understood my innuendo.

The song changed to a tango, effectively ending our conversation as we danced.

After a handful of dances, Lucien returned from his office below and I delivered Viva back to her husband. I was hopeful that her performance on the dance floor was an indication of how well we would partner on the tennis courts.

SHANGHAI, CHINA
16 MARCH 1933

It would have been unacceptable to have ended the evening by sitting alone in my room at the Astor House, so I stayed a while longer in the Cathay ballroom. I smoked and enjoyed the music and watched the dancers, politely declining the odd invitation to step back out onto the floor. I did not care to dilute Viva's touch by dancing with another woman so soon.

While most other reputable Shanghai night spots shut down around two o'clock, the band at the Cathay sometimes played until dawn. When the orchestra finally set down their strings and horns, one of the patrons convinced the staff to throw open the ballroom's windows and let in the air from the river.

A shrill voice, whose owner's ears were still adjusting to the absence of the music, shouted with an American accent: "Who wants to go to Del Monte's?" Even I had heard of the joint, advertised as the "Livest Spot in Shanghai," owned by Al Israel. Trying the much-publicized ham and eggs at Del Monte's was tempting, but I had other plans.

I slipped out of the ballroom with the rest of the crowd. As they went down and caught cars to Del Monte's, I rode a lift the other direction. The operator took me to the building's rooftop access point. I buttoned my overcoat, donned my hat, and stepped out into the night. The enormous green copper pyramid rose from the rooftop. I went to the railing and looked out into the pre-dawn.

Across the Whangpoo, plumes of white smoke hovered over the factories of Pudong. To my right, across Nanking Road, I could see the roof of the Palace Hotel. The Customs House loomed further down the Bund, with Big Ching nearly ready to chime another hour. Lights dotted the riverfront down to the French Bund and beyond. To my left was Hongkew, with the Astor House, the looming Broadway Mansions, and the German corner with its new Nazi flags. I turned my back on the scene.

THE SUITCASE

Behind me, the setting half-moon hovered over Nanking Road and all of Shanghai.

To think that, a mere twenty-four hours before, I had been on a pony, trudging through the mud, and now here I was enjoying the same views of the city as Sir Victor Sassoon himself.

Back at the Astor House, I removed my overcoat and smiled when I saw the scarlet carnation in my boutonniere.

We had done nothing more than exchange a glance and share a few dances, yet I felt as if I'd somehow betrayed my friend. I would have to be careful with Viva, I knew. Especially when I drank. To indulge in my attraction to her would have been the ruination of my friendship with her husband. It was obvious to me that, in a perfect world, we would have met at some other time, in some other place, and might have had a chance to be together. She looked good on my arm. She enjoyed the same activities. She was clever, candid, beautiful, and strong.

And married. A faithful wife to a rather dull, overworked man whose entire existence hinged on not taking risks. Whereas I was only in Shanghai at all because I had taken risks.

Shanghai, China
Tuesday, 30 May 1933

Drove out to Hungjao at 6.0. Dined Ovadias...
There a Czechoslovakian called Taussig. Played Bridge.
— Sir Victor Sassoon's Diary

My collar was beginning to dampen. I slid a finger between it and my neck. Summertime in Shanghai was dreadfully warm and humid, even in the evenings. "How much longer?" I asked the driver. We had been away from the heart of the city for several minutes and were surely nearing our destination — the Ovadias' residence in Avenue Haig.

"Almost there, sir," came the driver's reply.

Good. I did not want to arrive for my first encounter with Sir Victor Sassoon spoiled with sweat. I was looking forward to the gathering. It was to be an informal send-off for Sir Victor before Thursday night's formal, public going-away party at the Cathay. Lucien would also be joining Sir Victor on his business trip to India.

When the car finally came to a stop, I paid the driver, then checked my reflection in the window before he drove away.

Inside the home, servants led me to the sitting room. The Ovadias' little dogs yapped happily at my arrival. I was glad to see Lucien's balding pate and Viva's handsome smile. Sir Victor had not yet arrived. As I sat, a servant brought a glass of scotch, neat, unbidden. "You know my tastes too well," I said to the Ovadias with a grin. "Thank you. It is good to see you."

"And you," Lucien said. "You look well."

"You really do," Viva said.

"Shanghai agrees with me," I said. I took a sip of my whiskey.

"How are you getting on with Uncle Simon?" Lucien asked.

"Rather well, I think," I said.

I had begun working for S.E. Levy & Company, which bought and sold securities and commodities and was a member of the New York Cotton Exchange and Commodity Exchange. Their offices were in one of the many banking buildings in Kiukiang Road, a side street off the Bund.

Our new friend Ed Toeg, an exchange banker and equestrian from the Race Club and polo set, had also begun working for Levy. After Viva's participation in Sir Victor's "Movie Queen" photo contest to raise money for the Russian school, we had all attended the Movie Queen Ball at the Canidrome. The following morning, Viva and Edmund Toeg volunteered together at the silhouette booth at the Ministering Children's League Bazaar. Now Toeg and I also worked together.

"I quite enjoy working for Levy," I said. You did me a great favour by introducing me." I raised my glass to Lucien. The position was indeed a step in the right direction, though the small commission I received in exchange for acquiring customers for the firm was hardly a liveable wage. "Although, I must admit, I have considered casting a wider net."

"How do you mean?" Ovadia asked.

"Perhaps I could also acquire customers for other, non-competitive firms?"

"Who do you have in mind?"

"What about E. Elias & Company?" I asked.

"Eddie and Freddy?" Lucien asked. "They used to work with Uncle Simon too."

"I sometimes see their racing ponies in the papers. 'Western

SHANGHAI, CHINA
30 MAY 1933

Star' and "Smiling Morn.'"

"They also live in Avenue Haig," Ovadia said. "We are practically neighbours. I'll introduce you, if you would like," he offered.

The following month, June 1933, I would begin acquiring customers for their firm too.

"And how has business been for you?" I asked Lucien. His answer was stopped short by the arrival of Sir Victor Sassoon, whose entrance was heralded by the servants bustling, and by more yapping from the dogs.

The legendary bon vivant himself, whose photographs I had seen in the paper, whose racing ponies were near-royalty at the track, whose buildings I had marvelled at and spent time in — the man himself was just another British bloke in a suit, with a big smile under his moustache and a walking cane in either hand. Both of his legs had been broken in an accident during his time in the Royal Air Force, leaving him with legs of different lengths, chronic hip pain, and a dependence on his canes.

The Ovadias stood to receive him. I stood too.

"This is Captain Vladimír Taussig," Lucien said, introducing me to Sassoon, "a Czechoslovak."

I shook Sir Victor's hand. He said, "I confess I do not know many Czechoslovaks. My favourite architect, László Hudec, is from Hungary, and my brother-in-law, Doctor Weisweiller, hails from Austria. But we do not see very many Czechs in Shanghai."

"Well, I am glad to be here," I said, "and fortunate to have met Lucien."

"And I have been partnering with Captain Taussig for mixed doubles," said Viva. "Our styles are quite complementary."

"Yes. I stay close to the net and intimidate the competition while Viva dashes about," I said. I enjoyed the intimacy of seeing her shortness of her breath, the flush in her cheeks, the small beads of sweat on her brow as she rushed determinedly about the court. "We are quite the formidable pair," I added.

"I think that, with a bit more practice, we'll be ready to participate in some of this season's tournaments," Viva said.

"Splendid," said Sir Victor.

"Well, that should certainly keep you entertained while we are in India," Lucien said. "Play tennis. Go dancing. Whatever you like."

Whatever I liked? I wondered what she liked. For a moment the sitting room melted away and I saw the Cathay ballroom, heard the orchestra, felt Viva's firm body beneath her silky gown, one hand on the naked skin of her perfectly fit back. I had not danced with her since that night at the Cathay. Sometimes during our tennis play, we had near-intimate moments, but I always firmly reminded myself not to risk the relationship with my elite friends. And besides, tennis courts and dance floors, and even residences, were such public places, and the servants and amahs were vicious gossips.

Instead, I had been releasing steam with the young women at Casanova's on Avenue Edward VII. It had new décor and a new manager, Joe Farren. There was dinner every night, breakfast every morning, and, in between, I enjoyed a variety of entertainments, such as the tap-dancing Sullivan Sisters; Hawaiian harmony singers David and Queenie Kaili; and the only all-girl dance band in the Far East, Jere Lee's Madcaps. It was great music for dancing, and often set the mood for other late-night exertions.

"Now then," Sir Victor said, jolting me back into the moment, "Whatever aperitifs you are drinking, stop this instant, because I have a new concoction and I should like you to be the first to enjoy." He disappeared into another room, one of the little dogs following at his heels. After a couple of minutes, he returned,

SHANGHAI, CHINA
30 MAY 1933

tailed by the dog, followed by a servant carrying a tray of bright-red cocktails in martini glasses.

"So," Sir Victor announced. "You have tried the *Conte Verde* before. In honour of next week's voyage, I give you the *Conte Rosso*."

Our lips met our glasses. Everyone took a sip. Everyone except for Lucien, who held his glass at arm's length. "I had the *Conte Verde* before all right," he said. "Which is why I am in no hurry to try this iteration."

Ignoring his cousin for the moment, Sir Victor said to me, "You are a man's man and would enjoy a good *Conte Verde*, which consists of gin, Cointreau, dry vermouth, crème de menthe, and a dash of lemon."

Gin and wine, with orange, mint, and lemon? The entire combination sounded intolerable, and I detested gin anyway. "Oh," I said, trying not to make an impolite face. "Well, I can speak only for the *Conte Rosso*, and it is a fine drink. Try it, Lucien."

Viva nodded with enthusiasm. "Lucien, do try it."

"Very well." Lucien took a hesitant sip. "It's certainly more digestible than the green one anyway," he said by way of approval.

"Apricot brandy, sloe gin, and lime juice," Sir Victor said proudly.

"I think it's delicious," Viva said. She took another sip.

"So how is your bungalow coming along, Victor?" Ovadia asked. Though they referred to it as a "cottage" or a "bungalow," the house was a large estate at the end of the Hungjao Road golf links, near the Lunghwa airfield.

"Quite well," Sir Victor replied. "I should think it will be ready in time for my return."

"When will you be back?" I asked.

THE SUITCASE

"Early November," said Sir Victor.

"Plenty of time," Lucien said with a nod.

Sir Victor took a sip of his cocktail, then asked the Ovadias, "What did you think of Mrs. Hayim's garden party? I understand it was something of a farewell gathering, as she will be spending the summer holidays with her sons at Harrow."

Ovadia explained that the Hayims, another prominent Jewish family, were related to the Sassoons through both business and marriage. Sassoon's forefather, David, had married a Hayim in 1828.

"The party was nice enough," Viva said with a shrug.

Lucien said to Victor, "She hasn't even been in Shanghai that long, and already she is tiring of seeing the same old faces at the same old functions."

"Not entirely, dear," Viva said. "There was just nothing notable about the party. Except for those strawberries they put out during tea. Delicious."

"Fresh berries from Mrs. Hayim's garden," Lucien explained.

"Maybe I will have strawberries planted at Eves next spring," Sir Victor mused.

"Another Eves?" Lucien asked with a short, wry laugh.

"Yes," Sir Victor said, "of course."

"If I may, why 'Eves'?" I asked.

"The name is representative of my initials," Sir Victor said: "Elias Victor Ellice Sassoon."

"I only laugh because he names everything 'Eve' or 'Eves,'" Lucien explained. "His stables, his homes, his boats, his ponies."

Sir Victor grinned broadly.

Just then, we were called in to dinner. Once we had been seated in the formal dining room, Sir Victor recited a prayer in Hebrew that was, as Czechs say, a Spanish village to me. I had been unaware that it was Erev Shavuot, celebrating the day God

SHANGHAI, CHINA
30 MAY 1933

gave the Israelites the Torah.

"If I may," I said, "what does the prayer mean?"

Sassoon translated, "'Blessed are You, Lord, our God, King of the Universe, who has sanctified us with His commandments and commanded us to kindle the holiday light... Who has granted us life, sustained us, and enabled us to reach this occasion.'"

"Ah," I said. "That is beautiful. It makes me think of my mother, and her Hanukkah prayers." I failed to mention that I'd never paid the prayers much heed.

"Yes, it is similar to the Hanukkah prayers," Sir Victor said. "I gather you are not very religious?"

The servants turned up the lights, breaking the reverential mood entirely.

"I confess, I am not, no," I said. "Not only do many from Prague share my more secular views, but also my father was not deeply religious, so I wasn't raised in it." I hoped my unorthodoxy wasn't a strike against me in Sassoon's eyes.

"My own family is quite religious," Sir Victor said. "And it has been engrained in me. My father and my Uncle Jacob built the Ohel Rachel synagogue here in Shanghai."

I nodded. I had heard of, but had not visited, the synagogue, the largest building of its kind in the Far East, constructed in memory of Jacob's wife Rachel.

"But many of the Jews you'll meet in Shanghai are less-than-observant," Lucien said, as if to say, "Don't feel bad."

The first course was brought in.

Viva changed the tone and topic. "I had great fun at the spring race meeting. Lobster and champagne and all that. And it is always a treat to see 'Nunky.'" She smiled at Sir Victor.

"Nunky?" I asked. "Is that a pony?"

Laughter erupted around the table. "Heavens no," Viva said, "but how would you know? 'Nunky' is what the family calls Sir

THE SUITCASE

Victor's uncle, David."

The laughter quieted.

"Yes," Lucien said, "it was great fun indeed, worshipping at Shanghai's other sacred temple, the Race Club. And now the temple has been destroyed." The race club building had been demolished a fortnight earlier, at the end of the spring race meets.

"Destroyed, yes," Sir Victor mused, "but the old clubhouse was simply falling apart. Decrepit old thing. Those sentimental goats wailed and moaned that their precious clubhouse would be ruined, while chunks of plaster were quite literally falling from the ceilings down onto their heads. The new grandstand will be open by the time I return," he added with satisfaction. "New, and modern."

"We must bring Vladimír when the clubhouse reopens," Viva said.

"Yes, certainly you shall have to come, Taussig. My race day tiffins are legendary," Sir Victor said.

"So I have heard," I said with a grin.

The next course was brought in, and the conversation shifted to a recent visit from a Hollywood comedic duo, Wheeler and Woolsey, or, more informally, Bert and Bob. Woolsey was the fast-talking troublemaker to Wheeler's smiling naïveté. They had come to Shanghai at the beginning of the month, and I had often seen their names in the papers as they visited popular venues like the Cathay and the Race Club, and attended cocktail parties and private dinners.

"Bob Woolsey was a jockey before Broadway and Hollywood, you know," Viva said. "He told me at the Ezras' party."

"He should have mentioned it," Sir Victor said.

"Woolsey didn't mention horse racing?" Viva asked. "Whatever did you talk about?"

"Women," Sir Victor said with a smile.

SHANGHAI, CHINA
30 MAY 1933

"I thought Woolsey was the married one!" Viva exclaimed. "Didn't we meet Mrs. Woolsey?"

"We did," Ovadia said.

There was a brief lull in the conversation before I was met with a much-dreaded and much-anticipated question.

"So, Taussig," Sir Victor said, "what brought you to Shanghai?"

I cleared my throat. "There is heavy unemployment in my country," I said. "Especially for bachelors. And for veterans."

Viva said, for Sir Victor's benefit, "Captain Taussig was an equestrian instructor in the Austro-Hungarian and Czechoslovak armies."

"Among other duties," I said. "During the war there were difficulties with the horses in the Italian mountains, so we all served as infantry," I said. "I am still in the reserves."

"Yes," said Lucien, "hence 'Captain' Taussig."

"Veterans struggled with employment in England too," Sir Victor said. "But I suppose, with the Depression on, it can't be helped."

"I had hoped to find a position through my father, who is the agricultural commissioner in Prague, but it did not pan out. He also works for Georg Schicht, an industrial company near the German border that handles agricultural commodities." I wondered if he had heard of the firm. How easy it would have been for someone in Shanghai to inquire about my past in Prague — and then decide to blacklist me! "I thought I would have more success, and more fun, if I tried my hand at Shanghai," I finished.

I had recently received word from my family. Maglič had not attended the early-May trial, and I certainly had not been present. The hearing was adjourned and given to the state attorney for a decision. Months hence, the case would be shelved until my whereabouts were determined, and what was to have been a temporary trip out of country became a more permanent arrangement.

"My father was also a businessman," Sir Victor said. "My forefather was a merchant in Baghdad. As he fled anti-Semitism there, a palm reader advised him that great fortunes awaited him in India. He moved to Bombay and founded the David Sassoon Company."

"But Lucien tells me you run the E.D. Sassoon company?" I asked.

Sir Victor nodded. "Once Shanghai opened as a port, David's son, Elias David, was sent here, and branches of the company were founded in various Chinese port cities. Elias David then founded his own company, E.D. Sassoon and Company, which was passed to my father, Edward Elias, and which is now my firm. I also inherited his title, and am now the Third Baronet of Bombay."

"Hence the 'Sir,'" Lucien said.

"Well, after hearing so much about you, I must say it is truly a pleasure to meet you," I told Sir Victor.

"And you," he said. "The Ovadias do go on about you."

"Do they?" I asked.

"And I so often find I am far too busy to entertain my favourite couple with the appropriate frequency."

"Though you dragged us here to Shanghai," Lucien said with levity.

"Yes, because you are essential to the company," Victor said with a nod to his cousin. He turned his attention to me and said, "Viva has found a suitable tennis partner. Lucien, a friend. Levy, an employee. And I, for one, am glad you are all here." He raised his glass and gestured to Lucien, then to Viva, then to me.

"Hear, hear," said Lucien.

"And I am glad to be here," I said as servants cleared our

SHANGHAI, CHINA
30 MAY 1933

dishes. Others followed on their heels, placing desserts before us.

*****

After Tuesday's private going-away dinner came Thursday's very public going-away at the Cathay. Hundreds of Sir Victor's "closest" friends drank *Conte Rossos* and danced until near dawn. Even Lucien stayed up late, and managed a few turns on the dance floor.

He and Sir Victor arrived in Bombay three weeks later, on 22 June.

In Shanghai, the end of the fashionable season travelled in with the storm clouds, and the plum rain season began. Most of the visitors left Shanghai and returned to their native climes to avoid the oppressive heat, constant humidity, and rains from watering cans, as we Czechs say.

When the rains passed, I returned to the tennis courts and represented Czechoslovakia at the Davis Cup. In early August, I played men's doubles in the Rotary Club's tournament. In mid-September, I competed in the Shanghai Lawn Tennis Association's Men's Singles Championship.

That fall, Viva and I partnered in tournaments. On Czechoslovak National Day, 28 October, the French Club's Hard-court Championships began, and Viva and I played mixed doubles. She also played in ladies' doubles. For men's doubles, I partnered with our friend Edmund Toeg. Toeg and I lost our match on 5 November, just after my thirty-fourth birthday.

By October, Lucien had returned from his travels and was engaged in his own tournaments — squash rackets.

The weather changed again, and the muggy Shanghai summer gave way to a crisp fall. After the crops in the fields

THE SUITCASE

around Shanghai were collected in the autumn harvest, Ed Toeg provided my introduction to one of Shanghai's favourite pastimes, the Paper Hunt.

Shanghai, China
Saturday, 30 December 1933

> *"Paper-hunting is not such an old sport in Shanghai as racing... [S]mall parties of men used to ride across country from one point to another, as in the first form of steeplechasing. And after the Taiping rebels were driven away from the neighbourhood of the Settlement, some of the residents and officers of the regiments which were stationed in Shanghai began to go paper-hunting, as had been done in the Crimea – where it was made a substitute for fox hunting – and in India. They rode out on Saturday afternoons, and sent away one of their number as fox, who laid the paper, and after a certain start had been given him the others made after the fox and chased him until they caught him... The first paper hunt was run in December 1863..."*
> —J. W. MacLellan, *The Story of Shanghai, from the Opening of the Port to Foreign Trade*

I WAITED WITH the other riders by the Stone Bridge near the Shin Chawing Station. We were in the midst of the sixth Paper Hunt of the season, and riders who had fallen to that point were being given a rare chance to catch up—something that was not usually done during a Hunt. I watched some of Shanghai's most distinguished citizens trot towards us on those ridiculous-looking Mongolian ponies.

That afternoon, the paper had led almost immediately to jumps, nicknamed things like "Spence's Finish," and "the

THE SUITCASE

Cocktail Jumps." Then the paper had led to two deep wades. The frigid water had risen to my pony's belly, and to my boots. As we emerged, steam rolled off his flesh.

The Hunt had crossed over a railroad, then we had chased the paper trail along "Otter Creek." We had passed what they called the "Blue Temple," then had ridden into the lowering sun, traversing more deep and cold wades before finally arriving at the Stone Bridge, where we now paused to wait for stragglers.

I didn't like that we had paused the event. The wait was deteriorating both my pony's temperament and my own. The longer the Hunt idled, the stiffer my muscles felt. My sweat had begun to dry in the winter air, producing chills.

"Have you seen Edmund Toeg?" I asked a nearby horseman.

"Not lately," came the reply.

"Could he have fallen?" I asked.

The man scoffed. "Toeg? Never." He turned his pony and walked away to join a nearby group.

After another few long moments, the Master of the Hunt resumed our chase.

The paper was found running southwards, back on the other side of the railroad tracks. "Tally ho!" came the shout. Riders stampeded towards the voice, racing towards the Gulland Bridge. I nudged my pony towards the others. He jerked from a standstill to a gallop—in the wrong direction.

He ran hard across an empty field. I heard hooves approaching and wondered who would be idiotic enough to race against me, when I was obviously heading the wrong way.

When the hoofbeats finally passed me, I saw an empty saddle. It was a riderless pony with its neck eagerly outstretched, running full-steam ahead. On seeing the stray horse, my own pony increased his efforts and shot across the frozen field.

Neither the pony nor I saw the unnatural ditch in our path.

SHANGHAI, CHINA
30 DECEMBER 1933

The pony's leg caught in the little trench and his step faltered; he slammed into the cold ground. We both cried out as we struck the earth. I deftly avoided being crushed under the pony's weight.

I stood, brushed myself off, and surveyed the scene. The pony was tilted toward the ground with one leg almost shoulder-deep in the dirt, while his free legs scrambled to regain footing. He whinnied and tossed his head, his eyes wild. It was difficult to tell how badly he was injured.

There I was, stranded in the cold, twenty-five kilometres from the city with an injured rental pony, while any possible help was stampeding towards the finish on Minghong Road.

I spotted a group of riders at a distance. I waved my arms and shouted, "You there!"

One of the riders left the pack and came my way. He slowed to a trot. As he neared, he called, "I say, are you all right?"

"Yes, but—"

"Which way's the trail?"

I pointed in the appropriate direction. "But—"

"Jolly good!" He rode off, shouting, "Tally ho!" so his group would follow.

I lit a cigarette and peered toward the horizon.

After a few minutes, the red-pink coat of a former Hunt winner drew near. It was Ed Toeg.

"Toeg!" I called, waving my hand.

"Taussig? Is that you?" As he neared, he began to laugh. "Come, that's no way to Hunt!" he teased. "The pony goes over the ditches, not into them. I thought you were supposed to be an expert horseman."

"Thank goodness you found me. The last fellow only paused long enough to ask which way the trail had gone."

He laughed again. "Oh, he probably knew that the surgeon

would be along to help you eventually. One always brings up the rear."

"We were already heading the wrong way when my noble steed decided to chase a loose pony. Neither one of us saw the ditch."

"Sure, blame the pony. Blame the ditch," he joked. Then he frowned down at the frantic pony. "Leg's not broken, is it?" he asked with seriousness.

"I don't think so, no. Difficult to say. I believe he is more frustrated and restless than he is in pain," I said.

"I heard they charge extra if you bring rentals back broken." He was trying to joke.

"You should go on and catch the others," I said. "Especially if help is on the way."

He waved his hand dismissively. "The leaders are probably nearing the finish by now. Today wasn't my day anyway. Besides," he said as he dismounted, "I helped you lose in tennis last month. Now you have helped me lose the Hunt. It's only fair, Taussig." He frowned at the pony. "Well, we can't very well lift him out. What should we do?"

"If we had something to wedge beneath him, he might be able to find footing enough to free himself," I said.

We scanned our surroundings, but we were in the middle of a field, with nothing that might serve our purpose.

"We'll just have to make do," Toeg said. He approached the horse, knelt on the cold ground, and prepared to put his shoulder on the pony. "I'm going to roll him towards you as best as I can," he said. "You help him with that leg."

"You're mad," I said, "He'll kick us."

"Ready?" he asked. He was already moving, so I took up my position. "Now!" Toeg said. He threw his weight into the pony and pushed so hard his boots left divots in the frozen ground.

SHANGHAI, CHINA
30 DECEMBER 1933

Meanwhile, I purposefully grabbed the pony's leg and helped it find solid footing. We managed to get it clear of the ditch.

The leg wasn't broken, but we agreed the pony shouldn't run on it or carry my weight.

"If we cut across this way," Toeg said, pointing, "we'll reach the finish in no time."

So we walked. In the distance we could hear the intermittent shouting and stampeding of the Hunt.

"I haven't seen you since Freddy Elias's going-away party," I said. "When was that? The end of November?" A cocktail party had been held by brothers Eddie and Ronald at the Elias Apartments in Avenue Haig to bid Freddy farewell. The usual Who's Who had been there. I had also made the acquaintance of Mr. Edward Gerald Smith-Wright, whose friendship I would retain for many years to come.

"Yes. How was your first holiday in Shanghai?" Toeg asked.

"Exhausting," I half-joked. "Haven't had a dull moment since my birthday."

"When was that?" Toeg asked.

"The second of November. Then Sir Victor returned in the *Conte Verde* on the fifth—the day of our tennis match—just in time for the fall race meeting." The enormous five-hundred-foot-long grandstand had barely been finished for race day, though the Race Club was still under construction.

"Did you have a big Hanukkah?" Toeg asked.

"No. I don't observe it, really." I had considered making an appearance at Ohel Rachel, but would have been a fish out of water. "I did spend one night during Hanukkah at the Cathay with Sir Victor's dinner party; then we went on to the Little Club," which had been Shanghai's first real nightclub. "I suppose that was the highlight of my 'Hanukkah.'"

"Ah, yes, I read about your outing in the papers. Mostly

young unmarrieds, I dare say."

"Yes. Quite the crowd of young women." We paused to watch a group of eager Hunters stampeding nearby before continuing our walk.

"What did you think of the Little Club?" Toeg asked.

"It was okay. We saw Laura Guerite's new burlesque number. The bandleader, Al Uhles, joined her on the floor. It wasn't half bad."

"Hm. Earlier in the year, Miss Guerite was making quite some anti-Semitic jokes," Toeg said.

"Really? That seems in bad taste. There were rather a lot of Jewish patrons in attendance."

"How was the dancing?" he asked.

"So-so. Maybe I have spent too much time with taxi dancers to appreciate these tepid socialites," I said. Toeg laughed. "The only one who didn't dance was Rose Marie Meyer," I continued. "Do you know her? She took a tumble from her pony, so she sat the dancing out with Sir Victor."

"Lucky him," said Toeg. "If she had only waited, you two would have had so much in common—falling from ponies," he joked.

I laughed and jabbed at him with my elbow. "Fair enough," I said. "What was I saying? Ah yes. You asked about Hanukkah. A few days after that, on the twentieth, we celebrated Sir Victor's birthday. His Christmas Eve party soon followed. You should have seen the ballroom—a big purple canopy was hung overhead, glittering with hundreds of stars. It was like looking into your telescope. There were four Christmas trees. Everyone wore paper caps and popped crackers.'"

"How very British. Whose party did you join?" he asked.

"Denzil Ezra's," I said. "It was quite the table."

He gave a short laugh. "I probably had more fun on the

SHANGHAI, CHINA
30 DECEMBER 1933

houseboat. Though I am sorry to have missed the Christmas Day Hunt. I heard it was one of the best hunts in recent years. But," he waved his free hand dismissively, "there will be others."

"How was your boating trip?" I asked. Toeg had taken me houseboating during the previous summer. During the voyage we had feasted on items catered from our favourite restaurants, listened to records, played the piano, taken dips in the water, and sunned ourselves on large rocks. Our guests included Viva Ovadia, Vera Nickells, whose Pekingese Jou Jou, had won several local dog shows, and Eileen Webster, who would become another life-long friend. Our laodah, or captain, had navigated the shallow creeks and calm lakes with ease. When, on occasion, our craft was taken by strong tides, we relied on the laodah to hire a steamboat to tow us out of trouble.

"It was a good trip," Toeg said, "but damned cold. Lou and Hope were good sports though."

"I saw they held a going-away party before your excursion. As if they were leaving on some long journey," I laughed. I was passingly jealous that Toeg had chosen the Andrewses to share the Christmas holiday in this way, and not me.

We walked in a comfortable silence for a moment. Then I said, "I had hoped to see your latest sketches and drawings, but the December issue of 'Town and Sportsman' is entirely sold out." The local periodical featured all manner of local sports, "from rugger to polo and yachting to the kennel." Toeg's work had also appeared in 1923's *Celebrities of the Shanghai Turf* and 1930's *History of the Shanghai Paper Hunt Club*.

"I have a few extra copies socked away at my office," Toeg said.

"Speaking of your office, I said, "working for Levy isn't the same without you. Congratulations on your nomination to the Exchange Broker's Association, by the way," I added. "I hope to join someday."

"We would love to have you," Toeg said. "And when I get back to the office, once the holiday's ended, I'll fetch a copy of 'Town and Sportsman' for you."

"Thank you," I said. After a pause, I added, "'Once the holiday's ended.' Do the holidays ever end in Shanghai?" I asked, half-jokingly. "A week-long banking holiday at Christmas, and another for New Year's…"

Toeg laughed. "What are your plans for New Year's?"

"New Year's Eve? I haven't yet decided. New Year's Day, I will be having tiffin at the race meeting," I said.

"Will you be attending the New Year's Paper Hunt?" Toeg asked.

"I dare say," I said. "I suppose I will be seeking redemption for today's performance."

"Arrive early," he said. "We'll be out beyond Chapei, in Tarzan country, so they are starting a half hour earlier than usual, at three o'clock. We certainly don't want anyone stuck out there after nightfall," he said.

I thought about my not-so-distant early mornings spent exercising ponies in the mud of Chapei. "Oh, it might not be so bad," I said.

Toeg laughed. "I suppose you are more adventurous than most. And mind the red paper. It marks where vegetables are planted. That's when you know Paper Hunting season is almost over, when the crops, and the angry farmers, begin to sprout. In fact, I wouldn't be surprised if an angry local…" he trailed off, but I had an inkling of where the thought was headed. "Well, never mind all that," he said dismissively.

"No, go on," I said. "Clearly the hole my pony fell into was created intentionally."

Toeg nodded. "The farmers and villagers have been known

SHANGHAI, CHINA
30 DECEMBER 1933

to meddle with the Hunt. That's why we lay the paper as near to the starting time as possible — to prevent anyone from interfering with it. And that's why we go around and distribute $5,000 to the locals each season. It's meant to pay for use of their land, and to account for any damages caused by riders."

"I see," I said.

The landscape was changing. We had left the field and were passing areas with trees and Chinese grave mounds. The Paper Hunt riders often used them as jumps.

"As for your remark about the holidays never ending," Toeg said, "after New Year's, we celebrate Russian Christmas. The businessmen's tai tai wives like to present gifts at the Russian orphanages and schools, and there'll be tea dances at the Astor House. After Russian Christmas comes the Chinese New Year; usually it falls in mid-February. Beware of Nanking Road and Avenue Joffre that day. They are impossibly packed with people and vendors and street performers. Then it will be late-February, and the Paper Hunt season will end. We will hold our usual Annual Race Meeting at the Race Club, where we are able to full-on race one another."

"That does sound fun. I would pay membership dues for that," I said. Toeg laughed. "And I should think that the new Race Club building will be finished by then," I added.

"I should certainly hope," he sighed. "And after the Race Meeting, you will read the sad notice that is given each year: 'Owing to the advanced state of the crops, the country is closed to cross country riding.'" He dramatically faked wiping a tear. Then he quickly said, "Then, during the first week of March, training for May's Spring Race Meet will begin, and on and on it will go!"

"Endless diversions," I said. Keeping so busy had certainly made my time in Shanghai fly by, but Toeg didn't know the half of it. We walked quietly for a moment. Our ponies kept pace behind us, mine favouring one leg but otherwise doing fine.

"Here we are then," Toeg said. We were nearing the gay flags that established the finish line near Minghong Road's Third Bridge. Spectators, reporters, and mafoos crowded loosely around, their breaths swirling in the cold air.

Many riders were still on the course, completing the final jump, a challenging high-low affair, then stampeding towards the flags. Some ponies crashed within sight of the finish line, while others swept triumphantly past to join the other finishers.

Judging by the swarm of people surrounding Billie Liddell on "Coke" and her husband John on "Bobbie Barker," one of the two had won. I recognized a few other faces, like that of John Keswick of Jardine Matheson. Lou Andrews, of Toeg's recent houseboat excursion, was another.

"Toeg! Where have you been?" Andrews asked.

"Stayed behind to help Captain Taussig," Toeg said. "Bit of trouble back near the Stone Bridge."

"Sabotage?" Andrews asked.

"Appears so," said Toeg. "Ditch in the middle of a field."

"Wasn't necessarily dug this season, though," Andrews said. He looked me and the pony over. "They look all right to me."

"A little sore, but neither of us broke anything," I said.

"Say, did you hear the shot?" Andrews asked, looking back and forth between me and Toeg.

"What happened?" Toeg asked.

"Ted McBain was riding Willie Middleton's pony, 'Cloister.' Broke the pony's back." The McBain family was well-known in Shanghai, as evidenced by the existence of McBain Road, and the McBain Building at the corner of the Bund and Avenue Edward VII. Lou Andrews continued: "And William Hu broke his ribs and collarbone."

SHANGHAI, CHINA
30 DECEMBER 1933

"Well. I am truly grateful that my own difficulties are nothing that can't be undone by a hot bath and plenty of rest," I said.

"If you can ever manage to get any rest, that is," Toeg said with a chuckle.

"Endless diversions," I repeated.

We were approached by "Chuck" Culbertson, a partner in Swan, Culbertson and Fritz, a firm that dealt in stocks, securities, underwriting, commodity brokerage, investment, and short-term financing.

Toeg briefly introduced us.

"A pleasure to meet you," I said. "I have seen your offices in Sassoon House." The firm occupied an entire floor just below Lucien Ovadia's office, and their large, wall-mounted boards displayed the latest stock prices, which were updated every ten minutes, even late into the night. Exchanges around the world were represented there, including Hong Kong, Singapore, Manila, Buenos Aires, New York, and Montreal.

Of the firm's three partners, Chuck Culbertson was known as much for his skill with horses and hounds as for his business prowess. The second partner, Joe Swan, had been the first man to establish New York Stock Exchange offices in the Far East. The firm's third partner was Chester Fritz, one-time manager of Shanghai's Kodak Company, and a genius metals broker.

"I would love to tour the offices," I told Culbertson.

"You should show Taussig around some time," Toeg said. "He has a keen business sense. You would be lucky to steal him away from his current position. He would be an asset to any firm."

"Is that so?" Culbertson asked. "You shall have to pay us a visit after the holidays, then." Toeg gave me a wink.

After I said my goodbyes to Toeg, I returned the pony to the stables, with my apologies for his injuries.

At my hotel I soaked in a hot bath, then dressed in one of my

THE SUITCASE

best suits. After a dinner downstairs, I went out into the city and made something of that Saturday night.

A car took me down Bubbling Well Road, past the Race Club, past circus tents that had recently appeared on the corner of Gordon Road. We turned after Bubbling Well Cemetery and arrived at the Paramount Ballroom, on the corner of YuYuen and Jessfield Roads, about a block away from Marble Hall.

The outside of the building was dramatic, with a central tower that held neon lights spelling "Paramount." The entrance was styled like a cinema. Inside, the main dance floor was the largest in Shanghai. Upstairs, a second dance floor overlooked the main ballroom. The upstairs dance floor was made of glass, and coloured lights beneath the floor shone up onto the dancers. With certain dress fabrics, the light revealed what women wore beneath their gowns.

I found a table in the open and people-watched, hoping to spot someone with whom I would want to dance. Manager Joe Farren, who had also run Casanova's, continually drew my attention as he flitted around the room.

Once I had found the right woman, we spent some time on the dance floor before disappearing into one of the more secluded booths.

Shanghai, China
Thursday, 24 January 1935

One of the largest events of the social season took place at the Cathay Hotel last night when Sir Victor Sassoon was host at a "Circus Party," his guests appearing in the traditional garb of the sawdust ring. The ballroom was decorated in keeping with the spirit of the evening...
— *North-China Daily News*, 25 January 1935

Two LION tails rose between the tails of my dinner jacket and stood parallel to my back, held by invisible wires. My costume was inspired by the Czech national symbol of a split-tailed lion, standing rampant.

I had taken a position with Swan, Culbertson and Fritz, and had brought my costume to the office earlier that day, in order to avoid crushing my "tails" while sitting in the car. As I continued dressing, I slipped my "paws" on. They were fur-covered gloves with golden claws that had been designed in such a way as to leave my palms and fingertips mostly free. This would allow me to hold a glass, or a woman, and to navigate my cigarette case without difficulty.

Finally, I donned the hood that covered my head and shoulders. A jawless lion's face sat atop my own face, with his fangs and upper teeth on my forehead, and his mane covering my neck and shoulders. A golden crown, similar to the Czech symbol, rested atop the lion's head. The piece was heavy to wear, but impressive to behold.

THE SUITCASE

I checked my reflection in the mirror in one of my boss's offices. I did not have my own office, so to speak. My job with the firm was to acquire new clients. I targeted wealthy Chinese who were often trading internationally for the first time. Thus far, I had been sent to various areas within vast China—Nanking, Chungking, and Peking.

Using my earned commissions, I had purchased new luggage from the Cathay Trunk Company in the arcade of the Sassoon House. With my leather-veneered suitcase in hand, I travelled first-class through China, taking photographs and collecting coins as I went. That summer, banks had collected silver dollars to send to the mint for melting into new silver dollars and bars. I had saved many a coin from that fate.

Satisfied with my appearance, I headed up to the fancy dress ball. Upstairs, the Cathay ballroom had been transformed into the "big top" for Sassoon's party. Long Tack Sam's Chinese acrobats rolled past me as they cartwheeled their way around the ballroom. Men circled the room pushing wheelbarrows that contained tiny Chinese women in long scarlet brocade tunics holding little bamboo fishing poles. All around these performers, guests were dressed according to the circus theme, as elephants and elephant-shit sweepers, acrobats and dancing girls, tattooed women and strong men. One couple formed a donkey when they stood together. The donkey wore a racing tag that read "Opera Eve"—a jab at Sir Victor's prize-winning racing pony.

I spotted Sir Victor in a ringmaster's costume. He wore a red coat and tails over a white taffeta shirt, framed by a black velvet top hat and polished tall black boots. He carried a whip.

Since the German Hagenbeck Circus and Menagerie's visit to Bubbling Well Road in late '33, Shanghai had seen a variety of circus-themed plays, movies, and fancy dress parties. I knew Hagenbeck as a pioneer for his cageless zoo in Hamburg, where

SHANGHAI, CHINA
24 JANUARY 1935

animals lived in natural landscapes, separated from the public by moats. In Shanghai, his circus act was met with protests. Some who had lived in India objected to the captivity of sacred elephants and to Hagenbeck having trained them to "dance."

I found Lucien Ovadia, who looked supremely uncomfortable in an old-fashioned bathing costume.

"That's some outfit," Lucien commented as he looked me up and down.

"Your wife's seamstress crafted it," I said, turning so he could admire my tails — dinner jacket tails and lion tails. "Isn't it something?" I was quite proud. I looked him over. "That's quite an interesting costume you've chosen for yourself," I said. "I don't think I have ever seen you in swimming clothes — not even last summer when we travelled to Japan. I think you spent the entire time sunning yourself on the rocks while Viva and I swam with those finless porpoises."

During our visit to Miyajima, we had climbed the steps of Mount Misen and spun the prayer wheels there, watched the deer and monkeys in Maple Valley park, and taken tea with the famous maple-leaf pastries. On our final night, we visited the bay before dinner, during low tide. While locals dug for clams, we walked out to the ancient torii gateway and left coins at its base for luck, hoping the coins would be taken on by a clam and become part of the gate itself.

"This," he gestured to his bathing outfit, "will make sense when you see Viva," he explained. "She's a seal." The Ovadias' outfits coordinated with Marty Sands and Mildred Dawn, the regular musical comedy act at the Cathay Ballroom. "And to think I nearly did not attend tonight," Lucien said. "So much has happened since the accident."

"Yes, what's the latest?" I asked. A few weeks previously, Ovadia had struck a pedestrian with his car on Bubbling Well

THE SUITCASE

Road. He and Viva had been travelling towards the Bund on their way to watch *Transatlantic Merry-Go-Round* at the Metropol Theatre when Wong Ah-kiu, a blacksmith, walked right out in front of their car. Lucien swerved, but the blacksmith's right leg was struck by Lucien's running board. Now the man was suing for $12,000.

"The man says he's been in the hospital since the accident. His shin bone is broken, and there was some trouble resetting it. He might miss months of work and can't provide for his family." Lucien continued, "I did feel sorry for him, until his friends turned up as witnesses and claimed that I was drunk at the time of the accident."

"You? Drunk?" I rolled my eyes. "Next time I am low on funds, remind me to 'not see' a car when I cross the road. Make sure the driver is a nice, wealthy taipan with a pretty, well-kept tai tai wife."

Lucien laughed.

"I should think Judge Grant-Jones will dismiss the case," I said.

"Surely he will do what is just, and not what is best for his social set," Lucien said. But eventually, he did indeed dismiss the case.

"How is Viva?" I asked, gesturing to the seals and swimmer. "Whichever seal she is…"

He laughed. "The one on the left. She's doing well. She vacillates between being annoyed by the same-old same-old, and actually enjoying the tai tai wife routines."

"I haven't seen much of her since our last tennis tournaments," I said. We competed together in the Mixed Doubles Hardcourt Championship at the French Club in October.

"Yes, well you have been busy all winter gallivanting around with the likes of those fellows," Lucien said with a smile,

SHANGHAI, CHINA
24 JANUARY 1935

gesturing to the approaching Ed Toeg and David Innes-Ker. Toeg wore a strong man costume. Innes-Ker, dressed as a juggler, was a fresh face in our Shanghai circle, having only just left London a few months previously, in mid-October.

"What do you think, Taussig?" Toeg asked, "Better than last month's 'Ancient Egypt' ball?"

"Well, I'd take the Cathay over the Canidrome any day," I said, "but I did enjoy all the Claudette Colbert Cleopatra costumes. I suppose comparing these circus acrobats to those harem girls is mixing apples and pears." December's Egyptian ball had featured eighteen harem beauties lounging on colourful Turkish carpets and pillows beneath a draped Egyptian tent. Their eyes sparkled above their silken yash-maks which, when removed, revealed the beauties to be none other than Shanghai's own Western young women—Misses Lorna and Kay Lucas, Misses Itala "Itsie" and Matilda "Mats" Chieri, and others.

Nathan Rabin's scarlet-fezzed orchestra had performed wild tunes on their horns; the Six Hollywood Blondes had presented an "Egyptian Fantasy" dance; Miss Margery Marshon had given a dance she called "Oriental Mood"; "Itsie" Chieri had presented a "Dance of the Orient"; and tap dancer Vie Wong had delighted us with his "Chinese Bing Crosby."

Toeg said, "I'm sure Sir Victor was eager to make this ball even more extravagant."

"I dare say he succeeded," Ovadia said.

As we looked around at our fellow guests in their fancy circus dress, Ovadia, Toeg, Innes-Ker, and I fell into guessing which costumes were inspired by, or were direct copies of, costumes from various films.

"*The Circus*," Toeg said, gesturing towards a woman in a little tutu.

"Yes, that's right, the Chaplin film," I said.

THE SUITCASE

"She looks just like Merna Kennedy," Innes-Ker said.

"How about Mae West?" Toeg asked, directing our attention to a beautiful lion tamer who might have stepped straight off the set of *I'm No Angel*. The feathers on her cap, the decorative fronting of her jacket, the leggings and boots and riding crop she carried, were all perfect replicas of the 1933 film costume.

"Did she come here with a lion?" I asked. "Did anyone see?" My friends snickered and laughed. "I'm serious!" I protested. "Just wait, before the end of the night, she will be putting her head in this lion's mouth," I joked, referring to Mae West's stunt in the film.

"There's *Tonight is Ours*," said Lucien. In the film, Claudette Colbert wears a sequined ruffle-necked harlequin costume with a little sequined cap.

"That's a good one," I said, aware that the Colbert film was based on Noël Coward's *The Queen Was in the Parlour*, and that Shanghai loved Noël Coward. He had written *Private Lives* in his suite at the Cathay when the hotel had been newly-built. A few of my friends could recite Coward's fast-paced song, "Mad Dogs and Englishmen," a take on English life in the Far East based on a saying coined by Rudyard Kipling. The "song" refrained with the idea that, in the Far East, only "mad dogs and Englishmen go out in the midday sun."

"You know," Innes-Ker said, "*The Circus Queen Murder*, with Greta Nissen, is playing at the Cathay Cinema. We should go."

"I think after tonight I will have had quite enough of the circus," Lucien said.

Innes-Ker chuckled. "Fair enough."

"I'll go," I offered. "I would like to visit the new Park Hotel," I said. "We could make an evening of it."

The hotel that loomed over the racecourse had finally opened its twenty-two storeys for business. The Park was advertised

SHANGHAI, CHINA
24 JANUARY 1935

as "Shanghai's Newest... Tallest... Smartest... most up-to-date HOTEL and SOCIAL RENDEZVOUS."

"I have not been," Ovadia said, turning up his nose dramatically. "It's in direct competition with Sir Victor, you know."

"Oh, a dinner and a few cocktails won't hurt him one way or the other," Innes-Ker said.

Toeg said, "I've visited the Grill Room. It was open during the race meetings in November. It's on the fourteenth floor. What a view of the racecourse!"

Ovadia said, "I'm sure it cannot surpass the view from Sir Victor's private box."

"It is a massive building, isn't it?" I asked rhetorically. "Looks like it should be in New York, not Shanghai."

"Actually," said Lucien, "It was modelled after the 'Radiator Building' in Manhattan. László Hudec, that Hungarian architect, designed it. He's done design work for many of Sir Victor's buildings," he added for Innes-Ker's benefit.

Innes-Ker nodded. "I see. It looks a bit sinister, I think. All that black granite and brown tile. And so tall."

"Only three feet taller than the Cathay," Ovadia bristled. But the Park was indeed taller. It would remain the tallest building in the Far East for nearly fifty years. From the Park Hotel, one could see Big Bertie, the new clock face that glowed high over the Race Club; the neon tower of the Paramount Ballroom; the tiered rooftops of the Great World Amusement Centre and the glow of lights all the way down Nanking Road to the Bund.

Our chatter was interrupted by a commotion on the dance floor. There was a great to-do of shrieks and laughter and a sudden shifting of bodies. The tittering crowd made a circle around the cause of the excitement—a real donkey.

It seemed that John Keswick and Sylvia Chancellor had

rubbed themselves into the party. Keswick, whom I had seen at the Paper Hunt, was a director at Jardine Matheson. For the ball, he had dressed like a clown. Sylvia Chancellor, wife of Sir Christopher Chancellor, head of Reuters in the Far East, had dressed like some sort of French harlot.

The pair had brought a live donkey with them.

The beast had been convinced to step onto the dance floor, and when Keswick attempted to mount it, the donkey stood, brayed, and shat in the middle of the floor, causing the uproar.

"Remove this animal at once," Sir Victor ordered Keswick. Ovadia went to be of use to Sir Victor, and Toeg wandered off. Innes-Ker said, "That was exciting."

"Indeed," I said. "It's unusual for something like that to happen at a Sassoon party."

"The incident gave the whole thing quite the circus atmosphere—including the smell," he said. "If you'll excuse me, I'm going to go try my luck with that 'acrobat' over there. Why don't you try the 'lion tamer'?" he asked.

"Maybe. I suppose it would be fitting, but I don't know if I'm in the mood," I said.

"You? Not in the mood?" He held a hand to my forehead and peered into my eyes. "Are you feeling well? Do you need a doctor?" He dropped his hand and turned away, laughing and repeating, "'Not in the mood!'"

I smoked a cigarette and scanned the room for the tall white feathers the lion tamer wore on her hat. I soon located her and used my lion's claw to tap her on her spangled epaulet. She turned and looked me over. My lion's head and crown were as tall as her long plumes of white feathers.

"That's quite the outfit," I said.

"Gee, thanks!" she said. An American. "Mae West. *I'm No Angel*," she said, gesturing to her costume. I smiled; I already

SHANGHAI, CHINA
24 JANUARY 1935

knew. "Hey, that's some lion costume!" she exclaimed. "I don't suppose you need to be tamed?" she asked playfully.

"Oh, I just may," I replied with more seriousness. Her cheeks were flushed. "You look warm," I said.

"It's this jacket! Unbelievably heavy! It's all this beading!" she held her arms out as far as she could in the crowd and did a little spin.

"I bet it is heavy. This lion head is heavy too," I said. "And being jammed in this crowd doesn't help matters. I don't suppose you would like to go get some fresh air?"

She thought for a moment. "Gee, I don't know, Mr. Lion. What's your name, anyway?"

"George," I said, using the English version of my middle name. "I hear the view from the rooftop is incredible. Won't you join me? It simply isn't safe for a lion to undertake such an adventure without proper supervision."

"The roof?" she asked. She looked furtively around the ballroom. "All right," she said with a grin. "Show me."

As we exited the ballroom, I noticed that Sylvia Chancellor had fallen asleep on the ballroom floor.

SHANGHAI, CHINA
Thursday, 19 December 1935

> ...*to compel our men
> to sign a pact of peace,
> we must make war.*
> – Aristophanes, *Lysistrata*, Act I

I SAT IN the audience at the Capitol Theatre, located on the banks of the Soochow Creek behind the British consulate grounds. The eight-storey building also contained apartments, as well as the offices of Hollywood Studios, Columbia Films, Twentieth Century Fox, and Paramount. The theatre usually functioned as a cinema, but that night the stage was being used for a play. It was the final night of the International Arts Theatre's three-night run of *Lysistrata* – the contemporary Gilbert Seldes version.

I watched as, just beyond the footlights, the Old Men's Chorus prepared to set fire to the locked Acropolis gate in hopes of gaining entry. The leader of the Old Men's Chorus said: "Philurgus, you are at Number One Post..."

I straightened in my seat; Philurgus was the role I was to have played. But I had backed out of the role, owing to the dizzying number of other obligations I had been juggling.

"Fire carriers – light up! Now ready! Close ranks! Now forward!" As the Acropolis gates caught "fire," the Old Women's Chorus doused the flames with pitchers and urns of water. Their act could be seen as a metaphor for the entire play. In every iteration of the work – Aristophanes's original, Seldes's contemporary, or the French version by Donnay – the title

SHANGHAI, CHINA
19 DECEMBER 1935

character, Lysistrata, attempts to end the twenty-one-year-old Peloponnesian War by convincing women to withhold sex until their soldiers are driven to negotiate a peace treaty. The women also lay siege to the Acropolis, seat of the Greek treasury, keeping vital funds from the men.

Emily Hahn, called "Mickey" by friends, held the titular role. Hahn, a thirty-year-old American, had come to Shanghai in March on a cruise with her sister, and had stayed behind when the sister departed. She was a journalist for the *New Yorker*, and kept busy in Shanghai writing for the local papers. Hahn had fallen in especially well with Sir Victor; the two were carrying on an affair.

She made a splendid Lysistrata.

David Innes-Ker sat next to me in the theatre. He was to have been the play's Spartan Envoy but, like me, he had relinquished his role. We watched as another actor delivered the Envoy's lines to the Old Men's Chorus. As the Spartan Envoy informed the Chorus that he sought to deliver terms of a peace treaty, his exaggerated erection drew laughs from the audience. It seemed Lysistrata's plan to end the war was working.

There had been laughter throughout the play, which had been advertised in the papers as "the most amusing comedy Shanghai has ever seen." The audience really began to roar when Myrrhina, played by Grace Darroch, and Kinesias, played by Reggie Meyer, began their part.

Myrrhina had only grudgingly agreed to Lysistrata's plan, as she had been looking forward to her husband, Kinesias, coming home on leave from the war. Now that Kinesias had returned, Myrrhina had to dodge her husband's advances in order to keep her promise to Lysistrata. The two dash about the stage, attempting to find a suitable place to copulate, but every possible location has been taken by other couples.

THE SUITCASE

Having finally found a private spot, Kinesias all-too-happily lays down to receive his wife's attentions, but Myrrhina, true to her promise, continually delays the deed. She is always on the brink of unpinning her tunic, and keeps leaving Kinesias to seek various "necessary" items for their lovemaking.

First it is a bed. Kinesias protests, "A bed! To Hades with beds. Here, lie down on the ground." She runs off to find a bed anyway. Then she exclaims, "Oh, plague take it! This mattress is hard. I'll have to get another one." Then, "But mercy! We haven't got a pillow." Then, a blanket. Then, some perfume. Each time, Kinesias protests that they do not need the item she seeks. The audience's laughter grew along with Kinesias's frustration.

When the pair are finally about to engage in the act, Myrrhina says, "You remember, Kinesias, you'll vote to make peace."

He replies, "One thing at a time, my dear. We'll consider that later."

Myrrhina then runs off, leaving Kinesias more frustrated than ever before. "Myrrhina, Myrrhina, aren't you going to love me?" he calls after her.

"I'll consider that later," she says.

The audience erupted in laughter.

Meanwhile, on the stage, other women and their husbands were emerging from similar near-lovemaking situations. I knew the end of the play was nearing.

After a few minutes more, the Chorus for the Ballet came on stage—twelve young Shanghai socialites led by Miss "Itsie" Chieri, joined by "Sandy" Tittman, who was a close friend of Sir Victor's and the niece of American Judge Milton J. Helmick, and others. Their Bacchanale was exceptionally well-performed. As their dance came to its conclusion, the Men's and Women's Chorus gathered to shout their series of "Hails" to the Gods, ending with "Hail, Pallas Athena..." the same sentiment with

SHANGHAI, CHINA
19 DECEMBER 1935

which Aristophanes's original version also concludes.

The audience applauded. The cast members made their bows. Applause drew Mickey Hahn back once more for a curtain call. Then the amber glow of the house lights returned. I stood and stretched, and asked David Innes-Ker, "Shall we?"

*****

As the car rolled down the Bund, I enjoyed the distant view of the Palace Hotel and the windows of my office there. I had left Swan, Culbertson and Fritz in August with good wishes and high recommendations, and had taken a salaried position at another firm, Drakeford, Davis and Wilson. I was their Tokyo liaison.

David followed my gaze.

"I love my office," I said. "I can see Ovadia's window from my desk on one side, and the Bund and the river on the other. And I am glad I will be travelling to Japan."

Innes-Ker said. "I should like to see Japan sometime myself, while I'm out here."

Just before we reached the Palace, we would pass the entrance to Nanking Road, the Sassoon House, and the Bank of China lot which was then under construction.

"I would hate to listen to the construction all day," Innes-Ker said.

"Thankfully, it's on the far side of Sassoon House and isn't directly next-door. They demolished the old Club Concordia building last month. Construction on the building itself will be underway soon enough, I'm sure."

"Yes, well, I don't envy you the noise."

He was right. When construction began in February, pine piles up to a hundred feet in length were driven blow-by-blow into the swampy ground by a steam hammer. Two thousand piles were driven, each requiring up to three thousand hammer blows. The noise was maddening, even on the far side of the work zone.

As the car turned down Nanking Road, I caught one more glimpse of the Palace Hotel. "I should go in and check messages soon. It will give me something productive to do," I said with a sigh. "When I first came to Shanghai I quite enjoyed having a fortnight's leave from work while the banks were on holiday for Christmas and New Year's. Lately I grow restless around the holidays, with only ponies and parties to pass the time."

David Innes-Ker laughed. "Aren't you strange, to be given a holiday and still want to work." The car passed the Race Club. "Have you considered extending the break? Taking a long leave and visiting home?"

Other people, who worked for larger firms, took a "long leave" of six months every four years, and returned home to England, or to India, or to the States.

"I have not been with the firm long enough to merit a long leave. If I left, I would be replaced. Besides, two weeks out of work is bad enough. Can you imagine how restless I would be after spending a full quarter in Prague? A man can only stand so much visiting and dining and pleasantries."

"All play and no work makes Vladimír a restless boy," David said.

I laughed.

We arrived at the Cathay Mansions and went up to my rooms.

"What, no Hanukkah decorations?" Innes-Ker joked. He knew I wasn't very observant.

"I think the first night is tomorrow," I said. "No, no menorah for me. I would have preferred a Christmas tree. I do rather enjoy the smell. I miss the forests of my homeland." The talk of taking a long leave had only sharpened that sense of homesickness.

SHANGHAI, CHINA
19 DECEMBER 1935

"Why didn't you get a tree?" he asked.

I waved my hand. "Such a fuss," I said.

He nodded. "I suppose. If you had a Boy it would be no bother at all. I don't see how you manage without proper servants."

I laughed. I then poured two whiskeys and joined David where he had gone to stand at the window. We looked out onto the tennis courts and had views of the French Club's enormous white building glowing with lights.

"It's a shame," I said. "I finally live right next to my favourite courts in all of Shanghai, yet I hardly have the chance to use them." All summer, until my August resignation, I travelled on behalf of Swan, Culbertson and Fritz. When I should have been practicing for tournament play, I was all over the Far East, visiting Surabaya in the Dutch East Indies, as well as Sarawak and Singapore. Owing to my travels that year, I had hardly seen Viva at all, let alone on the courts.

Innes-Ker, meanwhile, was thinking on the French Club building itself. "This really is the perfect location for our New Year's cocktail gathering," he said. "Afterwards, we can hop right over from your flat to the French Club for the big party there."

"I only wish I had a balcony," I said.

"It's too cold to be out on the balcony, Taussig," Innes-Ker said with a short laugh.

"You are right," I said. "But the building really could use some balconies. I had a friend at Swan, Culbertson and Fritz, Desmond O'Neill, who lived at the Broadway Mansions. He's gone now; he left in September for an 'indefinite stay' in England. He had an incredible balcony, with views of the Bund. We would invite women over for play-acting and use the balcony as our stage. It was quite a lot of fun."

"What sorts of things did you act out?" Innes-Ker asked.

THE SUITCASE

"Oh, mostly comedic duo bits. Laurel and Hardy. Arbuckle and Keaton. Wheeler and Woolsey." I turned from the window and went to the desk. I took some photographs in hand and gave them to David. "In those photos, we are doing *So This is Africa*. We are, obviously, Wilbur and Alexander—Wheeler and Woolsey's parts—and our girlfriend Nellie obliged us and played Raquel Torres's part as Tarzana."

"Interesting film you two chose," Innes-Ker said with a laugh. "If I remember correctly, the tag line is, 'Two Big Sexplorers Go Big Dame Hunting.'"

"That's the one," I said. "We were both familiar enough with it to do a passable job of acting. Speaking of acting..." I finished the last sip of my drink and checked my watch. "Shall we go on to the cast party, then?" I asked. "I'll call for another car."

From the Cathay Mansions, the car turned onto Rue Cardinal Mercier, then onto Avenue Joffre, Louis Dufour, and Route Frelupt. The next cross-street was Route Ghisi, our destination.

*****

About a hundred cast members, crew members, family members, and friends gathered for the *Lysistrata* party that evening at the home of the Finkelstein sisters, Annie and Sophie.

When Innes-Ker and I made our entrance, the play's director, Aline Sholes, born Szold, was engaged in an impassioned debate with her sister, Bernardine Szold-Fritz, wife of Chester Fritz of Swan, Culbertson and Fritz. Bernardine's turbaned head bobbed and her dangly earrings waggled as she opined passionately about Aristophanes's position on women.

Innes-Ker and I took drinks from the roving serving staff and circled the room to find a good vantage point from which we could watch the other guests.

SHANGHAI, CHINA
19 DECEMBER 1935

"There's Toeg." I said, pointing to our friend in the crowd. "Though he seems a bit distracted at the moment." His attentions were occupied by Grace Darroch, the actress who had elicited so much laughter with her portrayal of Myrrhina.

"Isn't that the same woman he was talking to at the Horoscope Party?" Innes-Ker asked.

"It may be," I said. Earlier in the month, the International Arts Theatre had opened a new headquarters and had held a Horoscope Housewarming Party. Toeg had provided a telescope, and gave interested partygoers the opportunity to see Venus. There had been horoscope tellers and numerologists, phrenologists, card readers, palm readers, tea readers, automatic writers — all sorts of fortune tellers.

"She was wonderful tonight. Really makes me wish I had stayed involved with the play," Innes-Ker said. "I would have attended rehearsals just to spend some time with her!"

I laughed. "I'd rather have her sister. She was one of the ballet girls in the play. Both of them teach at the Public School for Girls in YuYuen Road, near Toeg's family's home. Let's walk over near Toeg and have a listen," I suggested.

I heard Grace Darroch tell Toeg: "My friend and I are planning a trek through the Yangtze Gorges to visit Mount Omei."

Toeg said, "Excellent choice. The Giant Buddha of Leshan is there." The Buddha was the largest in the world, standing at two hundred thirty-two feet, only forty feet shorter than the Cathay Hotel. "And you'll also want to see the oldest Buddhist temple in China."

"Certainly," Grace said. "Do you anticipate we will have any difficulties navigating?"

"That depends. When will you be travelling?" Toeg asked her. Innes-Ker and I walked past Toeg just then. "See you Saturday at the Hunt, Taussig?"

THE SUITCASE

"With knobs on," I replied.

David and I planted ourselves in a new spot and sipped our drinks. I scanned the crowd, looking for the Ovadias. I spotted them chatting to Princess Giulia Ottoboni.

"Have you met the Princess?" I asked, gesturing discreetly towards the impeccably-dressed noble-born Italian beauty. She was about fifty years of age. "In 1921, when she was forty years old and a Baroness, she married Sir Victor's brother Hector. Just two years later, Hector died during an operation, and Giulia became known as 'the million-pound widow,' though she was rumoured to be wealthier. In 1928 she married an Italian nobleman, Prince Ottoboni, thus becoming Princess Ottoboni."

"Clearly she is still in good favour with the Sassoon family, if she is chatting to the Ovadias and spending time with Sassoon," Innes-Ker said.

"Oh yes," I agreed. "I understand she visits from time to time. She came this spring, quickly earned the title as one of the fiercest bridge players in the Far East, then left during the summer to accompany Sir Victor's uncle Nunky to Vancouver for a medical procedure. She returned this fall, in time to win Shanghai's International Bridge Club tournament."

Innes-Ker chuckled. "I should like to play bridge with her sometime."

"No you wouldn't," I said. "Not unless you'd like to be soundly beaten. Let's go and chat," I said, leading Innes-Ker towards the Ovadias and Ottoboni.

"Princess Ottoboni, how are you?" I asked. "I haven't seen you since the farewell party for Sir Victor." In late-November, Cecil and Denzil Ezra had hosted a dinner at the Cathay before Sir Victor's departure for India in the SS *Corfu*. Many of our friends had attended: Princess Ottoboni; the former Laura Chieri who had become the Countess de Courseulles in May 1934, and

SHANGHAI, CHINA
19 DECEMBER 1935

in whose company the Princess was most often seen; Sandy Tittman and Judge and Mrs. Helmick; Dallas Lee Franklin; Tony George; Lorna and Kay Lucas, and others.

"What did you think of the play?" Princess Ottoboni asked. I hesitated to answer. The Princess was known for her sharp tongue, and, because she was Sir Victor's sister-in-law, I did fear her displeasure. Hopefully she was only using our remarks as a stepping stone to her own opinions.

"I enjoyed it," Innes-Ker said. "Sound acting. Good staging."

"Are you disappointed to have missed out?" Viva asked me and David.

"Oh, I'm not too sad that I was unable to perform," I said. "It turns out we were far too busy to devote ourselves to rehearsals and line-learning after all. It was a more serious production than we anticipated. So well-done for an amateur cast."

"I think so, too," Viva said. "I don't see why some found it so objectionable. Yes, it was bawdy at times, but anyone familiar with the work would expect it."

"In the papers someone called it 'frightfully unsuitable,'" I said. "They claimed to have walked out in the middle."

"With the crème de la crème of Shanghai promoting and participating in the production, I'm surprised anyone raised any objections at all," Ottoboni said.

Lucien said, "I think some people were only disappointed that Seldes's version was used, and not the Donnay."

"Surely even the Donnay would have been deemed 'bawdy,'" I said.

Viva said, "Someone in the editorials compared it to The Marcus Show."

"The Marcus Show?" Innes-Ker asked.

"Before your time," I said. The Marcus Show had opened at Shanghai's Carlton Theatre in April '34, six months prior to

THE SUITCASE

Innes-Ker's arrival.

"The Marcus Show featured a variety of acts," Viva informed him, "and probably a full half of their one hundred performers came in the form of the 'Marcus Peaches' whose bare chests decorated the stage."

"Was that all?" Innes-Ker asked.

"Well," I said, "there was La Fanette, a fan dancer, who did the 'Danse D' Eventail.' She claimed to be the originator of the fan dance. Her sister, Ha Cha San, 'The Silver Goddess,' danced in nothing but a coat of silver paint."

"To be fair," Viva said, "she was wearing knickers, skimpy though they were."

"Yes," I said, "but the painted lady and the fan dancer were no more incendiary than anything else that might be found between here and Timbuktu."

David nodded. "Doesn't sound like this 'Marcus Show' had anything to do with *Lysistrata*. Whoever has made this complaint has failed to make an essential distinction between high and low art. It's chalk and cheese."

"Well said, Mr. Innes-Ker," Ottoboni said with an emphatic nod.

Ovadia said, "One would think that, if anything, people would object to the idea of staging a play about war when, all around us, China is engaged in her own Peloponnesian War of sorts."

"It was a very timely performance, whether Shanghai realised it or not," Ottoboni said. "Though I should hardly think that, in China's case, withholding sex would dissuade Emperor Hirohito." Her remark was met with laughter, some polite, some genuine.

Innes-Ker said, "From what I understand, the Emperor has only his wife, and not the traditional concubines. He probably

SHANGHAI, CHINA
19 DECEMBER 1935

isn't having much sex in the first place." This, too, was met with laughter.

Lucien said, "The Emperor might not mind it, but his men would. I suppose there is some merit to the playwright's argument. If Aristophanes was wrong, would the Japanese have their 'comfort women'?"

"It would be more suitable to call them 'comfort girls,' from what I understand," said Viva with a bit of venom. It was true, the women and girls the Imperial Japanese forced into sexual slavery were generally quite young.

Lucien asked the group, "I'm sure you have all heard the latest news from the North?"

"I might have seen something about it in the papers," Innes-Ker said.

"Do elaborate," I said.

"This is, perhaps, an oversimplification, but, it seems the Japanese gave the Chinese an ultimatum for North China: either establish a new regime, or face invasion. Though Japanese troops were positioned at certain cities along the Great Wall, ready to invade, Generalissimo Chiang Kai-Shek has, thus far, resisted the goading and has not attacked."

"It sounds rather dire," Viva said.

"If our friends here in Shanghai are not worried, it's because they haven't a clue what's happening. Perhaps they should read more than just the sporting and society pages," Lucien said, half-criticising, half-good naturedly.

"That's not fair," I said, "I work the crossword puzzle, too!" This elicited laughter.

"In all seriousness," Ovadia said, "I would like to think we aren't in danger. After all, breeching the bounds of the International Settlement would be a disastrous provocation of the Western powers. But, one never knows." He took a sip of his drink.

THE SUITCASE

"No," I said, "I don't suppose one does."

"It may not happen tomorrow, or this month, or even next year, but," he paused for effect, "I can assure you that when Sir Victor has undertaken the effort and expense of relocating his ponies, there most certainly is cause for alarm."

The comment hung in the air for a moment, then Princess Ottoboni spotted someone she simply had to go chat with, and she and Viva took a polite leave: "I'll see you again at the Cathay on Monday for my going-away party?" The Princess would be leaving on Christmas Eve in the *Potsdam*, to sail to her villa in the South of France. We were left to speculate whether she'd reached the natural end of her stay, or if her departure was due to tensions in the North.

After the Princess and Viva left us, I asked Lucien the usual question: "How's business? Do you know that I recently heard there are still shops giving out little slips of paper with a 'change' amount, instead of giving patrons actual coppers for change?"

"Is that so?" he asked. "It has been nearly a year since our little 'copper trick.'"

"What are you two on about?" Innes-Ker asked.

I explained: "At the end of last year, the United States's position in the world copper market resulted in a decrease in European copper production. By the end of January, a British penny was worth nearly twelve times its weight in copper. In late February and early March, a World Copper Conference was held in New York City. At my suggestion, some forward-thinking individuals were able to collect copper locally and hold it until the time of the conference, when speculative interest grew, and, correspondingly, so did the price."

Lucien nodded. "We collected coppers from Sir Victor's fleet of double-decker buses, along with exchange copper from his firm, and from Swan, Culbertson and Fritz. Taussig went all over

SHANGHAI, CHINA
19 DECEMBER 1935

the city visiting little exchange shops and buying what he could."

"More than just exchange shops," I said. "I went to gambling houses, temples, bars, brothels—anywhere that might have a worthwhile amount of copper on site. We held it all in a godown and waited for the perfect price to present itself."

Lucien said, "By mid-February there was even an article in the news: 'Coppers are disappearing in this little place.'"

Innes-Ker's eyes were wide. "You two managed all of that?"

"Well…" I shrugged. "The firms did the brunt of the work and handled much of the logistics." I received a reasonable share of returns and was given a very, very small percentage of Sassoon's business. I would soon hire a Boy. Ovadia had purchased a racing pony, "Cambist," a chestnut sub-griffin who'd placed in the Autumn Meeting. I had a photograph of Viva leading Cambist into the weighing enclosure, her gloved hand on the pony's halter. Sir Victor remodelled the Cathay, probably owing more to competition from the Park and other Shanghai nightspots than to our "copper trick." When it reopened, the Cathay's ninth floor Tower restaurant had become a nightclub, and the ballroom had been renovated.

"And to think," Innes-Ker said, "I have been in the presence of exchange masterminds this whole time, and never would have guessed it."

Ovadia and I chuckled. "Masterminds? No," I said. "Opportunists, yes." I grinned. "Speaking of opportunists," I see that the Darroch girls have no one to entertain them."

"Say no more," Innes-Ker said. He put his glass down and made his way over to the sisters.

"Is the situation in the North quite serious?" I asked Lucien.

"Time will tell, my friend," he said.

*****

THE SUITCASE

On Monday the 23rd we met as promised for Princess Ottoboni's going-away at the Cathay, which was all decorated for Christmas. The Count and Countess de Courseulles joined us, as did Mickey Hahn, our Lysistrata.

"First Sir Victor left, and now you are leaving," Viva complained to Princess Ottoboni. "Shanghai will be a bore without you."

"Oh, I am certain Shanghai could never be boring," the Princess said with a smile.

The conversation felt stale, and we all seemed to know it. It was all just niceties.

The women began chatting amongst themselves. I half-listened as Lucien Ovadia and David Innes-Ker talked about a recent visit to the Seekingjao Golf Course.

I felt disconnected from my warm and cheery surroundings. My mind wandered, fast and far, to the Christmastime confession I had made in Prague four years before that had resulted in my journey to Shanghai. Four years!

As I watched my friends chat, I heard Lucien's warning echo in my mind: "It may not happen tomorrow, or this month, or even in the next year, but I can assure you that there most certainly is cause for alarm."

What would I do if trouble came to Shanghai? Would it ever be safe for me to return home to Prague?

Shanghai, China
Saturday, 7 November 1936

> *More about Ciro's:*
> *Opening parties were continued*
> *again last night... To-night there are*
> *just as many parties arranged*
> *as the club will hold.*
> *— North-China Daily News,*
> *7 November 1936*

It was the second week of the Autumn Hardcourt tennis championships. After the day's matches, I left the French Club and walked next door to the Cathay Mansions. My Boy, Cheng, had laid out my best suit. Only the smartest would do that evening. He had then gone to fetch the hors d'oeuvres for the cocktail party I was hosting with David Innes-Ker. We would then go on to the opening of Sassoon's latest venture, a standalone nightclub called Ciro's.

After bathing, I poured myself the usual whiskey, neat, and began dressing for dinner. As I was fastening my cufflinks, I heard Innes-Ker enter the flat. He was fresh from the Autumn Race Meet.

"How were the races?" I called to him. "I hate that I missed them."

"Oh, it was just another race meet," Innes-Ker said. "The expected crowd. The usual ponies. You know." I heard him throw his overcoat on the settee and pour himself a drink. "How was your tournament?"

THE SUITCASE

"It went as well as I could have hoped, I suppose," I said. I echoed his remarks: "The expected crowd, the usual players." He laughed. "With Viva being away all summer, I have been partnering with Mrs. Dvorjetz. Her husband owns D.D.'s Café-Restaurant, a Russian place on Avenue Joffre, whose food I've ordered for the evening's hors d'oeuvres. But, when it came time for the tournaments, I was partnered with Madame Caplain de Prisque, the wife of a French banker. Her playing style was quite different. You can imagine the struggle I had on the courts."

"I should like to watch the Madame play tennis," David said. "I shall never forget her performance at the Lyceum in *The Two Mrs. Carrolls*."

"Oh?" I asked. "I missed that one."

"The Amateur Dramatic Company put it on. Madame de Prisque played a French maid."

"I see," I said with a chuckle.

"When will you have your regular tennis partner back?" David asked.

"Viva? She returned a few days ago, on the fourth. She and Ovadia should be here momentarily."

"I didn't see her arrival in the paper," he said. "No matter. What about your singles match? Against the German?"

"I defeated him fairly easily," I said.

"Good!" said David.

"But as for men's doubles, I'm afraid I am out. I was defeated last week, when I partnered with Bob Biesel, an American jack-of-all-sports. But no matter," I said. "They took photos today. I hope they got some good shots." My photograph would indeed appear in local magazines. My favourite photo captured me in mid-air, twisting to reach the ball.

"I hope you are not tired," Innes-Ker said. "I'm looking forward to our party. Where's the Boy with the food?" he asked.

SHANGHAI, CHINA
7 NOVEMBER 1936

I emerged, smartly dressed. "The food is on the way. We have booze. I will have Viva put a record on. What more do we need?" I sat and lit a cigarette. "Have you heard from Jean?" I asked. Innes-Ker's mother and sister had visited Shanghai for some months earlier that year, after Lady Alastair Innes-Ker, or Anne, had lost her husband in March. She had brought David's sister Jean along. We had all dined at the Cathay on their arrival.

With the twenty-year-old Jean in town, it was not uncommon to see her and David's names in the society pages along with other Shanghai siblings of the society set: the Chieris, the Lucases, the Ezras, and others.

"I have. She wired me. She just arrived back home in England earlier today. She and Mother are still talking about Tokyo," he said.

I'd taken the Innes-Kers to Tokyo that summer when I had gone on business. It had been an excellent time to travel—not only was I still acting as Drakeford, Davis and Wilson's Tokyo liaison, but Japan was also promoting tourism at that time, and was eager to put its modernity and civility on display, in spite of, or perhaps because of, the ongoing tensions with China.

We took rooms at the Imperial Hotel. It had been the beginning of the warm and wet "plum rain" season. I had busied myself with work. While I worked, the Innes-Kers explored the city's gardens, temples, restaurants, and shops. In the evenings we reunited to dine, drink, and go dancing. At the end of our visit we sailed to Nagasaki, then back to Shanghai, arriving in the steamer *Shanghai Maru* on 5 July.

"They said they wish the Far East was closer," he said with a laugh. "If it wasn't such a long trip home, they would come right back and do it all again."

"As they should," I said. There was a comfortable lull. I looked at the clock. "You are right. Where is the Boy with the food?" The door to the flat opened. "Ah. Here he is now."

Cheng carried three large trays: one contained blini with caviar and smoked salmon, and sweet syrniki with jams and honey; one held hand-sized pirozhki pies with savoury fillings; and one was filled with small medovik honeycakes. They reminded me of home.

By the time he had set the food out, the Ovadias were knocking.

As soon as he had shed his overcoat into Cheng's waiting hands, Lucien went straight for the food. "You got D.D.'s," he said. "Wonderful."

"A courtesy, since Mrs. Dvorjetz tolerated me as her partner all summer while your wife was away," I said. Viva gave a short laugh.

"Delicious," Lucien said as he spread toppings onto a little pancake.

"How did you make out with de Prisque today?" Viva asked.

"I missed my regular partner dearly," I said as I smiled to Viva, "but we did well enough. We play again on Tuesday."

David added, "And he's got a singles match tomorrow."

"I'm happy for you." Viva said.

"And how are you? How were your travels?" I asked.

"I'm glad to be back in Shanghai," she said. "But," she paused, "I will be leaving again after the holiday. I have booked passage for London in the *Carthage*."

"She leaves on Russian Christmas," Lucien said in between bites.

"Oh?" I was crestfallen.

"So," Viva said, putting on a smile, "Are you excited for Ciro's? Have you been?"

"I have not," I said.

"This will be my first visit, too," Innes-Ker said.

SHANGHAI, CHINA
7 NOVEMBER 1936

"It's been open for a few days now," Lucien said. "I would expect you two to have gone every night." Sassoon held a three-night opening; we would be attending the final night.

"It's been booked," Innes-Ker said.

"And I was waiting for you two," I added.

There was a knock at the door. My Boy answered, and a few other guests arrived. They helped themselves to the food, and Cheng kept everyone's glasses full until, at the appropriate time, we donned our overcoats and loaded into cars.

We travelled a short distance down the Route des Souers. At the French Concession's boundary with the International Settlement, the street became Yates Road. Just after Love Lane, we turned right onto Bubbling Well Road and arrived at Ciro's.

"I already like it better than the Paramount," I commented as we pulled into the long U-shaped drive. Whereas, at the Paramount, guests' cars cluttered the roadway for at least a kilometre in each direction, Ciro's provided room for autos. A plot of grass and a floodlit fountain occupied the middle of the U-shaped drive.

"It certainly looks like the Paramount," Viva said. Both buildings had clean, modern lines. Both buildings sported a neon-lit tower, and both featured the club's name rising in lights above the building.

"I don't think so," Lucien said. "Ciro's will be Shanghai's first standalone nightclub. The Paramount has the hotel on its upper floors."

"And the Paramount isn't open," I said. "It's been closed since August for 'repairs and reorganisation.'" It wouldn't reopen until the following month, December '36.

"Come; let's go in," Viva said.

Inside, some patrons sat and stood layers-deep at the bar. Others had gone in to the dining area. There, the tables rested on elevated platforms, so that each table had unobstructed views of the stage. The dining areas bordering the dance floor featured a metal railing that, with the push of a button, sank down, allowing guests instant access to the parquet. There was already a crowd on the floor, moving in rhythm to Henry Nathan's Orchestra, on loan from the Cathay ballroom.

We were shown to our table and, once settled, we busied ourselves looking around the nightclub, and down at our menus. We ordered some dishes to share so that we might sample the fare.

"If Chaplin and Goddard came to Shanghai now, they would insist on dancing here this time — not at the Paramount." I said. The famous couple had visited for one night in March, just before *Modern Times* opened at the Tivoli.

"It's certainly the smartest nightclub in all of Shanghai," Viva said.

I said, "I heard gossips that Sir Victor only built Ciro's because, when he asked for the best table at the Paramount, some ignorant staff member looked at his canes and said, 'You can't even dance. If you want the best table, you'll have to build your own nightclub.'"

"I didn't hear about that," Viva said. "Are you sure?"

"It's possible," said Lucien. "It's not as if he tells us everything."

"Well, don't gossip too loudly, because here he comes now," Viva said as Sir Victor approached our table.

There were congratulations all around on the success of Ciro's. Sir Victor was gracious but didn't linger. With two hundred guests in attendance that night, he had many rounds to make.

After dining, drinking, and dancing into the wee hours, the Ovadias went home, as did Innes-Ker.

I went on to the Venus Café, located in Hongkew on Jukong Road. It was not terribly far, as the bird flew, from the bombing

SHANGHAI, CHINA
7 NOVEMBER 1936

debris and mud of Chapei where I had once exercised Mongolian ponies. The whole area had been built back up almost entirely.

An address outside the Settlement bounds meant that the Venus wasn't subject to Shanghai's regular closing times, and that the neon lights could burn until dawn. The Venus Café was at the height of activity between three and five o'clock in the morning.

It was one of my favourite places, with some of my favourite women, but not somewhere I would have been proud to be seen. It was more popular with sailors than with society types — somewhere to go slumming. There had been protests earlier that year when a German man had beaten two of the Asian dancing girls. And on another occasion, a man was stabbed outside the café during an argument over taxi dancers.

I had a somewhat sobering early-morning meal at the Venus. Dance halls and nightclubs were in stiff competition in those days, and giving free food to patrons was one way to attract customers. The Venus Café's menu was as multi-national as the community they served. It featured Arabian curry and rice, Dublin ham and eggs, Coney-Island hot dogs, and Moscow beefstrogen. They also offered coffee that had won an award at the previous year's Better Home Exhibition and had since been referred to as "Gold Medal Winning Coffee": "Free from chicory. Definitely contains no China beans. An honest, clean-cut Blend."

As for the dancing girls, in 1936 they were mostly Japanese and Koreans. There were also some Chinese girls, and a few Russians. When I did dance, I liked girls who could actually dance and not just rub themselves all over the front of me to keep me "dancing."

Near sunrise, the musicians and girls began slumping sleepily in their seats, I went back to my flat for a moment's rest, and to change from my tails into my tennis whites for Sunday's singles match at the French Club against Ronald Ma. My opponent hardly gave me a chance to establish myself; I was only able to win one game in the second set before my defeat.

On Tuesday, I would have my final tennis championship match at the French Club, partnering again with Madame Caplain de Prisque for mixed doubles. We would not move on to the semi-finals.

Wednesday was the Autumn Race Meet's Champion's Day.

Friday, I would don my tails once more, with a white bow tie and, for that occasion, a white carnation, and would join several hundred guests at the French Club for the Pan-Pacific Ball. It would be "International Night," hosted "for the purpose of bringing together various nationalities in a gala party." The ballroom would be decorated with national flags and multi-coloured streamers.

Several Czechoslovaks were in attendance. Because the years had placed some distance between myself and the troubles I had left behind in Prague, and because I had grown increasingly successful in business, society, and sport, I had become less hesitant to appear at Czechoslovak gatherings. Most notably, the community met on 7 March each year to celebrate the birthday of our first president, Tomáš Garrigue Masaryk, a day that retained its importance even though our former Minister of Foreign Affairs, Edvard Beneš, had become our new president in December '35. The community also gathered on 28 October each year to celebrate National Day. That holiday had taken place about a fortnight prior to the Pan-Pacific Ball.

And so I was familiar with members of the Czech Legation on Kiaochow Road, and members of the Czech Consulate on Yuen Ming Yuen Road, as well as the few Czech businessmen. I should perhaps especially mention the President of the Czechoslovak Association, Eduard Kann, who attended the Pan-Pacific Ball,

SHANGHAI, CHINA
7 NOVEMBER 1936

and who became an important figure in my life.

It was also becoming vital to distinguish myself among the Czechoslovaks so that the small group of established Czechs would not confuse me with the newly-arrived refugees that the city was beginning to see. People had begun to arrive in Shanghai from Czechoslovakia, Austria, and Germany, seeking refuge from Nazism. Shanghai's Sephardic community was gradually becoming involved in ensuring the welfare of those refugees who had found in Shanghai not only less-than-stringent entry requirements but also a well-established Jewish community.

I made my rounds at the Pan-Pacific Ball, visiting tables where several acquaintances were playing host to large parties: Judge and Mrs. Helmick and "Sandy" Tittman; Chester Fritz; Denzil Ezra. I then found my seat.

After dinner came dancing and a good deal of mingling. Joseph Shick, the roving photographer, snapped my photo with Miss Goldberg, a blonde in a smart dress who threw her arm over my shoulder for the shot. Another couple stood next to us. The handsomely-painted walls, decorated by Russian artists, made quite a backdrop for many photos that night, some of which appeared in the *North-China Daily News*.

The photo taken at the ball with Miss Goldberg was one I decided to send home to my family. My father's birthday was approaching, and I thought, what better gift than that photograph to show him how respectable I was, and how much I had changed from the son who had fled from Prague with his tail between his legs. This photo would be a testament to the sort of man I had become.

I drafted a letter to my family using company letterhead and enclosed the photo, sending it via airmail so that it would arrive just in time for the occasion of his seventieth birthday in early January.

Ústí Nad Labem, Czechoslovakia
Friday, 7 May 1937

> *Die Zeit ist da!*
> *[The time is now!]*
> – Sudeten German Party Slogan

Jaromír Taussig's gaze settled on the antlered stag logo on the wall before him, its image bounding eternally forward. When the stag appeared on the famous Shicht soap wrappers, the word "jelen," meaning deer, was printed beneath its hooves. The once-humble Sudetenland soap company had since grown into one of the nation's leading industrial concerns.

Jara assumed he had been summoned to the factory to be offered his father's position, and to discuss the details of Julie's widow's pension.

Karel's death was still fresh. Jara would never forget giving him the final prescribed injection of nitro-glycerine that was supposed to help his heart, but instead had only seemed to cause more misery. "Jara, I will shoot myself!" he had cried. Those had been Karel Taussig's last words. His final days ended in suffering.

Vladimír should have been the one to handle that sort of thing. Vlada, the soldier, who had stomached death many times over, should have been there during the night when Karel woke time and time again, short of breath, clutching at his arm or chest, complaining of the contractions near his heart. And Vladimír might have been better at handling the doctors when their trusted old family physician disagreed with the clever young

ÚSTÍ NAD LABEM, CZECHOSLOVAKIA
7 MAY 1937

cardiologist's course of treatments.

The rest of the family certainly hadn't been there to help with Karel's final illness, especially not when Francy had also been gravely ill.

His sister had always suffered from respiratory troubles. The family suspected that her latest spell may have been caused by prolonged exposure to cold winter air on her drive from Karlovy Vary to visit Prague on Karel's seventieth birthday in January. Francy had become so sick that Julie had taken both daughters away to the Adriatic Sea, to a spa in Opatija amid the bay laurel-covered hills in Western Croatia.

Since the time of the Habsburgs, Opatija had been a popular destination. Visitors danced in chandeliered ballrooms, ate Viennese-style pastries, and gazed out at the sea and the islands of Cres and Krk in Kvarner Bay. For those of ill health, Opatija had long been a popular place to convalesce. The Hotel Imperial was famous for its healing treatments, and it was to the Imperial that Francy had retreated. She rested, took the healing waters, and, on warmer days, she let Julie wheel her down to the Lungomare promenade to breathe the ocean air.

Instead of improving at Opatija, Francy's condition had worsened. The doctors had discovered an infection in her lungs. When she'd undergone an operation to remove the infection, she had been poisoned by a blood transfusion. Francy, Julie, and Marietta stayed for two long months in Opatija while Jara had remained in Prague to look after Karel. Julie and Mitcka had attempted to hide the seriousness of Francy's illness from Karel, fearing that the troubling news would aggravate his heart condition.

When they had finally returned from Croatia, Julie had taken Francy home to Karlovy Vary and stayed on with her. In the meantime, Karel had travelled to a health spa of his own — to

Dubí in the Ore Mountains, just beyond Ústí. He had gone "to put his nerves a little bit in order," as the family had explained to those who inquired. But the reality was that Karel's brief trip could not truly help his heart condition. The doctors had prescribed bed rest, but he had resisted their orders and had worked until the last.

Six weeks after his visit to Dubí, Karel Taussig had died. His body was cremated, as had been his wish.

Julie had balked, but Karel had insisted. "It's cleaner. Cremation is the way of the future. 'Save the soil for the living,'" he had said, quoting a slogan he learned at the International Cremation Conference held in Prague the previous September.

Now it was a Friday in early May and there was Jaromír, spending his first free weekend in months in Ústí nad Labem, called Aussig by the Germans.

As he waited, Jara crossed and uncrossed his legs. He corrected his posture, then let it slouch, then straightened again. He yawned. Stretched. Fiddled with his hat, his collar, the creases on his trousers. There he sat in a waiting room in Ústí, while his brother was living the high life in China. Jara was certain of it, for Vlada had begun sending home relics of his success in Shanghai — letters, photographs, gifts.

Karel had loved Vladimír's letters, and he had written: "For us it is a great feast every time we receive a letter from you." Karel had stared at the photos from Shanghai and "imagin[ed] all kinds of nice things and virtues in them." He'd asked Jara, "Doesn't your brother look like a lord?"

Their mother fawned over jade jewellery Vlada had sent, affixing sturdier clasps to the bracelet, adjusting the backs of the earrings to accommodate her ageing earlobes. When she wasn't wearing the pieces, she would stop each time she passed her wardrobe to take the bracelet out, lay it across her hand, and sigh

ÚSTÍ NAD LABEM, CZECHOSLOVAKIA
7 MAY 1937

at it wistfully.

Vladimír had even sent a visitor, some businessman from Shanghai. Even Francy, who had been ill, had gone with Marietta to the Hotel Alcron to meet that man and his wife. Though his wife had not been present after all, they had a pleasant visit, and the man delivered a gift from Vladimír, a silk blanket, embroidered in Soochow. The blanket featured a garden scene exploding with colour. Flowers, butterflies, birds, fish in a stream — all had been carefully worked into the fabric.

After the meeting, his sisters had returned home gushing about how earnest Vladimír was, how respectable, and how everybody in Shanghai loved him. Their father had actually wept with happiness! "What a difference," Julie had said, from the person Vladimír had been when he had asked Zikmund for a bailout. "With God's help, he has profoundly changed," the family said. "The Taussig character has prevailed in him."

Jara had been disgusted. What of his own "Taussig character"? While the rest of the family believed what a fine man Vladimír had become in his absence from Prague, Jaromír had gone thanklessly through another drudging day of caring for their father, certain that Vlada hadn't really changed at all. A few gifts and a friendly visitor were not sufficient evidence that his brother was in any way reformed.

It was almost sickening to Jara when, at the end of Karel's seventieth birthday, Julie had asked what her husband's favourite part of the day had been. He had said that his greatest joy that day was receiving the airmail with a photo of Vlada at some party, along with written birthday wishes.

Jara scoffed, remembering Karel falling asleep with the photo in hand, while Jara slipped Karel's glasses off, pulled the blankets around him, and dimmed the lights, and, later, when Karel's illness intensified, he checked his pulse, dabbed at his brow, prepared needles and performed injections. Sometimes, when Julie had been away with Francy and Marietta, Karel would wake and call for his wife, and Jara would clasp his father's hand in his own, and stroke his thinning white hair until he fell asleep.

These thoughts were interrupted by the Schichts' receptionist, who finally showed Jaromír into the handsomely furnished office. Jara entered, hat in hand. Patents for various mechanical parts and processes filled the wall behind the desk. A framed document from the 1920s welcomed the Schichts into the Unilever Corporation.

Behind the desk sat Jara's least-favourite Schicht, Heinrich, the scientist. If he had been given the choice of the three Schichts, Jara would rather have met with Heinrich's brother Georg, or even with their cousin, Franz. But Georg had moved to London a few years before and was dividing his time between London and Berlin. Franz was also living in London.

Heinrich Schicht, who had been president of the company for the past thirty years, did not rise to greet Jaromír. Perhaps Heinrich was thinking that, if he had to meet with either of the Taussig brothers, he would rather it be Vladimír.

As if knowing Jaromír's thoughts, Heinrich greeted him by asking, "How is your brother, the big businessman in China?"

Jara bristled. "How is your brother, Georg?" he asked. "I shall never forget when everyone came from far and wide to see the first talking picture in Czechoslovakia, filmed right here in your factory." Heinrich's brother, Georg, had been given the talking role in the film—not Heinrich.

Heinrich took no insult and answered cordially enough: "He is well, thank you. I saw him just this week. We have villas next door to one another on Lake Wannsee in Berlin. But," Heinrich leaned back in his chair, "no need to walk around hot porridge. I have called you here about the matter of a widow's pension for

ÚSTÍ NAD LABEM, CZECHOSLOVAKIA
7 MAY 1937

your mother."

"I thought as much, and I am also ready to assume responsibility for my father's accounts."

"That will not be possible. Nor do we plan to give a pension for your mother."

Jaromír was taken aback. "For decades my father spent more time with your family than with his own. Not a day of his life passed without his toiling away. He gave you his time, and his health. At the end, the doctors pleaded with him to rest, but he went to his office anyway. Then, later in the night, he would beg me for injections because he felt so unwell. And to think you were off in your villa, counting the money in your books while my father died to earn profits for you."

"So dramatic," Heinrich said. "Karel loved his work. Who am I to stop a dying man from engaging in an activity that gave him joy, and purpose?"

Jara's eyes narrowed. He did not share the same poker face that Vlada possessed. "And the whole family certainly noticed that no one from the company visited him on his seventieth birthday. The doorbell never stopped ringing that day. Where were you?"

"Busy, I'm sure." Heinrich continued, "As to the matter of your assuming Karel's position, his accounts have been distributed amongst others within the firm." He paused to look at Jaromír then said, "Mr. Taussig, I think you'll find that, in the months to come, many of your kind will be relieved of their positions at Schicht. Consider yourself one of the forerunners. We are Aryanising. Now, if that will be all, I bid you good day."

Jara had heard that the Schicht company had been the main financial backers of Konrad Henlein, leader of the Sudetenland's version of the Nazi party. Henlein's ideals were quite popular in the heavily German-populated border region. The anti-Czech, anti-Semitic Henleinists wanted to break with the government in Prague. The Great Depression had caused special problems in the heavily-industrialised Sudetenland region that, many thought, necessitated separate governance.

"Lieber Hitler," posters around Ústí read, "Mach uns frei von der Čechoslovakei." "Dear Hitler, make us free from Czechoslovakia."

Unbeknownst to Jaromír, in May of 1936, a year prior to his visit with Heinrich Schicht, the Schichts had met with Hermann Göring, who was rapidly becoming the Reich's economic head.

"Will that be all, Taussig?" Heinrich asked, returning his focus to papers on his desk.

"No. It won't be all." Schicht did not raise his head from his desk; Jaromír continued anyway. "Money and villas and factories can come and go—everything material can be taken from a man. But not his character. Perhaps if you had bothered to spend more time with my father, you would have been able to see an example of a good, upright man."

Heinrich looked up at Jara, smirking, but he said nothing. As Jaromír turned to leave the office, Heinrich exclaimed, "Oh, I almost forgot!"

Jara turned once more and watched Schicht take something from the desk. He grabbed it as if he had been quite sure of its place all along. He held the envelope at arm's length and stared at Jara, waiting for him to approach and take it. After a few moments he gave the envelope an impatient shake.

Jaromír received the envelope wordlessly and left the office, letting the door shut behind him.

He found his way through the building, past changing rooms, smoking rooms, washrooms, shower rooms, rest rooms, an employee library, a kindergarten, a doctor's office, and lecture halls. The Schichts had always been one of the best employers

ÚSTÍ NAD LABEM, CZECHOSLOVAKIA
7 MAY 1937

in the region. And Jara would never work for them. Beyond the factory grounds was housing for thousands of employees. In the streets, Jara noticed Henleinist posters. "Die Zeit ist da!" one read. "The time is now!"

At the train station, Jara watched a load of Germans arrive. Were they refugees from, or spreaders of, Nazi ideals? Refugees would be welcomed in Czechoslovakia, where they would be provided with resident permits and would trade their German passports for stateless passports, as Francy had done.

On the train back to Prague, Jaromír opened the envelope from Heinrich Schicht. Inside was a little slip of paper, stamped with a generic message of thanks. Someone had penned his father's name into the message's empty lines: "Thank you for the donation of 100 korunas from the Schichts in memory of Karel Taussig . Your gift is appreciated." A small gift to the poor.

Jara could have laughed, he was so frustrated. Without the widow's pension and the position at the firm, the Taussigs were in danger of becoming "the poor" themselves.

From the train's windows Jaromír could see Ústí, its riverbanks dotted with factory chimneys, its cliff faces with new villas, and Střekov Castle watching over it all. In the city's cemetery, Heinrich and Georg Schicht's father rested beneath an enormous stone monument.

*****

From the Bubny station in Prague, Jaromír took his time walking home through Stromovka Park, dreading the coming conversation with his mother.

As he left the park, Jara looked towards the Magličs' old villa. Jara's former sister-in-law, Maglič's daughter, Ann, had remarried in 1933. Estate Nový Berštejn had been sold in 1935.

THE SUITCASE

Back at the villa, Barry and Eda greeted Jara's arrival with joyous loud barking. Julie had acquired a black poodle since Karel's death and had named her Molinka, "little black bird." Molinka was quiet and careful, not unlike Julie. The poodle disappeared into the villa to find its mistress.

The servants, who had lately been working abbreviated hours with reduced pay, had departed for the day after making dinner preparations. They had depended on the Taussigs for a livelihood for so long, but soon would be released entirely from employ. The servants' absence, after the chaos of the dogs' greeting, made the villa eerily quiet, especially in the fast-fading daylight. Lights shone in the empty kitchen, where the remnants of warm beef goulash with bread dumplings awaited him.

Jaromír peered into his father's office, untouched since his death. It gave him the feeling as if the man might walk in at any moment, switch on his lamp, and take up his usual position behind his desk. Jara passed the empty dining room, where, in January, they had celebrated Karel's seventieth birthday. The table's centrepiece had been a large "70" fashioned by Mitcka out of violets. She had meant for the violets to symbolise the loving thoughts that everyone possessed towards their dear father. The "70" had been echoed in the garlands that Jara and the chauffeur had hung on every doorway and banister. The Taussigs' doorbell had trilled so frequently with birthday wishes that the chauffeur eventually had to let visitors show themselves in unescorted. Karel was so highly esteemed that Czechoslovak President Edvard Beneš's wife, First Lady Hana Benešová, had sent an azalea bush.

That evening, at the birthday dinner, Francy and Mitcka had cried when they wished their father a happy birthday. Jara had announced that he refused to cry, because he knew that when Karel turned eighty, they would have to repeat the whole

ÚSTÍ NAD LABEM, CZECHOSLOVAKIA
7 MAY 1937

performance, so he planned to save his tears for that occasion.

Karel's condition had already deteriorated significantly by that time, and everyone knew he would not live to see even his seventy-first birthday, much less his eightieth.

Jara found Molinka waiting in the doorway to the parlour, where Julie sat weeping in the last of the day's light. Near her feet, the fabric of her mourning dress had become indistinguishable from the dark floor. Marietta sat near the window, holding a book. Classical music played faintly over the wireless. Molinka jumped into the empty armchair that Karel had sometimes occupied in the evenings. Jara turned on a lamp. Julie's grey hair shone in the light.

The Soochow-embroidered silk blanket on the wall behind Julie caught the lamplight. Jara recalled the day his sisters had met the visitor from Shanghai and noted his wife's absence. Julie had remarked, "She must have thought [we] would be some vulgar Jewesses, so she didn't find it worth coming along." At the time, Jara had thought her statement to be exaggerated, but today's experience in Ústí made him reconsider. Perhaps his mother had been right.

Julie sniffled and took a breath, attempting to stifle her tears. "I don't mean to weep so much," she said with a brave smile.

"You are allowed to weep, Mother," Jara said, taking a seat.

"It's just—and I know it's an ugly thought, but—why did God save Francy but not our dear Father?"

"Mother!" Marietta admonished, looking up from her book.

"Oh, Mamicka..." Jara said with tenderness.

Julie sighed. "I know Francy has a son to live for, but your father had me and you children to live for. He might have stayed with us for years yet, if he had received the proper treatment. Why did we ever listen to that new doctor, with his constant nitro-glycerine injections—kilos of medicine! And what for?

THE SUITCASE

He was miserable in the end. Nothing we did spared him that suffering! And now he's gone."

"Yes, Jara," Marietta said placidly, "we were thinking over Father's treatments and recalling how, when you yourself delivered the injections, you were instructed to give them at a much earlier hour than those the doctor himself usually administered."

Julie nodded. "Don't you think that had some effect on the outcome? Why didn't we listen to our regular doctor?" she asked. "What is so wonderful about new breakthroughs in cardiology when he is dead either way?"

Marietta had returned her gaze to her book. She said, "He should have rested more. He shouldn't have worked so much."

Jaromír looked at his father's chair, occupied by Molinka. "At least we had many happy years together. Our family is lucky."

"Of course you are right," Julie said. She dabbed at her tears with a handkerchief. "Our life is not so easy, and yet, still, I thank God a thousand times for it. When one hears about other people's problems, we happily return to our own, do we not?" She presented another smile. "Now. Give me some good news! Tell me, how was it with the Schichts?"

Jaromír's stomach sank. "It did not go well. There is to be no pension, and his accounts have been given to other employees." He omitted Heinrich Schicht's comments about Aryanisation. "There was only this," he said, fishing the envelope from his pocket and handing it to his mother to read.

"A donation to the poor." Julie said. "But what about the rest of it? What will we do about money?" Julie asked, crying anew. Molinka stepped down from Karel's armchair and moved to put her head on Julie's lap. "How hard he worked," she said between teary breaths, "and yet we find ourselves in such a position."

Marietta said, "That means we can't afford to stay here! What

ÚSTÍ NAD LABEM, CZECHOSLOVAKIA
7 MAY 1937

will we tell the servants? Where will we go?"

Jara shook his head. "I don't know. There will be a little bit of money from Father's estate, but the probate court will not be able to complete their work until Vlada signs and returns the papers I sent." He shifted in his chair and took a more authoritative posture. "We might have to live below our accustomed lifestyle, but it may not be so bad. I will see how much money I can give you each month. I will do the numbers right away. Maybe you can keep the villa."

"What numbers?" Marietta asked sourly. Jara shot her a look. He was trying to make their mother feel better, but Mitcka knew that Jaromír had no prospects, and no savings.

Jara glared at his sister. "Why don't we ask Vlada to help? He seems to be getting on quite well in Shanghai." Jara knew that, though he sent nice photographs and expensive-looking gifts, their brother was in no position to help. Jara was certain that it had all been a show to impress their father. He let his gaze return to the brightly-embroidered Soochow blanket.

Julie was petting Molinka's head absently, repetitively. "Money isn't the only reason why my heart is heavy. You know, some of the aunts and uncles refuse to speak to me because of the cremation."

"It's what Father wanted!" Jara said.

"They think it was sacrilegious. I admit I had my misgivings at first, but it was his choice, and he convinced me. Now, you know I don't want it for myself."

"No," said Marietta. "Who would?"

Jara gave a little chuckle. "I imagine they are not too happy we didn't sit shiva, either."

Julie sighed, "Well, you know your father. He requested nothing religious. But no. They are not happy. Uncle Arthur's daughter, Hana? She had the baby in October—remember I embroidered that clothing for him? I spent all those hours on that gorgeous needlework. I have not seen the baby since your father's birthday. Now they are not speaking to me. The child's probably crawling by now. And Olga and Aka are so focused on themselves, and this illness Olga's had recently… I have not seen them since they brought food after your father left us."

To change the subject, Jaromír said, "Speaking of births, I know a happy topic we can discuss," Jara said. "What's on the menu for your birthday, Mamicka?" Never mind how they would afford it…

Julie let slip the day's first laugh. She would be turning sixty-four in a little less than a fortnight, on the twentieth. "I haven't given it much thought because it will be my first birthday without your father…" She let out a deep sigh. Molinka looked up with love and concern. "I am trying not to cry, my dear," she said to the dog, giving it a pat. "It's just… how many happy family occasions am I to spend alone, without my dear husband, the head of our family?"

"Cakes from Berger?" Jara asked.

"Cakes from Berger, certainly," Julie said with a sniffle. She took a breath, "And a walk in the park, perhaps, with all of us together. That would be the best way to spend the day. I expect Francy and Jiří will be over from Karlovy Vary, if Francy is well."

"She had better not miss it," Marietta said. "By your next birthday, they may be living in the States."

"Mitcka, you'll make Mamicka sad," Jara said, glaring at his sister.

"It is fine. I want only what is best for them, even if it means we cannot all be together," Julie said softly.

"Yes, think of the opportunities they will have there. Like how well Vlada is doing in China," he added wryly.

"One by one, you are all leaving me…" Then Julie smiled.

ÚSTÍ NAD LABEM, CZECHOSLOVAKIA
7 MAY 1937

"You know, I am thinking about the first time your father helped me celebrate my birthday. I had a brand-new ball gown, with a bustle—this was forty-some years ago—and bows all down the side, and a bodice so tight I could hardly breathe. He took me dancing and we waltzed, and waltzed..." Her eyes welled with happy tears. "Now that was a good birthday. To think those dances in our younger days would lead to so many years of happiness..."

"I hope that this will be a good birthday too," Marietta said. "I am excited for you to see the surprise we have planned."

Jara and Mitcka had obtained Francy's signature on a photograph of their father. They'd then sent it to China for Vladimír's signature. They had recently received the photograph and placed it in a silver frame.

Vlada was quick to sign the photograph and send it back from Shanghai, but when it came time to sign the all-important probate paperwork to finalise Karel's estate, how could the Taussigs not notice how Vladimír dallied?

Shanghai, China
Saturday, 14 August 1937

> *Mostly it is loss which teaches us*
> *about the worth of things.*
> — Arthur Schopenhauer
> *Parerga & Paralipomena*

My Boy woke me at nine with a glass of water and two tablets of Alka-Seltzer. He paused as he collected my dinner jacket.

"Hm, still warm," he said with a joking tone before disappearing to fetch my breakfast. Even after a long night at Farren's, Cheng could make me smile.

In the dinner jacket's place, he set out an outfit appropriate for the day's weather and business — a summer suit, linen for the drenching heat, formal enough for the office and anyone I may encounter there. If my hangover, and the weather, cooperated, I hoped to play tennis that afternoon.

As I dressed, I looked over at the photo of my friend Nellie and her dog, taken earlier that year when I had treated her and her girlfriend to a trip to Lake Tsetai. Owing to recent tensions, she had left Shanghai. In the photograph she holds my hand, and I am joking with her. She is laughing with her head tossed back — not an entirely flattering angle. Her friend, seated behind her, looks better in the photograph. She gazes directly at the camera, held by Ed Toeg.

While transfixed on the photo, my father's words came to mind. After receiving my Pan-Pacific ball photograph he had

SHANGHAI, CHINA
14 AUGUST 1937

written, "Do not limit your life by marriage." I had scoffed at his letter. Marriage? Hardly! And to think that the advice came from the man who had encouraged and arranged my marriage to Ann Magličová. "There is nothing like having your hands free and not tied down by a commitment," my father had written. When I revisited the photograph from the ball, I did notice the awkward angle of Miss Goldberg's left hand on my shoulder, as if she was showing off an engagement ring.

My desk also held photos recently sent by an old friend, Karoline Fischerová, called Karly or Fischerka. The photos showed her, her husband Otto, and their infant son, Petr. Nothing like not being tied down by commitment, indeed. I chuckled to think how my mother disdained my old friend Karly, and suspected that the baby did not belong to Otto.

Cheng returned with coffee, a simple breakfast, and my mail. He had gone down to the dining hall between the two southernmost buildings in the Clement's Apartments, a "First-Class Residential Hotel," where I was then living. The three- and four-storey brickwork apartment buildings were arranged around a central lane. My kitchenless flat was ideal for a bachelor who rarely took meals at home. Cheng then tiptoed off once more, overly mindful of a hangover headache that was fast fading. The combination of movement, water, and Alka-Seltzer had done me a power of good.

I clicked on the wireless. A typhoon was heading towards Shanghai, and the palm fronds outside my window whipped at the glass in a gust of wind. Maybe I would not be playing tennis that afternoon after all. With an ear to the radio and my mouth to the coffee — prepared just how I liked it, because Cheng made everything just how I liked it — I reached for the daily stack of mail and picked up the letter from home, addressed in my mother's familiar hand — handwriting that I knew like my own shoes — which my Boy had knowingly placed on top of the pile. I glanced at the photograph of my family that I kept on my desk. It had been taken earlier in the year, around the time of my father's seventieth, and final, birthday. They had all changed from the way I remembered them. But then, it had been five years since I had seen them face-to-face.

Next to the photograph, I kept a small bundle of letters from them.

The month before my father's death, he had sent a tabloid article, carefully clipped from *Pragger Mittag*, a "gunboat tabloid" established in Prague "by German immigrants who moved in after Hitler's coup." The article, my father wrote, "brings news which will be of interest to you." It described the status of the actress Renata Hohnová's estate. She had died intestate in 1935, and the article listed her sister, the "friend," and the rich industrialist boyfriend who were all chomping at the bit to be awarded her inheritance.

My father's hand had underlined: "Many men courted her. Out of the multitude of worshippers stand out two favourites, the industrialist, and a commercial councilman's young son, who for some reason suddenly emigrated to China..." In addition to the clipping, he had written disturbing news that he was being threatened to settle my financial affairs by the legal representative of her estate who had discovered my old promissory notes. Attempting to resolve the debts before the fate of her estate would be decided by the courts, he demanded five thousand korunas to make the promissory notes disappear. My father wrote that he offered two thousand korunas, but it was refused.

In between the sending of the tabloid article, and the news of my father's death, I had received letters telling of his heart palpitations and fatigue. He wrote, "Those stresses I have had

SHANGHAI, CHINA
14 AUGUST 1937

all my life make themselves felt." Without a doubt, I knew that the Hohnová matter had exacerbated his condition—and over promissory notes that Renate herself had never seriously intended for me to repay.

My father's last words to me—and I thought of them often—had been: "So, my dear boy, continue working and try to better yourself. See that you make a lot of money, nevertheless honestly and correctly, or else bring us some rich bride," he had joked. "I am awfully looking forward to your visit, and I pray to God that I live to see you in the midst of us all who belong together and love one another. Be in good health and good bye. Thousand kisses from Your Old Daddy."

I opened the newly-arrived letter from my mother and sighed to see that she had only written to inform me that the absence of my signature was delaying the settlement of my father's estate. It had been months since his death, and my family undoubtedly needed the money. It was assumed that my well-to-do father, as a long-standing member of the Schicht firm, and the agricultural commissioner, had left a sizable estate, but he had confessed in his letters that even before his final illness, business had been slow, and that health treatments and travel expenses had depleted his savings. The family had been living off capital for some time even before his death. I would later come to suspect that the Schichts had also been depriving him of contracts, owing to the impending Aryanisation of business.

My family was not the only ones eager to receive my father's estate. After his death, the inheritor of the Hohnová estate had once again begun hounding my grieving family. This time, the industrialist had demanded twenty-eight thousand korunas. "You should have urged your father to settle when it was just five thousand," my mother wrote. What I wouldn't have given to have been in Prague then, to run the man off myself!

THE SUITCASE

Cheng returned to tell me my car had arrived.

I asked, "Do you remember what we did with those important papers I was supposed to sign and send home?"

"Used for firestarter, like you say," Cheng joked. "No, no. One moment," he said, returning an instant later with the documents in question.

Who needed a wife when one had such perfect domestic help? I signed the papers, penned a short note both apologizing for the delay and sending words of love and encouragement, then slid the papers into an envelope to be posted by airmail.

Outside, I clutched at my hat with one hand and gripped my camera strap in the other. Even the four-storey apartment buildings that surrounded me couldn't keep the fierce gusts at bay. My driver struggled to open the car's door against the wind.

Somewhere inside the flat, Cheng was collecting my breakfast dishes, turning off the wireless, changing my bed linens, laundering my pyjamas, ironing my suits, shining my shoes, and dusting and cleaning. "Don't limit your life by marriage" indeed!

The car rocked as we left the sheltering walls of the courtyard and slid out onto Rue Lafayette. Had we turned left and travelled just over a kilometre I would have found myself at the Ovadias' new residence, the Picardie Apartments, flat 38, where they had lived since the spring — when they weren't staying at Eves in Sir Victor's absence.

Viva and I had partnered for tennis in May and June. I imagined her as I had last seen her, in a golden chiffon evening gown, sliding from the table at Ciro's straight onto the dance floor, where she joined a similarly gold-draped Mickey Hahn. The Ovadias and I had plans to visit Ciro's later that evening, if the weather held.

Mickey Hahn was spending less time with the Shanghai elites and more with the Chinese poet Shao Xunmei, whom she had

SHANGHAI, CHINA
14 AUGUST 1937

met at one of Bernardine Szold-Fritz's salons.

The car turned right, away from the Ovadias' apartment, towards the Canidrome, and towards the Bund.

The driver knew that I liked to approach my office at the Palace Hotel a certain way. He turned onto Avenue Joffre for a moment, then onto Route Cardinal Mercier so we could drive past the French Club, which I missed seeing every day.

I hadn't been to the club since February, when I had attended the Mardi Gras "Gypsy Ball." There had been several hundred guests at the ball, with fiddlers borrowed from Farren's — Joe Farren's latest nightclub enterprise. "Itsie" Chieri was among the ball's amateur dance performers. Countess Nesselrode, well-known in Paris as an expert fortune teller, played "gypsy fortune teller" for the night, predicting the future for those who queried her. Innes-Ker and I sat at Denzil Ezra's table that night.

The following night, on Chinese New Year, many of those same "gypsies" had come to the Cathay as toys for Sir Victor's Toy Shop Party.

Sir Victor, who had converted the ballroom to suit the fantasy, had worn a toymaker's apron with an exaggerated grey wig. People dressed as a variety of national dolls — Dutch, Austrian, Russian, Swiss, Japanese, Afghan, Italian, Spanish, and more. There were Sinbad the Sailor dolls, U.S. Naval sailor dolls, clown dolls, farmer dolls, Mexican straw dolls, Chinese yarn dolls, Alice in Wonderlands, Little Red Riding Hoods, and others. Mr. Culbertson was Little Boy Blue. Viva dressed as a peasant doll. I was a toy soldier.

The car turned into Avenue Foch, which became Avenue Edward VII near the Race Course where, earlier that summer, the city had celebrated the Spring Race Meets one week, and the coronation of the new British King the next.

Owing to the scandal with Wallis Simpson, the coronation

THE SUITCASE

date originally intended for Edward VIII, known to his family and friends as David, was instead used to crown "Edward's" brother, George VI, also known as Albert.

Edward, who had, coincidentally, once been Sir Victor's golf buddy, had ascended to the throne on 20 January 1936. Soon after, he created a sensation by announcing his intention to marry a twice-divorced American by the name of Wallis Simpson. Edward abdicated and his brother Albert, or George VI, was crowned as king. George's wife Elizabeth became the queen.

Edward and Wallis were wed in early June. They became the Duke and Duchess of Windsor and, as their first official state visit, they went to see Hitler in Germany. Some thought that, after the English royal family had snubbed Wallis so badly, Edward just wanted her to experience an official visit and feel important. Others thought Edward had intentions of winning back the throne with Hitler's help.

For the coronation of George VI, every British-owned building in Shanghai had been festooned with extra lights, British flags, crowns, the King's initials, and other decorations. Pressed into my scrapbook back at Clement's Apartments, stored away Cheng-only-knew-where, were badges I had worn to gain access to the members' enclosure for the races, and into the grandstand for the coronation activities.

Many garden parties had preceded the coronation celebrations. I had attended one of the more important parties, hosted by Brigadier-General and Mrs. Alexander Patrick Drummond Telfer-Smollett, the Brigadier-General being the Commanding Officer of British Troops in Shanghai. A photo in the North China Daily News memorialized this event and was already glued to a scrapbook page.

Even the Chinese celebrated the coronation. The Chinese Minister of Foreign Affairs, Wang Chung-hui, extended his

SHANGHAI, CHINA
14 AUGUST 1937

best wishes to the English, saying that, while Britain and China had their differences in the past, the similarities between the two countries were evidence of an enduring friendship and understanding. Both nations, he said, "prefer butter to cannons," desire to conquer no other lands, and seek peace at home and abroad. The English Shanghai papers urged the Chinese to take an active interest in the coronation, since the British had been so instrumental in establishing the city as an international port and fostering its growth.

We continued driving towards my office. Just beyond the Race Club, at the corner of Edward VII and Thibet Road, sat the Great World amusement centre with its tiered, cake-like rooftops, then being used as a refugee centre. That particular Saturday morning, thousands of Chinese refugees were crowding the sidewalks surrounding the building. The wind whipped at their hair and clothing as they waited for whatever food or shelter the building would offer.

These were not refugees from the stormy weather.

In July, Peking had fallen to the Japanese, and, while I was having barbeques and ice cream with the Americans, the Second Sino-Japanese War had begun. Many Chinese families abandoned their homes in hopes of escaping the fighting, and the rape, looting, and executions that attended the Japanese military presence. In their arms and on their backs, in buckets, in baskets, in wheelbarrows, they carried everything they ever hoped to see again. Shanghai's refugee centres had quickly filled, leaving people huddling in alleyways, in doorways, beneath stairs, in vacant lots, and on sidewalks.

Owing to the influx from the interior, there were more refugees then, in August of '37, than I had ever before seen in the city. Entire families had set up their homes right there on the sidewalk alongside the buildings, with their baskets and cooking pots, their shoes lined neatly beside their straw mats. I was grateful to be away from them, in the safety of the car, which whisked me quickly past their misery before I had much chance to see or smell them. The sight of such obvious desperation on such a grand scale was overwhelming.

The conflict had followed them to Shanghai. All week, the crisis had been escalating. On Monday, there had been Japanese attacks in Hongkew. On Tuesday, when we had begun to take notice of the crowds of refugees at the Settlement's bounds, there had been incidents near the Shanghai airport, much too close to Eves for comfort. On Thursday, the Shanghai Volunteer Corps had been mobilised to help protect the Settlement's bounds from a possible Japanese attack.

I was taken down Avenue Edward VII to the French Bund, where the rest of the Bund curved before me, down to the Garden Bridge. That day, the Bund was just another place for refugees to cluster. Every available inch was packed with Chinese people hunkering down against the gusting wind.

The Japanese flagship *Idzumo* occupied its usual position at the end of the Bund, near the Japanese consulate and the Astor House. Among the other battleships present in Shanghai was the British cruiser *Cumberland*, flagship of the British China squadron, which had arrived with reinforcements for the extant 1,000 or so British soldiers in Shanghai. The American cruiser *Augusta*, flagship of the U.S. Asiatic Fleet, had joined her, carrying reinforcements for the 4th U.S. "China" Marines. I was one of many who snapped photographs of the multi-national "Warship Row" in those days; I had an especially good view of it from my office.

As we travelled down the Bund, my eye was drawn to the garish red banner that graced the Glen Line building, hanging from roofline all the way down to the building's doorway. The

SHANGHAI, CHINA
14 AUGUST 1937

Nazi German consulate had relocated their offices in the spring and was now prominently housed between Jardine's and the French Bank of Indo-China. They had used the opportunity to hang the largest possible swastika flag down the entire face of the building. Even in the newspapers, the German Imperial eagle that had once headed announcements had been replaced by a Nazi eagle that held a swastika in its talons.

The driver stopped the car near the hotel's Nanking Road entrance.

A small Czechoslovakian flag hung in one window of the Palace.

*****

After checking phone messages and markets, it was soon time to knock off for tiffin. I phoned Lucien to join me. If I could not pry Ovadia from his desk, then Desmond O'Neill, who had been back in Shanghai since the spring, would be my next attempt.

As expected, Lucien nearly refused to come take tiffin with me at the Palace. "But you must eat," I pleaded. "And think how much more efficiently you'll work once you have given yourself a short reprieve."

"I haven't the time to stop and eat. I'll take tiffin at my desk," he said stubbornly.

"Oh, come now," I prodded, leaning back in my chair, trying to see him through the windows. "When was the last time you ate somewhere other than your desk?"

After a thoughtful pause he admitted, "I suppose I could be at a stopping point. There are a few things I should inform you about anyway. But quickly!"

I smiled. "See you in a moment." I replaced the telephone's receiver.

THE SUITCASE

The ground floor of the Palace Hotel held a tea lounge and a grill room. I went down and took a table in the grill room. Moments later, Lucien arrived, dabbing sweat from his brow.

He gawked at me. "You are a sight! Did you sleep at all last night?" He took his seat.

"Farren's." I said with a shrug. Lucien was familiar with the casino on the outskirts of town. "Do I look so awful?" I asked. "I feel a far sight better now than I did on waking."

"I don't see how you have the time, or the energy, for such constant frivolity."

"I don't sleep," I said.

"Farren's..." Ovadia mused. "I haven't been to Farren's since the beginning of the year."

"Yes, after Innes-Ker's birthday. That was ages ago! I remember Mickey Hahn and Ed Toeg joined us. Vera Love has recruited almost an entirely new batch of 'Peaches' since then!" Likely inspired by the Marcus Show, manager Joe Farren had curated a group of eighteen barely-clad busty blonde showgirls.

"Which reminds me," Lucien began, "about Ciro's tonight, thank you for inviting me, but..."

I grinned. "I knew you would cancel! I should have wagered on it!"

"I have so much to do at the office," he protested.

"Which is why you should get out for one evening and relax. If you think this tiffin break will boost your productivity, then just wait until you see what a night out on the town will do for you. Food, drinks, dancing — if you are up for dancing." He had gained weight since he had traded squash rackets for golf.

"Taussig, how can I relax? Even if the weather holds and doesn't flood us out... Even if the war doesn't come today..."

I waved my hand dismissively. "All year we have heard how tensions are coming to a head. But there doesn't seem to be the

SHANGHAI, CHINA
14 AUGUST 1937

least bit of real danger." Lucien was shaking his head. "Sir Victor is riding you too hard, my dear horse. Now, you don't have to stay until dawn, but I demand you at least make an appearance at Ciro's tonight and have a genuine good time."

He was exasperated because I was not listening. "There are some things I really must attend to in case the situation deteriorates. Clearly you have not yet heard that bombs were dropped in the river this morning. They were aiming for the warships. The impact made tidal waves. I went down and moved my car on account."

"You willingly left your desk?" I asked with mock astonishment. "You didn't send a Boy?" He rolled his eyes. I laughed. "Who was aiming for whose warships?" I asked.

"It appeared to be the Chinese, aiming for the *Idzumo*." Lucien leaned closer and said, in confidence, "But I wouldn't put it past anyone to attack a Western ship, apologise later, and call it an 'incident.' They always provoke the Generalissimo with these 'incidents.' He never fights, and Japan comes away with another piece of China." He thought for a moment. "I don't think Japan would attack Westerners outright, or invade the Settlement, but I do think we could be caught in the midst of some very nasty business." He leaned back into his seat. "No one shares my concern. People who were here in '28 or '32 say, 'Oh, China is always at war, don't worry, it never reaches the Settlements.'" As the Japanese aggression had moved closer to the centre of the city, it was just a matter of time before Shanghai proper would be in the cross hairs. That time, it seemed, had come. "And I'm sure you have seen the stock market these past few days. You see how people have been sending assets to Hong Kong, just in case?"

"Or Singapore," I mused, thinking of my own company, Drakeford, Davis and Wilson, who had been doing an increasing volume of business there.

THE SUITCASE

"And when something does happen, how long will it take for help to arrive? Will it even come?" he asked. "By the time the small number of Western troops try to defend us, it may be too late. And why should they take a stand against the Imperial Japanese forces?"

Our food was delivered. Lucien dug in to his meal. When he came up for air, I said, "I suppose, if Japan sought a rapid victory, opening a second front here in Shanghai could be one tactic..." I thought about the Chinese troops, who were ill-equipped, under-trained, and prone to Japanese propaganda techniques and opium addiction. "Or," I continued, "perhaps it is China who may want a second front opened in Shanghai, to entice the Western powers to finally intervene on her behalf."

Lucien thought, then said, "Perhaps."

"With war on the river, and war in the skies, I'll be stuck here if there is a battle."

"Don't you have a pilot friend?" Ovadia asked.

"Chuck Sharp," I nodded. "Yes, but he flies Chinese planes and, if there is a war on, the Japanese will target him. He's been training the Chinese pilots." Chuck was an American from Texas who was known as "Apple Dumpling" on account of his dimples. Chuck loved ladies, cocktails, card games, tennis, golf, swimming, and his dachshunds. He flew internal mail routes for the China National Aviation Company, which was jointly owned by Pan American Airways and the Chinese government.

"There's a fair chance Sir Victor will send me to Hong Kong for safety," Lucien said between bites. "Neither the British government nor the Shanghai municipality have any plans in place in the event of attack."

"Could the British evacuate if they wanted to?" I asked. "There are not nearly enough ships."

"The British can carry maybe eight thousand of their own; the

SHANGHAI, CHINA
14 AUGUST 1937

Americans can take maybe three thousand, if the need arises."

"How many Westerners are there in all?" I asked.

"Oh, I would say a hundred thousand? Maybe fewer."

"Can you imagine the Chinese refugees watching the Europeans board their ships and leave all the trouble behind?" I mused. "I wonder what the Czechoslovaks will do. Maybe I will give Eduard Kann a call."

"Would you go if they did evacuate?"

"Difficult to say. Aside from my family, there's nothing for me back in Prague except ex-girlfriends and lousy tennis partners," I said. "A rare few do have the privilege of holding both titles."

"And Nazis," he said into his food.

"I do worry about my sister in Karlovy Vary, and her family. My family in Prague, I think, will be fine. My father's death was hard on them, naturally, but their letters do not reveal anything that would cause alarm."

"Well, clearly the situation with the Nazis is bad enough to send Jews fleeing to Shanghai."

By that time, Shanghai had amassed nearly ten thousand registered Jewish refugees from Europe, and an estimated one thousand unregistered exiles. Of these, only maybe two hundred and fifty held permits for destinations beyond Shanghai. The city's Sephardic Jewish community, including Sir Victor, Ellis Hayim, Eduard Kann, and others, had been assisting with funds to finance the refugees' passage. They had also created a Revolving Rehabilitation Fund for families who would be staying in Shanghai, which enabled newcomers to borrow money to start businesses. Once the loan was repaid, the money would be lent to the next refugee. It did not take long for that system to break down because of greed.

As we finished lunch, I asked, "You will give me warning if you're sent to Hong Kong, won't you?"

THE SUITCASE

"As much warning as I myself am given," he said, wiping his mouth. "Now, I must get back to it." He stood and buttoned his jacket.

"Perhaps I should see to a few things as well," I said, thinking of the most sensitive financial documents in the office, and where I might put them for easy destruction in the event of a hostile takeover. I stood too, and said, "If something does happen, you and Viva stay safe."

"Of course. And you."

"Oh, don't worry about old Vlada," I said. "I thrive in chaos." I grinned. But, to be honest, it had been half a lifetime since I had been in the midst of a battle. I had been twenty years younger during the Great War, and had been living a much more regimented life.

I sighed. "So, no Ciro's tonight, then. Well, do give Viva my regards."

"How about this?" He offered, "Unless something extraordinary prevents my attendance, I'll see you at Ciro's. Let's make it eight o'clock."

"You'll come? Really?" I asked.

"Why not?" he said. "It may well be our last hurrah."

But we never made it to Ciro's that night. We were just a few short hours away from the events of "Bloody Saturday," which marked the beginning of the Battle of Shanghai, and, for those of us in the Far East, the beginning of the Second World War.

*****

It was a few minutes shy of Big Ching's Westminster Quarters announcing half past four. I had stayed at the office much longer than intended, owing to my revised post-tiffin plan for the day. After conversing with Lucien, an attack, and a second front in

SHANGHAI, CHINA
14 AUGUST 1937

Shanghai had shifted from a vague possibility to a fairly definite eventuality in my mind.

When I heard the drone of an aeroplane, I moved to the window.

Along the Bund and down Nanking Road, the scene had not changed much since morning. The wind still gusted around businessmen and beggars alike. Refugees still sheltered in every available space, clustering around each tree, statue, and stairway. As people on the ground heard the aeroplane's mechanical humming, their necks craned back and their eyes turned skyward.

A bomber broke through the clouds, swooping down towards the city. In an instant, the *Idzumo's* anti-aircraft guns spun to target the plane. The guns fired with startling booms. Some of the onlookers screamed.

I turned from the window to grab my camera, thinking I might capture some excellent shots for the *North-China Daily News*'s photo contest—maybe for the action category or the news category.

I was not at the window to witness more planes descend below the cloud cover, or to see the one plane that broke from the pack. As I was bending at the desk to fetch my camera, my building shook with an explosion. Then, for a moment, all was eerily quiet. Or perhaps I had just been temporarily stunned. All at once, my senses were bombarded by a torrent of smoke, shrieks, and smells.

The screaming came from all directions—from other rooms and floors within the Palace Hotel, and from without, on Nanking Road and on the Bund. I could smell rubber burning, flesh burning, the building itself, burning. Careful to avoid the glass on the office floor, I inched toward the window, mindful there could yet be more planes and more bombs. I tried to look out at the scene but saw only smoke and dust.

People began moving inside the hotel, opening doors, shouting that the roof was on fire, and that the upper floors were on fire. Outside, a ladder was soon positioned for rescue.

Through the settling smoke, I realised that Sassoon House's Nanking Road entrance's glass arcade lay in shards all over the street. A large bomb crater, perhaps two metres across and at least a metre deep, had been created in the pavement in front of the building. One of the hotel's upper floors had been struck when the bomb glanced off the building, but the damage was minimal.

I looked to Lucien's glassless office window and actually smiled, in the midst of that scene, because I knew that my friend had been at his desk and should not have been badly injured by the blast. Indeed, the blast had thrown him backwards, but he suffered no visible injuries. The Cathay's doorman had not been so lucky. Nor had the hundreds who had, moments before, been standing on the sidewalks and in the streets, looking up to the sky.

All around the bomb crater, and all down Nanking Road, lay pieces of buildings, of cars, of humans. Unidentifiable pieces of people were plastered to sides of buildings or stuck in trees. Blood spattered the streets and filled the gutters. There had to have been at least a hundred countable corpses in the length of one city block.

The shock civilians must have felt — the shock I myself felt — on seeing such a grisly, unexpected scene, in the middle of an otherwise fine and stormy summer day in Shanghai, was incredible. I knew I was witnessing an historic event. So did others.

A "March of Time" cameraman had been in the Cathay when the bomb fell, and had come out to take photographs. And

SHANGHAI, CHINA
14 AUGUST 1937

Hearst's "Newsreel" Wong was quick to the scene. They would produce photos of the broken awning of the Sassoon House, of the military and volunteers digging through rubble, of foreigners with handkerchiefs over their faces tiptoeing through wreckage.

Other photographers captured other moments from the aftermath of that bombing: the traffic director slumped dead in his bird's nest; the rickshaw coolie lying dead with one arm still hooked over the rail of his cart. The masses of innocent civilians whose lifeless bodies awaited identification and burial.

The Shanghai Volunteer Corps, the Shanghai Municipal Police, and others in uniform had already begun searching for those who were injured but were likely to survive, and carrying them off in any suitable conveyance. Others were removing the dead and creating rows, and then stacks, of bodies against nearby buildings. Their efforts would continue for some time.

I helped briefly in the short stretch of Nanking Road between the Palace and the Sassoon House. There, Lucien was busy giving instructions to board up the hotel's windows, and to have the S.V.C. guard the arcade against looters. "I plan to stay and ensure all our guests are safe," he said. "I have already notified Victor."

I was impressed by his coolness in a crisis, but then, he always was calculating risks and possible outcomes.

He said, "I don't know the full situation, or what the plan will be. It's quite possible we may never see one another again."

"Or, who knows," I said hopefully, "maybe you will see me at the office on Monday morning, once this has blown over."

Lucien smiled, knowing that nothing would "blow over."

I began walking, hoping to find a car. Glass and stone crunched beneath my feet. I avoided the blood and flesh I encountered as best I could.

I spotted smoke ahead, near the Race Club; my stomach sank. Traffic was being re-routed into the French Concession. I made

THE SUITCASE

inquiries of a French Municipal Policeman.

"The Great World's been hit," he said.

The bomb had struck Avenue Edward VII, the border between the International Settlement and French Concession. On the Settlement side, turbaned Sikhs controlled the traffic, while on the Concession side, Annamites in pointed straw hats took the role.

"We are cleaning our side of the boundary," the policeman said. "It will be back to normal by nightfall," he added, waving me on.

"The Great World?" I asked. My outrage grew knowing of the masses of refugees sheltering in and around The Great World. Their corpses were now being stacked like sandbags near the racecourse in the sweltering August heat, while coffins were acquired or built by charity organisations, and mass graves were dug.

"Can you tell me whether the Race Club has been damaged?" I asked.

"I don't know," he said. "Now please..." he waved me emphatically onward.

After I walked a little further, I managed to hire a car. By the time I reached my apartment in the French Concession, aerial battles had ensued. Smoke coated Shanghai. It was especially thick and black over Pudong, where the Japanese had attacked the American Standard Vacuum Oil Company's oil tanks.

The Battle of Shanghai had begun.

Part Two

Historical Interlude

The bombs dropped on Shanghai's Bund and at the Great World were, in fact, accidentally loosed by Chinese planes. The three bombs dropped on the Bund were meant to hit the *Idzumo*; the two that struck the Great World were released by a damaged bombing plane.

Following the events of 14 August 1937, or "Bloody Saturday," Shanghai suffered several more large-scale bombings of civilians. On 23 August, Wing On and Sincere, two of the city's main department stores on Nanking Road, were bombed by the Japanese at midday.

On 28 August, the South Railway Station was the target of Japanese bombs, as Chinese refugees waited there for transport to Hangzhou. Most of these refugees were women and children. This bombing resulted in the famous crying baby photograph featured in an October 1937 issue of *Life* magazine. On 30 August, the North Railway Station was also bombed.

The Battle of Shanghai was an urban battle. The Chinese and Japanese fought street by street, building by building. During the battle, China lost a significant number of troops and failed to arouse any international intervention from Western powers.

Shanghai's last stand, dubbed "Shanghai's Alamo," took place from 26 October to 1 November on the bank of Soochow Creek. There, in the Sihang Warehouse, the last Chinese battalion to be withdrawn from Shanghai was surrounded by the Japanese.

Westerners watching from the International Settlement begged their representatives to make Chiang Kai-shek withdraw his men before the Japanese destroyed the building. The remaining troops were eventually evacuated from the warehouse. They crossed the bridge into the International Settlement under heavy machine gun fire, resulting in the loss of more men.

Then, after weeks of battle, the city of Shanghai finally fell quiet. Sihang Warehouse sat in ruins, as did the Chinese parts of the city, Chapei and Nantao. The Japanese surrounded, but did not occupy the foreign-controlled sections of Shanghai.

The Imperial Japanese forces held a victory parade through the city. Artillery, tanks, and soldiers travelled right down Nanking Road, the heart of the city, at midday on a Friday, in order to halt business and be as much of a nuisance as possible. The parade, which was three kilometres long, was not received quietly.

During the victory parade, one man leapt from the spires of the Great World, shouting, "Long live China!" on his fatal descent into the mass of telephone wires above Thibet Road.

Elsewhere in the crowd, a middle-aged British lawyer grew frustrated after a small Imperial Japanese flag was thrust repeatedly into his hand by a fellow spectator. When the lawyer broke the flag stick over his knee, Japanese onlookers chased the man, who eventually had to be protected under lock and key by municipal police.

A grenade was thrown at the recently bombed Sincere department store, wounding three Japanese soldiers and two Chinese policemen. Japanese troops opened fire into the department store, spraying parade spectators with bullets.

After leaving Shanghai, the Chinese troops retreated westwards towards the capital, Nanking, attacked at the heels by the Japanese the entire way. In Nanking, in December '37 and into January '38, the Japanese conquered and famously "raped" the Chinese city. Another victory parade was held through

HISTORICAL INTERLUDE

Nanking's ruins, witnessed by tens of thousands of Chinese corpses.

*****

Czechoslovakia faced her own series of crises. In September '38, a meeting was held in Munich between German, British, French, and Italian powers; no Czech representative was invited. At the meeting, it was decided that the Czech Sudetenland would be ceded to Germany. Not only were vital industrial concerns, like the Schicht factory, now in German hands, but also, the control of Czech border defences shifted to Germany. Following the Munich Agreement, called the Munich Betrayal by Czechoslovaks, the name "Munich" became synonymous with appeasement — giving in to intimidation to avoid war.

The following month, October '38, President Beneš resigned and went into exile. Emil Hácha, a noted lawyer and judge, was designated as Beneš's successor.

In March 1939, six months after Munich, Hitler demanded a total occupation of Czechoslovakia. Emil Hácha suffered a heart attack during his meeting with Adolf Hitler and Hermann Göring, wherein he agreed to the occupation and signed the Czech lands over to the Nazis. The democratic nation of Czechoslovakia was occupied by Nazi Germany on the Ides of March. The western Czech lands became the Nazi Protectorate of Bohemia and Moravia. The eastern lands of Slovakia became independent.

Emil Hácha remained nominal President of the Protectorate and swore an oath to Hitler. Hitler then appointed Konstantin von Neurath as the first Reichsprotektor of occupied Bohemia and Moravia.

The Nazi occupation obliterated Czech status abroad.

THE SUITCASE

Consulates around the world were given a directive to transfer control to local Nazi German authorities. Some complied, but others resisted, remaining loyal to the exiled President Beneš. Beneš formally notified Paris, London, and the entire League of Nations that, "despite the Nazi occupation, Czechoslovakia continued to exist." But no foreign government was prepared to formally endorse that position.

In August of 1939, the Germans and Soviets signed a non-aggression pact that shocked the world. The agreement allowed the former enemies to focus on their respective interests: Germany would invade Poland without backlash from a major power and could deal with the French and British without worrying about a second front with the Soviets, and the Soviets could focus on building their military strength.

Six months after the Nazi occupation of Czechoslovakia, on 3 September 1939, World War II in Europe began when Germany invaded Poland. On the 17th, the Soviets crossed Poland's Eastern borders. On the 29th, Warsaw fell.

An eight-month-long period of inaction, or "Phoney War," began.

In October '39, Beneš established a Provisional Government in France, with former Ambassador Jan Masaryk, the son of first Czechoslovak President Tomáš Garrigue Masaryk, serving as Beneš's Foreign Minister.

Though the Czechoslovak Army had been officially disbanded by Hitler, newspapers announced the reconstitution of the Czechoslovak Army in Exile on French soil.

Vladimír Taussig travelled to the nearest open Czech consulate to report for duty.

New York City, United States
Wednesday, 1 November 1939

> *After the tempest of wrath has passed*
> *the rule of thy country will return to thee*
> *O Czech people.*
> – Czechoslovakian Pavilion Inscription
> 1939-1940 New York World's Fair

NEW YORK City's Hotel Edison stood slightly taller than the tallest building in Shanghai, the Park Hotel on the racecourse. But the Edison was dwarfed by the other skyscrapers in Midtown Manhattan—the Empire State Building, the Chrysler Building, the nearby RCA Building in Rockefeller Center.

I had only just arrived in the city. I was too tired to go dancing, but too wide-awake for sleep. The Central Theater next-door to the Edison was playing *Le Quai des Brumes*, or, *Port of Shadows*, deemed the best foreign film of 1938.

In the film, an army deserter attempts to escape France by boat. At the titular foggy French port, he meets a runaway young woman and dreams of a life with her, but the deserter runs afoul of gangsters.

Amusingly enough, one of the gangsters was named Lucien. Because of this, I found myself chuckling at odd times during the film, despite its ominous tone.

My laughter drew the attention of a young woman seated nearby. Our eyes met as she glanced my way in the half-light.

THE SUITCASE

When the house lights came up, the young woman stood and smoothed her skirts and checked her wristwatch. She did not look at me. I spotted her again in the lobby, where she was buttoning her coat, slipping on her gloves, and straightening her hat. She looked to be half my age. Her blondish, light-brown wavy hair framed her face becomingly. When her blue eyes finally looked my way, her generous mouth spread into a smile.

"I hope my outbursts did not spoil the film for you," I said.

"It was definitely not a laughter-inducing picture," she said, "but no, you did not ruin it."

"Did you enjoy the film?" I asked.

"It was all right. I like all the foreign films, don't you? But then, you sound foreign yourself. I suppose to you, they are just 'films,'" she said with a smile.

I dialled up the debonair when I said, "I'm Czech. Captain Vladimír Taussig. I just arrived today from Shanghai."

"Just today? Aren't you exhausted?"

"Quite. So much so that I knew I should never be able to sleep. I came over from the hotel to see the picture." I paused, then asked, "What brings a lovely young woman like you to see such a film tonight?"

"I had a free evening, and my acting coach says there's something to be learned from every film. He has me watching comedies, tragedies, mysteries, romance, horror, foreign films, children's films—you name it."

"Ah, an actress. And what do you think? Is there something to be learned from every film?"

She smiled. "For an actress, yes. Most definitely. Even the worst films could be seen as examples of what not to do." We laughed. At that point she might have excused herself, but instead she stayed and asked me a question. "So, what do you do in Shanghai, Captain?"

NEW YORK CITY, UNITED STATES
1 NOVEMBER 1939

"I am a partner in a brokerage firm."

"And a military captain?" she asked. "Is there a Czechoslovak military in China?"

"No. I am a member of the Czechoslovak Army Reserves. I will be reporting for duty in the morning. As a reserve officer, it is my duty to report, in the event of war, until I am fifty years of age. It just so happens that the nearest open consulate is located here in New York City."

"Yes," she said with a little frown, "I suppose they were all closed when your country was occupied by Germany. There was a big to-do here in New York to raise funds for the Czechoslovak Pavilion at the World's Fair. It's too bad, really. You've just missed it. The Fair won't reopen until the spring."

"Maybe by then, the troubled times in my homeland will be over," I said with a smile. "It is up to us who live abroad to oust the Germans. I hope to be headed to the front in France, post-haste."

"Captain Taussig," she said thoughtfully. Her wide smile returned. "I'm Elizabeth Wragge. Everyone calls me Betty."

"Pleased to make your acquaintance, Miss Betty Wragge," I said, gently taking her gloved hand and kissing it. She giggled and grinned.

"How do you like New York?" I asked her.

"I love it. But, as a native, I suppose I am a bit biased. What do you think so far?"

"Everything I have seen thus far, from the skyscrapers, to the cinemas, to the audience members, has impressed me." She laughed again.

Ushers opened the theatre's front doors onto the street. I gestured to the Edison. "I have a room here," I said.

"No wonder you couldn't get any rest! You've got Times Square and Broadway just outside!"

THE SUITCASE

"Within sniffing distance," I said. "Won't you come in for a drink?"

"Like to the Green Room? Tonight? Oh, I don't know, Captain. I have rehearsal in the morning." She lifted her wrist, pulled back her coat sleeve, slid the edge of her glove away from the face of her dainty wristwatch, and frowned.

"The Green Room? How fitting, for an actress."

"Yes, the Green Room is the bar and restaurant attached to the Edison Ballroom," she said. The Edison's doorman was opening the doors. The hotel's lobby beckoned, warm and brightly lit. "I suppose one drink wouldn't hurt," she said. "I'm not at all dressed to be seen here, but I really would like to hear more about Shanghai."

In the Green Room. Blue Barron and his orchestra were playing "sweet, not swing" music—songs like "I'd Be Lost Without You," "That's Where I Came In," and "When Am I Gonna Kiss You Good Morning?" Patrons were peppered around the dining room and dance floor. My companion turned heads and elicited whispers.

"How do they know you?" I asked. "No wonder you were worried about being smartly dressed!"

"Well, I act on the radio. And I have done Broadway, so some folks around here in the theatre district know me from *Dead End*. I also did a film, as a child, but I was only three years old."

"Oh? What film?" I asked.

"A Marion Davies silent film. *Yolanda*. I doubt you know it."

"It rings a distant bell…"

"I had some screen tests in Hollywood not too long ago, but nothing's come of it, which is just as well."

We arrived at a small table near the dance floor. The staff had definitely known well enough to give her one of the better seats!

I ordered my usual whiskey. She asked for a champagne cocktail.

NEW YORK CITY, UNITED STATES
1 NOVEMBER 1939

"Tell me more about your radio show," I said.

"Well," she said excitedly. "The show is called *Pepper Young's Family*, and I play Peggy Young, the title character's sister."

"Do you enjoy radio acting?" I asked.

"Oh, immensely. "I have been doing radio since I was a child. As a young girl, I played in *Gold Spot Pals*. My brother Eddie did too." She laughed, "But you would have no way of knowing that." She smiled that wide smile. "Radio is great fun. Some days we perform live; other days we rehearse and record it 'in the can.'" It was then common for cast members to read through a script with a timer, allowing for adjustments to speed or slow the final performance, adding or removing lines as needed. "Sometimes I even get to suggest lines," Betty added. "I have been playing Peggy Young for so long that I often find that the very thing I would say, is what the writers have Peggy say!"

"I shall have to tune in and listen to you," I said.

"Please do. It's on NBC Blue at three-thirty."

"NBC Blue," I repeated.

"In fact, the studios are just a couple of blocks from here, in Rockefeller Plaza. You should see the Plaza while you're here. And Broadway."

"Broadway, movies, radio—what can't you do?" I asked, grinning.

"Honestly, I could use some dancing lessons." That wide smile of hers brightened her face. "Now, tell me, what is Shanghai like?"

I described the balls and dances, teas and tiffins, pony races and paper hunts, play acting and film viewing, and so forth. But the vibrant city I described to her had changed since the Battle of Shanghai. Social life had since become tinged with the ever-present possibility of terrorism—bombings, kidnappings, shootings, robberies, that sort of thing. The fun had also been

THE SUITCASE

spoiled by the loss of a few of our best, who had departed the city either to avoid the tensions in China, or to join the conflicts in Europe.

Betty Wragge, being a clever young woman, saw beyond the picture I painted. "Isn't there a war in Shanghai?" she asked.

"Oh, there's always some conflict or another," I said. "At the outset of the Battle of Shanghai, I was in one of the buildings that was bombed. I was checking telephone messages at my office on the riverfront when the excitement began." I silently recalled the typhoon, the aeroplanes, the bomb craters, dust and debris. The blood- and dust-covered volunteers lifting rubble to search for survivors and extract the dead. The gutters filled with blood and flies. The smell of days-old bodies in the summertime. The unexpected sight of gore lingering in tree branches or plastered to billboards and buildings.

Our drinks were delivered. I took a sip, then continued: "Owing to the damage from the battle, we had to move our offices to a new building." Drakeford, Davis and Wilson had moved to the Hongkong & Shanghai Bank building on the Bund—that domed edifice with bronze lions symbolising Protection and Security crouched out front. Its exterior walls were stacked with sandbags. I had taken photos of our office with its sandbags.

"As far as the fighting on the ground went, we were fairly safe. The Japanese advanced through the Chinese parts of the city, creeping quietly with their gas masks and bayonets, pillbox by pillbox, barricade by barricade, conquering what they were able. Then the Chinese would retake the area in a similar manner, one street at a time."

"My goodness," she said. "And you all were living there during this fighting?"

"I worried about aeroplane bombs, and shrapnel from AA fire, but we were mostly fine. We Westerners in the international

NEW YORK CITY, UNITED STATES
1 NOVEMBER 1939

zones were largely unaffected." Sir Victor continued to hold parties at the Cathay, which had fully reopened within a month of August's "Bloody Saturday" bombing.

Betty asked, "What has life been like since the battle?"

"Mostly the same as before. The Japanese surround the city. Chinese and Westerners now have to stop at the boundaries of the international zones and show our papers, and we are expected to bow to the Japanese sentries."

"Are you really?" she asked.

"Oh yes. And they have been known to slap a Westerner for failing to bow, or to take him in for questioning. They represent the Emperor, and any insult to them, is an insult to Him. They are harsher with the Chinese, but then, the Chinese are the enemy." I had heard of Chinese people being beheaded for refusing to bow to the Emperor's soldiers. Chinese people in Shanghai were often dragged to an old hotel in Hongkew, "Bridge House," to be punished for such insults, and for other various "crimes." Any Chinese person might, at any time, be subjected to searches, manhandling, slaps and punches, strikes with rifle butts, and prods with bayonet points. The Western armed forces and Shanghai Volunteer Corps watchmen saw all of this happen each day, but were powerless to intervene. "But if you were to visit Shanghai today, you would never think China was at war at all."

"Where would you take me, if we were to go out on the town in Shanghai?" she asked, grinning.

"Well, if you arrived during the fashionable season, that is, April until June, the weather will be wonderful, and the flowers will be out along the river. We could visit the Race Club. Play tennis or golf. When it is safe to do so, my friend takes parties in his houseboat through China, up and down the rivers and through the gorges. And Shanghai's nightlife is incomparable. We would go to the Cathay ballroom and the Tower nightclub, both in my friend Sir Victor's hotel."

"It sounds delightful," she said.

"Maybe sometime you could give me a tour of your own city."

"Oh, maybe! If I can ever get away for any amount of time. I'm always dashing here and there, you know. Auditions, rehearsals, lessons, performances, press appearances, dinners, dances — always something to do!"

"It sounds a lot like Shanghai," I said. "Have you travelled much?"

"Not too much. I have had my few jaunts to Hollywood." She smiled. "But someday I do hope to visit Holland. My parents are Holland Dutch."

"One of my business partners is Dutch," I said with a smile, "Frederik Mijsberg. So," I continued, "a Dutch girl, born in New York City. I was born in Prague." I gently took her hand. "May I?" I asked, turning her wrist to see the face of her dainty little watch. "In fact, I was born in Prague forty years ago today — since in Prague it is now after midnight on November the second." I gently returned her wrist. "They are six hours ahead of your city."

"Oh! You should have said so before! Happy birthday, Captain! In Dutch they say, 'Gelukkige verjaardag.'"

"In Czech, 'Všechno nejlepší,' or 'Best wishes.'"

She smiled. "On that note, I really should be going."

As we parted, she said, "It's been awfully fun chatting with you, Captain. I do hope you enjoy your time in the city."

"I'm sure I will. So far, my visit has been just splendid." I smiled at her. "It was lovely to have met you." I reached inside the pocket of my overcoat for a calling card. I bent and kissed her gloved hand and slid the card into her palm.

*****

NEW YORK CITY, UNITED STATES
1 NOVEMBER 1939

In the morning I fulfilled my military obligation. Had Maglič not died in 1938, freeing me from the shelved court case, it would have been a far sight more difficult to do my duty as a Reserve officer while hoping to maintain some mystery about my whereabouts.

Headlines that day read: "Chinese Nationalist Army Begins Disastrous Winter Offensive against Japanese Forces." Perhaps it was a good time to be away from Shanghai.

I exited the Edison into a bright and crisp early November morning and began a ten-minute walk through the lively theatre district and into the open space of Times Square, where lights and signs for Planters Peanuts, Coca-Cola, Camel cigarettes and Chevrolet cars were flashing and blinking even in the morning sun.

I soon arrived at 1440 Broadway, a tallish corner building that housed, among other offices, the WOR radio station and the Czechoslovakian consulate. Inside, I found the military attaché to the Czechoslovak Government-in-Exile in France, Colonel Oldřich Španiel, a slim, bespectacled man about five years my senior who had only just arrived at his post about a month previously. His chest was filled with ribbons.

I felt brotherhood. I felt homecoming. I felt relief. As long as there were men like Španiel, and men like me, Czechoslovakia would continue to exist.

"Reserve štábní kapitán Vladimír Jiří Taussig, reporting for duty from Shanghai," I announced as I presented my military book. "After I heard about Poland, I immediately booked passage."

He scanned the book's various training dates, advancements, and awards. The entries dated to 1924. I made it a point to tell him of my first engagement, the Battle of Caporetto, fought when I was in the Austro-Hungarian Army at the tender age of eighteen, as well as my post-war transfer into the newly-formed Czechoslovak Army. I wanted him to know how seriously I took my commitments.

Španiel frowned and said, "A Czechoslovak Captain from Shanghai, reporting to a consulate in New York City, to serve the military of an occupied 'Protectorate.'" He cleared his throat. "What business do you do in Shanghai?"

"I am a member of the Exchange Broker's Association," I said. I had been elected and voted in in February, and was still paying instalments on the $6,500 I'd borrowed for my membership dues. "I have two business partners." Our offices were at 45 Kiukiang Road, just steps from the Bund. "We specialize in bullion." My partners were treating my absence as a "long leave" and continued executing necessary transactions on my behalf.

"And prior to that?"

"Before that, I was with a brokerage firm, Drakeford, Davis, and Wilson. I left near the end of the Battle of Shanghai and formed my present partnership."

"An exchange broker," Španiel said thoughtfully. He returned my military book. "There are no open consulates in the Far East to which you might have reported?"

"I am sorry to say that, in an appalling show of weakness, the consulate in Shanghai followed Hitler's order and transferred control to the local Nazis." If anything, they might have given control to municipal authorities instead. Or they might have gone the route of consulates in New York, London, Paris, Moscow, and Washington, which had defiantly remained open.

"With the consulate closed, who is leading the Czech community in Shanghai?" Španiel asked.

"Some would say Jaroslav Stepan," I said. "Others would say Jan Seba."

"Yes. I know Seba's name," he said. "The former Romanian

NEW YORK CITY, UNITED STATES
1 NOVEMBER 1939

Minister who resigned amid a scandal over his book." That was 1937's *The Soviet Union and the Little Entente.*

"The very same," I said. "He left his post in Bucharest in February of '37 and was hosting parties in Shanghai by late-October. He was the Legation Chief in Shanghai who surrendered to the Germans, whereas Jaroslav Stepan, Chancellor of the Legation, wanted to surrender to the British, if the Legations were to be surrendered at all."

"I see."

I continued, "Because of Seba's betrayal, and the surrender of the Embassy to the Nazis, we Czechs have been without any diplomatic representation. Stepan now heads the 'Czech Circle,' the Czechoslovak resistance organisation in Shanghai. My task, through the Czech Circle, has been to establish contact with representatives of the Western democracies."

"What does that entail?"

"I was given the job of approaching the American, British and Chinese press to persuade the publishers to accept from me, without compensation, informative articles pertaining to the injustice of the Munich agreement and the danger of the inevitable Second World War. In this capacity, I supply newspapers with articles, buy time on local commercial radio stations, write scripts, and even speak over the airwaves in English, Czech, and German. I have also engaged Chinese translators and supplied native newspapers and commentators with my scripts."

"Seems like a great deal of effort on your part, on the behalf of what is surely a small group of Czechoslovaks in Shanghai," he said with a frown.

"We firmly believe that our efforts will, and do, extend far beyond the bounds of Shanghai. The city is brimming with members of various nationalities who will surely be impacted by our messages in some way. We understand that the rewards may not be readily apparent, and we are willing to assume the necessary risks."

"Risks?"

"A broadcaster named Carroll Alcott is a prime example. He speaks on an American-owned station, XMHA. The station's signal reaches all the way to Japan. Since the summer of '38, Alcott has been making broadcasts and speaking the truth about the Japanese. Therefore, since the summer of '38, station XMHA, and Alcott himself, had been victims of terrorist attacks. Alcott's broadcasts are sometimes jammed, and his voice replaced by the sounds of gongs and horns, bells and buzzers."

"But you are not making anti-Japanese statements, only pro-Czech?" Španiel asked.

"That is correct. But that is all behind me now anyway, as I hope to be transferred immediately to the front."

"How many Czechs are there in Shanghai?" Španiel asked.

"A few hundred. There were only about one hundred — until the situation with Germany began to heat up. Though we are outnumbered by the Austrian and German refugees, the Czech presence in Shanghai is not insignificant." I did not feel it necessary to inform Španiel that most of those latecomers to Shanghai were Jewish and had come to China as a last resort.

Španiel thought for a moment. "It might be some time before Beneš and General Ingr," the exile government's Minister of National Defence, "reach a decision about you. Buďme upřímní," he said, "Let's be honest. You are a forty-year-old broker whose last formal military training was in the 1920s."

"I am an active athlete and fearsome tennis competitor," I said. "I am hardly out of shape," I said. "As for awaiting instructions, I have a sister in New York whom I have not seen in several years, and I shall be visiting with her in the interim." Francy, Zikmund, and Jiří had recently immigrated to the United States.

NEW YORK CITY, UNITED STATES
1 NOVEMBER 1939

Španiel dismissed me, saying, "I shall summon you when I receive further instruction."

I was released into New York. After the weeks of preparation and travel, my meeting with Španiel was over in a matter of minutes. The waiting began.

*****

I walked back to my hotel, passing again through the lights and crowds of Times Square. When I was nearly back to the Edison, I came across someone whose presence in New York promised to make waiting to hear from Španiel and the Government-in-Exile infinitely more exciting.

"Captain Taussig!" a woman called.

For a moment I failed to recognize the familiar face. Who was the lovely lady wiggling her gloved fingers at me, cheeks flushed above an elegant fur stole, hair carefully marcelled beneath a tiny Parisian hat? "Helene Freeman, is that you?"

Helene, a New York City native, had come to Shanghai when she married Jo Fisher Freeman, accounting adviser at the Central Bank of China. Apparently, Helene and Jo had parted ways, and she had returned to New York. Since July, she had been performing as Sandra Wilson on a radio program called *Meet Miss Julia*. The show, she said, was set in a boarding house in a place called Gramercy Park. "Tune in at two thirty!" she told me.

With *Meet Miss Julia* at 2.30 and Betty Wragge's show at 3.30, I would be spending many afternoons within earshot of a radio set.

Helene was bound by an appointment at the NBC studios at Rockefeller Center and could not stay and chat. "Why don't we meet later this evening?" she suggested. "I'll introduce you to my new beau, Eddy Jerome. There will be some other friends of mine for you to chat up."

"Where shall I meet you?"

"Where are you staying?" she asked.

"The Edison."

"Meet us at the Cotton Club," she suggested. "You won't even need a car. It's right on Broadway; you can't miss it."

New York City, United States
Thursday, 2 November 1939

> *I'm living in a great big way.*
> — Bill "Bojangles" Robinson

That afternoon, in between my visit to Španiel and my first trip to the Cotton Club, I visited my sister Francy. It was the first time I had seen any family since my departure from Prague nearly seven years before.

Though a subway line had been constructed for the World's Fair which could take me almost directly from my hotel to my destination, I ordered a car to deliver me to my sister's new American home, giving the driver the address—98-09 65th Road, Forest Hills.

"All the way out in Queens?" the driver asked.

"In Forest Hills," I said, reaching into my overcoat to produce the envelope I carried with me, to show him the address. "Here."

"No, it's all right," he said, waving the envelope away. "I mean, I know where Forest Hills is and all. I'm just sayin', the address you want ain't in Forest Hills. And anyway, you'd do better taking the E train."

"Forest Hills," I said, looking ahead.

"Sure." He pulled away from the Edison. After a moment's pause, he began filling the silence with his own voice.

"I don't usually leave the city, but I was just over in Forest Hills several weeks ago," he said. "Drove a few tennis pros doing the National Championships up there. The address you want, though, that's Rego Park. Right down the road from Forest Hills, but very different."

We drove out of Manhattan and across the East River, taking the Queensboro Bridge into Queens.

As we drove, the driver chatted at me intermittently.

He pointed to a distant shape, a tall, narrow white obelisk: "That's the Trylon. Big monument at the World's Fair. Fair's closed now though. Until spring, anyway."

"Yes, well, I won't be here in the spring," I said.

"Oh yeah? Just visiting?" he asked.

"Yes." I shifted in my seat and looked out of the window.

The driver slowed on a broad and busy avenue called Queens Boulevard. We stopped in front of a group of eighteen brick apartment buildings called Queens Boulevard Gardens.

"Now," the driver said, "just so you know, Forest Hills is right down the road there," he said, pointing down the boulevard as I gathered my packages. "Just off the main road. Tennis club. Mansions. You'll know it when you see it."

I stepped from the car out into the cold and began walking amongst the buildings, looking for Francy's exact address. Once inside and upstairs, I found myself knocking on my sister's apartment door. How strange to find her here, in an apartment building in the United States.

I was admittedly not extremely close to Francy. Even when we were children living in the same household, we had operated within very different spheres. She was six years my senior.

I thought of the last times I had seen her, before my sloppy departure from Europe in 1933. I had been sent photographs of her in the past couple of years, but the forty-six-year-old woman who opened the door was greyer and more heavyset than I expected. "Francy!"

"Vlada!" She grinned, and for a moment I lost sight of the

NEW YORK CITY, UNITED STATES
2 NOVEMBER 1939

wisps of grey near her temple and the wrinkles beaming from the corner of each eye. When the smile faded, I again saw how her illnesses, and the events surrounding her family's emigration, had aged her.

"Look at you!" she exclaimed. Her smiling brown eyes looked me over. I was the same old Vlada, same grey eyes and brown hair—perhaps a little less hair than she remembered, but still very fit and handsome. She laughed, "Here I am going grey while you have hardly changed at all." She squeezed my shoulders. "How strong!"

I clasped her hands in my own and noticed an angry callus. "What is this?" I asked.

"I have been learning to help Zikmund with the clerical duties in the office. There have been some long hours, but it will be worth it someday. Thankfully, Jiří is at an age where he can look after himself if I work late."

"You? Working?" I asked as we entered the apartment.

"Mamicka would have a fit if she knew," she said.

We paused for a moment in her foyer and looked at one another, the invisible stretch of years and continents between us.

"Oh!" She exclaimed, "How rude of me! Allow me to take your overcoat, sir," she said in a tone that recalled one of our household servants from childhood. How strange, it occurred to me, to find ourselves alone—no chauffeur, no doorman, butler, maid or cook. I mentioned it to Francy. "I do the cooking and cleaning," she said, "I have been in the kitchen all morning!"

"And you work?" I asked. "I do hope you can manage it all."

"Once we are a little more well-established, I'll engage someone to come help once or twice a week."

"In Shanghai you could have an entire house full of servants for the price of that one maid. That said, the Shanghai servants may not be as proficient as you would like. And they will definitely gossip about your affairs. They may steal from you, and, whether they steal or not, they will definitely expect extra 'squeeze' money from time to time."

She laughed. "That sounds awful. I look forward to having one trustworthy woman to help keep house, not a bevy of meddling Chinese."

I laughed too. After the laughter quieted, I said, "We had some good servants in Prague, didn't we?"

"We did," she said. "What I wouldn't give to have a real cook again! When we left Karlovy Vary, we had to let our servants go," she said. I had never visited them there. Entire chapters of my family's life were unknown to me. "And in Prague, Mamicka did all of the cooking. She couldn't afford the help after Father died. Luckily, she is a wonderful cook."

"I could hardly believe it when I heard that the Schichts offered no widow's pension."

"I could," Francy said. "I am told they are Nazis. Why should they help our family? When Jara met with them, he was told outright that the firm was Aryanising. I have heard that Franz is living in London and organising the Germans living there. They call his home 'The German House.'"

After a moment's pause, I attempted to lighten the mood by circling back around to the topic of hired help. "I cannot believe how domestic you've become. I suppose I had imagined you and Zik and Jiří going to restaurants to eat each day, like we do in Shanghai."

"Zigi would never allow the expense," Francy said. "It's so much more economical to cook," she said. She ushered me into the bright sitting room and bade me to sit.

In the past, Francy's household had always been exquisitely decorated; she had taken great pride in the fashionable arrangement of her rooms. Here, she had only two armchairs,

NEW YORK CITY, UNITED STATES
2 NOVEMBER 1939

a settee, and a few tables adorned with a couple of lamps and some framed photographs. There was a photo of Francy and Zikmund as newlyweds; a professionally-made portrait of Jiří as an infant; the photo I also owned a copy of, showing the Prague Taussigs gathered for our father's seventieth birthday. My own face did not appear in a single photo.

Francy noticed my tacit examination of the room. "I'm sure you had hoped to see some familiar things from Prague. We lost a lot when we left Karlovy Vary, and then more when I left Prague," Francy explained. "We even sold some things to finance our journey. We had to pay taxes on, and pay shipping fees for, anything brought with us to the States. I wish I had been able to bring everything. I was always so proud of my home and my decorating, and now look at me."

"It looks fine," I said. "A much nicer arrangement than many who've left Europe have." I placed my packages on a table. I plopped into an armchair and casually crossed my legs.

"So, how was your journey?" she asked.

"Long!" I laughed. "How was yours?"

She took a seat on the settee.

"Everything leading up to our travel was more difficult than the journey itself," she said. "The interviews. The paperwork. The separation. But we can discuss that later. Tell me, what are these packages you have brought?"

I grinned and presented a gift to her. It was another Soochow blanket. It was beautiful, it was versatile, and it had been easy to carry in my luggage.

"Oh!" she exclaimed. "Just like the one you sent Mamicka. Oh, I do love it," she said, gazing down at the blanket in her lap, her fingers tracing the embroidery. She looked up at me, "Thank you," she said. "I will hang it, and when I look at it, I will think about Mamicka and Jara and Mitcka and their parlour. And you and your adventures in the Exotic East," she laughed. "Zigi will like it too. He is due home before too long."

"Before he arrives, tell me, how did Mamicka really handle the move from the villa to the new apartment?"

Francy sighed. "She kept saying that when she finally did leave the villa, at least she wouldn't 'feel the lack of our dear father in every step.' She went on and on about how she needed to sell the villa, which, to be sure, financially, she does need to, but she has only been able to find a renter. Some English attaché, last I knew." She sighed again. "But their apartment is very nice," she shrugged. "Fashionable. Upscale. Modern. She goes for walks with Molinka. And you know, it broke her heart to give up Barry and Eda before the move."

"I know. An apartment is no place for those two anyway. They need room to run. I hope they are happily strolling in the park, or hunting birds with their new owner."

"One can hope. Mamicka takes Molinka everywhere. They used to frequent the Café Imperial, but now there is a long list of places which Jews are forbidden to visit. She still takes the tram to visit Father in the cemetery. She sits and talks to him."

I said, "I suppose today she'll be visiting and lighting candles, for dušičky," All Saint's Day. Francy nodded. I added, "I can't imagine all of you squeezing into an apartment. Mamicka, Marietta, Jara, then you and Jiří too."

Francy nodded. "And her dog. And occasionally Jara's girlfriend."

"Girlfriend!" I exclaimed.

"Haven't you heard? It's quite scandalous, really. She lounges in bed all day, and Jara brings coffee to her. When she wasn't staying with us, Jara would send her lunch—even though our dear family is living well below the usual standard. She eats enough for three."

NEW YORK CITY, UNITED STATES
2 NOVEMBER 1939

"Is she pregnant?" I asked.

"Doubtful. She's so slim."

"Is she at least pretty?"

"I think so. When she makes herself up, anyway. But Mamicka says she would rather look at a dead rat." I laughed. "Our dear brother wants to marry her, but Mamicka is set against it. 'What would our dear Father have thought?' she asks."

"Why does she hate this woman so?"

"The girlfriend slept with another man for four years," Francy said, eyebrows raised.

"I see," I said.

"Mamicka tries to keep quiet, and to not get mixed up in it. She says Jara is no little boy, and that hopefully, with God's help, he will see for himself that she is no good. It makes your gallivanting around not seem so bad. At least you never brought girls home." Francy sighed. "Mamicka misses you terribly, especially since Father died. She weeps each time she sees your stationery—your letterhead that looks just like Father's. She was worried sick about you during the battle in Shanghai, you know. It was like the Great War all over again. You were off in another country, in the midst of a battle, and we couldn't get much information."

I smiled. "Oh, it wasn't so bad. I was never in too much danger," I said dismissively.

With raised eyebrows she said, "Your office building was bombed."

I waved a hand. "I was lucky. As for Mamicka's letters, I remember them very well."

She had written: "Can you imagine, Vlada, how worried I was, and what a fright I lived through when the war broke out and the newspapers were full of the worst horrors about what was going on there? Such terrible things, and you are so far away, and almost in the middle of it all. I was desperate for news of you, and though your siblings and Zigi did everything to comfort me, and tried to find out any information they could and contact people who would be helpful, nothing helped."

Francy said, "We were saying to ourselves that if our precious father had read all those horrors about China in the newspaper, the poor man would have suffered one stroke after another from being so upset. And Mamicka looks like a little old lady now, after all that has happened — the stresses she's endured."

"Well, I hate that I have contributed to that stress. But you all needn't have worried, truly. The battle itself took place in the Chinese parts of the city. Shrapnel from anti-aircraft guns was the only real danger. And aside from the bestial and uneducated soldiers, the Japanese themselves aren't half bad. And Japan itself is quite lovely. More refined, less garish than China. Quieter. Cleaner. In fact, I just visited earlier this year."

"Japan? Why?"

"Oh I have been plenty of times. Actually, the ship just stopped there on our way to the States. And I bought my car there in March. A Ford."

"A Ford? You?"

I nodded. "What, did you think it would be a Škoda?" I laughed. "There actually is a Far Eastern branch of Škoda, run by a man named Urbanek, who knows nothing about my dealings with Tomáš Maglič. But no, definitely no Škodas for me. There are very few Czech cars in the Far East. No Tatras or Wikovs or Walters. But Japan did have a Ford factory, which has closed. The car was something of a mercy purchase. The Japanese are rabid for scrap metal just now, tearing down iron lamp posts, railings, benches, removing manhole covers, resurrecting submerged ships. How long before they begin sacrificing autos? I got the car for a steal."

NEW YORK CITY, UNITED STATES
2 NOVEMBER 1939

"So you go there often?"

"In my last firm, I was the liaison to Tokyo. But for this most recent trip, I was actually visiting with the Ski and Winter Sports Club of China. I am missing their annual meeting this month, while I'm here in New York. Membership has doubled since the refugees from Europe began to arrive in Shanghai."

"I believe it," Francy said. "What was the skiing like in Japan?"

"It was great fun. There were three resorts, all centred on Akakura village in the Myoko Kogen ski area, which boasts the longest runs in the country. I stayed in Akakura Kanko. The rooms had traditional Japanese onsens to soak one's tired limbs in after a long day on the slopes. You would have enjoyed the resort."

"Maybe the hot springs," she said, "but I haven't skied in years. Jara still skis, when he's able."

I shook my head. "Not anymore. The family shipped a container of household items over to Shanghai, including three pairs of skis. It arrived in August." The wooden container sent by the Taussigs was the size of a small room. In addition to the skis, it contained furniture, linens, and other household items that would help the family establish themselves.

Francy said, "To be honest, I'm worried about them. Our family and Zikmund's too. Who knows what is happening since I left. They have been censoring the post for some time. And the telephones have been tapped. Everywhere the Gestapo is watching, listening, recording."

"I am certainly careful with what I write to Mamicka," I said. "I would not want to draw unnecessary attention to the family."

"But you already have. Anyone with family living abroad is subjected to Gestapo interrogations, our family included. Myself included," she said. "When she wrote to you about invitations to parties, and having conversations there about the villa, those were half-veiled statements to pass the censor. She was trying to tell you about Gestapo interviews."

Our mother wrote: "Can you imagine how happy we all were! You know Mitcka, what she does when she is 'happy.' Before she went, she took three tranquilizers in order not to be nervous. They spoke [to her] there about our villa and had also other kinds of conversations! I would have loved to be there, but I am too old for them, after all. As you can see, at least one happy event appeared in this monotonous life of ours! ...Thank God your father isn't here to share in such worries!"

So many thoughts flooded my mind that I was unsure what to say. But Francy continued, "And I had to deal with them again while making preparations to come to America. I was terrified that they would discover I had been living in Czechoslovakia illegally."

"What do you mean?" I asked.

"Where do I even begin?" she sighed and looked to the ceiling. Then she said, "So, when I married Zigi, I lost my Czechoslovak citizenship. After you left for Shanghai, we moved from Berlin to Karlovy Vary, at which time we had to obtain special permission to reside in the Czech lands for a number of years. That was April of '33."

"I know. I wish I had been able to visit you there. Oblatten wafer cookies. Thun porcelain. The Grandhotel Pupp," I said wistfully.

She waved her hand. "You were long gone," she said. "But yes, I loved living there. By the time Father died," Francy continued, "the year I was so ill and Mamicka and Marietta and I went to Opatija?" I nodded. "By then, my permission to live in Czechoslovakia had lapsed. And there was no chance Zigi and I would return to Germany. Too much had developed with the

NEW YORK CITY, UNITED STATES
2 NOVEMBER 1939

Nazis by that time, and I was worried, always, about Jiří."

"Naturally."

"Zikmund left for New York via Antwerp last May. At that time, Jiří and I moved to Prague to live with Mamicka and Jara and Mitcka at their apartment at 23 Revoluční. Prague had changed since the occupation. The main square was dominated by this horrible banner, a multi-storey affair that read: 'To each his own.' Quite a homecoming."

"I should say."

She continued, "Jiří and I lived there for a little over a year. That was..." she paused. Her back was straight. Her hands were firmly clasped in her lap. "That was a difficult year," she said. "We pretended to be divorced."

"Why would you pretend that?" I asked.

"Well, for one, Zikmund was already in New York. He returned to Czechoslovakia once, briefly, in September. The Munich Betrayal was unfolding. Then he travelled back here to New York, arriving in early October, two days after President Beneš's resignation. By that time, the fall of '38, they had begun stamping German Jews' passports with a big red 'J,' making it even more difficult to be accepted by a destination country."

"Damned Nazis."

"It was the Swiss," she corrected me. "They wanted to make it easier to deny Jews entry."

"Interesting. But if you were divorced then you wouldn't be German anymore?" I asked.

"Right. Just as I lost my Czech citizenship by marrying a German, I was no longer considered German when we 'divorced.' I became stateless. They did not stamp a 'J' on my passport. With Zigi in the States, I was able to use him as one of my sponsors, calling him my 'cousin.' The Americans issued me a quota number and approved me for immigration.

All the while, I was frightened that our divorce ruse would be discovered, or my illegal presence in Czechoslovakia—or rather, the Protectorate—would be discovered, and that Jiří and I would be stuck in Prague, and possibly punished."

"I'm glad you were in Prague. It was lucky that you were there for Kristallnacht, not in Karlovy Vary," I said. I knew that in Karlovy Vary, Jewish heads of households had been taken to Buchenwald and forced to sign their property over to the Reich. The Great Synagogue on Park Street, where Jiří's Bar Mitzvah was held just the year before, was burned.

There was a quiet moment. Then she said, "They say there are only four Jews left in Karlovy Vary now."

"Four? Surely that can't be."

"That is what I have heard. Especially after Kristallnacht, everyone went running to the emigration offices. People waited in lines for days, through rain or cold or beating sun." She paused, then added, "Since the occupation, the Nazis have been actually encouraging emigration. A man named Adolf Eichmann, from the Central Office for Emigration, came to Prague in July and established offices there." Before his arrival in Prague, Eichmann had been responsible for processing one hundred thousand Viennese Jews who emigrated from Austria after the Anschluss.

Eichmann once said of his office: "This is like an automatic factory, let us say a flour mill connected to some bakery. You put in at one end a Jew who has capital and has… a factory or a shop or an account in a bank, and he passes through the entire building, from counter to counter, from office to office—he comes out at the other end, he has no money, he has no rights, only a passport in which is written: You must leave this country within two weeks; if you fail to do so, you will go to a concentration camp."

Francy said, "But while the Germans are pressing emigration,

NEW YORK CITY, UNITED STATES
2 NOVEMBER 1939

it has become more and more difficult to find a destination country." The July '38 Evian Conference had revealed that, of thirty-something countries with a stated desire to help the emigration crisis in Europe, only one nation had actually agreed to take on an increased number of Jewish refugees — the Dominican Republic.

Francy continued, "To get into America, I had to provide five copies of my visa application, two copies of my birth certificate, and an immigration quota number. I needed two citizen or permanent resident sponsors to provide affidavits of support and sponsorship — six notarized copies of those. And then, let's see, an affidavit from my bank regarding the status of my accounts, a certificate of good conduct from the local police authorities, and a clean bill of health following a physical exam at a United States Consulate. And everything was to be filled out in German, and in duplicate. For myself, and for Jiří."

"That's quite an overwhelming list," I said.

Francy shook her head. "That's not even the financial portion. We were forced to pay the Reich Flight Tax and a Jewish Property Tax. Since Kristallnacht, we also have to pay our 'share' of a billion-Reichsmark 'punishment fine.'"

"So many fines and taxes," I said. "The Nazis know that destination countries will be more reluctant to accept impoverished refugees."

"But we made it, and we have been here since August."

"It sounds exhausting," I said. "It's not like that at all in Shanghai. Since the Battle, with Greater Shanghai under Japanese control, the docks and customs are also under Japanese control. Or rather, lack of control. There are more European refugees entering the Settlement than the established Jewish residents are able to help. Eight ships docked in July. Eight more in August. There will have been even more since I departed."

THE SUITCASE

"Well that's wonderful," she said. "I am glad those families were able to emigrate."

"It is going to get more difficult, though," I said. "The International Settlement has long been an 'open city,' with no entry papers or visas of any kind required, but, as of August, the Japanese authorities have begun to impose some restrictions."

"What do you mean?" Francy asked.

"Last month, a new permit system was introduced," I said. "The Jewish leaders in Shanghai assured the Japanese that 'world Jewry' would not be upset if the Japanese began limiting European refugees to 'a few desirables from time to time.'"

An acquaintance of mine, Godfrey Phillips, of the Shanghai Municipal Council, had conferred with the Japanese authorities in Shanghai and, in August '39, had sent letters "to the Committee for the Assistance of European Jewish Refugees, [to] members of the consular body, and [to] three leading shipping companies informing them of the council's decision 'to forbid any further entry into the International Settlement of refugees from Europe.'" The French Concession was expected to follow the International Settlement's suit. It was also unofficially made clear that "very few refugees would be permitted to enter" Japanese-controlled Hongkew.

In October, after I had left Shanghai, the Council's decision had been amended and the announcement made that the restrictions didn't apply to people who had, "available for use in Shanghai," not less than $400 for each adult; people who had "immediate family relations... of certified financial competency resident in Shanghai, or [had] a contract of employment with a resident in Shanghai, or intend to contract marriage with a resident in Shanghai."

I continued, "People like my friend Sir Victor have committed much time and numerous resources to relief efforts and refugee

NEW YORK CITY, UNITED STATES
2 NOVEMBER 1939

committees. Sir Victor especially has done a lot—financing and chairing committees, providing and raising funds, furnishing loans, allowing use of his buildings. For instance, his enormous Embankment Building has been transformed into a refugee centre. That sort of thing."

"And he is unable to continue doing more?" she asked thoughtfully.

"Well, yes. There are simply too many people to help. And we cannot have our countrymen and co-religionists living in squalor. We will lose face, that is, respectability. The decision to limit refugees was met with almost unanimous approval in Shanghai. You must understand, before the Jewish refugees there were Chinese. Before the Chinese there were the White Russians. Before the Russians it was another group. The city is quite at its capacity as a safe haven for the downtrodden." I explained: "There are maybe fifty thousand foreigners in Shanghai. Of these, there are only about one thousand affluent, English Sephardic Jews. And it has fallen on them to see that the fifteen-or-so thousand European Jews who have recently arrived in Shanghai are cared for in a way that neither burdens nor disgraces the community. As I said, we cannot allow decent, educated Europeans to live like the Chinese refugees or to compete with uneducated coolies for pennies-a-day labour, living in mud huts amid cesspools, dying from poor hygiene and nutrition. Starving! Freezing! Shitting themselves to death! Their corpses left exposed, unburied. That is precisely what will happen if more refugees continue to arrive."

The image of the dead, muck-spattered infant I had once seen in Chapei flashed through my mind. It was compounded by all the years of misery, poverty, and mistreatment I'd seen since.

She gave another sigh. "I don't like it. Now Shanghai is no different from anywhere else—just more impossible hoops to jump through and juggling acts to coordinate. People must be

THE SUITCASE

able to escape somewhere. People are killing themselves to avoid going back to Prague. There was recently a story in the papers about a Mrs. Charles Langier. The Langiers came to the States on a six-month visitors' visa. When the visa was due to expire, the family applied to the Canadian authorities for permission to move there. There had been no reply, and time was running out. So Mrs. Langier took her two little boys, four and six years old, and checked into a Chicago hotel. There, she jumped out of a window with her children."

"Oh?" I asked stoically.

"The mail was delivered just after she departed for the hotel," Francy continued. "In the mail was the letter granting permission for the family to reside in Canada. When the husband arrived home and read the letter, he couldn't wait to tell his wife and children the good news. He waited and waited for them to return. Eventually, he went looking for them, which was when the police informed him of his family's fate."

Francy's voice had started to shake by the end of her anecdote. I had been hardened to situations of that nature. People killed themselves every day in Shanghai.

"All of which is to say, people are desperate not to be in occupied territories, Vlada. You should not be stopping them from coming to Shanghai. And what about our own family? Our siblings at least have their banking and background information in order. And what about the household goods they sent this summer?"

I asked, "Do you really think our family would leave? Especially if I am no longer in Shanghai? Besides, we both know good and well that it is one thing to prepare documents and make plans. It's quite another thing to pack up, say goodbyes, and leave for the unknown."

"I suppose you are right. I am lucky Zigi was able to pave

NEW YORK CITY, UNITED STATES
2 NOVEMBER 1939

my way. Think of Marietta's nerves—can you imagine her going through with it?" After a moment, she added, "Well, they are not likely to go anywhere unless they can sell the villa. They cannot afford to leave. Jara gave the last of his savings to me for my journey. Even if they had the funds, Mamicka recently wrote to say she is worried that once they clear the apartment out, and the trip is paid for, they'll stop granting visas and they'll be stuck there as beggars."

"I understand their concerns. I only wish I had the means to help them, but even I have been borrowing," I said. "So, tell me, how bad is it? Occupied Prague? Nazi occupation?" I asked.

Francy sighed. "There was a lot of anxiety leading up to March the fifteenth. A lot of tension. Demonstrations took place, especially on Wenceslas Square. On the morning of the fifteenth, the Nazis were not exactly met with open arms as they were in Austria, but they came in peacefully enough just the same. They want to 'Germanize' the Czechs. They forbid the singing of patriotic songs in public. They won't let *The Lantern* be performed at the National Theatre."

"Ah," I said. "'I will defend my country even if I have to die as a result,'" I recited the drama's popular line.

"Yes," Francy nodded. "They quickly learned that when that line is said, the audience stands and sings 'Kde domov můj,' and the Nazis can't bear it. After they banned *The Lantern*, people began spontaneously singing it at any performance—music, theatre, cinema."

I was smiling like mad, imagining the audiences in song.

"And there were other small forms of protest. On President Beneš's birthday," 28 May, "someone left the streetlamps burning all day long. The lamplighter was later arrested, but, people do continue to make gestures. But every outright protest, and some subtle ones too, have been brutally squashed by the Nazis."

THE SUITCASE

"If the Czechs can outlast four centuries of Habsburgs, then surely they can survive Hitler," I said.

"They hope to. They boycott all things German. Shops. Newspapers. Films. The German language."

I nodded. "I have seen a similar situation with the Chinese and Japanese. The Chinese boycott Japanese products, until they can no longer afford to do so. Eventually the Japanese will see to it that only Japanese goods are available, and only Japanese goods are affordable. But," I added, "I have no doubt that the Czechs will continue on for as long as they are able."

"I am not so sure. After the occupation, their first order of business was to block Jewish bank accounts and limit even Aryan withdrawals. They closed the schools; many were then used as barracks. Before we arrived in the States, Jiří had not attended a proper class since March. Food is being rationed because the Germans 'need' it. They creep about at night, making arrests and hauling people away. Everyone knows somebody in a concentration camp."

"Terror tactic," I said. "The Japanese do the same to the Chinese."

"You seem so dismissive," Francy said, "as if this is all normal." She was quiet for a moment, then said, "You were in transit and missed Jan Masaryk's Independence Day broadcast. He said that he did not know how long this war will last, but that he did know that our faith, love, and hope would last longer than the horrors of the war. He said, 'Your task in this struggle is... difficult but important.' He said, 'Calmly and determinedly wait for the moment when, at a given sign, the Mountain of Blaník, the mountain of our resistance, will open up again, and you, its knights, will expel the hated invaders for ever from our land flowing with milk and honey.'"

"Ah, Mount Blaník," I mused. As legend holds, when the

NEW YORK CITY, UNITED STATES
2 NOVEMBER 1939

Czechs are beset by enemies too numerous to count, Saint Wenceslas, Václav the Good, will summon his knights from the massive cavern beneath Mount Blaník and emerge to rescue the Czech lands and their people. "Well," I said, "you can have some relief in knowing that you needn't wait for the Knights of Blaník, because your dear brother is on his way to go oust the Nazis. I have, just this morning, requested to be sent to France to join the Czechoslovak troops there."

"Dear God, Vlada, what if you are killed? Or captured? We were told that those who join military organisations abroad are committing treason against the Protectorate. You would be executed."

I scoffed. "Oh, they shan't catch Old Vlada," I said with a smile. I was thinking of the "damned, elusive" Scarlet Pimpernel, the man whose status as a wealthy Englishman was a front for his role helping French elites escape the guillotine.

Just then, we heard a key in the door. "Now, no more talk of this," she said. Francy rose, straightened her skirt and her hair, gave me a smile, and went to meet her husband.

As I awaited his entrance, I recalled the second-to-last time I had seen Zikmund, when I had confessed to him that a date had been set for the criminal trial, and informed him of my gambling debts to Renate Hohnová. The very last time I had seen him had been on the docks at Trieste, after he had escorted me to the Shanghai-bound ship.

Zikmund entered the room and stood before me, his head tilted back. He gazed down his nose and looked me over. He was more rotund than I remembered, and had thicker glasses and less hair than I recalled.

"Well," he said, "who ever would have thought we would be reunited this way?" He had probably hoped never to see me again.

"Certainly not me," I said. "Here, I brought you this," I added, handing Zik his gift from the table—a handsome leatherbound ledger from a shop in the Cathay arcade. "For your office."

He thanked me without letting on whether he was actually pleased with the gift. "How are things in Shanghai?" he asked. "Last I knew, a fellow came to Prague to boast about your big exchange career. It's funny, people trusting you with money."

"Yes, I am trusted. All things change in time. Who could have known that my escape to Shanghai was a one-way ticket to happiness? I have been able to surround myself with some of the world's wealthiest and most influential people. I have worked my way up as a broker and joined the Exchange Broker's Association. And," I said pointedly, "at the outbreak of war, put all of it on hold to fulfil my obligation to my military, my country, and to democracy itself."

Zikmund was unmoved. Francy looked at the clock then excused herself to attend to dinner.

"Are there Nazis in Shanghai?" Zikmund asked.

"There are. The German presence is quite well-established in Shanghai, both the Nazi-Germans and the ever-increasing Jewish German refugee colonies. Aren't they everywhere?" I asked.

"I suppose so," he said. "They held a rally at Madison Square Garden earlier this year. Twenty thousand people attended. Then, a few weeks ago, they held a parade, right through downtown Manhattan, with their Nazi uniforms and flags. But I suppose I should add that, when Beneš was in the States, there was a great deal of support shown to him, and to the Czech cause," Zikmund said. "I understand that the Czecho-Slovak Pavilion at the World's Fair is only open because the Americans raised funds. When your ex-President spoke at the Pavilion's opening, he said, 'The dictatorial regime can rule the country temporarily, but it cannot kill the spirit of the people…' Five thousand people

NEW YORK CITY, UNITED STATES
2 NOVEMBER 1939

gathered to hear Beneš speak at the Fair in the Court of Peace, and countless others heard his message broadcast over the radio the following day, on three different stations."

"Good," I said.

"As visitors leave the Czecho-Slovak Pavilion, they see the phrase, 'Pravda vítězí,'" Zikmund said. The truth prevails.

"Yes, well, I must believe those words to be true."

Francy bustled back into the room, warm smells wafting in behind her from the kitchen. The arrival of my nephew changed the atmosphere from seriousness to excitement.

When I saw Jiří, I could not believe how he had grown. The boy of seven or eight I had last seen, and the awkward adolescent who appeared in occasional photographs, had become a young man of fifteen and possessed a fairly strong family resemblance. He spoke fine English as he greeted me and spoke to his mother, saying, "I hope I'm not late. I stopped at the park to play football."

"American football?" I asked. "Perhaps I should have brought you a football, instead of these," I said, reaching to retrieve his gift. I had brought him toy soldiers, like the ones he and I had played with before I left Prague. But these were modern, more detailed, and with contemporary weapons. "Remember how I used to show you formations? We had such battles. You were just a boy then."

"I hope he remains 'just a boy' and far away from battles for some time yet," Francy said. "Jiří, why don't you go and get cleaned up for dinner?"

*****

In the dining room, we found an impressive spread. It was clear that Francy had spent considerable time and expense planning and preparing for the occasion.

THE SUITCASE

"We wanted to celebrate your arrival," my sister said, "and your birthday!" She smiled.

"You remembered!" I exclaimed.

"Certainly. Have I ever forgotten a holiday, birthday, or name day? Especially a kulatiny!" Round-numbered years were celebrated in grand style.

I smiled down at the sandwiches, salads, canapes, and cakes. "This is wonderful. Thank you," I said.

"I thought you would appreciate foods that remind you of home."

"This is true, but, dear sister, you may laugh to know that I can eat 'like home' any time I like in Shanghai, especially now that there are refugee-owned restaurants. When the British came to Shanghai, they brought their pubs and clubs. The Russians brought their many courses punctuated by sips of vodka. The French established their cafés; the Americans built their hamburger and ice cream joints. The newly-arrived German and Austrian refugees have introduced their coffee house culture. And I have helped two friends establish one of the smartest restaurants in the city."

I told them how Fritz Strehlen and Hans Jabloner, big names in Austrian theatre world, turned to me for advice before opening a Viennese-style restaurant of their own. I had cautioned them against opening their business in Hongkew, where most refugee-established business were located, and where the vast majority of the recent arrivals were living. The popular Café Louis on Ward Road, with its wonderful apfelstrudel, was one example.

"But now, since the Battle of Shanghai," I said, "to sample the fare in Hongkew, one has to venture past Japanese sentries and across the Soochow Creek. I convinced Strehlen and Jabloner that the International Settlement and French Concession needed a high-end Viennese-style eatery." The men found space on the

NEW YORK CITY, UNITED STATES
2 NOVEMBER 1939

ground floor of the seven-storey Weida Hotel in Avenue Joffre, and Fiaker was born.

"I promised Strehlen and Jabloner that so long as they maintained a first-rate food and drink standard, I would bring my friends along and help make their establishment popular. Since their opening last December, they have been patronized by the highest class of clientele. They spoil their guests with Viennese and Hungarian baked goods: melange with Gugelhupf cake, striezel sweet bread, buchteln yeast buns. They advertise 'the most delicious Sachertorte outside of' Vídeň, or rather, 'Vienna,' made from a family recipe. I haven't had such sweets since Berger."

"Forget Sachertorte, Vlada," Francy said with a girlish grin. "When was the last time you had medovník? Now, I know it's not as good as Berger, but have some," she said, as she served me a slice. How could she have known that I had medovník whenever I liked in Shanghai!

"I'm sure it's even better than Berger." I grabbed my dessert fork and sank its tines into the honey cake.

And so I celebrated my fortieth birthday in my older sister's apartment in not-Forest-Hills-but-actually-Rego-Park in Queens, New York, eating cake.

I met my car beneath a streetlight and turned my thoughts to my next engagement.

*****

Helene Freeman had been right—you couldn't miss the Cotton Club. It was just one block away from the Edison, where I had stopped to rest, freshen up, and grab my signature scarlet carnation. At the club, enormous neon letters glowed red over a row of taxis idling in steam—COTTON CLUB.

THE SUITCASE

The interior was decorated to look like a Louisiana plantation. A mural on the back wall depicted a riverboat scene. Seating areas ringed the dance floor, and an elevated, columned, porch-like area overlooked the lower level. The décor was reminiscent of the soon-to-be-released film, *Gone with the Wind*. The atmosphere was compounded by the presence of mostly-Caucasian patrons, in contrast with the coloured serving staff and entertainers. The racial segregation in the States was both fascinating and appalling.

I spotted Helene at one of the best tables, on the raised "porch." On our table, amid the cocktails, were plates of finger foods.

I settled in and we started chatting. "What ever happened to David?" Helene asked, her voice raised to shout above the band.

"David?" I thought for a moment. "Oh! Innes-Ker?"

"Yes!" she said. To her beau, Edwin Jerome, she explained, "They were practically twins. Wherever you saw Vladimír, you knew David was nearby."

"I'm afraid I have been separated from my twin. The 'famous bachelor' is getting married this month. He returned to Montreal and joined the Royal Artillery." By the time I left New York City, David's sister, Jean, would be married, to Reginald Baron Black, a squadron leader in the R.A.F. Thus went my Shanghai bachelor "twin" and his sibling.

"What about that Edmund Toeg?" she asked.

"Oh, he's still around. He's been increasingly involved in amateur theatre. Just this spring he designed the dresses for *Orpheus*. He did the costumes and sets for *Dido and Aeneas*. He's quite good. He played 'The Hangman' in last year's production of *The Beggar's Opera*, directed by none other than Sylvia Chancellor. You would have laughed to see the various prostitutes and pickpockets played by the usual Who's Who—

NEW YORK CITY, UNITED STATES
2 NOVEMBER 1939

Mats Chieri played Mrs. Baggage; Lionel Sackville-West" of Jardine's — writer Vita Sackville-West's cousin — "was Ben Budge; and Hugh Barton," also of Jardine's, "was Crook-finger'd Jack."

Helene giggled, imagining high society playing such sordid characters. "I have a great admiration for stage actors," she said. "After all, when I perform on *Meet Miss Julia*, I only have to worry about being Sandra Wilson with my voice, not my entire instrument." She smiled at her beau. "Eddy is doing radio now, too."

"Yes," he said, "I do mid-day radio like Helene. I have two shows on CBS: *Aunt Jenny's Real Life Stories* at quarter 'til noon, and *When a Girl Marries* at quarter past."

"He wasn't always in radio, though," Helene said.

"I would say I'm best known for my impersonations," Edwin said. "Stalin, Franco, King Alfonso of Spain..."

"He performed so cleverly that it even fooled King Alfonso's son," Helene added.

Edwin nodded. "Before that, I was an opera star. I trained in Paris. Once, when I was singing in Spain, I lost my voice and performed for the Queen as a clown until I could move on again. I took theatrical and film roles here in the States, then quit to sell oil in Texas, then brokered land in Florida. I lost the oil in a 'duster' and the real estate to hurricanes."

Just then, the rest of our party arrived. I was amazed to see the very same beautiful young woman with the big smile whom I had encountered the previous night at the cinema.

"Oh, Captain, it's you!" Betty Wragge exclaimed.

"You two know each other?" Helene asked, eyebrows raised.

"Betty Wragge, my Holland Dutch friend."

"It's nice to see you," Betty said with a grin. Have you met Elizabeth Reller?" she asked. "She plays in *Young Doctor Malone* on NBC Blue at quarter past eleven, then at two o'clock she does *Doc*

THE SUITCASE

Barclay's Daughters on CBS." I shook the young woman's hand.

"And this is Alfred Zeisler," Helene said. "He is an actor, director, producer and writer. He recently arrived here from Vienna."

Zeisler was Jewish, with an Austrian father and a German mother. He and his wife, actress Lien Deyers, the daughter of a "mixed marriage," had left Europe together just months previously. They had settled in California but had since parted ways. Helene had likely invited Zeisler so I would have someone to talk to, unaware that I had already fallen in with the brightest young star of the bunch.

The others placed orders for roast prime beef and broiled filet mignon and breaded sword fish. Betty requested the chowder and a salad. Though I was not hungry, I couldn't resist the special: for two dollars I received half of a Southern fried chicken, served with candied yams, corn fritters, and warm biscuits with honey.

As we dined, we were treated to the dancing of Bill "Bojangles" Robinson, known for tap dancing in films. He performed his signature dance, tapping up and down a set of stairs with a smile, and keeping that smile no matter how difficult the steps became. We heard Louis Armstrong, with his gravelly voice and his trumpet. Everyone knew the song "Jeepers Creepers" from the recent film by the same name. Armstrong talked and sang until the Master of Ceremonies came on—Bobby Evans, the man responsible for dance crazes like the "boogie-woogie" and "Susie-Q peckin'."

Soprano Avis Andrews took the stage. The sleek songbird did a little comedy routine and sang "Night Fall in Louisiana" and "I'm Always in the Mood for You." She left everyone wanting more when she winked and waved and slinked offstage. The applause stirred me from a comfortable, sleepy, overfed state. It had been a long day, and I had eaten two full dinners. When the

NEW YORK CITY, UNITED STATES
2 NOVEMBER 1939

waiter appeared offering a demitasse, I assented.

The program then shifted gears. Drums started up and a lovely Cuban woman, Princess Oreila Benskina, began a rhumba, showing us her "Cuban Shake." We watched her sway and shimmy, a train of ruffles jerking and swaying from her hips down her bare legs, to the floor. Her high-heeled feet kicked out, then ground into the stage as backup dancers rhumbaed in from the wings.

My coffee soon arrived, as did the others' desserts—Jell-o, petit fours, fruit cake, rice pudding. The server whispered to Betty Wragge, who pointed at me. I was presented with a slice of ice cream-laden apple pie, with a candle sparkling on top. My tablemates smiled broadly. "Happy birthday! Make a wish!"

Make a wish? I closed my eyes against the din of the club and smiled, though my inner thoughts were grim. Would I live to see another birthday? I would soon be at war, while my American companions would still be safe in Manhattan, speaking into microphones and dining in nightclubs, unaffected by my fate.

I wish to survive this war.

I opened my eyes and blew out the candle. My companions, and a few onlookers from other tables, applauded. I smiled and raised my glass. "Na zdraví!" My companions repeated the toast and took a drink. Then a trombone wailed, a cymbal crashed, and a pair of tumblers took the stage.

I sat, slightly vacant, for the briefest moment.

Betty nudged me with her elbow; I snapped to attention at the sight of her broad smile. "Captain, your ice cream, before it melts!"

*****

Time passed quickly as I waited to hear from the Government-in-Exile via Colonel Španiel.

THE SUITCASE

On Thanksgiving, I awakened with a start to the sounds of the nearby Macy's parade: marching bands and applauding crowds. Uncle Sam, the Tin Woodman, Pinocchio, Mickey Mouse, and many more floated past New York's high-rise windows. The parade's grand finale included a Santa Claus balloon larger than a small house that drifted into and out of my view through the hotel's windows.

Not long after Thanksgiving came a big announcement. An article in *The New York Times* entitled "A New Czech Army Mobilized in France" read:

> The Czech army, as created by a Czecho-Slovak national committee after a meeting here Thursday, was mobilized officially today.
>
> All Czechs between 18 and 50 years were called to the service in mobilization orders posted throughout the world where Czech legations are still functioning.
>
> Service in the Czechoslovak army will be compulsory for all Czechoslovaks abroad... Fit recruits will be concentrated, drilled and incorporated in the United Czechoslovak Army in France...

Yet still I sat, awaiting orders in New York City.

*****

I saw Francy and Zikmund and Jiří as often as we could arrange, including a visit during Hanukkah. I brought a gift, in honour of Francy and Zikmund's upcoming anniversary on the 18 December. It would be their sixteenth anniversary. "And may we all be alive and well to celebrate your stříbrná svatba," their silver anniversary, I toasted. We also talked about those who

NEW YORK CITY, UNITED STATES
2 NOVEMBER 1939

could not be with us—our parents and siblings, and Zikmund's. I ate more than my fair share of Francy's kolaches.

Just before the Christmas holiday came word in the paper: "Every Aid Put at Disposal of National Body's War Aims." A fund had been established to help recruit Czechoslovak soldiers. It seemed I should soon receive notice from Španiel that I had been assigned to duty. And yet, no word came. Each time I inquired at Španiel's office, I was told the same—he still had yet to hear from the Government-in-Exile. Maybe the Exile government was waiting for the right opportunity to transport me to the front. Maybe they were busy organising men for my command. Whatever the case, when a decision was finally reached, I would be alerted at the earliest possible moment.

At Christmastime, the city was decorated with lights. The shop windows on Fifth Avenue glowed and glittered. Ice skaters filled Rockefeller Center. Cinemas played Reginald Owen as Dickens's Scrooge.

New Year's passed with Times Square ball-drop festivities, ritzy parties, and champagne toasts. The Chinese New Year passed—dragon. Valentine's Day passed—blizzard.

I spent innumerable evenings in the theatres, restaurants, and night clubs that surrounded me in Midtown Manhattan. I collected matchbooks everywhere I went. Just on the other side of Broadway, on the 65th floor of the RCA building in Radio City, lifts whisked me up to the Rainbow Room with its views of the city lights, and its rotating dance floor.

Within sneezing distance of Radio City, on West 51st Street, were Toots Shor's for drinking and being seen, The Golden Horn with its world-famous shish-kebab and ekmek kadayif dessert, and the Stockholm Restaurant's smorgasbord. West 52nd held the 21 Club and the Yar Russian Restaurant, popular after theatrical shows. The snobby Stork Club was on East 53rd. On East 54th was

THE SUITCASE

Elmo's, short for El Morocco.

Sometimes I went up to East 61st to visit The Colony, haunt of the very wealthy. Sometimes I went down to East 14th to visit Luchow's, a German restaurant. In November they had hosted a Venison Festival; in December, a Goose Feast; in March, a Bock Beer Festival.

It was mid-March before Španiel gave me my orders. They were not at all what I had been anticipating.

Between Hawaii And Japan
Friday, 12 April 1940

> ...*seas between us broad have roared*
> *since auld lang syne.*
> —Robert Burns

THE *PRESIDENT Coolidge* had just left Hawaii, and I was sitting in the first-class Smoking and Games Room. It was a cosy room, with West African bubinga panelling on the walls, a dark carpet, low overstuffed chairs, rare wood tables to hold cocktails, and glass-topped smoking stands. Heavily-draped windows looked out to the promenade deck.

I had my back to the baize-covered walnut gaming tables and was sipping my whiskey and staring at the antique marble fireplace and its "Magicoal" grate, glowing red even on a spring evening in the Pacific. Over the fireplace, a large steel and iron frame held a Majolica panel carving of an Elizabethan woman in a pink gown standing before a white rampant unicorn.

The Elizabethan woman had gold at the hem of her dress. The golden decoration climbed her skirts all the way to her waist. Golden fetlocks covered the unicorn's hooves. Gold graced the flower by its feet. Gold were the mane and tail. Gold, the woman's hair.

It called to mind a night at Ciro's when Viva Ovadia and Mickey Hahn had both worn gold evening gowns. It had been a Saturday night in June. We had all gone drinking and dancing. How we had laughed and carried on, as if nothing would ever change.

Since then, Ciro's had been sold to the Chinese and converted to a taxi dance hall, complete with dance hostesses and dance tickets.

Mickey Hahn, who found adventure everywhere she travelled, had left Shanghai for Hong Kong and Chungking to write a book, and had not returned. Her subject was the Soong sisters — the three most important women in China. Soong Mei-ling was the wife of Chiang Kai-shek. Soong Ai-ling was married to finance minister H. H. Kung, China's richest man. Soong Ching-ling had been married to Sun Yat-sen, the first president of the Republic of China. I wondered how the south of China was treating Mickey, or if she had already moved on.

I also had to wonder whether Viva would still be in Shanghai. I had not seen her in some time, and, with the interruption of the world's conflicts, gone were the days of our regular tennis tournament play. During the Battle of Shanghai, in the late-summer of '37, the tennis courts had been closed. We had played at the Swiss Club in the summer of '38 — but then Viva had left for London. We had played in the summer of '39, a few months before my departure from Shanghai. Would we partner again for that year's summer and fall tournaments?

As I stared at the Elizabethan woman and thought about a golden-gowned Viva Ovadia, I heard Sir Victor Sassoon's distinctive laugh erupt behind me in the Games Room. I stood and turned and spotted him just across the salon. Other passengers were gathered around him like a peacock's tail feathers. He had turned fifty-nine in December; his hair and moustache were greyer than ever. He smiled when he saw my approach.

"Taussig! I thought I saw your name on the ship's list. AWOL already, are we?"

He stood to greet me, standing cane-free and with ease. He

BETWEEN HAWAII AND JAPAN
12 APRIL 1940

had been working with a new masseuse and felt better than he had in years.

"I was told it would be impossible to deliver me safely to a command post at the front, where there are, apparently, an abundance of officers anyway. They decided to send me back to China as a representative of the Czechoslovak Army-in-Exile. It is good to see you."

"Have you met my companions?" Sir Victor asked. At that point in the voyage, I had been on the ship long enough to see my fellow first-class passengers, but I had not yet made everyone's acquaintance.

"May I introduce Mrs. Douglas Frank Bonamy and Mrs. Isaac Newton Perry?"

I bowed to kiss their hands. "Mrs. Perry, I believe I have seen your husband in the ship's stock exchange, if I am not mistaken."

"I am certain you have," she said.

"And this," Sir Victor said, "is Mrs. Myron Zobel, the young wife of 'Global Zobel.'"

"I go by 'Freckles,'" she said as she extended her hand to me. Sassoon was disappointed to find "Freckles" to be "straight-laced" and still very much in love with her husband of three years.

"And you know Mrs. Cornelius Van der Starr," Sassoon said. I was given a polite nod. Mr. Van der Starr was best known for founding the AIG insurance company, and for publishing the newspapers *Shanghai Evening Post and Mercury* and *Da Mei Wan Bao*, a vernacular version of the *Post*.

One of Van der Starr's best friends was Christopher Chancellor, the President of Reuters, and husband to Sylvia, the woman who had once brought a donkey into Sassoon's Circus Party and who would work for the Czech Institute in England during the war. Cornelius's other best friend was John Keswick of Jardine's. Cornelius Van der Starr was also, unbeknownst to me, head of the American Office of Strategic Service, or O.S.S.'s "Starr Group."

Sir Victor asked, "Where will you be staying in Shanghai, Taussig? Everything suitable has been let out with long-term leases, you know."

"If only I had a dear friend who owned hotels and apartment buildings," I said, hoping to elicit a chuckle instead of a scowl. I never let myself forget that Sir Victor hated people who were overly familiar.

Thankfully, Sir Victor laughed. "I'll help find you something. Maybe the Metropole?" The residential hotel was located at the junction of Kiangse and Foochow Roads – the "Piccadilly Circus of Shanghai." The intersection was dominated by the Metropole Hotel; its near-twin, the Hamilton House; and the fifteen-storey China Development Building, then home to the American consular offices. The American Club, the Shanghai Volunteer Corps headquarters, and the Shanghai Municipal Council's administration building were all nearby. I would be only blocks from the Bund, and just steps away from my brokerage office in Kiukiang Road.

"I should like that very much," I said. "Thank you."

I secretly hoped I could afford to live there. Surely it would be a bit pricey, even with its discounted rates for diplomats and military officers. A proper diplomat would receive a salary from his home government and would be able to afford the Metropole. But, as a representative of an exiled government that could not afford to pay either their civilian or military officials abroad, and as a businessman who had been "on leave" for many months during his visit to the States, I was unsure how I would handle the expense of keeping a Metropole address. It certainly did not help matters that I had made an extensive shopping trip on Fifth

BETWEEN HAWAII AND JAPAN
12 APRIL 1940

Avenue once I knew I was being sent back to Shanghai.

"Then it's settled. We can sort out the particulars later," Sir Victor said reassuringly.

The rest of the voyage was filled with happy activities as we steamed on towards the Far East. The Top Play Deck featured an eighteen-hole Tom Thumb golf course and courts for tennis, hardball, squash, quoits, and other sports.

The promenade deck was enclosed with plate-glass windows and wrapped around the first-class common rooms in a U-shape that terminated at the after end of the ship. The ship's aft held the Marine Tea Garden with its teak deck for dancing; the African-walnut and Sienna-marble soda fountain; and the first-class tiled swimming pool, filled daily with fresh sea water, its nearby "beach" of Monterey white sand dotted with canvas chairs and coloured umbrellas.

Sometimes I even saw Sir Victor in the ship's gym, which contained not only the expected punching bags and pommel horses, but also featured adjoining facilities for massages, electric baths, steam cabinets, and ultra-violet ray treatments. Owing to these various diversions, the voyage flew by.

In no time, we had reached Japan. On one of our final nights at sea, as we sailed between Yokohama and Kobe, we sat in the ship's Continental Lounge and watched *The Cat and the Canary*. Sir Victor grinned as the shape of Paulette Goddard's breasts, visible through the fabric of her gown, projected onto the silver screen. "Charlie's a lucky man," I whispered jokingly to Sir Victor. Goddard had been married to Chaplain since their 1936 visit to Shanghai.

In *The Cat and the Canary*, Goddard's character stood to inherit a Louisiana estate — if she could withstand a streak of madness, a prowling murderer, and the ill intentions of other potential inheritors. We watched Goddard survive a night of terror, earn her inheritance, and announce her engagement to Bob Hope's character.

Then we danced. The staff moved the Continental Lounge's satin armchairs and overstuffed davenports to access the carpet. The centre of the dark-green rug was removed, revealing the lounge's parquet dance floor. The cathedral windows leading onto the promenade were opened and the music began.

Sir Victor took snapshots that evening. One shows me in my suit, relaxed and being my usual jovial self, while, seated next to me, Sally Brewster Perry sits with arms crossed, occupying the furthest possible corner of her armchair. In an attempt to make her smile, I had told her she looked like Paulette Goddard, but she was not flattered. Sally was a Chicago-born nineteen-year-old. She, along with her parents, Mr. and Mrs. Isaac Newton Perry, were en route to visit her older sister, who resided with her husband in Manila.

After the movie and the dancing, I returned to my cabin to ensure I was ready for our arrival in Shanghai. It was already the 25th, and we were expected to arrive on the 29th. Once there, it would be time to fulfil the objectives with which I'd been tasked.

I had fairly well memorized the two letters I carried which confirmed my status—one from Španiel's office in New York, and one from the Czechoslovak consulate in Chicago:

> March 12, 1940
> To Whom It May Concern:
>
> This is to certify that Vladimir Taussig of Shanghai, China enlisted in the reconstituted CZECHOSLOVAK ARMY IN FRANCE and is authorized to register all Czechoslovak volunteers living in CHINA, who desire to fight in this army with the Allies against

BETWEEN HAWAII AND JAPAN
12 APRIL 1940

Nazi-Germany.
Chicago, Illinois, March 12th, 1940
Dr Jan Papanek
CZECHOSLOVAK CONSUL

And:

March 14, 1940
Mr. Vladimir Taussig reported on the 2nd of November at the Czechoslovak General Consulate in New York, U.S.A. and joined the Czechoslovak Army.

Since it is impossible to move from the United States to France, Mr. Taussig will return back to Shanghai.

For now, I am entrusting Mr. Taussig, with the approval of the Czechoslovak National Council-Military Administration in Paris so, that in agreement of the Trustee of the Czechoslovak National Committee Mr. Stepan in Shanghai, he would work on Czechoslovak volunteers who are reporting to the Czechoslovak Army.

At his arrival in Shanghai, Mr. Taussig will notify the Military Administration in Paris and also notify me.

Colonel O. Španiel
CZECHOSLOVAK CONSULATE-GENERAL
New York, New York

The tasks that were not put into writing included reporting on the situation in China from a military perspective, and transferring money when necessary by using my position as a broker. Of particular importance was my ability to funnel funds to the Czechoslovak Ambassador in Tokyo, Frantisek Havlíček.

THE SUITCASE

I knew that reintroducing myself to Shanghai would not be easy. Since Shanghai was completely surrounded by Japanese armies, Czechoslovakia had no extra-territorial rights, therefore she was not entitled to keep forces in Chinese treaty ports. Considering that outer Shanghai was under the rule of pro-Japanese Chinese authorities, my task would not be simple at all.

Beneš's government-in-exile, the Czechoslovak National Committee, had been recognized as a non-governmental agency by Britain and France, strengthening "the morale, strength and spirit of resistance of the Czech nation," but the Allies were "non-committal to Beneš himself," mainly because of the "murky situation" in the then-independent Slovakia.

So many of my new duties also depended on the British. My mission to recruit and train military volunteers would come to depend on the cooperation and goodwill of the British. My ability to transport those men to the front would depend on British transport ships. My directive to produce and disseminate pro-Czech, pro-Allied, anti-Axis propaganda would depend on Allied cooperation, especially that of the British. But before I obtained their cooperation, I would first need their recognition. As we sailed, I hatched a plan for my reintroduction to Shanghai society and making my diplomatic debut.

The *Coolidge* arrived at the customs jetty on the morning of Monday, 29 April, under the watchful face of Big Ching. The familiar Bund was a happy sight. I looked to the windows of the Astor House where, several years before, I had hung my Czech flag. I took in the dark-green pyramid atop Sassoon House that held Sir Victor's penthouse suite; the Palace Hotel where I might have perished in the '37 Bloody Saturday bombing; the Hongkong & Shanghai Bank building where I had worked behind rows of sandbags during the Battle of Shanghai.

When I surveyed the Bund, the only things that stole my

BETWEEN HAWAII AND JAPAN
12 APRIL 1940

smile were the red flags bearing swastikas and rising suns. The nineteen-storey Broadway Mansions, which Sir Victor had sold the previous March, proudly flew the Japanese colours. A Nazi flag flew from the top floor of the Glen Line building, the latest home of the German consulate.

But Sassoon House, the highest point on the Bund, flew a Union Jack.

Sir Victor took his own launch to his private wharf, as always, and went off to lunch with Sandy Tittman. I would see both of them that evening for dinner at Eves.

Shanghai, China
Monday, 29 April 1940

> *Arrived S'hai.*
> *Sandy Tittman to lunch.*
> *To dine: Viva... Sand, George Taussig.*
> *Lucien, Chuck & Lorraine Culbertson joined after.*
> —Sir Victor Sassoon's Diary

My arrival at Eves was met with hugs and handshakes and wagging tails. Lucien and Viva had been staying at Eves since Sir Victor's January departure. They had been playing golf and letting their dogs roam the grounds. Viva was present, but not Lucien.

"I was not expecting to see you back in Shanghai," Viva said.

"Nor was I," I laughed.

"And fresh from the ship, too. You must be tired."

"Oh, I wouldn't miss this little gathering for the world," I said, grinning at her.

"Where is Lucien?" Sir Victor asked.

"Out with the Culbertsons," Viva said. "They'll join us later. How was the trip? How was New York?" she asked.

"Terrific," I said. "Do you remember Helene Freeman? I fell in with her and some of her radio friends." Viva brightened. "I stayed in the theatre district. It was great fun."

Sandy Tittman said, "I love New York. I was just there last year, modelling for the John Powers Agency and haunting the Rainbow Room."

SHANGHAI, CHINA
29 APRIL 1940

"There are worse places to spend eternity," I said. Sandy chuckled politely. "How have things been in Shanghai?" I asked, looking back and forth between the two women to invite an answer from either or both.

"Oh, the usual," Viva said. "In one sense, you have missed everything. In another sense, you haven't missed a thing at all."

"Isn't that always the way," Sir Victor said.

I used my hand to stifle a yawn.

"See, you are tired," Viva said.

Until seeing Viva, I had been quite tired. After disembarking from the ship, I had retrieved my car from storage, noting that the date on the car's bill of sale, 15 March 1939, was the day Czechoslovakia had been occupied by the Nazis. I called on my business partners. I called on my Boy, Cheng, to inquire whether he was available for reemployment. I sent word to the Government in Exile in Paris and to Španiel in New York that I had arrived back in Shanghai, and I contacted Stepan, as directed. I had then driven "home" to the Metropole, where the trunk I had filled on Fifth Avenue had already been unpacked by hotel staff. On instruction, the staff had not touched my suitcase. I removed my scrapbook, much-expanded with photos of my family, headshots of New York City starlets, matchbooks, ticket stubs, and the like. I had poured a drink, dressed for dinner, then gone to Eves to enjoy the company of friends, good food, soft music, and plenty to drink. No war, distant or close by, could encroach on that happy, golden bubble.

After dinner, we were joined by Lucien and the Culbertsons. It was late before I left Eves and went out to Farren's, where I met a woman worthy of my attentions.

The wee hours found me on my new roof terrace at the Metropole. From the rooftop terrace, I could see all the way to the Whangpoo, dotted with boats from the smallest sampans to

THE SUITCASE

the largest warships, and beyond, into Pudong, which the rising sun was just beginning to touch.

When I woke, Cheng was standing over the bed and grinning down at me. He held a glass of water in one hand, and a bottle of Alka-Seltzer tablets in the other.

"Welcome back, Boss," he said with a laugh.

*****

About a week later, on 5 May, I was back at Eves. Late-afternoon sun rolled across the golf course and streamed into the windows. The guests who gathered to play bridge and share supper that day included Godfrey Phillips, secretary and commissioner general of the Shanghai Municipal Council, and his wife; and Tony Keswick, chairman of the Municipal Council, and his wife. Lou and Hope Andrews sat at Sir Victor's bridge table. The Ovadias, Edward Smith-Wright, and I occupied another table. The serving staff skirted the room. Little dogs lay beneath the card tables, occupying laps and hovering near feet.

Godfrey Phillips said, "I quite liked your gathering at Fiaker on Thursday, Taussig."

"Thank you." I said with pride.

Keswick agreed. "Quite right. I enjoyed myself."

I was relieved that my diplomatic debut had been deemed a success. I had decided to make my arrival as official as possible, so as to present my new status as a *fait accompli* — as opposed to proceeding with an official request for recognition. There was no doubt in my mind that such a request would get me nowhere. Instead, the way I presented myself to the British and other Allied civilian and military authorities would decide everything. Therefore, I had called on all Allied diplomats, most of whom I knew socially anyhow, and presented myself as a representative

SHANGHAI, CHINA
29 APRIL 1940

of the Czech government. I distributed invitations that read:

> A Cocktail Party will be held at Fiaker on Thursday, 2 May 1940, from 6 to 7 p.m.
>
> Will all Allied and friendly-neutral ambassadors and staffs, consuls and commanding officers, and aides of the Allied armed forces who wish to attend, be good enough to communicate with the undersigned as soon as possible:
> Captain V. G. Taussig,
> Honorary Military Delegate of the Czechoslovak Provisional Government

To my mind, by appearing at my party, the attendees had given recognition of my status, which depended less on the letters in my pocket from distant representatives of an occupied nation, and more on whether the men I had invited would, on that day and in the future, agree to confer that status upon me and cooperate with my aims. My invites went out to, among others:

- Sir "Archie" Clark Kerr, the British Ambassador, and a friend of Sassoon's
- Tony George, Commercial Counsellor since 1938; British Consul since January
- John Alexander, the British Press Attaché
- Colonel Burkhardt, the new British Military Attaché
- Richard Butrick, the American Consul-General
- Monroe "Rhody" Hall, a senior American vice-consul
- Emil Fontanel, Swiss Consul-General
- Poul Scheel, Danish Consul-General
- Gideon Boissevain, Dutch Consul-General
- Gother Herbert Mann, Brigade Major of the S.V.C., and
- Colonel Hornby, Commandant of the S.V.C.

THE SUITCASE

At Fiaker, I had prepared cocktails for the event, à la Sir Victor. They were something like a Diplomat or a Manhattan, featuring whiskey with vermouth and bitters. I called it "The Delegate."

During cocktails, Tony George had made one of his famous speeches, then I had given a little speech of my own. The gathering had been over in no time. I considered it a success.

At Eves, after Godfrey Phillips and Tony Keswick bestowed their brief accolades, Viva said, "I wish you had invited me."

"Yes," said Lucien, "I love the menu at Fiaker."

"Oh, we didn't have a whole meal, just cocktails," I said. "Besides, I only invited representatives who are unaware of my new role and you, my friends, already know about my new official capacity."

"I understand," said Viva. "I still wish you had invited me. I suppose I could have attended as a representative of the British Women's Association. Who do you think the diplomats and support staffs are married to?" she asked rhetorically, speaking into her playing cards, then raising an eyebrow and catching my eye.

I smiled. I shifted the conversation back to Phillips and Keswick: "I must ask, why such security precautions? It seemed everyone had bodyguards and protective vests. What have I missed?"

"Well, even during the battle, it was made clear that Westerners who strayed from the Settlement's boundaries were not safe," Phillips said. Japanese planes had "accidentally" shot at two separate groups of pony-riding Westerners out near Columbia Country Club on Great Western Road. Lieutenant Commander Burnett of the H.M.S. *Cumberland* had his pony killed beneath him; two other ponies had been killed that same day in similar incidents.

SHANGHAI, CHINA
29 APRIL 1940

Keswick said, "The area has only gotten more dangerous. They call the Western Roads area 'The Badlands' now. It's become a hotbed of nightclubs, cabarets, gambling houses, opium dens. Gangsters and terrorists run rampant while Chinese puppet police stand passively by. Japanese Gendarmes demand that the Chinese and Japanese business owners pay 'squeeze' in order to be allowed to operate businesses."

Sassoon nodded, "I intend to sell Eves. Other estate holders nearby hope to do the same."

Phillips cleared his throat. "In January, I was in my car in Avenue Haig when I was approached by gunmen. They emptied their chambers into the car at point-blank range."

"Thank goodness you weren't killed." I said.

"The Municipal Police said I was targeted because of my involvement with the Municipal Council. At that time, the Japanese Military Police and the Chinese puppet government were attempting to undermine an arrangement for the Western Roads to be policed by the municipality. Thankfully, the assassination attempt failed."

"I should say," I said.

"Since then, the general chaos, accompanied by anti-British sentiment, have led many of the councilmen and other officials to take certain precautions."

Mrs. Phillips chimed in, saying, "Come, let's not talk of such things."

It seemed polite society did not care to dwell on the prevalence of anti-British sentiment in the Settlement. The Japanese were pressing the ideals of "Asia for the Asiatics" and were tapping into the anti-British talking points that the puppet Chinese president, Wang Ching-wei, had long espoused.

Determined to change the subject, Mrs. Phillips addressed Smith-Wright: "Edward, I see you and the Amateur Dramatic

THE SUITCASE

Company have a new play premiering soon?"

He shifted in his seat. "We do, yes. *Youth at the Helm*. Tickets at Moutrie's, as usual," he grinned. "Taussig, you and Sir Victor missed our most recent production. We did *Night Must Fall*, about a fortnight ago," he said.

I had seen the film, a 1937 MGM production starring Rosalind Russell and Robert Montgomery. "I'm sure you did a stellar job," I told Smith-Wright.

"They certainly did," Mrs. Phillips nodded. "The Amateur Dramatic Company should be called the *Expert* Dramatic Company." This was met with polite laughter.

We would indeed attend *Youth at the Helm*. The play's lead role was played by Jimmy Barton, a member of the British Embassy offices, and the eldest son of the man who had been Shanghai's British Consul-General in the 1920s. I enjoyed his portrayal of a "charming, cheeky young man who cons his way through the ranks at a bank... form[ing] a bogus company [and] fooling all of the directors" and "bluff[ing] his way through" the jobs.

"Speaking of actors and performances," Viva said, "Victor, I saw you in the papers with some film stars. What was that like?"

"I did spend some time at Metro-Goldwyn-Mayer studios," Sir Victor began. "I used my new film camera on Bette Davis. She's on loan from Warner Brothers and is filming something called *The Little Foxes*. I visited the sets of *Waterloo Bridge* and *Pride and Prejudice* with Chester and Bernardine Fritz and with Sir Herbert and Mrs. Phillips." Sir Herbert had been the British Consul-General from 1937 until January 1940, when Tony George had taken charge. "We saw Robert Taylor, Maureen O'Sullivan, Virginia Field, Vivien Leigh."

The bridge games were ending. There was a shift in the room and the dogs' ears stood at attention as the servants invited us in to supper. The dogs followed us as we migrated into the other

SHANGHAI, CHINA
29 APRIL 1940

room.

At dinner there was a discussion of that day's race meet. Highlights were recounted for those of us who hadn't been in attendance. Chatter swirled up around me, amid the polite clinking of dining utensils. I listened disinterestedly to the gossip.

"'Bober' fell," someone said. "The rider was thrown and kicked in the face."

"The bleeding was frightful."

"Then, during the Commonwealth Handicap, 'Star Turn' ran into the rails and took a tumble. The jockey went down with him.'"

"Those were the most shocking incidents anyway. The finishes of some of the races were not very exciting. Plenty of daylight between the ponies."

"They are still racing now, in the dusk."

I was quiet, contemplative. I recalled my first days in Shanghai, when I had exercised racing ponies at the old Race Club, before I had graduated to watching ponies run from private tiffin boxes at the new club. Sir Victor made a comment that stirred me from my reverie.

"You must all come to my box for tiffin on Champion's Day," he said.

We did attend that Wednesday, 8 May – the Ovadias; Sandy Tittman; Anne Arkwright, the wife of Sir Victor's personal representative in Shanghai; Michel Speelman, the banker and Jewish relief committee chairman; and others.

On the tenth of May, the Battle of the Netherlands began; France also became embattled. The Phoney War had ended, and I was not in France to fight alongside the Czechoslovak troops there.

I was to see Sir Victor again on the evening of 12 May, a Sunday.

Cheng had left the perfect dinner jacket ready for dinner and a night out. After dressing, I descended from my thirteenth-floor room to the Metropole's bustling lobby. I found Sir Victor in the American Bar. We went into the restaurant to dine.

Sassoon inquired after my Kiukiang Road brokerage business.

"Things are a bit different than I remember," I confessed. "More... lawless. I was checking the phone messages at the office on Friday evening when I witnessed the tail-end of an armed robbery. Five men attempted to rob a Yokohama Specie bank lorry; one of the robbers ran down Kiukiang Road, firing shots at those in pursuit."

I had already been a bit on edge when the incident took place. I had gone there after-hours not to check phone messages, as I told Sassoon, but instead to wire money to František Havlíček, the Czech ambassador in Japan.

Sir Victor nodded. "I heard about the robbery. I suppose things will only get more and more hectic here," he said. "How are things going with the Czechs?"

"They held a tea dance this afternoon. A damned long one, too — from four-thirty to eight o'clock. The American Women's Club hosted." I'd visited their Bubbling Well Road club to see Stepan. "I intend to form a committee," I said. "I want to establish a group of men to assist refugees who are having an unsatisfactorily slow time dealing with the officials, who are overwhelmingly German and Austrian."

I wanted our new committee to assist the refugees with their paperwork and provide them with official addresses if needed. If their passports had been confiscated by the Gestapo, we would provide them with new papers. We would help the municipal police evaluate Czech applicants to the International Settlement, verify their information, and guarantee they would not become a burden on Shanghai.

Once created, the Czechoslovak National Committee,

SHANGHAI, CHINA
29 APRIL 1940

consisting of myself, Jaroslav Stepan, Emil Jan Štembera, Leo Lilling, and Frantisek Urbanek, had dealings with the Czechoslovak Ministry of Foreign Affairs in Exile.

"And it was nice to rub elbows with my countrymen." I encountered many recently-arrived families, like the Votickys. After travelling for many weeks, they had only just arrived at midnight on the tenth. They sailed from Trietse in the *Conte Rosso*. Because they came from Nazi-occupied Czechoslovakia, they were considered stateless and were unable to disembark when the ship stopped at port in Venice, the Suez Canal, Aden, and Singapore. It was not until they reached Manila, Hong Kong, and Shanghai that they were allowed off the ship.

"So, who is she?" Sir Victor asked.

"What's that?" I asked.

"Why else would you display this newfound desire to assist refugees, if not for some woman?" he laughed.

"No, there's no woman. I am taking a page from your book and helping my co-religionists. Speaking with my sister in New York impressed upon me how important it is to help any who seek refuge, especially the Jewish Czechs who have so few friends in the world."

"Perhaps you could provide them with a destination beyond Shanghai. You could make arrangements in the same manner the Frieder brothers did in the Philippines. Two of the five brothers, Alex and Philip, manufacture cigars there. They have collaborated with both President Quezon and the American diplomats to arrange for visas for refugees to enter islands as skilled labourers." Quezon had donated an estate, Marikina Hall, and several acres, for that use. It had just been dedicated on 23 April. By 1941 it would house thirteen hundred workers. "The Frieders' model may work elsewhere," Sir Victor suggested.

I did end up visiting the Philippines that month, May 1940. I brought my new girlfriend, Raya, along for the trip. We stayed at the Manila Hotel, that enormous mission-style affair sprawling alongside Manila Bay. We lounged under palm trees beside the tiled pool and visited the poolside champagne room. After we watched sunsets on the bay, we danced in the open-air Fiesta Pavilion where the orchestra played until two.

My actual business there, meeting the Frieder brothers and touring Marikina Hall, took only one morning. The rest of the time, we enjoyed ourselves. In the ensuing months, I would enter into negotiations with British Commercial Attaché for the mass placing of Czechs as technicians, foremen, and labourers in munitions factories in India and Malay States, where factories existed without sufficient workforce. But, in the end, we were not granted the required working permits.

"So, what's in the cards for this evening?" I asked Sassoon.

"Farren's," he said. "The Hartnells are performing."

"Ah, yes. 'The King and Queen of Swing.' I never know if you are simply appreciating the acts we see, or if you are scheming to poach them for your own nightclubs."

He laughed but made no reply.

I said, "I shall bring my car then. I imagine you'll be going on to Eves after Farren's."

"And I assume you'll be staying until sunrise," he laughed.

I stood and buttoned my jacket.

"I enjoy Farren's well enough, but I do miss the Tower," I said.

"It will reopen soon. Hopefully by July," Sir Victor said. "I'm having the air conditioning repaired." Sassoon stood with relative ease.

"Those massages were good to you," I said.

"Best I have felt in years," he said.

"Off to the Badlands, then." I said. "Shall I bring my bulletproof vest?" I joked. I did not own one, but I did carry a set

SHANGHAI, CHINA
29 APRIL 1940

of brass knuckles in my jacket pocket in those days.

He laughed. "I'm sure that won't be necessary." I wondered that he did not concern himself with kidnappers seeking hefty ransoms, or other violence.

"I don't know how you feel safe," I said.

"So long as His Majesty's troops are in Shanghai, I feel certain that I shall be safe," Sassoon said.

*****

His Majesty's troops withdrew from Shanghai in mid-August.

I sat in the Race Club's stands with the Ovadias and several thousand other onlookers, watching the soldiers marching as they prepared to depart.

I shifted uncomfortably in my seat. "I wish we were in Sir Victor's box," I said. Sir Victor had left Shanghai in early July, shortly after the Tower nightclub reopened.

"I don't mind it so much," said Lucien. "At least for this occasion. It's nice to be down here, everybody all together."

"It's nice to see you away from your office," I said.

"Yes," said Lucien. "I have taken the day."

"How was your tennis match?" Viva asked. I had just played men's singles at the French Club.

"Lost to Indrickson," I said.

"I hear his game has improved a great deal," Viva said. "You know, it's a shame you and I didn't partner for mixed doubles." She had played singles and women's doubles that year, but we had not managed to coordinate any mixed doubles matches or tournaments.

"Viva and I have been playing golf so often anyway," Lucien said.

"I wonder what next tennis season will be like," Viva said

distantly as she watched the troops marching and counter-marching. "Everything might be different by next summer." I understood her meaning — we might have missed our last chance to play together.

"I can tell you what it will be like," Lucien said. I smiled. He was like the fortune tellers, in his own way. "If I had to wager a guess, there won't be a 'next tennis season.' This is the beginning of the end," Lucien continued. He gestured to the soldiers. "When they leave, who will we have for protection? The United States Marines and the Shanghai Volunteers. That won't do us much good when the Japanese finally decide to claim the remainder of Shanghai."

"It's just the International Settlement left," Viva said.

"Yes, now that France has fallen," I said. After several weeks of fighting, France fell to the Nazis in June. The French Concession came under Vichy collaborationist control.

"I heard the Czech troops in France fought well," I said. After the fighting, they were evacuated to England, to be housed and trained on the grounds of Cholmondeley Castle, which belonged to Sir Victor's cousin Sybil, The Most Honourable The Marchioness of Cholmondeley. "You know," I said furtively, "Even though my countrymen are there to stand and fight alongside the British, Beneš still has not been recognized. But when France fell, de Gaulle was recognized within a week as the 'leader of all Free Frenchmen, wherever they may be.' Isn't Beneš the leader of all free Czechs?"

"Well," Lucien said, "Maybe now that Churchill has replaced Chamberlain, he will support the Czechs."

"He's been Prime Minister since May!" I said. Viva shushed me a little, but I was confident that the general din of the crowd would cover any comments I made. "How long will it take for Beneš to receive official recognition?"

SHANGHAI, CHINA
29 APRIL 1940

"I understand your frustrations," Lucien said.

"All I hear," I said, "is how the British are fighting 'alone.' It simply isn't true. The Czechs have always been there to support them. There are forty-four hundred Czech troops in Great Britain now. I just read an article about how valuable the Czechs have been as allies since their escape from France. And yet..."

I trailed off and stared at the troops. Despite my irritation, I did understand. We were a small country, occupied by the Germans, and, since the seizure of the Sudetenland, virtually weapon-less. We needed aid in order to even fight.

"Well," Viva said, "the French are collaborating with the Nazis. The British are leaving. I suppose that when the Japanese do decide to come knocking, Shanghai may be in a bit of trouble."

"A bit of trouble," Lucien repeated with a scoff. "You're grossly understating the situation, darling." He watched the troops march for a moment before adding, "Mark my words, change is going to come."

"It has already changed a great deal," I said. "The Japanese surrounding the city. The crime. The dreadful flooding. Have I told you? My family sent a shipment of household goods last summer when they thought they were coming to Shanghai—before the war in Europe, and before I left for the States. I put their things with my own, in that Kiaochow Road godown, not far from Soochow Creek."

Viva gasped. "You didn't."

"I did." I nodded. "And now it's all been ruined. I was recently provided with an amended inventory so I could gauge the extent of the damage." Upholstered furniture had been ruined. Tables were legless. Wood had become warped with water damage. Bare metal frames were left where chandeliers had been. Cake stands and tea sets were broken. Clothing, linens, books, and carpets had been destroyed. Only mundane items remained

THE SUITCASE

undamaged — the ironing board, the three pairs of skis, and some entirely replaceable kitchen utensils.

Lucien said, "Well, if the Japanese were dredging the silt from the riverbeds, like the Whangpoo Conservancy Board has always done, this could all be avoided." But the Japanese had seized the dredges and decommissioned them. Shanghai's drainage system has become completely clogged with silt. For a time, areas of the city only flooded during typhoon season. Then floods began occurring during high tides too. In some areas, standing water caused epidemic illnesses — like in refugee camps, where hundreds died. Some refugees decided to return home rather than suffer the conditions in Shanghai.

"I'm sorry about your family's effects," Viva said.

"Thank you. I am too. Just one more straw that is beginning to weigh on this camel's back." I stared out at the race course for a moment, then added: "Here's another thing — the way we can't show popular or patriotic films, but the Nazis can."

Lucien laughed. "Well you certainly know why."

"Yes, the Municipal Council's film censorship department doesn't want to incite any disturbances or interfere with business," I said.

"Yes," said Lucien. "Remember back in '37 when the Italians rioted after seeing *Abyssinia* at the Isis in Hongkew?"

I laughed. "It's a documentary. It's not as if there was any exaggeration. Anyway, the British and American films are being censored to death in the Settlement, while over in Hongkew, pro-Nazi films are being screened, for free, with grand introductions by the Japanese Naval Landing Party's marching band. It's ridiculous. And thousands turn out to see the films."

Viva said quietly, "Well, you do have your Allied film-viewing club..."

"Yes, but it's not enough. Everyone should be able to see

SHANGHAI, CHINA
29 APRIL 1940

newsreels, especially the ones concerning the development of the war in Europe. People should know."

"Speaking of which," Lucien said, "will I see you tonight, Taussig?"

"At The Nine-Fifteen Club? I wouldn't miss it," I said. It was a good thing I attended, as there was a newsreel showing the Czech Legion landing in Britain, along with segments on the British fleet in action, a barrage balloon squadron erecting a curtain, and Churchill inspecting troops.

The Nine-Fifteen Club had originated when the British Press Attaché, John Alexander, and his cinema department volunteer, Richard Hubert, showed films privately, in the Cathay, to the founding members like myself, Sassoon and Ovadia, Ellis Hayim, David Toeg, Cecil and Denzil Ezra, Charles Arkwright, former Sassoon employee E.H. Adams, H.E. Morris of the *North-China Daily News*, and British Military Attaché Colonel Valentine Burkhardt. Many of them were spies, as it turned out.

These gatherings to watch newsreels in privacy with like-minded friends had since morphed into a way to raise funds, spread awareness, and subvert Axis efforts. The club had gone semi-public that summer, inviting hopefuls to apply for membership to watch films under the protection of the club.

Our membership cards were encased in black leather-bound tri-fold affairs. In one plastic-sleeved pocket was my membership card. To the other plastic-covered pocket I would soon add a lucky four-leaf clover and a copy of the Shema Yisrael, a prayer often said by Jews in desperation. My feelings regarding organised religion had not changed, but my sense of hopelessness soon would.

Viva shifted in her seat. "Seems they are winding down," she said. "I can't believe they really are leaving the Settlement. Goodbye British military in Shanghai," she said with a sigh.

THE SUITCASE

"Goodbye, Shanghai," Lucien added.

I looked at my friends, then at the soldiers, in silence.

Music began. The Seaforth Highlanders' pipes and drums joined the East Surrey Regiment's horns and drums. The familiar tune rolled across the Race Club's grounds and echoed through the city's streets. The audience joined in, singing:

> ...*We two have paddled in the stream,*
> *from morning sun till dine;*
> *But seas between us broad have roared*
> *since auld lang syne...*

SHANGHAI, CHINA
Saturday, 21 December 1940

...do not let perish us nor our descendants.
— Inscription on the Statue of Saint Wenceslas
in Prague's Wenceslas Square

MY SQUAD of thirty-three Czech volunteers stood at attention in British uniforms in the Shanghai Volunteer Corps drill hall on Foochow Road. The Czech squad was a part of the S.V.C.'s Headquarters Company's "A" Battalion, headed by a British instructor named Whitaker. It was significant that the Czechs were included among the ranks of the British volunteers. German refugees tended to join the Jewish Company of the S.V.C., formed by Russians in the early 1930s.

By arrangement with the British authorities, I had joined the S.V.C. the previous month and had been immediately promoted. Since that time, I had been using the Volunteer Corps as a façade — what appeared to be S.V.C. training was in fact actual military training, and preparation for my men to be sent to the front. The most common route to Europe, via the Mediterranean, had been blocked by Italy's early-June entry into the war, but there were other fronts on which the men might fight, and other routes which they might take.

In a Scarlet Pimpernel-esque victory, the British Military Attaché, Colonel Burkhardt, in conjunction with The Nine-Fifteen Club's financial support, had recently successfully moved French troops, right under the noses of the Japanese. In

THE SUITCASE

late-September, the soldiers had been evacuated to China after fighting in French Indochina. They had since left to join the Free French forces. I was certain that, once my men were up to snuff, the British would also aid them with travel to the front.

As my troops were inspected, the photographer I had hired snapped photos. I probably would have hired him anyway, but I had been especially compelled to use his services after sending a November telegram to the Government-in-Exile via Colonel Burkhardt, and receiving no reply. I had told President Beneš and General Ingr that I recruited thirty volunteers, "consisting of eight officers (including two physicians), twelve reservists, one degreed female nurse, nine recruits (including one physician)," who were all ready for transport. "Instruct by wire if volunteers could be transported at government expense or at a greatly reduced rate to an Allied training centre. Of the above, four men require that their wives be permitted to leave Shanghai for British territory and be taken care of according with the Army Regulations."

Since there had been no reply to my November telegram, I decided to make a special display of our scheduled December S.V.C. training. I intended to show the Czech Government-in-Exile how serious and how ready we were, and also that we had been working in unison with the British. We stood ready to fight alongside the British Empire. Photographs would be more impactful than a few lines in a telegram could ever be.

After the men passed inspection at the Drill Hall, we marched into the late-December chill to the rifle range in Hongkew, where we would spend the next two days at camp. Visiting the Hongkew Rifle Range was the capstone on what had been, for some, three months of training. The men had undergone physical exercises focusing on basic fitness and running, as well as weapons drills with rifles and bayonets, small arms, Lewis guns,

SHANGHAI, CHINA
21 DECEMBER 1940

and Browning guns. In Hongkew we would be able to put our weapons knowledge to use and would qualify in marksmanship at various distances.

We marched through the cold towards the Metropole. As we passed the hotel, I said a silent farewell to my comfortable rooms, and a good riddance to the lectures on "yoga," which Bernardine Fritz and Indra Devi and those types had instituted, and to the raucous Rotary Club meetings that also took place in the hotel — like their recent two-hundred-guest Christmas meeting, which had made it impossible to get to my rooms without seeing dozens of familiar faces and having as many conversations along the way. We turned at the Metropole and began marching towards Soochow Creek.

The only difficulty came when we passed the sentries on the bridge. The Japanese Gendarmes were supposed to have been expecting us, yet they made us stand in the cold while they chatted among themselves. Becoming irritated with the situation would do nothing but cause the sentries to delay us even longer, and so I masked my frustration behind a fairly jovial front, and, eventually, we were through.

The Japanese had officially joined the Axis in September when the Tripartite Pact was signed. I was now training Allied troops in plain view of the enemy. To think what might have happened had the Japanese realised I was actually enlisting men for Allied war work and not just training them for duties within the Settlement! And Francy's warning about being executed by the Nazis for joining the armed forces abroad was rarely far from my mind. I could only imagine my fate if I was found to be leading, recruiting, and training men.

Once we had made it over the bridge and into Hongkew, we continued our march straight down the road. We entered the camp and the formalities began. The photographer snapped away as my old Czechoslovak flag was ceremonially hoisted over the camp. Instructor Whitaker and Commander Barraclough saluted. There, in Shanghai, our colours flew, and the British acknowledged them!

With our red, white, and blue flag overhead, we divided the men into groups and began the main work of our visit. One group qualified in marksmanship at thirty, one hundred, two hundred, and three hundred yards' range. From a cement-lined trench they fired on a set of mechanical targets that moved on a hill at the range's far end.

Meanwhile, another group was drilling with the British instructors, learning new marching formations and methods of assembly according to the latest British military rules. The third group of men practised constructing trenches and erecting wire and wooden fencing, skills necessary for battle. At certain intervals, the groups would rotate duties.

A semi-official awards dinner was held the following afternoon. The photographer returned to capture the dinner and its special guests. Invitees included Lieutenant Colonel Gother Herbert Mann, Brigade Major of the S.V.C.; Jaroslav Stepan, as a temporary delegate of the Czechoslovak Provisional Government; and Stanislaw B.M. de Rosset, the Polish charge d' affaires.

Three long tables were arranged in a horseshoe shape, draped with linens, decorated with flowers, and topped with trophies I'd had specially made. The officers and notable guests sat at the front of the room in their dress uniforms or formal wear.

I stood and addressed my men and our guests. "Thank you all for being here this evening," I began. "We are especially honoured by the presence of our diplomatic and military officials. Now, for our generous instructors..." I said, taking two of the awards in hand, "Instructor Whitaker and Commander Barraclough,

SHANGHAI, CHINA
21 DECEMBER 1940

thank you for allowing us into the 'A' Battalion, for opening your facilities to us, allowing use of your equipment, and imparting your knowledge. Your goodwill is heartily appreciated."

"Hear, hear," the group murmured.

"Commander Barraclough, we are especially grateful to you, as we understand you are missing rehearsals for *The Dover Road* in order to be with us. I shall send my special thanks and apologies to Smith-Wright and the Little Theatre Company, and to the production's patron, Consul Tony George."

This was met with polite laughter. Barraclough was also part of the Cathay Land Company with Ovadia and others, so I felt comfortable addressing him in this way. I handed both Whitaker and Barraclough a silver paper weight in the form of a Czech lion, with a gilt Slovak coat-of-arms and the Czech national flag on the base.

"And now, for marksmanship awards," I said, taking a trophy in hand. "The first prize," I said, "to Second Lieutenant Steirer." He rose to receive the award. "Ninety-five percent accuracy," I said. "Well done."

After a few more awards were presented, our British instructors led the group in a toast. "To the health of Czechoslovakia!" Our men cheered and drank. "To the health of President Beneš!" Another cheer, another hearty swig. "To the health of the Czech Army!" Roaring cheers. "And to the Czechoslovak Squad, one of the sharpest units in the whole Corps, if not the sharpest of all."

After the toasting, my men sang staropražské písničky — "Old Prague Songs" — with great enthusiasm. The songs had always been a source of strength for the Czechs in the face of oppression. When it came time for our festivities to end, I launched into a song I had prepared as a surprise. Our men sang a Czech rendition of "There'll Always Be an England." Our instructors and guests joined us, emphasizing the chorus in English: "There'll always be an England, and England shall be free, if England means as much to you as England means to me." It was the perfect show of our mutual cooperation and respect.

When the photographs were processed, and when my reports on our visit to Hongkew had been prepared, I sent it all to the Government-in-Exile, along with a special Christmas card I had commissioned. The card depicted troops marching together beneath side-by-side Czech and British flags. Inside, the card read: "A free Czechoslovakia in a Free Europe." I also added the information that, a week hence, another thirty-five recruits would be joining the S.V.C., increasing our Czech squad to a half-company of nearly seventy men.

I posted one copy to our government in London and another to Španiel at the consulate in New York City. Španiel would use my reports in a book about the Czechoslovak armed forces abroad. He clearly shared my feeling that my efforts were worthwhile. The Exile Government in London, on the other hand, was apparently not impressed.

At least the British in Shanghai were appreciative of our efforts. In January, our Czechoslovak National Committee had been recognized by the Municipal Council. Beginning 1 February 1941, the committee became the sole authority which granted or refused requests for admission of Czechoslovak citizens to Shanghai. Thus, the immigration of those who could not make the deposit of $400 American, as required by Shanghai Municipal authorities, was eventually possible.

And Stepan, Štembera, and Urbanek, heads of the Czech Circle, had recently been honoured at the weekly R.A.F. tiffin, held in The Dome at the Hongkong & Shanghai Bank.

After the S.V.C. awards dinner, I spoke to Stepan: "I have been meaning to tell you how much I enjoyed your National Day speech." I had been one of hundreds who gathered at the Czech

SHANGHAI, CHINA
21 DECEMBER 1940

Circle on Rue Bourgeat in late-October to celebrate the day and hear Stepan speak.

Stepan said dismissively, "I was only parroting what Foreign Minister Masaryk has said." The National Day speech had recalled our two decades of Czech democracy. Jan Masaryk, and Stepan, had said: "[I]f a nation stands firm in good times—and those twenty years really were good times—it will stand firm in bad times; such is our history." They had said, "We are always at our best when in adversity," and that, "The final victory will be a victory of those ideals which inspired our beloved nation for a thousand years and fortified it through good and evil." After the speech, Stepan had led the audience in a heartfelt singing of "Kde domov můj."

"I especially enjoyed when you called to mind the statue of Saint Wenceslas," I said.

"It is an especially poignant message, in these times." The base of the statue reads: "Svatý Václave, vévodo české země, kníže náš, nedej zahynouti nám ni budoucím," or, "Saint Wenceslas, duke of the Czech land, prince of ours, do not let perish us nor our descendants." Precious words from our Czech Hymn.

"I was glad to see such a large turnout," I told Stepan. "Those people chose to celebrate National Day with us at the real Czech Circle, instead of gathering with Seba." Traitorous Seba had held a National Day gathering of his own at his "Czech Circle" on Avenue du Roi Albert, with a flag-raising and ceremony.

"I am sure you have not failed to notice that the press continues to refer to him as 'Minister Seba,'" Stepan said.

"I have attempted to correct them," I replied.

"And Seba has continued to deliberately sow confusion." The real Czech Circle—the one Stepan and I were part of—had previously been known as the Czechoslovak Association of China. Seba had created an organisation called The Association

THE SUITCASE

of Czechoslovak Residents in China and had announced in the papers that the Association had "resumed" their activities.

I had blitzed the newspapers with the truth: Seba was in no way connected to our organisation and never had been. The original Association had been founded in 1933 and dissolved in 1936, and Seba had only presented his credentials as Minister in October '37, after the group's dissolution. Seba was "not the Czechoslovak Minister to China and [was] not a member of any Czechoslovak organisation in China which may be considered as such."

Seba did eventually change the name of his "Association" to "The Czechoslovak Club." But, infuriatingly, newspapers would continue to refer to him as "Minister" for the duration.

Not-Minister Seba and his phoney organisation had planned a concert to benefit St. Tichon's, which, ever since the orphanage's founding in 1935, had been a popular thing for society types and charitable organisations to do. Carnivals, cabarets, concerts, tea dances, costume balls, bridge parties — Shanghailanders engaged in all sorts of activities in order to raise funds for "Saint T's." Seba tapped into this and used a well-timed concert to detract from his scandalous behaviour. When all was said and done, the event only raised $420. But it showed that he still had many members of the community fooled.

In less than a fortnight, Jan Seba would display his true character to all of Shanghai. At the French Club's New Year's Eve ball, Seba assaulted a man named Pisarevsky, manager of Shanghai's Škoda office. After Pisarevsky was down, Mrs. Seba and Jan Seba Junior gave him some kicks, and thus became involved in the eventual court case. Shameful idiocy. Aside from this incident, we had managed to keep Czech problems out of the papers by handling our issues amongst ourselves in a separate court.

SHANGHAI, CHINA
21 DECEMBER 1940

I took my leave of Stepan, saying, "I shall see you after the holiday, at the next committee meeting." In the meantime, I hoped to hear from the Government-in-Exile regarding my volunteers.

I did not know that, earlier in December, the Middle Eastern Czechoslovak Unit, one of the possible destinations for my men, had assisted Britain in their North African offensive. I was similarly unaware that, within the Czech unit, some soldiers had refused to serve under Jewish officers. Would the Exile Government receive my hopeful Christmas Card and reports of mostly-Jewish Czechs in Shanghai, around the exact same time as they heard unsavoury reports from Syria?

How could I have known that President Beneš and General Ingr were concerned with whether the Army-in-Exile had a "highly-Jewish character"? When did I begin to suspect that my supposedly democratic government had its own anti-Semitic streak?

*****

Boxing Day was also the third night of Hanukkah. I was at Eves, visiting with the Ovadias, "Tita" Clark Kerr, Edward Smith-Wright, and others. We awaited Sir Victor's return. He had been away from Shanghai since July.

When he arrived, we filled him in on the recent highlights: Fundraisers. Parties. Performances. The new act at Farren's — Lantzoff and his Blonde Darlings and their "Lambeth Walk." The previous month's Paper Hunt season opener that featured Chinese farmers protesting near the finish. Plans for the upcoming Christmas at the Russian School, co-financed, that year, by Ed Toeg and Princess Sumair Patiala, a fairly recent addition to our little society.

THE SUITCASE

As we chatted, Viva rose and turned the knob on the radio to provide some background music. We were startled by the shrieking and banging of whistles, gongs, buzzers, and bells. The Alcott Jam—an attempt by the Japanese to silence the most popular Western newsman.

"Sorry!" Viva cringed. "I forgot!" She quickly adjusted the dial.

"It must be eight o'clock," I said. Alcott's broadcasts were then at 8 a.m., 1 p.m., 8 p.m., and 10 p.m.

"Have they started the jam again?" Sassoon asked. "What did Alcott do this time?"

I explained: "Earlier this month, the Japanese blockaded the Badlands, which trapped a quarter of a million people in the area without food, or fuel. Between the cold and starvation, several hundred corpses were left to rot in the streets, amid the ever-accumulating garbage heaps and refuse piles. So Alcott started making comments about 'The New Odour,'" a play on the Japanese intent to establish a "New Order" in East Asia.

"He is lucky to be broadcasting from behind that grenade-proof mesh wire at the station," Sassoon said with a chuckle. The XMHA studios on Race Course Road also had an iron grill fitted over its door, and armed Chinese guards on duty.

That summer, the Japanese had published a "death list" of journalists and broadcasters they wanted killed. Prominent men were targeted, including Cornelius van der Starr, president of the *Shanghai Evening Post and Mercury*; Randall Gould, editor of the same publication; J. B. Powell, editor of the *China Weekly Review*; J. A. E. Sanders-Bates, managing director of the University Press; Hal P. Mills, publishers of the *Haw Mei Pao*; Norwood Allman, owner of a pro-Kuomintang paper.

Severed heads, mostly Chinese, were found propped against homes and lampposts, with messages attached: "This will be

SHANGHAI, CHINA
21 DECEMBER 1940

your fate." Journalist "Sammy" Chang was shot in a café in Bubbling Well Road. Hallett Abend, Far Eastern correspondent of the *New York Times*, was attacked by two armed Japanese men in his apartment on the fifteenth storey of Broadway Mansions. He was "robbed of various manuscripts" by the gunmen, and nearly thrown to his death from the balcony I had once enjoyed with Desmond O'Neill.

"Sounds like they've still got it in for old Alcott," Sassoon said. "Clearly they have lifted the blockade, though."

"Only just," I said.

"They wanted the casinos to be open for the holidays," Lucien added. "After all, the Japanese can't get their squeeze if the casinos aren't open for business."

"But, as you just heard," Viva gestured to the radio, "the jam remains."

"This time they not only jammed Alcott's broadcasts, but also the children's shows, the Sunday religious specials, and all sorts of programmes," I said.

Lucien added, "The studio eventually put Alcott out over a second wavelength. It took the Japanese, what, a week?" he asked the room. "Then they had another transmitter up and running to block that frequency too."

"Well, it's about time we boys head off to our meeting on the Bund," Lucien said. We were going to a Nine-Fifteen showing with Sir Victor.

"We have certainly got plenty of British Women's Association business to keep us busy here," said Viva.

"Tita" Clark Kerr, wife of Ambassador "Archie" was famous for her fundraising abilities. That May, she had used showings of *Snow White* to raise $16,000 for a charity run by Madame Chiang Kai-shek, Soong Mei-ling — one of the Soong sisters Mickey Hahn was then writing about.

THE SUITCASE

Most recently, Tita had organised Shanghai's War Work Bazaar, held a fortnight previously at the Race Club. The turnout had been so massive that some people could not even enter the venue. Inside, it was too crowded to move between the various stalls. Viva had run the raffles; Ed Toeg had done silhouettes; Kay and Lorna Lucas had sold tea and cakes, coffees, and hot dogs; elsewhere there were stalls with ice cream, tombola games, second-hand books, a fortune teller, Christmas decorations, and so on.

"I'm sure you have another winning fundraising idea in the works," Lucien said.

"You be careful," Viva said, looking from Lucien to Sir Victor to me.

We gentlemen rose, buttoned our jackets, straightened our ties. Viva stood and went to Lucien and fiddled with his scarlet carnation. I wore one too, as usual, and had seen to it that Sassoon had a carnation as well. Overcoats and hats were donned, and we were off to the Bund. On the way, we chatted about the Nine-Fifteen Club.

"The films have been excellent," Lucien told Sir Victor. "Most of November they showed one with R.A.F. battles—Spitfires and Hurricanes. Don't worry, I have already asked to borrow it." Sir Victor gave a little laugh. Lucien continued, "You are about to see the first change in programme since they have gone semi-public with the club."

"What do you mean?" Sir Victor asked.

Lucien explained: "There was a membership drive over the summer. The original 9.15 p.m. showings turned into 6.15 and 9.15 showings. Then they added more times. Now they're up to four showings a day, plus three on Saturdays, and two more on Sundays."

I added, "To accommodate the expanded membership, we've

SHANGHAI, CHINA
21 DECEMBER 1940

begun meeting in the Glen Line building," home to the Cinema Section of the British Press Attaché.

Ovadia continued, "The German consulate is also leasing space in the building, and carrying out Nine-Fifteen activities within sniffing distance of the Nazis provides some of us with a certain delight."

I chuckled.

"The funds the club has raised were used, in part, to the evacuation of Free French troops that were stuck here in Shanghai after the fighting in French Indochina," Ovadia said.

"Snuck them right out under the nose of the Japanese, did they?" Sassoon laughed. "You all played Scarlet Pimpernel and slipped right past their guards."

"'A thousand ways to cheat the poor, stupid officials of the Republic,'" I said, quoting the film.

"Now I see why you have placed particular emphasis on the scarlet carnations this evening," Sassoon said.

At the Nine-Fifteen Cub, the late-December programme was perfect for Sassoon. The newsreel featured a British plane with a camera affixed to its wings. The film recording begins just before its take-off and follows its subsequent engagement with German bombers. We watched and cheered as the British pilots sent Nazi bombing planes crashing down.

The crowd hushed as reels changed and the film began its presentation of extensive damage to London that had been caused by the Nazis' Blitz. To lift spirits, undamaged parts of the city are then shown on film: businesses opening, traffic flowing, pedestrians walking.

Some riveting footage is then displayed—an enormous time bomb, a 1,000-kilogram "Hermann," named after the "spherical" Göring—is removed from St. Paul's Cathedral. It is a delicate surgery, with high stakes. As the featurette progressed, some audience members moved from sitting comfortably, to perching at the edges of their seats, to standing as breathlessly as they would at the finish of a championship race.

In the end, the bomb did not detonate, and the Cathedral, and the workers, were spared. The audience sighed with relief and broke into applause.

After the spectacle, the lights in the auditorium returned to their full strength, and the men joined in sing-songs. The acoustics in the auditorium were not the best, and the singers were especially enthusiastic after such moving newsreels. I am sure I visibly cringed a few times before the evening's end as they shouted in happy song:

> *We're going to hang out the washing on the Siegfried Line.*
> *Have you any dirty washing, mother dear?*
> *We're going to hang out the washing on the Siegfried Line.*
> *'Cause the washing day is here!*

Shanghai, China
Tuesday, 22 July 1941

> *I love-a-you and love-a you true*
> *And if you-a love-a me.*
> *One live as two, two live as one,*
> *Under the bamboo tree.*
> — Bob and Robert Cole
> "Under the Bamboo Tree"

I WAS SWEATING beneath my black tie. My scarlet carnation was fairly wilted from the late-afternoon heat. The tickets from Moutrie's in my jacket pocket were probably limp with humidity. I turned near the French Club and drove down past the Canidrome to Route Joseph Frelupt to fetch my date for the evening.

I stopped in front of number 390, a spacious villa. My date, Eliska Kanturek, called Liza, was the pretty, young, tennis-playing sister of Anka Voticky, the refugee woman I had met at the Czech tea dance the previous summer. Liza had left Prague in December 1940 in possession of a trans-Siberian railway ticket. She'd arrived at the end of January, homesick and clutching a Dvořák record. Liza was one of only a few dozen refugees who managed to reach Shanghai in 1941.

Since then, Anka and Liza's brother, Vilda Kanturek, had arrived via Switzerland. He and another brother, Erna, had become privates in my Czech company in the Shanghai Volunteer Corps.

THE SUITCASE

The S.V.C. had come under the command of Lieutenant Colonel G. H. Mann. Our former commandant, Colonel Hornby, who had assumed control in '37 and who had seen the city through many troubling times, left for England in February '41.

Lately, the city's workers had been protesting, and the S.V.C. had spent many a night standing guard. In late March, bus drivers of the Compagnie Française de Tramways et d'éclairage Electriques de Changhaï went on strike to demand higher pay and living allowances. In late April, thousands of workers went on strike at the Ewo Cotton Mill, owned by Jardine Matheson. Force was used and some municipal police were injured before the situation was resolved. Then, just a week previously, on 15 July, we had been called again when the ongoing strike at the China Electric Company had grown to some two thousand workers.

In between all of the striking, I had also added some twenty-two members to Headquarters Company, including the Kanturek brothers, and a man named Frank Popper, who would be a friend for as long as I lived.

When I rang at the villa, one of the servants answered the door.

Liza soon materialized. She was about half my age. She wore a becoming summer gown, perfect for that evening's "Moonlight Follies" event, sponsored by the XCDN radio station. Most of Shanghai was entirely ignorant of how deeply involved I was with XCDN's radio broadcasts. Thankfully, with their studios located in Sassoon House, my activities there appeared, on the surface, just like my usual comings and goings, when in reality I had been making regular broadcasts on behalf of the Czechs and the Allies. Another Czech in Shanghai liked to write under the name "Tomáš Pravda," meaning "Thomas Truth." I, too, had been using the name "Truth," broadcasting as "Doctor Truth" to

SHANGHAI, CHINA
22 JULY 1941

add another layer of intrigue to my identity. "Doctor Truth" had been inviting listeners to the Follies for some time, but twice the event had been postponed by rain.

My social life that summer was certainly not what it had been in years past. As I greeted my date, I was genuinely glad to be having some fun.

"Thank you for coming with me," I said. "It promises to be an eventful evening."

"I hope the long-awaited Follies live up to the expectation," Liza said.

"Next Friday will be Czechoslovak night," I said. Each week, the Follies would feature a different country. "I don't suppose you would like to be my date again?"

She gave me a coy smile. "I'll check my calendar."

It was a short drive to our destination in Avenue Haig.

"You certainly know your way around the city," Liza commented.

I chuckled. "I have lived here nearly ten years now."

"I'm still not very fond of Shanghai. I did not want to come."

"Where would you have gone, if not Shanghai?" I asked.

"Oh, I don't know. There were various near-misses. In the summer of '38 there was the possibility of going to Yugoslavia. The following summer, we shipped some of our items to Chicago, but nothing came of that either. Early in September '39 we had plans to emigrate to Britain, but then the war began. At one point there was the idea of joining an illegal transport to Palestine, but that fell through. And then, last year, the route to China surfaced." She sighed. "Have you heard from your family in Praha?"

I said, "My mother once wrote, 'You have no idea about the things here, and I would not want to get into any kind of trouble.'"

THE SUITCASE

Liza was quiet, thoughtful. She finally said, "We recently received a letter from home, saying only, 'Why didn't you insist?' I have to wonder how things might have changed since we left Praha."

An alarming feeling filled my stomach with hollow panic. "'Why didn't you insist,'" I repeated. "I don't think my family is going to make it out. The money, the permits, the timing. You understand." I could see her nodding in my periphery. "I still owe $1,200 for permits I sent them earlier this year to enter the International Settlement. Then my mother wrote to say the permits were the wrong thing, that they had missed their chance to leave, and that my siblings are both enamoured and don't want to come to Shanghai anyway."

Liza sighed. "Yes, I understand that position rather well," she said wistfully.

"My sister has apparently found 'a wonderful person' and is quite in love. He comes to visit her every day."

Liza scoffed. "He would have to come visit her. It would be their only chance to spend time together. Jews are no longer allowed in most public places."

"So I hear." I drove quietly for a moment before continuing. "My brother, Jara, is seeing someone my mother hates. Apparently he has diabetes. He is doing labour now, but he isn't strong enough for the work. He comes home exhausted. My mother said I would hardly recognize him. I wish they had come to Shanghai, but now she says that 'nobody is allowed to travel abroad,' and that men under forty-five are not permitted to leave the 'Protectorate' anyway."

"I'm sure she's right," Liza said.

"Now," I said, "my money for the permits is stuck with the Manchurian authorities, and it will take months for me to recoup it. And it will only be twenty-eight percent of the original sum."

SHANGHAI, CHINA
22 JULY 1941

"Why did they think the permit was wrong?" Liza asked.

"They were told that the entry permit into the International Settlement needed to be certified by the Japanese Consul-General."

"A transit visa, maybe," Liza said. "My family was able to obtain transit visas from a man named Sugihara. Otherwise we never would have been able to cross Japanese-controlled territory. Most were not so lucky."

I nodded. "The Jewish Council in Praha told my family that I would need to go to the Japanese-Russian border at Tsuruga and deposit $120 per person with the Japanese Tourist Office there. Then Tsuruga would send authorization to the Japanese Consulate in Praha, who would, in turn, notify my family when they were able to travel. They would then apply to Hamburg for the transit permit to Manchuria. They were also told that they would have to pay in dollars to get across Russia. If that is true, they definitely wouldn't have the funds. They say the going rate is three hundred korunas for one American dollar. They were told it would be sixty- to seventy-thousand dollars for their tickets and for exit taxes. My mother wrote: 'We don't have that much, and neither do you, unfortunately.'" She had been right.

"What if they sold their villa?" Liza asked.

"The letters stopped mentioning the possibility of selling. I know my brother gave the last of his money to my sister in New York, to finance her trip. My mother has written that they are 'beggars' now. They have taken on a renter in the apartment who pays them room and board. She says they are living on Havelská now, and that the apartment is cold."

I did not tell Liza about the things my mother had written to Francy: "You are right that we did not take things seriously enough. Unfortunately, I am not strong enough to have said, 'I am going.'" She closed that letter by saying, "So as you can see,

THE SUITCASE

we lead a great life. I don't care anymore. I hope we'll be able to endure what God has reserved for us. And if not, then... the world will go on."

"Well," Liza said, "Even if they could, or wanted to, make the journey, they would be in for a rough trip. While we were still in the 'Protectorate,' we were not allowed to use sleeping or dining cars. I think I held my breath the entire time the train was stopped in Berlin. I am sure my parents paid some bribes there, and then again at the Russian border. Then we crossed thousands of kilometres of frozen-solid Soviet territory. And then we boarded the ship to Kobe. Then, finally, the ship to Shanghai," she finished. I had heard that the Votickys had taken a rowboat out to meet the newly-arrived Kantureks, waving a Czech flag and buzzing "Kde domov můj" on a harmonica on the waters of the muddy Whangpoo.

I sighed. "Well. I am glad you made it. Whether you like it here or not, I'm sure it's infinitely safer."

"Is it?" she asked with an air of scepticism.

We were nearing our destination, but I was actually enjoying speaking with someone who sympathized with my family situation—a situation for which my socialite friends had no understanding. I sighed. "Now I would like to go to the States, and I can't because even if my visa is approved, my funds have gone to their unused permits."

Liza thought for a moment. "I wouldn't mind going to the States if I could get permission," she said. "I should like to go anywhere, really. I don't see how you stand it here. All the mindless dancing and drinking atop all the disease and destruction. The rickshaw coolies, the blind and crippled beggars, the mud-covered corpses, the opium and heroin addicts, the prostitutes. The Japanese fighting the Chinese. The Chinese fighting each other..."

SHANGHAI, CHINA
22 JULY 1941

"Maybe we can all go to America," I said with a sigh. "My mother says that 'when things get better,' she will go to America, and if I ended up there, nothing would make her happier. I was told that the Czechoslovak quota for immigration into the States hasn't yet been met, and that if I apply for an entry visa it should be granted in short order. A friend of my brother-in-law provided affidavits of support to help expedite my case. You know—the sort of thing from someone who owns businesses or land or properties, saying that I shall never become indigent or be a burden on the U.S."

I did not tell her that I had also requested these same affidavits for Štembera and his wife and daughter, and for Karel Gustav Aschenbrenner, who had been an officer in Prague. I asked that the papers be sent directly to the U.S. Consulate General in Kiangse Road, the same consulate where American Judge Milton Helmick's court was located. By sending the papers there, the British censor in Hong Kong wouldn't delay the mail—and wouldn't know what I was up to.

I continued, "I am concerned about staying on in Shanghai. Business is lousy, and if war comes between Japan and the States, we will be shut off completely from the outside world and business will be non-existent. The thing is, I can only go to the States if Beneš and the Government-in-Exile allow it. I am writing by every boat."

There was a quiet moment.

I parked the car near our destination in Avenue Haig. We were in view of the enormous Nazi radio tower near the Kaiser Wilhelm School. The powerful tower of XGRS radio was responsible for transmitting propaganda throughout most of East Asia. In the Park Hotel overlooking the Race Course, Baron Jesco von Puttkamer, "the Goebbels of the Far East," was running a well-financed "information bureau" from his penthouse. In the nearby

Badlands, uniformed Nazi officers were being entertained at the Argentina Nightclub. There were about a hundred Gestapo in Shanghai, including Colonel Meisinger, the notorious "Butcher of Warsaw," who had arrived in Shanghai in May.

"The damned Nazis are everywhere," I said as I glared at their radio tower. "If they'd like to start something out here, they are welcome. I have not organised a Czech company for simply attending Easter Processions."

After a moment, Liza said, "When we were young, our parents wanted us to know German. Whenever our nanny scolded me for failing to use German, I would begin singing 'Kde domov můj.'"

My anger dissolved. I had to laugh. "Did you really? I knew I liked you!"

I exited the car and walked around to open and to hold the door for her. We could hear distant music coming from Hayim's garden. The newspaper had promised that the grounds would be lit as splendidly as Disney's *Fantasia*. Over the garden wall, the treetops were glowing in the fading daylight. Chinese lanterns punctuated the scene, adding to the enchantment.

Liza and I crossed the Bridge of Chance and passed a number of tents holding attractions. There was a food bar, and drinks were being served to patrons around the garden at tables large and small. When I spotted Hayim, I shook his hand and thanked him for hosting the event.

I then spotted Stepan. Liza and I went over to say hello.

"Stepan," I said, shaking his hand. "You know Miss Kanturková."

Liza said, "Major Stepan, I have been meaning to tell you how much I enjoyed your lecture on Beneš's life and work," At the end of May, on the occasion of President Beneš's fifty-seventh birthday, three hundred people had gathered at our Czech Circle

SHANGHAI, CHINA
22 JULY 1941

to hear Stepan speak.

"And your Jan Hus talk on the eighth was wonderful," I said. That year, the *North-China Daily News* had even run the story of "John" Hus, enlightening those in Shanghai about the man who was martyred for his views that opposed components of Catholicism. Hus originated our Czechoslovak motto, "The truth prevails."

"Thank you," Stepan said.

"It was nice to hear something besides how the British are fighting alone, and how the British can take it, and how the British 'would rather stand up and face death, than kneel down and face the kind of existence the conqueror would impose upon them,'" I said, quoting, in the last instance, from "London Can Take It." In April, the short film had played all over Shanghai—at special R.A.F. picture shows, at Nine-Fifteen meetings, and, in audio-only form, over the XMHA and XCDN airwaves.

I had seen "London Can Take It" so many times, I knew every flash of AA fire, every swipe of the searchlight, every comment about "nightly visitors" and image of public shelters. I knew how, after the night-time bombing raid, the kitten would be freed from rubble the following morning. I knew the narrator's words as he praised the British people for continuing their lives without panic, without fear, without despair—with determination, confidence, and courage—that was the Londoner's way. "Great fighters get up after being knocked down, like London each morning," the film proclaimed.

Czechoslovakia's feet had been kicked out from under her, and she had been held down for the past two years while the British withheld recognition of President Beneš. I had found the commentary deeply offensive, especially since the British had decided at the Munich "Agreement" that Czechoslovakia would "kneel to the conqueror." The Czechs had not been given the opportunity to choose a different path for themselves. Instead, we had been betrayed.

"I suppose you have not yet heard the news?" Stepan asked.

"What news?"

"Just a few days ago, on the eighteenth, Beneš gained official recognition."

I was floored. "Did he? Finally! What changed?"

Stepan said, "As you know, the Czechs offered assistance to the Soviets when the Germans turned against them last month and invaded. In return, the Soviets immediately granted official recognition. The British have now followed suit."

"After all this time. Who knew the Soviets would be the ones to do the right thing?" I asked.

"Yes, well, I suppose there's nothing so unifying as a common enemy," Stepan said.

"If you'll excuse me, gentlemen, I'm going to go see some of the entertainments." Liza stepped away.

I asked Stepan, "Will the British even be able to finish the job? Perhaps the Soviets are a better ally anyway." Even Beneš "had little confidence in the determination of the British to fight for complete victory."

"We need as many allies as we can get, Taussig," he said.

"I wonder whether this latest development has had any bearing on the recent opportunity for some of our numbers to join the Army Abroad? The Government-in-Exile has finally offered to subsidize travel expenses for Czech troops under the age of forty. Almost every member of my Czech platoon has volunteered for transport to the front." Unfortunately, the Ministry of Defence believed I would arrange everything. "I was beginning to think that Attaché Colonel Burkhardt, who is retiring anyway, was not delivering my messages as he should. Back in November I wrote to the Exile Army officials that my

SHANGHAI, CHINA
22 JULY 1941

volunteers were ready. To further confirm my suspicions, in January '41, reserve Corporal Feder was directly ordered by the Exile officials to get on a ship to England. I was only later made aware of this directive."

"Yes, well, perhaps the proverbial wires were crossed somewhere along the line. Besides, how would they be transported when the British Admiralty's ships have been ordered to the Atlantic?"

"That may be, but I had been trying to transport my men to the front for several months without any result. I saw no possibility of our volunteers getting to our army until our government settled the financial question and offered transports free of charge. I explained to the officials that the idea of having the Shanghai Czechoslovaks finance the transport would not work. They needed to take into consideration that fact that there were no more than three hundred and fifty new Czechoslovaks and that most of them have no means. There are only five of us old Czechoslovak inhabitants here, also without funds to assist."

"If I were you, I would just be grateful that there have been positive developments," Stepan said.

On 7 September, twelve of my men would be transported; another ten departed two weeks later.

As I had told Liza, my Czech company had not been organised only to march in parades and police local protests.

Unbeknownst to me, ten days after I had written and sent my January letter to the Government-in-Exile, the British Embassy in Shanghai had added a caveat before sending it on to London: "As some doubt exists as to Mr. Taussig's pro-British sentiments," it was "suggest[ed] that [the] contents of [the] envelope [I had sent] might be censored."

When my letter was eventually examined, someone in the British Foreign Office had written: "The letter seems quite all right and should go on." There was agreement at the next desk it crossed: "Rather creditable. A copy of this might perhaps be sent to War Office and Ministry of War Transport?" By that time, it was mid-June.

On 28 June: "Yes, please send accordingly."

Was it a coincidence that I had, shortly thereafter, been given the green light to move my troops?

Also present in Hayim's garden that evening were many members of the newly-formed Inter-Allied Federation, organised in early May by British Press Attaché John Alexander with the aim of promoting inter-Allied publicity, and gathering nationals who supported the Allied cause.

I was bitter that the *North-China Daily News* had lauded the Inter-Allied Federation and, by extension, Alexander, as being so brave to unite against the "Axis bandits." They wrote: "...the sponsors of this Federation are required to have courage and determination to struggle toward their glorious darkness, they should be proud of themselves being bearers of torches illuminated with light, and stars of justice and righteousness." It was sticky-sweet enough to induce nausea. What of my own courage and determination, and that of all the others who worked thanklessly for the Allied cause?

Because membership in the Inter-Allied Federation overlapped with membership of the Nine-Fifteen Club, associates I knew all too well were circulating near John Alexander in Hayim's garden. Chatting away. Laughing at their own cleverness. I hated them just then.

I was also sour because Alexander had been freely given time on XCDN on Friday nights, from 21.45 to 22.00. I, on the other hand, had originally been made to pay for airtime on that station. Alexander was also receiving money from the British government, whereas I was, financially speaking, on my own.

SHANGHAI, CHINA
22 JULY 1941

Thankfully, Sassoon had eventually given me time to broadcast on behalf of Czechoslovakia on XCDN. I was offered a regular time slot along with Portugal and the Netherlands, broadcasting each Monday, Tuesday, and Wednesday from 18.30 to 19.00.

With XMHA, the station that hosted Carroll Alcott, I had negotiated on delicate grounds before I succeeded in getting the station's manager, Roy Healey, to accept thrice-weekly broadcasts during the rush hours, enabling me to take advantage of Alcott's quarter-of-a-million listeners. Alexander's air time was freely given, while mine was only possible through careful negotiations.

As I took my leave of Stepan, I noticed an unfamiliar face seated near John Alexander. Rather stern. About my age. Precisely groomed. Definitely former military. He stared directly at me.

The man was John Helier LeRougetel of the British Foreign Office. He had just arrived in Shanghai about a week previously. He would cause a good deal of trouble for me.

In Hayim's garden, I found Liza queuing before a tent, waiting to meet with the fortune teller. When it was her turn, she went in alone. A few minutes later, when she returned, she said, "You should do it, Vladimír."

"Should I?" I asked with a bemused smile.

"Just go," she said, giving me a gentle push. "You have already skipped to the front of the queue by coming up to wait for me."

What did I have to lose? After all, had it not been for a fortune teller's encounter with David Sassoon, the family never would have found prosperity in the Far East. "All right," I said. I gave Liza a wink and entered the tent.

The inside was draped with scarves in reds and purples and oranges, with gold stars and moons and swirls painted here and there. The fortune teller, a woman I had seen at many Shanghai

THE SUITCASE

functions in the past, was seated at a table with an array of mystical devices at her disposal—a mirror, a crystal ball, a deck of cards, the makings of a tea ceremony.

"Hello," I said. "Which one should we try?" I gestured at her table.

"I think the cards for you," she said.

"How appropriate," I grinned. "I love cards."

She picked up the deck and began to shuffle. "Is there a particular question you wish to ask the cards?"

One question? That, I did not know. I was only there because Liza had sprung it on me. "I suppose I wish I knew what was coming next."

"We all do," the fortune teller said, smiling. She drew a single card and set it on the table, face-up, in between us. "The Tower," the card said. The image on the card showed a tall tower on a mountain top. The tower was being struck by lightning and was enflamed. People were jumping from the window to escape the fire.

"Chaos," the woman said. "Upheaval. The tower itself is sturdy, but it was built on a cliff. With no solid foundation, the lightning could easily bring it down." She waved her hands. "Revelation. Awakening. What is real? What is true? What can be relied upon? What cannot?" She looked into my eyes. "You cannot avoid the Tower. Do not submit to fear and act in terror," she added, tapping her finger on the people jumping from the tower's windows. Fear? Terror? I would never. "Instead of panic, welcome the trial ahead. Stay prepared, so that you may enter the fray with confidence. After the ordeal, you will be stronger. Wiser. You will have a new perspective." She finished by saying, "As the Tower crumbles, it creates space for more life." Then she returned my card to the deck and began to shuffle.

"Thank you, I suppose," I said. I drew a bill from my pocket

SHANGHAI, CHINA
22 JULY 1941

and tried to hand it to her. She pointed to a little box. I deposited my money there and exited the tent, allowing the next person to enter.

Liza was waiting for me outside. She took my arm. "What did you think?" she asked.

"It was interesting, all right," I said. She laughed. I wondered what her reading had been.

We wandered over, arm-in-arm, and found an empty table near where the entertainments were just beginning.

The Masked Singer took the spotlight and we all listened to his performance. Then Margaret Sinclair emerged, carrying an enormous dark-blue feathered fan for her number. We saw chorus girls in conga costumes, chorus girls in pastel organdie, chorus girls in scarlet-and-blue military getups.

One particular chorus girl attempted to catch my eye. I had dallied with her earlier in the year when, back in March, and again in May, the "XCDN Calling" show, benefitting the Central British War Air Raid Relief fund, held their rehearsals at the Metropole. And rehearsals had been endless—the three-hour-long variety show featured nearly one hundred entertainers. Long Tak Sam had come out of retirement to perform. Noël Coward's "Red Peppers" had been part of the show. Owing to the proximity and frequency of the rehearsals, I'd had a fling with one of "Queen Victoria's Floradora Girls" from the Gay Nineties.

The same chorus girl now danced before me with an eager smile. I avoided making eye contact with her and hoped that Liza hadn't noticed. It was not that I feared her jealousy or displeasure, since she had had many suitors too, but I certainly didn't want her to know that I had been carrying on with chorus girls.

Finally, the dancers quit the stage. The orchestra was given the go-ahead, and the patrons rose from their seats to dance. As soon as Liza was in my arms, she casually asked, "So who's the chorus girl?" Sharp as a tack, she was.

We danced for a time, until little beads of sweat on our lips and brows glistened in the fairy lights in the trees. We paused to have a drink. I spotted Sassoon and the Ovadias at their table, and Liza and I went over to have a chat.

Lucien asked his customary question: "How's business?" I had established a partnership with Eduard Kann, born in Austria and sympathetic to the Czech cause.

"Business is good," I said. "And you?" I asked, looking between Ovadia and Sir Victor.

"Oh, the usual," Ovadia said. Sir Victor was quieter than usual. "Don't mind him," Lucien added. "He's feeling blue about his pal Sand."

Sir Victor's good pal Sandy Tittman had left Shanghai and was marrying John Morris, the Far Eastern manager of the United Press. Sandy's uncle, our friend Judge Milton Helmick, had departed to attend his niece's wedding.

I suggested, "Why don't we all go out after this? Chase those blues away?" I looked from Lucien to Viva to Sir Victor. None seemed too enthused about the idea.

"Is it safe to go out?" Liza asked. "Aren't you terrified you'll be shot?" She had no trouble saying what was on her mind.

"Are you yourself terrified you'll be shot in this garden party?" Viva asked.

"Passingly, yes," Liza said.

"I understand her concerns," I said. "After what happened to Keswick in January, and at Farren's in February, and who knows what other incidents since then…"

Lucien added, "Well, with the Japanese pushing the idea of 'Asia for the Asiatics,' they wanted to make a clear statement that Westerners should get out of the picture."

SHANGHAI, CHINA
22 JULY 1941

"Who is Keswick and what happened to him in January?" Liza asked.

"Tony Keswick," Sir Victor said. "He was shot in broad daylight, in front of a crowd of witnesses, while attending a Shanghai Municipal Council meeting."

"The Keswicks are known for Jardine's, for the Race Club, for their involvement with the Municipal Council and the Chamber of Commerce," I said.

"Keswick didn't die," Viva said. "But the man who shot him hasn't been punished."

"I suppose I don't understand," Liza said. "What happened at the council meeting?"

We explained how the Japanese had attempted to seize control of the Shanghai Municipal Council, and the Westerners' apathy had nearly paved the way. In the end, the Settlement's administration was saved through a clever subdivision of business and residential holdings, so that British ratepayers' properties became thousands of smaller parcels, each with its own vote. In this way, eight British businessmen had cast five thousand votes.

This had been quite a dirty trick, especially since the Japanese did comprise the majority of ratepayers at that time. Following the underhanded victory, the Council proposed to raise taxes by forty percent, effective retroactively, which would heavily affect the Japanese-majority ratepayers.

On the late-January 1941 day in question, a special council meeting had been convened to vote on the tax increase measure. Councilman Yukichi Hayashi suggested an alternative to the tax increase, but his amendment was laughed down. The councilmen had already put forth the outcome they wished to see enacted — the tax increase.

"If my amendment fails," Hayashi warned, "this council

will be responsible." Keswick, the S.M.C.'s chairman, asked the Council to reject Hayashi's amendment. Then it was put to a vote. The ayes won by such a landslide that the nay votes were not even counted. Realising they had been overlooked, the Japanese audience members began to boo, hiss, and stomp. Some rushed at the stage, throwing chairs, while one of the Japanese councilmen called for order over the microphone.

Amid this chaos, Hayashi pulled a revolver from his overcoat and shot Tony Keswick in the chest. Keswick had not been wearing his bulletproof vest that day, but he did have on a thick overcoat, which surely aided in his survival.

"Keswick, of all people, is known for trying to work with the Japanese and protect his family's business interests by finding compromises," I explained to Liza.

"What ever happened with the tax increase?" Liza asked.

"The next S.M.C. meeting was to be held under a mat-shed, which 'someone' attempted to raze — but they failed. The Japanese boycotted the meeting, but no quorum was needed, since technically the old meeting was reconvening. The increase was approved by a ridiculous margin, something like several thousand votes against five."

Following this January incident, there had been a shooting at Farren's in February.

I had been upstairs at the chemin de fer tables when I heard screams and breaking glass downstairs. Then the chaos spread upstairs, and people dove beneath the tables and cowered next to the slot machines to avoid the sudden gunfire. Guards materialized, including the always-armed Wally Lunzer. Also joining in the fray were the club's co-owners — Joe Farren, the Ziegfeld of Shanghai, and Jack Riley, one of Shanghai's most wanted men who, until the incident, had been avoiding capture, using the club as his hideout.

SHANGHAI, CHINA
22 JULY 1941

In the excitement, Miss Daisy Alice Simmons, a fixture at the roulette wheel, was killed. She was an English girl, Shanghai-born and California-educated; she was also a bullion broker, and a partner in her father's firm,

"I don't know whether it is 'safe' to go out, but one can't spend one's life cowering in fear of random violence," Sassoon said.

I hoped Liza was not too ruffled by his remark. Knowing her, she would say something like, "I would be worried if I were you. If they can shoot a Keswick in broad daylight, they'd surely shoot a Sassoon."

Viva saved us from any such remark. "I can't go out tonight anyway," she said. "I'll be sailing for India in a few days. I have got to prepare."

"Oh?" I asked. It was the first I was hearing of her plans.

"Yes. I haven't had the chance to tell you," she said.

"And I'll be leaving next month," Sir Victor added.

"Yes, Victor's going in August, and I shall be joining him in September," said Lucien.

I suddenly felt as if I had been kicked in the chest. I had grown accustomed to Sir Victor's comings and goings, but what would Shanghai be without the Ovadias?

"Liza, do you mind if I have a dance with Viva?"

"Don't ask me; ask her husband," Liza giggled.

"Oh, he doesn't mind," Viva said.

Lucien nodded. "Go ahead, sport."

That night in Hayim's garden was to be our final dance. The orchestra played a popular melody, "Begin the Beguine." I held Lucien Ovadia's wife in my arms and swayed in the glow from the lights and lanterns in the trees.

"I shall be sorry to see you go," I said.

"It's Shanghai," Viva said. "We all come and go. Even you."

THE SUITCASE

After a pause she said, "She's a lovely girl."

"Liza? Oh, I haven't quite caught that fish," I said. "Many other, talented young fishermen in the sea."

"I see."

"She's a lot like you," I said. "Intelligent. Athletic. Modern."

"She's beautiful."

I nodded. "Yes, beautiful too. Except, you are better at tennis, and," I twirled her to the music, "she has never sold me vegetables." Viva laughed.

In June, Viva had worked the vegetable stall at the Market Garden Fair, benefitting the British War Fund. She had sold me a bag of potatoes. I had bought a hot dog, then wandered around to the "Horse and Hound," Sassoon's ground-floor Cathay pub, cleverly recreated in the Mohawk Lodge on Route Pere Robert, and had bought a drink from one of the "amateur barmen." Even after those exchanges — the warm hot dog, the cool glass — my hand had still buzzed with Viva's touch.

"India, then?" I asked.

"Lucien says it's time. So India it is," she said. "I can't very well go back to Britain. Why put myself in harm's way? Lucien would die with the constant uncertainty of attacks." The Blitz had only just ended in May.

"Well, there shall be plenty of tennis courts and War Work parties in for you in India, I'm sure."

"India's not entirely safe either, you know. Not for the British. The people are fighting for independent rule," she said.

"I don't know if there's a place in the world that's entirely safe right now," I said. "But I'm sure Lucien will know the least-dangerous path."

The music would soon end. We looked at one another. "I will miss my tennis partner," I said. The orchestra played the song's final strains. "I suppose I won't be seeing you here next week for

SHANGHAI, CHINA
22 JULY 1941

Czech night."

"No. I suppose I don't know when I shall be seeing you," she said. The song reached its finish. Those on the dance floor, and those seated around the nearby tables, began to applaud.

I held her for a moment longer, savouring the feel and smell of her.

She gave a short laugh and pushed me gently away. "You'll make me cry," she said. She walked past me, towards the table, towards her husband and Sir Victor and Liza.

I masked my feelings with a smile and gestured for Liza to join me on the dance floor, where we cut a proverbial rug until the orchestra launched into the night's final songs. The evening's festivities ended with Shanghai's zillionth singalong of "There'll Always Be an England."

Sir Victor and the Ovadias made their exit while we were dancing.

*****

Liza and I left Hayim's garden amid a flood of other revellers. I delivered her back to her family's villa on Route Frelupt.

Back at the Metropole, I went up to my room, number 1302. Cheng had left a good record in the player and a clean glass next to the whiskey bottle. I poured myself a drink and listened absently to the familiar strains of Dvořák.

My thoughts wandered. I recounted the conversation I'd had with Stepan that evening. I thought about the discussion Liza Kanturková and I had had in the car, the fortune teller's warnings about The Tower, the dance with Viva. Why did I feel as though I would never see Viva again?

Prague, Occupied Czechoslovakia
Thursday, 4 December 1941

> *Arbeit macht frei.*
> *[Work makes you free.]*
> — Archway in Terezín

THE ROOM in the apartment at 5 Kanálská, to which the Taussigs had been relocated in September, was cold. Jara stood in his overcoat, his packed bags waiting by the door. Mitcka wore her housecoat, her hair dishevelled. She had been up since the wee hours, scrubbing the bathroom they shared with the others on that floor. Julie wore a robe she had fashioned from the Soochow blanket by creating sleeves and adding a belt.

They were perpetually cold. Some of their winter things had been sent on to Shanghai; some woollens had been reclaimed by cousin Olga. To make matters more difficult, Jewish families had not been eligible for clothing coupons for over a year. That winter, the Taussigs had been spending much of their time trying to obtain warm clothes.

Jara shifted his stance. "I think I am ready," he said gently, all too aware that his imminent departure might result in an emotional scene. He was hesitant to upset Julie, or to wake the people sleeping in the corner of the shared apartment.

Julie said quietly, "I wish you hadn't volunteered to go. First Vladimír left us, then Karel, Francy and Zikmund and Jiří, then Molinka — and now you are going too." Pets with Jewish owners had been confiscated in July, after being taken to a collection

PRAGUE, OCCUPIED CZECHOSLOVAKIA
4 DECEMBER 1941

point. Molinka had been Julie's sole comfort and constant companion. She was devastated.

"Yes, I am going, but I'll be home on weekends, as was promised. And I will write at every chance. Besides, if I don't volunteer now for this Aufbaukommando, this construction unit, what's to say I won't be assigned to something worse later on?"

Julie sighed. "I know. You have told me. I still don't want you to go. You work too hard as it is. Who knows what it will be like there, or where you will even be."

Jara said, "I don't know. I haven't heard any bad news from the volunteers who left in the last week or two."

With an ominous tone, Marietta said, "No one has heard any news from them at all."

Jara shot his sister a look. "I will write to you as soon as possible," he told Julie.

"I will check for mail as often as I can," Julie said. Prague's Jewish population had been limited to one post office, which was only open for a few hours in the afternoon. It was located in a different section of town, and special permission from the Gestapo was needed in order to leave the neighbourhood.

Jara wrapped his arms around his mother. She seemed so small.

Marietta took a small bundle from the nearby table. "Here," she said, handing it to her brother.

He knew it was food. "No," Jara said. "You keep it." Good food had become scarce. It had become a punishable offence to sell certain foods to Jews: fruit, nuts, cheese, fish, poultry, game. And it wasn't as if they were free to visit parks or forests to forage or hunt.

"Please," Julie said. "You'll need your strength. You must take care of yourself, especially with these long days of labour."

Jara slowly took the bundle from his sister's outstretched

THE SUITCASE

hands. "Maybe the diet will be better there, since we are workers," Jara said hopefully. He tucked the bundle into his other luggage. "Thank you."

Jara was standing by the door. His bags were ready to be lifted. He had already embraced his family. What else was there to do?

"Take care of Mamicka," he said to his sister. "Take care of one another." He looked between the two women.

The yellow star on his overcoat was visible in the brightening room.

When the stars were first required in Prague, some non-Jews had donned stars of their own to show solidarity, but the Nazis had soon deterred them. Since Reinhard Heydrich's September appointment as Deputy Reich Protector of the Protectorate, there had been fewer and fewer displays of protest against the Nazis. No more Jan Hus day or National Day demonstrations. No more "v" for "ven" — meaning "out" — planted into flowerbeds or painted onto buildings and buses. Executions and deportations had become the rule.

On the first day of October, Heydrich had ordered a new Jewish registration be performed. On the tenth, he had announced his plan to build a settlement for Jews. On the twenty-third, he had declared that emigration from the Protectorate was illegal. On November 24th and 30th, the first workers had been transported to Terezín.

Jara opened the door. Then the yellow star was gone from the room, its wearer moving down the stairs and out into the street.

Jaromír stood outside the apartment in the cold and took one last look at the building that held his mother and sister, then he turned and began walking.

*****

PRAGUE, OCCUPIED CZECHOSLOVAKIA
4 DECEMBER 1941

As he waited for the tram, Jaromír thought of his girlfriend, who would normally have been sleeping at that hour, warm and soft and sweet. On waking, she always gave him kisses and made him coffee and brought it to him in bed.

But he couldn't hold that image of her in his mind just then. It was replaced by the memory of the way he had left her very early that morning. "I love you," she had said, as she wiped at her weeping eyes and running nose. "Come back to me as soon as you can." But when would that be? His stomach lurched with the thought that had haunted him since he had decided to volunteer, that she would not wait for his weekend visits and would take back up with her old beau.

On the tram, he was relegated to the last carriage, as all Jews had been since the previous September. The tram would take him directly to the railway station. What a shame he wasn't able to say goodbye to his city properly—and it did feel like a goodbye.

He would have liked to have gone the long way to the train station, walking from the flat on Kanálská, taking his time as the sun rose, passing the National Museum and the statue of Saint Wenceslas. The Statue made him think of the National Day protests, and murders, and the ensuing Nazi military parades. He and Marietta had then gotten their passports in order. Reason for travel? "For existence," his sister had written.

Jara could imagine stopping for freshly-baked pastries and just-brewed coffee on his way through Wenceslas Square, all restaurants open to his patronage, none barred to Jews. He might have veered off to see his father's old office on Jindřišská, near the Palace Hotel.

Just before he crossed the Vltava, he would arrive at the Revoluční apartment that his mother had rented when they had left the villa. They had since been forced out of that apartment, and had been required to move again. Conditions had steadily deteriorated from their villa, to the apartment they chose to rent, to an apartment they had been forced into, to a corner of a shared flat.

As Jara crossed the wooden bridge over the Vltava, he might have hummed a few bars from Bedřich Smetana's symphonic poem about the river, a work which had been banned since 1939.

From the far side of the river, he might have stopped to take in the city in the slowly-brightening winter morning light. He would have walked through Stromovka park, travelling familiar paths. There were a few secluded places he had always wanted to take a girl, and now that he finally had a girlfriend who would have been game, Jews had been forbidden entry to the parks. He might have turned his thoughts instead to family outings of years past, to afternoons spent strolling the grounds and stopping into the restaurant for lunch.

He would have continued moving towards the villa, imagining himself now with the dogs trotting alongside—Barry and Eda and Molinka— and thinking of the several happy years the family had spent there, and not about the tense months at the end of his father's life, the Shakespearian "second childishness," or about the container of ashes the great man had become.

Jara would have noticed that the street's name had been changed to "Führich-Strasse" to honour an Austrian painter who had lived in Prague. The Nazis had been desperate to get their hands on the Taussigs' villa and redistribute it to some deemed-worthy family of the Reich, but the Taussigs had so far been successful in evading the eventual handover.

Jara would have crossed back through the park as the birds chirped at the dawning of the day, and would arrive at the train station to present himself and his credentials to whatever official waited there.

But Jaromír Taussig had no business being anywhere except

PRAGUE, OCCUPIED CZECHOSLOVAKIA
4 DECEMBER 1941

where the occupiers granted permission to be. And so he sat, luggage assembled around him on the tram that carried him steadily towards the railway station where he was to gather with the other construction workers of the Aufbaukommando.

Soon he was delivered at the Prague-Bubny station and unceremoniously received as one of a thousand other "volunteers" to leave Prague that day. Jara rubbed his hands and stomped his boots to try to stay warm during all of the loading and counting and checking, re-counting and re-checking.

Then, Jaromír Taussig left Prague for what would be the final time.

Though he did not know it, he was bound for Terezín, where he was to join two previous transports of workers who would prepare the garrison town of seven thousand for the reception of an estimated fifty thousand Jews.

*****

Jara's train puffed to a halt at Bohušovice station and slowly dribbled the thousand men and their belongings back out into the cold. Bohušovice was not their destination. From there, they would walk. The trees lining the street lifted their winter-deadened branches toward the chilly sky where the sun approached its midday peak. Its cold light glinted from windows, behind which watchful townspeople shifted. The Ohře and Eger rivers flowed somewhere nearby; the new settlement lay somewhere further down the road. Later the volunteers — inmates — would build a railroad siding to carry transports two kilometres further, eliminating the walk from the Bohušovice station, and the eyes of the town's inhabitants.

Their destination was within a long hill covered with dead grass. A church steeple and a Nazi flag peeped from the hill's top. There was a town behind those grass-covered walls. The men had arrived at the fortress town of Terezín, enclosed by high bulwarks, encircled by an empty moat that was once flooded with water from the Eger for the town's defence, and which would become the camp's fruit and vegetable garden.

"This is Terezín," Jaromír said to himself. "This is where Princip and others were imprisoned for the assassination of Archduke Ferdinand and Sophie. Just across the river is Litoměřice, where Tomáš Maglič had his sawmill." Jara felt good, knowing where he was. "We aren't far from Prague at all," he thought, as the men passed through a normal-looking town, with ordinary homes and buildings lining a grid of streets. "Are we just passing through?" Jara wondered. "There is nothing here to construct."

By 1940 the Nazis had been tasked with turning Terezín into a ghetto and concentration camp. The Small Fortress at one end of the town had become a Nazi prison and the town itself became a Wehrmacht military base, with thirty-five hundred soldiers and thirty-seven hundred civilians living there in 1941. Now, with the departure of the soldiers and the arrival of the "volunteer" Aufbaukommando, the garrison town could be converted into a holding and transit centre for the Protectorate's Jews who were to be sent East. But Terezín would be disguised as a final destination, and billed as a resort for retired, famous, and decorated Jews. It would become a Potemkin village to fool the Allies into thinking the Jews were being well looked after.

On the surface, everything in the newly-converted settlement town was to be run by a Jewish council, the Judenrat, who would give the illusion of a self-governing society, while in reality taking orders from the Nazis concerning all facets of settlement life. The Jewish prisoners of Terezín would hardly see the Nazis. In fact, one of the Aufbaukommando's first orders was to construct tall

PRAGUE, OCCUPIED CZECHOSLOVAKIA
4 DECEMBER 1941

fences to separate the SS from the town's inhabitants.

Any remaining civilian residents of the town would leave. Their homes and the town's other buildings would have bunks built in them, from the ground floors up to the attics. A waterworks and appropriate sewage and sanitation facilities would be essential. A receiving area, with delousing and disinfecting stations would be required. Kitchens to feed thousands would be needed. During those early days, all the Aufbaukommando had by way of a kitchen was a single three hundred litre-capacity pot.

That night, Jara shivered beneath his overcoat, visions of his soft girlfriend and warm bed dancing in his head, as his hip- and shoulder-bones pressed painfully into the hard floor and his body shook with the inescapable cold.

SHANGHAI, CHINA
Monday, 8 December 1941

> *Get off my bloody ship!*
> – Lieutenant Polkinghorn
> Commander of the HMS *Peterel*

"AND THEN he said..." Captain Columbus Smith, commander of the USS *Wake*, paused for the punchline of his anecdote. "He said they were only curious about my whereabouts because they wanted to deliver a turkey to me!" He roared with laughter.

"A turkey?" I asked.

"Tonight?" asked Judge Milton Helmick, who had recently returned from Sandy Tittman's stateside wedding to John Morris.

"Those Japanese are up to something," Captain Smith said.

"Thanksgiving was two weeks ago? Here, free turkey!" Helmick joked.

"Never mind the food shortage, the inflation. Have a turkey!" I howled.

Captain Smith and I were at a dinner party hosted by Judge Helmick at his flat in Haig Court. Sir Victor was gone. Viva was gone. Lucien Ovadia was somewhere at sea, having travelled around the world for a business deal — the sale of the Metropole — that had then fallen through.

Captain Smith, who commanded the gunboat called the USS *Wake*, was one of the last American military officials in Shanghai — and one of the last Allied military officials at all. Following the August departure of the British forces, the 4th U.S.

SHANGHAI, CHINA
8 DECEMBER 1941

"China" Marines had been pulled out in November.

One battalion of China Marines had left in the rain, going by bus to board the boat that took them over silted waters to the ship. The following day had seen better weather, and Shanghai had an opportunity to say goodbye.

At 9.00 the other battalion had begun their march, with the Marine band playing behind them as they moved from the corner of Avenue Road and Ferry Road towards the Race Course. There, they passed fifty ponies whose jockeys held American flags. Just past the Race Club, at the Foreign Y.M.C.A., a kilted Scot played his pipes from the balcony as the Marines marched by. On Nanking Road, when the battalion passed Jimmy's Kitchen, it was joined by Jimmy's orchestra, who formed up New Orleans-style behind the parade, playing swing music down the final block to the Bund, where most of Shanghai had gathered to see the men off.

We had listened disinterestedly to Colonel Samuel Howard — who had only been in Shanghai since mid-May, after all — as he gave a short speech. Then the Shanghai Refugee Institute played the Marines' Hymn and we watched the China Marines float away to board their steamship, leaving Shanghai, more or less, on its own.

About two hundred regular forces and Embassy guards remained, along with a few-dozen Allied naval members like Captain Smith, and his British counterpart, Lieutenant Polkinghorn, who manned the HMS *Peterel*. Polkinghorn's ship was small, like the *Wake*, and functioned as a radio station for the Consulate more than she did as a ship.

There was also the Shanghai Volunteer Corps, which consisted of a mere twelve hundred men at that time. My Czechoslovak half-company had taken over patrolling the borders of the British-American defence sector.

THE SUITCASE

Captain Smith said, "If something does happen—if the Japanese do come bearing 'turkeys'—most of my men are on shore leave for the weekend and won't be back until Monday morning."

I replied, "I am sure the Volunteer Corps will assist in every possible way."

"You think they would strike tonight?" Judge Helmick asked.

"I wouldn't put it past them," Smith said. "Why else would they call me about that turkey nonsense?"

"If you are here with us, and your men are on shore leave, then who's on the *Wake*?" I asked.

"The Quartermaster," Smith said. "Possibly a few others."

"I imagined it would be peaceful," Helmick said, referring to the possibility of a Japanese takeover. "If it does in fact happen."

"Not if, but when," Smith said, parroting the popular sentiment.

"I don't see how it could be peaceful," I said.

"Yes, we are certainly prepared for the alternative," said Smith.

Just three days previously, on 5 December, the British had warned: "[T]here is reason to believe that the Japanese are planning to 'take over' the Concession... The project has been discussed at several dinner parties lately..."

Western civilians had plans in place for what had always seemed like a hypothetical, far-away day. People buried their silver, hid their art, prepared to burn stacks of documents.

I personally had disposal plans in place for my brokerage documents on Kiukiang Road, my military papers at the S.V.C. headquarters, my diplomatic records at my little Czech office, and certain letters and effects at my flat. I also kept a suitcase packed with personal mementos and necessities, just in case.

"I don't suppose I'll see you fellows," Helmick mused. "If—

SHANGHAI, CHINA
8 DECEMBER 1941

when — they take over, I expect they'll take me prisoner."

"You definitely won't see me," Smith said. "I intend to put up one hell of a fight."

"Let's have a toast then, shall we? For all the days to come during which we may likely be hungry, sober, and otherwise uncomfortable — if not dead."

We raised our glasses, not knowing that it really was the last night; the time had indeed come.

As we toasted, John Alexander's warning words to me, "The Embassy won't be able to offer you any protection," repeated in my head. Alexander had asked, "Won't you take one of the last boats evacuating British citizens?"

How I wished I could!

I had said, "I have orders from my Army-in-Exile to await further instructions."

Should I have known that my own position was deteriorating just as rapidly as Shanghai's? Though I was unaware, the cliff upon which I had built my Tower had eroded with each accusation thrown against it.

In September, the rumour mill had worked hard against me. It was reported to London: "There is nothing tangible, but [Taussig] is reputed to have surreptitious contact with Axis elements. As a banker he does little business but is always in funds. He inspires little confidence in those who have been in personal contact with him here."

Someone at the Foreign War Office in Whitehall had defended me, writing: "Captain Taussig is a leading member of the local Czech Committee. There [is] nothing… to support that he [is] anything but a patriotic and pro-Ally Czech."

"But," the argument came, recall "the caveat in the Chancery's letter" — a reference to the note: "We here [in Shanghai] are not absolutely convinced of Taussig's pro-British sentiments."

THE SUITCASE

The result: "We are telegraphing to Shanghai to inquire further about his alleged suspicious activities."

If only someone had asked, I might have had a chance to explain what others had, perhaps, seen as suspicious activity. The War Stabilization Board had put new banking regulations into effect in August, and had killed my budding business with Eduard Kann.

But our business was, in part, a front for me to funnel money to Havlíček in Japan at the request of the Czech Government-in-Exile. Our office had stayed open, and off the black market, by performing small money transfers for "friends," but was otherwise at a standstill. Our impressive bank of seventy-two telephones rarely rang.

Meanwhile, with business so dead and income down, inflation had continued to grow and expenses had risen. It was a time when less-than-loyal Czechs changed their passports to German so that they could receive the Germans' supplemental funds, up to hundreds of dollars for those with children. I reported these traitorous passport-changers to the Provisional Government as cases of Fifth Column activity. All the names on my list were people who had previously received benefits from the Czechoslovak Support Court in Shanghai. I, too, was going hungry, but I would rather have starved than take a German passport, and I had no pity for those on my list.

Others surely wondered how I, who did little business and received no government funds, could afford to eat at Fiaker with regularity.

To ensure I had at least one adequate meal each day, I had traded my fur coat for lunches at the restaurant. I also banked on the owners' gratitude for my assistance establishing their restaurant. Our arrangement was that I would eat whatever simple fare the staff threw together for their own meal. All the

SHANGHAI, CHINA
8 DECEMBER 1941

while, across the dining room, I watched Rhody Hall and other American diplomatic staff gorge themselves on lunches that could have fed two, while Hall drank martini after martini.

Was it any coincidence that the covert naysaying in secret telegrams and letters coincided with my finally moving troops out of Shanghai? Was it any coincidence that, that same month, September, Havlíček was arrested in Tokyo?

The October follow-up to Havlíček's arrest said that the arrest was "made by the Japanese Gendarmerie, at the instigation of the German Gestapo" and was "further evidence of the growing hold of the Gestapo over the police and the people of Japan... [O]ne of their aims in engineering these... arrests... is to... estrange Japan still further from the democratic powers, and tighten the Nazi hold on Japanese policy."

I had been warned by friends in the French police that I was being followed. I had been told that I was on the Nazis' "short list." Was I the next target for arrest? If, or rather when, Japan took control of the Settlement, what would be my fate?

A further complication:

On 8 November, John LeRougetel had received a message from General Ingr of the Czechoslovak Government-in-Exile that authorized me to "look after Czech military matters in the Far East." Ingr was two years too late in granting me that power. Ingr's authorization didn't matter—LeRougetel withheld the message.

"In the circumstances"—my alleged suspicious activities and anti-British behaviours—"I am deferring action," LeRougetel wrote. "Taussig is now stated to have expressed strong anti-British views when he thought it safe to do so. In view of this and of the suspicious factors reported in my telegram under reference, I cannot accept any responsibility for Taussig."

The recipient of LeRougetel's message replied with a warning that it would not be possible to withhold Ingr's instructions for me indefinitely. Then, about a week later, on 15 November, opinions changed and it was agreed that LeRougetel should not deliver Ingr's message for me. Might a suggestion be made for a suitable replacement? The Czechoslovak military authorities expressed a willingness to accept any recommendation that might be made.

When I tried to help the government, my messages were delayed for months. When outsiders defamed me, messages flew between desks in a matter of days.

On 6 December, the night before my dinner party with Smith and Helmick, the formal request had been sent between the British authorities:

6th December, 1941.
From: Frantisek Nosek, Czechoslovak Ministry of Foreign Affairs, London
To: Frank Kenyon Roberts, Esquire, British Foreign Office, London

Dear Mr. Roberts,
The Czechoslovak Military Attaché in London was informed during a visit to the War Office on the 17th ult., that according to the reports of the British authorities in Shanghai, Mr. V.G. Taussig, who was entrusted with the enrolment of Czechoslovak volunteers at Shanghai, has made disloyal remarks about Great Britain, and therefore cannot be further recognized as a Czechoslovak representative.

I should be extremely grateful for further particulars about this matter, and I am, therefore writing to ask if you would kindly let me know whether the British

SHANGHAI, CHINA
8 DECEMBER 1941

authorities at Shanghai, after conferring with Mr. Stepan, our representative there, could suggest to us some other suitable person to take charge of our volunteer organisation. This seems to us the most satisfactory method of dealing with the matter as rapidly as possible.

> Yours sincerely
> F. Nosek

Clearly, replacement would have taken place—not that there would have been anyone suitable available to fill my shoes—had the Japanese takeover of Shanghai not shattered our entire world.

*****

Captain Smith also kept a flat at the Metropole. He and I headed home from Helmick's at quite a late hour, sometime around four o'clock on the morning of Monday, 8 December.

"I expect an invitation to a full turkey dinner this evening," I joked to Smith as we parted. Then I was alone in the lift with the operator. I never saw Smith again.

"Thirteenth floor, sir?" the Boy asked.

In my room I found a copy of the bill, handed over to Cheng earlier in the day while I had been away. The bill showed a zero balance. The previous afternoon, before Helmick's dinner party, one of Sassoon's managers had erased November's bill at the Metropole and had paid me my small, but now-vital commission for the "copper trick" back in 1935. This was very important to me; I had no money.

On the desk sat a letter I had written to my mother in mid-

THE SUITCASE

October, before I had been instructed to "stay put" in Shanghai. My letter to Prague had recently been returned as undeliverable. "It's been a long time since I received news from you but I hope you are all well and in good health," I had written. "Many people have left and closed their businesses and I intend to do the same and go and see Francy in New York." This was written before I had been told to stay and await orders. "My dear sweet mother," I had written, "I have been thinking of you very much and I keep hoping."

Francy had told me how our mother had written, from the third relocation: "I have no idea how long we'll be staying here." And, "Don't send anything anymore. It would be in vain now because I cannot give you any further address."

What was going on in Prague?

I put my pyjamas on. I looked in the mirror. I look tired and boozy. I slipped on my housecoat and slippers and stepped onto my roof terrace to smoke. The thought of my bed, clean sheets turned down and waiting for me, was a happy one indeed.

I looked to Big Bertie. It was about four thirty; I would be able to get plenty of sleep before my next obligation.

My eye was suddenly drawn to movement down on the river. The moon had been full a few nights before, and was bright enough to make out the shapes of Smith's ship, and the British *Peterel,* amid the hulking Japanese and Italian battleships.

Had I looked closely enough, I might have seen two little boats, carrying small groups of Japanese officers who rowed their way through the murky waters towards the *Wake* and the *Peterel*. I might have seen the Japanese board the American and British ships.

On board, the Japanese sought the ships' commanders, in order to present written instructions of surrender. On the USS *Wake* they had found the ship's commander absent. Smith had

SHANGHAI, CHINA
8 DECEMBER 1941

only just returned to the Metropole. When the fighting began, he would take a car to the wharf, but he would be too late to save his ship. In Smith's absence, the highest-ranking officer, the Quartermaster, surrendered. In the course of the war, the *Wake* would be the only U.S. ship to surrender without a fight.

The *Wake* was anchored about fifty yards from the *Peterel*. On board the *Peterel*, the Japanese were met with resistance. Unlike Smith, the ship's captain, Commander Polkinghorn, was present that night, and had in fact just received a call informing him that the Japanese had bombed Pearl Harbour in America and British territories in the Pacific, that Britain was at war with Japan, and that since, "Obviously there is nothing [Polkinghorn] can do with the forces at [his] disposal," they "would suggest [he] strike [his] colours." He planned to do no such thing and was prepared to scuttle the ship using pre-wired depth charges.

Polkinghorn refused the command to surrender and ordered the Japanese off the ship. He instructed his crew, about fifteen of them, to man their battle stations, even though a few obsolete Lewis guns were their only real defence.

I did not see the Japanese rowboat moving away from the *Peterel*.

I only saw the red signal flare go up and cast the boats, large and small, in a garish light. The flare was a signal to the Japanese ship *Idzumo* and to the Japanese shore batteries to open fire from their positions along the French Bund and on Pudong Point. As soon as I saw the flare, before I could even take a breath, the concussion of massive guns rang out; shells whooshed into the river, spraying dirty water around the *Peterel*, whose Lewis guns rapidly rat-tatted at the ten-thousand ton Japanese battleship — a lapdog yapping at a bear. Alongside the *Idzumo* were torpedo boats, submarines, artillery boats, and even commercial boats that the Japanese had armed. It was a hopeless fight for the Allied

THE SUITCASE

gunboat. The *Peterel* soon broke into flame and began to capsize, but she still fired her guns until the moment the men abandoned ship. They swam toward the riverbank, even as they were being fired upon from that direction.

Lightning had struck the proverbial Tower.

I took a drag of my cigarette and turned towards my rooms. Inside, I began enacting my plan.

Since I had no idea how quickly the Japanese would occupy the International Settlement, especially with the help of two hundred members of the Nazis and several hundred uniformed fascists, I took all of my correspondence with the Ministry of National Defence, principally the names of our Czechoslovak volunteers, and burned all of it in the hotel furnace.

My overcoat lay where I had left it on my return from our dinner party. I put it on over my pyjamas. I then took my pre-packed suitcase down to the car. Letters, photographs, and important mementos were in that suitcase. I also brought down a small trunk containing clothing and supplies.

I drove to the brokerage office on Kiukiang Road and burned all the papers I could find there. No one stopped me on the road or at the office. In fact, there was no sign of Japanese troops anywhere. The only other hints of life were other small smoke trails springing up in furnaces and fireplaces around Shanghai.

The streets were still dark when I returned to my hotel. There was not much else to be done but perhaps to get a little sleep while such a thing was still possible. I laid down just before sunrise, leaving the door unlocked so the Japanese might let themselves in when they arrived.

I closed my eyes.

*****

SHANGHAI, CHINA
8 DECEMBER 1941

At daylight, the Japanese soldiers who had stood at the International Settlement's boundaries since the end of the Battle of Shanghai finally crossed into the Settlement. Some troops rolled down the Bund, others down Nanking Road and towards the Race Course—light tanks, armoured cars, lorries of Special Naval Landing Forces and Japanese Marines, columns of foot soldiers with bayonets at the ready. Twenty thousand men. As they marched, they plastered posters that read: "These premises now under Japanese control." "Rising Sun" flags rose in their path.

Aeroplanes flew overhead, dropping leaflets printed in various languages that read: "His Imperial Japanese Majesty has declared war on the United States and the United Kingdom and, for Shanghai's protection, the army will enter the International Settlement. Citizens should continue the pursuit of their normal avocations and avoid creating disorder."

I dozed as the Japanese marched their way towards the Metropole.

They entered the building and crossed the quiet, white lobby, bright with morning sun. They moved room by room.

After what seemed to me like mere moments of rest, there came a frightful pounding on my door. It was all but kicked in, even though I had left it unlocked in expectation of a visit.

Before I could sit up and say, "Good morning," I was harshly removed from my bed and escorted from my rooms.

"Impressive," I said, "I must be quite important to be among the first to be taken for questioning."

It was to be the first of many interrogations in what had finally become Jap-occupied Shanghai.

Part Three

Historical Interlude

WHEN THE JAPANESE finally occupied Shanghai on 8 December 1941, their "peaceful penetration" of the populace began. Banks and businesses were taken over. Rental properties were confiscated, and Western tenants were gradually dispossessed and replaced with Japanese tenants. The Japanese population in Shanghai would balloon from about ten thousand to two hundred and fifty thousand. The Shanghai Municipal Council was replaced by a provisional council and John Liddell, the last chairman of the S.M.C., was interned and replaced by a Japanese man, Katsuo Okazaki.

The various nationalities present in Shanghai were redefined by their relationship to Japan. Specific individuals were also targeted for financial or political purposes. Enemies of Japan were subjected to depraved treatments in facilities like Shanghai's notorious Bridge House. Desperation grew. Some attempted to escape into Free China. Others, knowing themselves to be stuck, hoped to wait out the invaders—a tactic they had, perhaps, learned from the Chinese.

Recently arrived stateless European refugees from Nazism were not considered enemies of the Japanese, but died from sickness and hunger in centres that housed thousands. One can only imagine the conditions the native Chinese, who were the enemies of the Japanese, faced.

*****

THE SUITCASE

In Europe, the Nazis held the Wannsee conference on 20 January 1942 just across the lake from the Schichts' Berlin villa. There, fifteen Nazi officials gathered to affirm their "Final Solution," and cemented plans for the mass deportation and murder of the Jewish population and other "undesirables."

The Wannsee conference also presented an opportunity to incorporate the role of Terezín as a waystation to the East, as a place to hold prestigious and important Jews whose absence would be apparent, and as a Potemkin village that would mislead anyone inquiring after those who had been sent eastward to their deaths in concentration camps and killing centres. Questions were anticipated because, by June, reports had reached the Allies that gas was being used to murder Jews who had been sent "East."

The so-called President of the Nazi Protectorate of Bohemia and Moravia, Emil Hácha, remained a collaborationist puppet. In September 1941, Reinhard Heydrich became the acting Reichsprotektor. Heydrich was fatally injured during an attack by Czech resistance fighters on 27 May. Jozef Gabčík and Jan Kubiš, along with other Free Czechoslovaks who had been airlifted to Czechoslovakia from Britain's Cholmondeley Castle, were responsible for Heydrich's assassination.

The Reichsprotektor succumbed to his injuries on 4 June.

As punishment, on 10 June, the Czech town of Lidice was destroyed, and its inhabitants were massacred, owing to suspicions about the town's involvement in the assassination plot.

A fortnight later, a second village, Ležáky, was also destroyed.

By the time of Ležáky's late-June 1942 destruction, both Julie and Marietta Taussigová had been sent to join Jaromír in Terezín.

*****

HISTORICAL INTERLUDE

By the late summer of 1942, Vladimír Taussig had managed to "wangle" his way onto a ship for inclusion in an arranged diplomatic exchange between Allied and Japanese-occupied countries. Six ships would descend on the exchange point, Lourenço Marques, Mozambique: the *Kamakura Maru*, the *Tatuta Maru*, the *Narkunda*, the *City of Canterbury*, the *City of Paris*, and the *El Nil*.

Since the Czechoslovak Government- and Army-in-Exile had relocated from Paris to London, Taussig was bound for England.

Leaving Lourenço Marques
Portuguese Mozambique
Sunday, 13 September 1942

> *"Send Airmail Madeira Care Diplomatic Ship* Narkunda
> *Proceeding London. Love Vlada Taussig."*
> —Telegram from Vladimír to Francy

I ENTERED THE SS *Narkunda*'s first-class dining salon. The supremely pleasing sounds of Edvard Grieg's Piano Concerto in A Minor reverberated all the way to the enormous open atrium. Already this ship surpassed our previous transport ship, the *Kamakura Maru*.

Most passengers smiled and chatted. We were escaping the grip of Japanese control. The mood was relaxed for the first time since we had left Shanghai, or, for many, for the first time since the Japanese takeover.

The top-ranking British passengers were already seated and talking amongst themselves. As I stood and scanned the room, I heard someone ask, "Can you really blame them for wanting one last jab at us?"

"I can, and I do," came the stubborn reply. "It was horrible. I haven't had clean water, a decent meal, or a good night's sleep since before we left Shanghai."

The Japanese captain of the *Kamakura Maru* had amused himself and his crew by subjecting the Allied diplomats and higher-ups to an embarrassing class-reversal. High-ranking diplomats had been given cabins in steerage, while junior staff

LEAVING LOURENÇO MARQUES
13 SEPTEMBER 1942

members and ordinary businessmen were placed in the first-class cabins.

As I scanned the salon, one table in particular drew my attention. There was Consul-General Sir Tony George, who still looked unwell. He was a month free from Japanese imprisonment in Bridge House. Next to him was John Alexander, Press Attaché, organiser of the Inter-Allied Federation, founding member of The Nine-Fifteen Club. Next, John LeRougetel of the Foreign Office. As I looked around the table, my heart leapt when I locked eyes with LeRougetel, who was staring directly at me.

I shifted my gaze to another table, where Ellis Hayim, the millionaire taipan in whose gardens the Follies had been presented, was seated. Like Tony George, Hayim had been deplorably mistreated by the Japanese during his imprisonment at Bridge House. Near Hayim was Charles Arkwright, Sassoon's representative, a fellow member of The Nine-Fifteen Club, and of various Jewish relief committees. Arkwright had served on committees alongside my former business partner, Eduard Kann.

Other tables were filled with junior diplomatic staff members and other underlings; businessmen and bankers of various sorts; and wives, nannies, and children.

I saw the Czechs and moved to find my seat amongst them. The Czechs on board consisted of men I had recruited and trained in the Shanghai Volunteer Corps who were now on their way to join the Army-in-Exile, as well as various others — businessmen, doctors, and the like. There were about thirty of us on board.

As I approached my table, I performed a mental roll call of my Czech squad: Aschenbrenner, Bock, the Feder brothers, the Groszmann brothers, Kroha, Kulka, Rebenfeld, Rebhuhn, Rosenfeld, Schick, Subert, and Wltzek. All present and accounted for.

The Czechs were seated near various other non-British

nationals. I was pleased to see my friends, Netherlands Consul-General Gideon Boissevain and his wife Daisy, adjacent to my own place.

"Boissevain, how have you been?" I asked. "I have not seen you since the night you turned yourself over to the Japanese."

On 16 December, shortly after the Japanese occupation, I had attended a bridge party where Boissevain was present. At that time, unbeknownst to us in Shanghai, the oil-thirsty Japanese captured three cities in Dutch Borneo to claim the oil fields there. When men from the nearby Dutch airfield retaliated, the Dutch became enemies of the Japanese—though Japan would not officially declare war on the Netherlands until 10 January.

Boissevain nodded. "Yes, that was certainly a shock. Imagine being in the midst of a bridge party and then the telephone rings with instructions to report to the Japanese embassy in an hour's time. At least we are now bound for England, and not interned somewhere."

Boissevain was now heading for Britain because his government, under Queen Wilhelmina, was in exile there.

"What did you think of Lourenço Marques, Taussig?" Boissevain asked.

Many had spent their time awaiting exchange in Mozambique enjoying the exotic scenery: the white beaches and palm trees, the hippos in the river, the grapefruit trees and pineapple plants. Many had gone for cocktails and iced Portuguese wine at the Polana Hotel, or a bit of fun at Costa's Casino and dance hall.

"I spent most of my time queuing in the telegram office," I said.

The office had been full of other repatriates sending messages, and with journalists who had been sitting on stories since the December occupation. No one had been able to publish stories or send letters the censors may have found disagreeable. Any

LEAVING LOURENÇO MARQUES
13 SEPTEMBER 1942

reports of life under Japanese occupation had to reflect the official standpoint of the Dōmei Tsushin, the Imperial Japanese news agency.

When it was my turn at the telegram office, I sent word to the Government-in-Exile, and to Francy in America. I informed Francy that I was en route to London and gave her the name of our ship, lest anything should happen to us. The waters we sailed contained pirates, as well as enemy ships. In spite of the repatriation ships' obvious markings — giant crosses, and even the word "DIPLOMAT" painted onto the hull — we remained a target for boats and aeroplanes.

I just hoped that the safe-conduct agreement under which we travelled would hold, and no enemies, or friends, would attack. We were well over capacity and there were not nearly enough lifeboats to accommodate the repatriates. What with all the children, women, and "important" British passengers on board, I had no doubt that, if trouble came, my men and I would be sunk with the ship.

While in Lourenço Marques, I had also asked Judge Helmick, who would be repatriated to the States, to reach out to Francy and inform her that I had been safe when last he saw me. Whatever happened to me at sea, news of me would eventually reach her.

Our meals were delivered to us, and the diners quieted. All were focused intently on the foods before them.

"You will excuse us," Boissevain said as he, too, turned his attentions downwards to the table.

I took the opportunity to speak to Aschenbrenner, who sat next to me. "Have you seen the exercise room?" I asked. "We should all be making use of it," I said, looking from him to the few others of my soldiers who were seated nearby. "And perhaps some jogging on the promenade decks is in order, hm?" Without giving obvious and direct orders in front of the other Czechs, I tried to make plain that I wanted the men to be as fit as possible when we arrived in Britain.

The men nodded, then tucked into their food.

I was pleased when, as the meal ended, Boissevain got my attention. "Taussig, I understand there are a few card games to be had this evening. Perhaps you'll join me later in the smoking room?"

"I shall be there with knobs on," I said. "But if the Japanese should happen to telephone you during this card game — don't answer!" Boissevain gave a weak smile but did not laugh.

As I left the dining salon, I stopped at the table of Brits where Tony George, John Alexander, John LeRougetel, and others were seated. Any warm welcome I might have received from Alexander, whom I had considered a friend, was dampened by LeRougetel's presence and comments.

"How did Taussig manage to weasel his way on board?" he asked his companions without looking at me, unmasked venom in his voice.

I bristled but did not take his bait. I had nothing to prove or to explain to the man, who seemed intent on demeaning and dismissing me. I gave a short, uncomfortable laugh but did not respond.

He scoffed and said, "Here is a man who, from what I understand, left Shanghai at the outbreak to join up, but then mysteriously returned, offering no explanation, then masqueraded around as some sort of military attaché. Now here he is in our midst, when other worthy individuals were left behind in Shanghai at the mercy of the Japs."

This did elicit a response. "You, who only arrived in Shanghai last summer, are one to talk!" I said.

"Because I have not been so long in Shanghai, I see things more clearly than my compatriots. I am not fooled by you."

LEAVING LOURENÇO MARQUES
13 SEPTEMBER 1942

Any one of the other men at the table might have defended me to their countryman—they had known me socially for some years before my diplomatic debut. But none chose to contradict LeRougetel. Instead, they shifted uncomfortably in their seats and took sips of their drinks or looked down at the tabletop.

"You are occupying a valuable place on this ship. You, who are nothing more than an exchange broker," LeRougetel sneered.

I laughed. Nothing more than a broker. I, who had been sent back to Shanghai specifically to fulfil certain military duties — reporting from a military perspective, disseminating pro-Allied and pro-Czech propaganda in print and on the radio, contributing to every possible Allied effort at my own time and expense. Nothing more than a broker! I, who, as we spoke, travelled with an entire squad of Czech soldiers that I myself had recruited and trained under the nose of the Japanese.

I said, "When we reach England, I wouldn't be surprised if I am given a special commendation for my work in Shanghai."

LeRougetel laughed. "Well I would be surprised. Quite surprised indeed. Good evening." He attempted to dismiss me.

"I work for the Allied cause. For truth. Freedom. Democracy. What do you know of those ideals? I thought others shared my position, but it is becoming starkly clear that you care only about the British. This conflict goes beyond any national lines—that is why it's called a World War, gentlemen." I looked from man to man, then let my sights settle on LeRougetel. "Good evening, you blithering idiot."

I turned my back on LeRougetel's reddening face and walked away before he could say anything further. It had not been prudent to speak to him in such a manner in front of so many important passengers, but they were clearly not in my corner anyhow.

I left the dining salon and went out on to the *Narkunda*'s

THE SUITCASE

lighted decks. The sun had sunk below the horizon a full two hours before dinner. By the time I finished my meal, it was quite dark out on the water. But the ship travelled fully-lit at night, and the white lights glinted off the waves for some distance. Above us, a sliver of moon pierced the sky.

This ship, at least, sailed smoothly and lightly over the waters. The *Kamakura Maru* had to traverse the Indian Ocean, and the summer monsoon current had pitched and tossed us along the whitecaps for weeks. The *Narkunda* would find much smoother sailing up the African coastline.

As I stared out at the ocean, other passengers around me on the promenade stood at the rail or sat in chairs and talked. Elsewhere on the ship, games were starting up: bridge, chess, checkers, mah-jongg. Some evenings on our voyage, films would be shown. Other nights, passenger-studded variety acts would be staged.

At the appropriate hour, I made my way to the first-class smoking room. I found Boissevain seated and talking quietly with a passenger the *Kamakura Maru* had mysteriously taken on in Singapore.

A week after leaving Shanghai, the *Kamakura Maru* had stopped and was slowly led through a minefield. Passengers had been ordered belowdecks for this process, so we would not be privy to the route. Then, somewhere near Singapore, the ship refuelled and replenished its stores without docking. At that time, we were met by a motorboat, and the man who now sat with Boissevain had joined us on board. The passenger hadn't spoken much to the other repatriates. Who was he? Why had we taken him on in Singapore?

"Taussig, meet my countryman, Arthur Hartog," Boissevain said.

"The enigmatic Dutchman," I said with a smile. "Pleased to

LEAVING LOURENÇO MARQUES
13 SEPTEMBER 1942

meet you." I shook Hartog's hand.

"And you," Hartog said.

"I must say, many people have been curious about you," I said.

"Understandably," Hartog said. "I am glad to have been evacuated. I arrived in the East Indies in October to negotiate a new soap plant for Malaya. But by February, the Japanese had captured Malaya and the East Indies, making glycerine extraction for the Allies an impossibility."

Until that time, the Dutch had done well resisting the Japanese. Unlike the American Philippines, for example, the Dutch East Indies had been almost impenetrable to the Japanese. There were only seven thousand Japanese residents in the Indies before the takeover, and their economic activities were tightly controlled.

On the other hand, some thirty thousand Japanese resided in the Philippines — two-thirds of them in Davao, a commercial centre. There, the Japanese controlled plantations, lumber, and ore — precious resources for the war effort. Though the United States and Philippine forces had defended the islands for months, the Philippines had fallen to the Japanese in May 1942. I was glad my Czechs were not working in factories there, as I had once planned.

"A soap plant in Malaya..." I mused. So, the man was of some importance to the war effort.

Boissevain explained, "Hartog is a senior board member with Unilever." Many of the board members were representatives of the families from whose businesses the corporation had grown, like the Hartogs — and the Schichts.

"Unilever?" I asked. "You don't say! I simply must ask you, Mr. Hartog, whether you are acquainted with the Schichts? Unilever grew from the Schicht company in the Czech Sudetenland. My father, who was the agricultural commissioner in Prague, worked for the Schichts most of his life."

Hartog straightened. "Is that so? I do know George Schicht. He became a British subject before the war. His sons, Georg and Roland, have joined the British forces. The other Schichts, however…" he trailed off.

I nodded. "Franz and Heinrich."

"Yes, well, their loyalties lie elsewhere," Hartog said. "Neither Franz nor Heinrich remain on Unilever's board. Unilever aids the Allied war effort by all possible means," Hartog said. "Everything has been put at the British government's disposal. Most everything is managed from the London headquarters."

"How are things in Singapore?" Boissevain asked Hartog.

"Oh, probably no different than anywhere else under Japanese rule," Hartog said. "Inflation. Shortages. Internments. The Japanese Army has taken Raffles as their headquarters."

"Speaking of Japanese rule," I said, "tell me, how were things for you on the *Kamakura Maru*?" I asked Boissevain. "I know they delighted in treating the diplomats poorly, but what happened belowdecks that had poor Daisy so out of sorts? I don't believe she said a single word to me earlier."

"Oh, it was awful," Boissevain said. "I knew there was an end in sight, but it still wore on me. I have hardly slept since we left Shanghai because our berths were so near the engine room."

"It was hot enough without being near the engines," I said. "And you had no portholes."

Boissevain nodded. "And the constant noise and rumbling was dreadful. Dreadful! The accommodations weren't the worst of it," Boissevain said. "I'm sure you have heard about mealtimes. We formed a line before a madly-grinning Jap who stood at an enormous pot and slopped unidentifiable mush into our mess kits."

"I am sure they were delighted if you showed any expression

LEAVING LOURENÇO MARQUES
13 SEPTEMBER 1942

of disgust," I said.

Our meals in first-class had been served on linens, with real dishes and cutlery. We had even been provided with menus, which boasted dishes like "sunflag ham" and "essence of chicken," followed by wine and brandy and cigars.

"The worst of it," Boissevain continued, "was that, since we travelled over capacity, they used some of the fuel tanks to store water. The water we were given reeked of diesel fuel. I don't care if I never smell that wretched stuff again in my life."

"No wonder Daisy had such a hard time," I said. "I am glad you are back in civilised hands."

"Quite," Hartog said.

Boissevain sighed. "Yes. Civilised is an understatement. I cannot believe the shit they put us through. And yet, when I look at those who were been interned in Bridge House, I think how much worse it might have been. How were things for you?" he asked.

"It seems almost trivial, compared to your own experiences," I said, "but quite a lasting impression was made on me by a monkey that belonged to one of the crew members."

Hartog nodded.

"Most of the Japanese I have known—the businessmen anyway—always treated animals quite well. But this poor monkey on the *Kamakura Maru* was constantly tormented by members of the crew. They would pet it, and, while its guard was down, they would affix pliers to its ear. They would then yank them away, nipping the poor thing's flesh, and howling with laughter when the monkey screamed and screeched. It angered me to no end."

Hartog agreed. "The son of the Swiss Chief Delegate also mentioned these incidents. He felt powerless to intervene, as upsetting as it was."

THE SUITCASE

"How cruel," Boissevain said. "Surely they only did it to get a rise out of the Allied nationals."

"Whatever their reason," I said, "you can learn a great deal about a man from the way he treats animals and other helpless creatures."

Boissevain asked, "Because you were above decks on the *Kamakura Maru*, I can only imagine that you were included as a civilian, and not as a Czechoslovak Military Attaché?"

"That is correct," I said. "As you know, Japan does not recognize Czechoslovakia as a country." I stopped short of sharing my feelings of gratitude that I hadn't had to endure the same treatments Boissevain and the other diplomats had faced.

While the cards were shuffled and we entered into a three-handed poker game, I told my companions how I had managed to find a place on the repatriation ship:

"When it came time for the evacuation from Shanghai, I was initially told that no Czechs would be included in the exchange. Then, three or four days before the ship's departure, the Japanese consulate informed us that eighteen Czechs would be allowed to board the ship. Through my connections with the Swiss, I sent a cable to Foreign Minister Jan Masaryk in London. Because the Swiss Red Cross was responsible for the evacuation, I asked Masaryk to have the Red Cross suggest to the Foreign Office in Tokyo that I be included in the exchange list, as a representative of the Czech Army. While I waited for word from the Provisional Government in London, I also took matters into my own hands. I thought of a pretext under which I could visit the Japanese Consulate and plead my case. I decided that the best approach would be an indirect one."

Boissevain agreed.

I continued, "The Japanese had issued an order that people who were to be exchanged could not take any gold or silver with

LEAVING LOURENÇO MARQUES
13 SEPTEMBER 1942

them, even in coins or gold bars. So, I gathered some souvenir silver coins I had collected from various places in the Far East, and I went to see Mr. Banjo, the Japanese Vice-Consul in charge of the exchange. I brought a Swiss consular official with me."

"Fontanel?" Boissevain asked.

I nodded. "Yes, Emil Fontanel. At our meeting with Banjo, I played stupid. I said, 'I understand the exchangees are prohibited from taking any gold or silver, but I wonder if an exception might be made for these souvenir coins?' And I showed him the coins in question. As I expected, Banjo immediately went to the list of repatriates. 'I do not see your name included in the exchange,' he said. That was when my Swiss friend intervened. He said, 'But Mr. Taussig is an official of Czechoslovakia; his name should be included in the list for exchange.' Banjo started in with the old song-and-dance about how my country was occupied by Nazi Germany and that Japan didn't recognize Czechoslovakia, and therefore did not recognize my position. That was all fine and well. The important thing about our meeting was that my name had appeared as a blip on Banjo's radar."

"Clever," Hartog said as he studied his cards.

"Two days after the meeting with Banjo, I was told that I would be allowed onto the ship. Then, a day before the *Kamakura Maru* sailed, more Czechoslovaks were included in the exchange." I did not mention it to Boissevain and Hartog, but I had tried to ensure that as many trained-and-ready soldiers as possible made it onto the ship with me.

Boissevain said, "From what I understand, you weren't the only one who managed to find a place on the ship. I have heard people refer to the *Kamakura Maru* as the 'Wangle Maru' because certain people 'wangled' their way on board."

I gave a little laugh. "It was certainly worth trying. I do not envy those we left behind."

THE SUITCASE

Hartog said, "May I ask, Taussig, what would have happened if you had stayed on in Shanghai?"

"In the worst case," I replied, "if the Japanese had any idea what I had been up to, I imagine I would have been imprisoned in Bridge House. I avoided that fate on a few different occasions. Surely you have seen some of our shipmates who were imprisoned and tortured there, and how it affected them."

Hartog nodded.

Boissevain explained, "Bridge House was a hotel that the Japanese used as a prison. After the Japanese occupation, even prominent Shanghailanders began disappearing into Bridge House in the middle of the night."

"Awful place," I said. "The Japanese Gendarmerie made Bridge House notoriously wretched. Prisoners were kept in conditions worse than those of the lowliest coolie, crammed together in wooden cages without room to either fully stand up, or to fully lie down. They relieved themselves in buckets, in full view of the others, and were tormented by lice, vermin, disease, and abuses both mental and physical… cigarette burns, kicking and flogging, blows to the head, the 'knee spread,' electric shocks, the 'water cure,' and constant threats of execution. And these were regular civilians, not people trained to withstand such mistreatments. My Boy, my former business partner, and my business partner at the time were all subjected to such tortures."

"Who?" Boissevain asked.

"Eduard Kann, and Frederik Mijsberg, your countryman," I replied.

Boissevain shook his head.

I sighed. "I am just grateful to be on this ship, with you fine gentlemen, and to be bound for London."

*****

LEAVING LOURENÇO MARQUES
13 SEPTEMBER 1942

THE *NARKUNDA* travelled slowly up the coast of Africa, staying within an assigned area each day.

I sent Francy another telegram from Cape Town, South Africa, when the ship stopped there on 17 and 18 September. From Cape Town, the *El Nil*, a smaller ship that had participated in the exchange, followed us the rest of the way.

After three more weeks at sea, we stopped again off the coast of French West Africa in St. Vincent Harbour in the Cape Verde Islands. As we left the Islands, we entered the danger zone. We were told to wear life vests at all times. The weather grew colder.

In the wee hours of 10 October, the *Narkunda* entered the Mersey Canal outside of Liverpool, and we encountered the soon-familiar sights of barrage balloons and AA guns, blued-out headlights and blacked-out buildings. These were grim reminders that the Germans were nearby in France. I was told that, in spite of precautions, German pilots navigated by the lights of neutral Dublin and easily found British cities.

The smaller *El Nil* docked first; the *Narkunda* waited midstream overnight before moving to Princess Landing Stage. The following morning, the nearly nine-hundred passengers crowded the ship's rails as we waited to disembark. I stood with my suitcase in hand, watching the dock workers, reporters, police officers, and Ministry of Health officials on the docks below.

It was then that we were boarded by the British Security Police.

I heard someone say my name, and, in an instant, I was met by grim-looking uniformed men, their bayonets pointed at me as if I was the enemy.

In full view of the other passengers, I was relieved of my luggage and escorted from the ship at bayonet point. Amongst the faces in the crowd I glimpsed the smug-looking LeRougetel, the surprised Boissevains, and the astonished Czech soldiers. Inwardly, I was mortified.

Outwardly, I joked as I was taken into custody: "Some porters they've got here in England!"

London, England
Thursday, 15 October 1942

"Something is rotten in the state of Denmark."
— William Shakespeare, *Hamlet*, I. iv

I SAT IN a dim and chilly panelled room in the London Reception Centre at the Royal Victoria Patriotic School, a sprawling Gothic building. I stared at the empty chair across the table and wondered when Weisner would enter for the day's interrogation.

I had been held since my arrest on 12 October. The whole ordeal was pointless, and frustrating. The gloomy weather and wartime atmosphere in Britain in general also lent themselves to my overall foul mood. To say nothing of the fact that, with each passing day I was detained there, my peers from Shanghai were loose in London, doubtlessly gossiping relentlessly regarding my fate.

Bedřich Weisner, my interrogator from the Czechoslovak Ministry of National Defence, had continually assured me that my treatment was entirely routine. In fact, MI5 interrogators would interview at least thirty thousand newly-arrived immigrants to England throughout the war, including others from my own ship. But as far as I saw it, I had been the only one embarrassingly and infuriatingly arrested at bayonet-point, as if I, Vladimír Taussig, posed a security threat. My attestations to Weisner had, I hoped, proved my status as a trustworthy and democratic-minded Czech officer who should be of use to the Allies.

THE SUITCASE

As I waited that day, I considered some of those who had looked smugly on during my arrest. Then there had been the surprised expressions of my friends, with whom I had surely lost face. I thought of my father, and his insistence that the Taussig character would prevail in me—as it had. The adventurous adolescent I had been during the Great War, the man I had been when I left Prague in disgrace, and the man I had been when I had lived the high life in Shanghai, had, at the outbreak of the Second World War, begun to give way to the sort of man I wished my father had lived to see. All the good I had done, for my people and for my country, and yet I had been treated as a criminal. It was clear that the Czech Government-in-Exile, who had entrusted me with such serious tasks in Shanghai, had not informed the British of my status.

The door opened; in came Weisner. "Shall we run through it once more?" he asked. I had repeatedly been asked to recount my story, in writing and through our interviews. It was a thorough questioning, and the letters, reports, and photographs I had sent to the Government-in-Exile in London since my return to Shanghai all reinforced my story.

Weisner took his seat across from me, placed a folder on the table in front of him, and opened it. "So, how long did you live in Shanghai?"

"About ten years. From 1933 to '39, and from 1940 to '42. At the outbreak of war in Europe, I reported for duty in the U.S. and spent some months there before being sent back to the Far East."

"And you travelled all the way to the States to report for duty because...?"

"Because that was the nearest open consulate. Ours in Shanghai had been handed over to the Germans."

"As you have detailed in the reports made since your arrival."

"Yes. And I should like to add that I had a very nice life in

LONDON, ENGLAND
15 OCTOBER 1942

Shanghai before the outbreak, yet I left and fulfilled my duty to the military, travelling halfway around the world at great personal expense, to report."

Weisner glanced down at his notes. "And then in the spring of 1940 you were sent back to Shanghai."

"That is correct, yes. Copies of my letters from Španiel and Ingr should be in your file."

"And what assignment were you given?"

"I was instructed to report to the Exile Government in London from a military perspective, to disseminate pro-Czech and pro-Allied propaganda, to organise the Czechoslovak refugees in Shanghai–"

"Jewish refugees?" Weisner interrupted.

"Yes."

"And you, yourself are Jewish."

"I am." I paused, put off by the question. "I did all that was asked of me, and more. I enlisted and prepared these men as soldiers, so that they could join the Czechoslovak Army at the front. This training occurred within the extant framework of the Shanghai Volunteer Corps, with use of British instructors and equipment. I employed my contacts in print news and in radio for propaganda purposes, and my business and diplomatic connections to assist the refugees with securing paperwork and finding employment. These efforts were often, if not always, financed from my own pockets. I used my position as a broker to make transfers to Ambassador Havlíček in Japan, at great risk to myself and my business associates."

Weisner nodded. Unbeknownst to me, Havlíček had arrived in Liverpool just two days before my own arrival. He had likely already passed through the interrogation centre, giving a complementary accounting of these transfers and of my vital role.

"What became of the troops you trained?" Weisner asked.

THE SUITCASE

"Some were sent to fight last September, and a number were passengers on the *Narkunda*," I said. "I have provided you with those details."

"And the Czechs that remain in Shanghai?"

"There are a handful of old-timers and there are perhaps a few hundred recently-arrived refugees." I had mentioned to him before the names of those I trusted. My men in the S.V.C. My friends in the Voticky and Kanturek family. Their friend Professor Pribram. "Stepan and Štembera, whose names are surely already in your notes, are the most notable Czech authorities there, in my absence. Seba, the traitor who turned the consulate over to the Germans, is not to be trusted. The list I furnished — the names of people who exchanged their passports for German ones — those individuals are also not to be trusted."

My list would later be independently confirmed by a second list sent from Shanghai.

Weisner nodded and turned to another page in his notes. "Can you speak further about the Czechoslovak-German passport switching?"

I said, "I worked with the Czechoslovak Circle to provide recently-arrived Czech refugees, who swore allegiance to the Czechoslovak Government-in-Exile, with documents and an official address. The Nazis had taken the refugees' passports, so we provided identification papers saying they were bona fide refugees in good standing with the Circle. Meanwhile, most of the long-time Czech residents, who were not refugees, asked the German embassy for German passports. Not only did this make them friends of the Axis Japanese, but also there was a financial incentive. Germans attracted our countrymen by granting those who held a German passport a certain amount of local Central Reserve Bank currency."

"Which was?"

LONDON, ENGLAND
15 OCTOBER 1942

"Japanese puppet money. The occupation currency I described during our first chat."

"Would you care to explain it again?" Weisner shifted in his seat.

I began a long, and hopefully not confusing explanation, hoping someone without a financial background would understand the complexities of the situation. "The Chinese Central Bank functioned about the same as the National Bank of Czechoslovakia," I explained. "In January this year, the Central Bank was transformed into the Central Reserve Bank of China, and was made an organ of the puppet Nanking government headed by Chinese quisling Wang Ching-wei. The Central Reserve Bank issued federated Chinese notes which became the legal tender in Shanghai. The old Chinese dollar had been circulated by the government in Chungking. A rate was established to exchange two Chungking dollars for one new dollar."

Weisner laid his pen on the table and listened.

I continued, "The banks were directed to liquidate. A forced liquidation would happen when a bank belonging to the Allies decided to do only minimal business, for example the National City Bank of New York, which controlled around two billion U.S. dollars. The bank could not issue any funds or payments during the first weeks of the occupation. The Japanese insisted that the Allied banks must conduct all transactions with the Chinese Central Bank in cash, so not a lot of money was left for depositor transactions.

"The effect of this situation on the economic life of the city may well be imagined. Starting in June, the federated Chinese notes became the only allowable legal tender in Shanghai—at least, until the Japanese began printing occupation currency with no serial numbers. The Chinese farmers were forced to accept this new 'military yen' that the Japanese Army introduced on a large

THE SUITCASE

scale in occupied China, trading their valid Chinese government bank notes for the new occupation currency.

"Japanese merchants, knowing the notes were worthless, refused to accept the notes for the goods they sold to the farmers. Eventually the farmers, through effective passive resistance, forced the invaders to give some purchasing power to the billion yen in bogus notes which they had spread throughout North China and the Yangtse Delta Region."

Weisner said, "So. All transactions with Japan had to be conducted with the new occupation currency. And you said the Germans were giving three hundred 'local currency' to people holding German passports..."

"Yes, three hundred Local Currency for a single man, six hundred for a married couple, and one hundred fifty for each child. Inflation was high; food was scarce. Those of us who remained loyal Czechs, and who would never touch German money, were in a difficult position. I parted with many of my personal effects in order to finance my activities." My Kodak camera and projector were sold to a Jewish refugee shop in Rue Edward VII; my golf clubs and equipment were bought by an American sporting goods store on Nanking Road, Messrs. Squires Bingham, Inc. I sold some of my Chinese art and collectibles to friends. I traded my fur coat for lunches. I won a few hands of cards at the Swiss Club. "But I most certainly did not take a German passport or collect support money from the Nazi German government. I would sooner have gone hungry. At times, I did go hungry. Even the Czech Support Court's best efforts could only provide cracked wheat and other pitiful Red Cross-supplied staples."

Weisner's attention briefly returned to the folder on the table before him as he checked my statements against my previous reports.

LONDON, ENGLAND
15 OCTOBER 1942

"I was lucky to have gotten out," I added. "I was instructed to stay in Shanghai long after it was safe for me to stay there. I requested to join outbound troops on their transport, and I was told, by General Ingr, to remain in Shanghai. Because I stayed on so long, I lost my personal belongings, including six rooms in a warehouse that was looted by the Japs. I was detained and questioned by the Japs on numerous occasions and am grateful to have escaped with my freedom." I looked around the interrogation room. "Or relative freedom, anyway."

Weisner closed the folder and addressed me directly: "Well, Taussig, we are going to release you into the military's care."

"I should like nothing better. I want only to be of service to my country and my military."

"And it seems you shall have your chance." He rose from his seat and took the folder. I rose from my seat as well. "Your effects will be returned to you before your release."

I did receive my luggage, but I never received an apology for the embarrassment of my arrest. I left the Royal Patriotic School paperless and nearly penniless — and filled with questions.

*****

For bus fare, I used one of the souvenir coins I had shown to Banjo when wangling my way onto the repatriation ships. Across the Thames and past Buckingham Palace, about seven kilometres from the Royal Victoria Patriotic School, the Dutch legation in London was headquartered near Green Park. I arrived, with luggage in tow, near cocktail hour, and was invited to drinks with the Boissevains.

"We were interrogated too, you know," Daisy told me. "It was all quite routine." Clearly, as they had already been released, theirs had not been an in-depth interrogation like

THE SUITCASE

mine. Just as they had not been detained at bayonet-point, as I had been.

"All foreigners are processed through the Reception Centre," Gideon said as he took a sip of his drink.

"It is actually surprising to see you here so soon," Daisy said. "Some of our mutual friends are still being held for questioning."

"We certainly are glad everything went smoothly as far as you were concerned." Gideon exchanged a glance with his wife, then added, "Some people in Shanghai were talking quite some rubbish about you."

My posture snapped to attention in my seat; I placed my drink on the nearest table. "Who?" I asked.

The Boissevains declined to give further details, saying, "Please don't press us further," and, "You understand how delicate these things can be." They continued politely sipping their cocktails. Why was there this wall now between us? What had happened to my once-candid friends?

"I understand your hesitation to provide specific details," I said, "but please, even the vaguest of clues might be of use. I am, after all, on my way to report to my government and my army, and I should like to know what's been said about me so I might mitigate any potential harmful gossip. Was it one of my own countrymen?" I asked, looking from Gideon to his wife. "I can assure you that whoever spoke against me did not know the extent of my activities, and I can imagine why some of my doings may have raised suspicions. If the gossips came from a Czech, then it is a product of in-fighting, with derogatory remarks made in hopes of some sort of post-war commendation."

The Boissevains did not comment.

"Or perhaps it was a Brit or an American?" I asked, with John LeRougetel in mind.

"I understand your desire for details, but we really cannot

LONDON, ENGLAND
15 OCTOBER 1942

provide specifics," Daisy said.

"All that we do remember was that somebody or other was spreading stories that you are a member of the Fifth Column—a Nazi spy, or some similar nonsense," Gideon said.

"Well, clearly it's not 'nonsense,' given the ordeal I have just been through," I replied with thinning composure.

"I assure you, the interviews are quite routine," Daisy said.

I could feel the stress and frustration tightening in my chest. "So you have said. But my arrest was not." I named another suspect. "Was it Rhody Hall?" I asked.

Gideon said, "I can't quite recall..."

Daisy gave a wave of her hand and sipped at her drink. "One hears things. You know how it is." She gave a quick glance at Gideon.

"If Rhody Hall was indeed the source, then I can explain his suspicions," I said. I told how I had sold my fur coat for lunches at Fiaker and how I was seen twice to three times a week by Hall, who went there with his girlfriend for lunch. Surely he had been suspicious as to how I could continue to lunch at his level. "Hall could have concocted the story that I have dealings with the Axis, otherwise I could not possibly have any money. He is a drunken louse and his stories are not to be believed."

But the Boissevains refused to give further information. They would neither confirm nor deny my suspicions about any particular individual. I was going to get nothing further out of them—that much was clear. I thought to myself, if an American had been the source of the unpleasantness, then why would they protect that person now, instead of helping me, their friend? The Americans had been repatriated to the States, and Shanghai society had been forever scattered to the winds. Why protect some long-gone American official?

Gideon said, "We have got to be getting off to a dinner..." He stood, relieved to be ending the conversation. I took a final swig of my drink. So that was that.

I did not see the Boissevains again. Soon after our meeting, Gideon was appointed as Counsellor of the Netherlands Embassy in Washington and also began acting as the temporary charge d'affaires in Ottawa, Canada. He would also work for the U.S. Office of War Information for the Netherlands. Perhaps there had been something behind protecting his American colleagues after all.

In actuality, the gossips had come from LeRougetel, and from Rhody Hall, and probably from other sources as well. LeRougetel claimed that he suspected me of working with the Japanese, saying that I was a "suspicious individual" and that I was "suspected by all of the British Offices in Shanghai." He expressed an assumption that the Japanese would not have let me depart Shanghai without having some way to use me. He reported this to Lieutenant Colonel Kalla, Czech Military Attaché in London, who told the British War Office. LeRougetel also wrote to London about "rumours that [I] had surreptitious contact with Axis elements."

Then there was the "former British Army Communication Officer in the British consulate in Shanghai" who reported that it was suspicious that I had left to join the army, then returned after several months, without offering a clear explanation as to why I hadn't joined up. Instead, I had settled down as a broker and started living the "high life." This was bolstered by LeRougetel's statement that, as a broker, I had done very little business, and yet always had money. And that I "inspired little confidence" in those who had met me in Shanghai.

Rhody Hall had reported that the American offices were also suspicious of me, but that they had nothing concrete against me. Could it possibly have been because there was nothing

LONDON, ENGLAND
15 OCTOBER 1942

"concrete" to be had?

*****

On leaving the Boissevains, I found myself with no money and, apparently, no friends — and no idea where to spend the night before reporting for duty the following day. Dinner would have done me a power of good. Wasn't there anyone in London who had known me before Shanghai, and whose opinion of me was untainted by gossip?

I found an old family friend to visit with that night. She lived about four kilometres away from the Dutch Legation, just past Regent's Park, in a lovely home in St. John's Wood.

The wife, Karla, was a driver for an army general. The husband was the director of Marks and Spencer on Church Street in Liverpool. Every fortnight he returned to St. John's Wood to stay with Karla for the weekend. He would be coming home after I had already reported for duty.

Karla was, at that time, being kept company by another Czech woman, Lady Luisa Raudnitz-Abrahams, a skilled golfer and a former junior tennis champion. We made pleasant conversation over dinner. It was no five-course dining event, as the family was limited by rationing, but it was a far sight better than the fare I had had at the Reception Centre.

"Lady Luisa, how did you come to find yourself in Britain?" I asked.

She replied, "After I won the 1938 Ladies' Open in Mariánské Lázně — do you know it?"

"Certainly," I answered. "My mother and sisters have been to the spa there many times."

"Indeed," she nodded. "After my win there, I was invited to play here in England. That was February 1939."

I inhaled sharply. "I see." I could tell where the story was heading—the mid-March occupation.

"I was golfing in Richmond when Czechoslovakia was occupied, and I have been here ever since. Thank goodness for Karla, who has become like family to me." She reached over and patted her friend's hand.

"Tell him about the trousers," Karla prodded.

"The trousers?" I asked.

Lady Luisa gave a little laugh. "Well, when I knew I would be staying on in England, naturally I went to purchase clothing. I went into a department store called Aquascutum to purchase some trousers–"

"Quite shocking in its own right," Karla interjected.

"To some, yes," Luisa said. "Although now, with the war, no one would bat an eye at such a request."

"I suppose not," I said.

Karla said, "She was shopping for trousers at her future father-in-law's department store. Her husband's father owns Aquascutum."

"You don't say?" I asked.

"Yes," Lady Luisa smiled, "I met my soon-to-be husband, Sir Charles Abrahams, while buying trousers that day."

"Isn't that something," I said thoughtfully. "He must have been understanding of your need for comfort, especially while golfing..."

"I also wear them when I'm working with the Air Force," Lady Luisa added.

"Do you? The Air Force is an admirable way to serve!" I exclaimed. "Well. Tell me, are there a great deal of Czechoslovaks in London?"

"If you want to see Czechoslovaks," Karla said in between bites, "then you should try the Czech Centre in Clifton Gardens;

LONDON, ENGLAND
15 OCTOBER 1942

it's only about a kilometre from here, two at most."

Lady Luisa said, "I never go there. Too crowded for my tastes."

"The food is good," Karla said.

"Oh, I visit Isow's when I crave home-style food," Lady Luisa said to Karla. She added, for my benefit, "You never know who you'll see there—film stars, that sort of thing."

"Sounds like my sort of place," I said.

"So," Karla said, "You have been in Shanghai all this time, under Japanese occupation." I nodded. She asked, "Have you heard from your family? Have you heard much news at all from Europe?"

"They told me some time ago not to expect further letters. I do not want to make any trouble for them now. If the timing had been different, they would have joined me in Shanghai, but that never did pan out."

The ladies had seen alarming headlines regarding the Jews in Europe and were, in their roundabout way, inquiring after my own level of knowledge. Earlier that year, in March 1942, buried in the middle of the newspaper, a headline had read: "10,000 Jews Used as Guinea Pigs in Poison Gas Experiments." By that time, the Nazis had been experimenting with gas as a means of mass execution for three years. In June '42, the BBC ran an article stating that seven hundred thousand Jews had been murdered in the past year.

I had no idea that Beneš had, in January '42, published an article in *Foreign Affairs* entitled "Organization of Postwar Europe," wherein he stated that the pre-war system of minority protections had become "a burden upon the states that supported them," blaming the national minorities—the ethnic Germans and the Jews—for the occupation and dissolution of Czechoslovakia. Was it a coincidence that his statements aligned with the Nazis'

THE SUITCASE

Wannsee Conference? Was it a reaction to their propaganda, which had called Beneš "The White Jew" and accused him, daily, of being under Jewish influence?

Beneš had stated: "Minorities in individual states must never again be given the character of internationally recognized political and legal units, with the possibility of again becoming sources of disturbance." Minorities, he said, should be allowed to emigrate, so "they may gradually unite with their own people in neighbouring states." Ethnic Germans would return to Germany. "Jews would either move to Palestine or assimilate to their home nations. They would be Czechs, not Jews." I had always considered myself a Czechoslovak, not defined by my religion. That is, before the Nazis had declared themselves the Master Race and separated and persecuted us because of our Jewishness.

Meanwhile, the Czech Government-in-Exile was officially denying that there was any difference in the way the Nazis were treating the Jews, as opposed to non-Jews. Lies. The Government-in-Exile, with its connections in the "Protectorate" puppet government, in the Czech Resistance, and in Terezín itself, certainly knew the truth.

In November '42, the month after my conversation with Karla and Lady Luisa, a representative of the World Jewish Congress, Gerhart Riegner, would reveal that he had heard from authoritative sources that Hitler had discussed and was considering a plan wherein "all Jews in countries occupied or controlled [by] Germany, numbering 3½ to 4 million, should, after deportation and concentration in [the] East, at one blow [be] exterminated to resolve once and for all [the] Jewish question in Europe."

The Czech Government-in-Exile would dismiss this report as alarmist. Beneš would tell the World Jewish Congress that

LONDON, ENGLAND
15 OCTOBER 1942

he doubted the existence of a German plan "for a wholesale extermination of all the Jews."

One is reminded of those who tried to warn the United States against an attack from Japan, and who were ridiculed for sharing their suspicions.

In December, the Polish Government-in-Exile would send a note to the Allied governments entitled, "The Mass Extermination of Jews in German Occupied Poland," detailing "the mass murder of Jews" which had "reached such dimensions that, at first, people refused to give credence to the reports. The reports, however, were confirmed again and again by reliable witnesses. During the winter of 1941-1942," the note would state, "several tens of thousands of Jews were murdered." Poland would plead with the Allies to "find a means of offering the hope that Germany might be effectively restrained from continuing to apply her methods of extermination."

The Czech Government-in-Exile would then change its tune. During a visit to the States, Foreign Minister Masaryk would say, in December, that "Hitler's anti-Jewish madness grows in proportion with the imminence of his defeat. I have reliable reports of frightful massacres... It seems that millions of Jews will be slaughtered."

One week later, on 17 December 1942, British Foreign Secretary Anthony Eden would read a statement to the British House of Commons:

> [A]ttention... has been drawn to numerous reports from Europe that the German authorities, not content with denying to persons of Jewish race in all territories over which their barbarous rule has been extended, the most elementary human rights, are now carrying into effect Hitler's oft-repeated intention to exterminate

THE SUITCASE

the Jewish people in Europe.

From all the occupied countries Jews are being transported in conditions of appalling horror and brutality to Eastern Europe. In Poland, which has been made the principal Nazi slaughterhouse, the ghettoes established by the German invader are being systematically emptied of all Jews... None of those taken away are ever heard of again. The ablebodied are slowly worked to death in labour camps. The infirm are left to die of exposure and starvation or are deliberately massacred in mass executions. The number of victims of these bloody cruelties is reckoned in many hundreds of thousands of entirely innocent men, women, and children.

...[S]uch events can only strengthen the resolve of all freedom-loving peoples to overthrow the barbarous Hitlerite tyranny. They reaffirm their solemn resolution to insure that those responsible for these crimes shall not escape retribution, and to press on with the necessary practical measures to this end.

*****

But on that Friday morning, 16 October 1942, I left St. John's Wood to travel about two hundred kilometres to Lowestoft, a town on the most easterly part of England, where the Czechoslovak Brigade had, since August, been engaged in coastal defence duties. There, I reported for duty at Brigade Headquarters at the Dell Road School.

"Everyone starts from the ranks," I was told, and Reserve Captain Taussig of the Czechoslovak Army became a First Lieutenant of the Czechoslovak Army-in-Exile. I was given three

LONDON, ENGLAND
15 OCTOBER 1942

medical examinations and declared to be an especially perfect specimen of health.

Nevertheless, when, a few days after my arrival, I finally met with the Commander in Chief of the Czechoslovak Forces, General Bohus Miroslav, I was not given favourable news.

"Lieutenant Taussig, as I'm sure you are aware, there are already too many officers in the Brigade. We have, at this time, over two hundred officers, two hundred and fifty unposted, and twenty-five hundred other personnel."

"I was, until a couple of days ago when I reported here, a Captain." I presented to him my military book.

"Forty-two years of age," he said as he scanned my book. "Almost forty-three. I suppose I could assign you to the commanding reserve of an artillery regiment, but then, as a reserve officer, you would only be receiving reserve pay, you understand. Minimum wages for an unneeded military officer."

Unneeded? Did this man know who I was? The work I had done on behalf of the Czechoslovak Government- and Army-in-Exile? The risks I had taken? It seemed that one hand was completely ignorant of what the other had been doing.

I simply said, "If you don't mind my saying, I believe I am most certainly needed. Especially with my knowledge of the Far East, and of languages."

"What languages?" Miroslav asked.

"Naturally I am fluent in both Czech and German, but also English — American English, the 'pidgin' English of the Far East. I have a fair understanding of Chinese, and I possess a detailed knowledge of China, Japan, India, the Malay States, the Philippine Islands..."

We were interrupted by a bombing alert. When our meeting resumed, Miroslav said, "The Americans are sure to be doing more business with the Japanese than the English will be. Perhaps

THE SUITCASE

they would welcome your assistance. Take a two week leave and sort things out. You will require General Ingr's permission, and approval from the Embassy in London. You'll receive a Ministry of Defence salary during this time."

The Americans! "I have no papers. Will you provide me with some sort of statement?"

The statement read: "This is to certify that it has not been possible to accept for service with the Czechoslovak Army Mr. Vladimír Taussig, who was a sub-Captain of the Reserve, owing to his age and as in the present circumstances no commission is available in the Czechoslovak Army which might suit his qualifications."

So, with papers in hand and pay pending, I made plans to return to London, interrupted at intervals by further bombing alerts.

That afternoon, in London, I applied to work with the American Office of Strategic Services. I wrote to Francy that I hoped to be on my way back to the States soon and looked forward to celebrating at Forest Hills.

The thought of Forest Hills in the spring was tantalizing — especially compared to wartime London in the winter. I hadn't played tennis in what felt like ages! Earlier in the war, most English tennis courts had been "abandoned or dug up for allotments." And I didn't know any members who might get me in to play at Wimbledon. Though the tennis club had been struck by two bombs, eight of the grass courts had been kept in action, but four of those were on loan to the fire services. Pigs, poultry, and rabbits inhabited the other courts.

But my Forest Hills fancies would have to wait.

Unbeknownst to me, a caveat was added to my soon-to-be-rejected O.S.S. application: "This man has been put through the cards and we have received the following comment from

LONDON, ENGLAND
15 OCTOBER 1942

MI-5 on him: He was interrogated at Royal Victoria Patriotic School... and the conclusion reached was that he appeared to be a genuine refugee with no apparent security interest. Although the Czech authorities in this country know of nothing against him and there is nothing very definite recorded, we cannot, on the information available, recommend that he is suitable for confidential employment."

*****

My two weeks' leave passed, and my leave period was extended. November and December crept by without any satisfactory developments. All the while, I was receiving minimal pay from the Ministry of Defence. At the end of December, I was informed that my leave period was ending – as were my payments from the Ministry – so my pittance of a salary was cut off before I received any affirmative decision on travel to, and secure employment in, the States.

In financial desperation, I requested a partial reimbursement for my activities in Shanghai – a sum of only £250. I thought it quite a reasonable amount, considering the scale and span of my doings in the Far East.

Instead of being reimbursed for my good to work, I was told that, regarding the expenses incurred during my "semi-official activities in Shanghai," as Ingr called them, my claim had no merit. It was deemed "not appropriate" to reimburse me because I was "not a member of the Czechoslovak armed forces and did not perform any military service." Ingr added: "I also want to remind you that a lot of groups and individuals are in the same situation as you and cannot get financial assistance from the military."

I was furious.

347

THE SUITCASE

This decision came from Ingr, the Minister of National Defence. When I had reported for duty in New York, it had been Ingr who had decided, after months of waiting, to send me back to Shanghai. When I had sent readied troops to the front and requested to join them, it had been Ingr who had instructed me to stay in Shanghai and await further orders. Now he was telling me that nothing I had done had been "official" and that the troubles resulting from the position he'd put me in were not his concern.

I had a growing suspicion that Ingr, and some of the other supposedly-democratic Czech authorities, didn't want a Jewish man like myself serving in their military. Apparently Sergěj Ingr, the very Minister of Defence himself, saw Jews as an "unreliable element" and "opposed the general mobilisation of Czechoslovaks living in Britain because most of the émigrés were Jewish and it was not in the interest of the army to have a 'German-Jewish character.'" He must have been thrilled when, months hence in mid-May '43, the Nazis' North-African retreat ended and the mostly-Jewish Czech forces who had been fighting in the Middle East were evacuated to England. A full third of his Army-in-Exile became Jewish.

For what it was worth, Jan Masaryk would soon occupy Ingr's role as Minister of National Defence. Whether this came about in reaction to Ingr's views, I wish I could say.

By mid-February 1943 I was dead broke. On the 13th, I went to the Ministry of Defence near Green Park where I had met with the Boissevains. I found the offices on Piccadilly in a seven-storey stone building called Latymer House. There, I was met by Colonel Chodsky. I explained my situation and appealed once more for payment.

When Chodsky inquired about my case, he was informed that I was no longer employed by the Ministry of Defence. The

LONDON, ENGLAND
15 OCTOBER 1942

people for whom I had worked so diligently, and sacrificed so much, were denying my authority and refusing payment. I had no civilian or military papers. If a civil or military policeman had asked me for my papers I would have been taken for a deserter and hauled in like a criminal — again.

I left the offices feeling quite low indeed. From there, I had about a five-kilometre walk back to the flat I had been renting on Priory Road. I had to make the trek on foot because I didn't even have six pence for bus fare at that time. During my journey through the February cold and wind, I began mentally composing a letter to President Beneš.

I wondered whether Beneš would remember the Taussig name. Back in 1937, his wife, Mrs. Hana Benešová, had sent my father flowers and good wishes on the occasion of his seventieth birthday. Was Beneš aware of all the work I had done in the Far East for the Government- and Army-in-Exile? Was he aware of the rubbish and rumours that had since tainted my name?

I arrived at my Priory Road flat ready to compose my letter — and found myself locked out by my landlord, Mr. Prokock.

"Let me have my luggage and you'll never see me again," I told Prokock. I hated the flat anyway — no heat, no running water, no telephone in the entire house, the bathroom that was located two floors below my own room.

"You shall have your luggage when you have paid what you owe in back rent," Prokock said, laughing at my plight. "Come back when you can pay."

If he had have given me the luggage, I might have sold a few of my remaining effects in order to make a payment to him. As it was, what was I to do? I was about a twenty-minutes' walk from my old friends in St. John's Wood, but I felt embarrassed to call on them in need, again, when I had failed to contact them since my visit the previous autumn.

THE SUITCASE

And so, I was locked out with the vagrants and the prostitutes, with no money, and no friends. I found myself tramping around, "down and out" in London like George Orwell. I wandered around town like a hobo all Saturday and Sunday. Sunday it rained heavily.

On Monday, while Prokock was away, I convinced his wife to allow me back into the flat in his absence. She liked me well enough; I always made her laugh.

About a month previously, on 17 January, a Sunday, the Luftwaffe had visited London for the first night raid they had made since May 1941. Mrs. Prokock knew how, that day, I had been in an underground cinema near Piccadilly and missed the greatest AA barrage ever put up over London.

"Didn't you see the notice on the screen?" she later asked.

"Yes, I saw the air raid warning on the screen just when I got in. I thought it was part of the newsreel!" I exclaimed.

She howled with laughter. "What about your date?"

"Oh, she wasn't looking at the screen," I said with a wink, inciting renewed laughter. "We were leaving the theatre and were at the top of the stairs when the sirens started. I said, 'There seems to be an air raid on,' and someone nearby replied, 'Oh no; that's the all-clear.'"

"'There seems to be an air raid on,'" she laughed. "I don't see how you could have missed it."

When the Nazis had returned the following morning, 18 January, I had been woken up by the last wail of the siren. I switched my light on and Mrs. Prokock, seeing the light, had knocked on my door to offer me a cup of tea.

"Yes, thanks," I said. "There seems to be another air raid on. I heard the siren."

She cackled and said, "Taussig, that was the all-clear!"

These incidents had endeared me to the woman enough for

LONDON, ENGLAND
15 OCTOBER 1942

me to convince her to let me into the flat at Prokock's.

Once I was reunited with my room and my belongings, it was a simple matter of going off and selling a few things before Prokock came home, including some furnishings I did not think he would miss. I then paid Prokock what I owed, plus a few more weeks. In the meantime, I placed myself on a waiting list for a room in a better neighbourhood, without knowing how I was going to be able to afford the accommodations.

I hoped that the appeal I wrote to Beneš, once I was back in my flat, would be key in awarding me some much-needed back payment.

Within three weeks of sending my appeal to President Beneš — before I finally moved from Prokock's on Priory Road — I received a reply.

Vladimir Taussig
39 Priory Road, London, NW 6
Military Office
The President of the Republic
7 March 1943

In response to your letter that you sent the 17th of February this year to the President of the Republic, the Military Office of the President of the Republic after investigation is informing you as follows:

The measures of British offices in questioning foreigners arriving in England are needed to insure state security in times of war and are the same for everybody. Part of it is a military escort from the port to the Patriotic School in London and an interrogation which is held in accordance with the needs and requests of British offices. Czechoslovak military

THE SUITCASE

and other offices have no reason or ability to request changes or exceptions to these procedures. British officers are acting the same with respect to all comers and surely you have no justifiable complaint in your case.

Privately, the author of the letter, Nizborsky, Divisional Commander, had consulted with Major Slama at the Ministry of Defence and had been told "escort from the Port to Patriotic School in London is compulsory for all new arrivals. The procedures, applicable to all and enhanced by a specific British interest in an individual, that Lieutenant Taussig is complaining about, were done by the Ministry of Defence under instructions by British offices."

Major Slama had informed Nizborsky "that the English had information about Taussig while he was in Shanghai that gave them a reason for a detailed interrogation," but that "English inspectors behave[d] the same with respect to Taussig as to any other arrival and it is completely without an exception, they do the process by a habit. The interrogation is detailed but respectful. The interrogation camps are well kept, and have good furnishings, club, libraries, etc. Physical needs of individuals are well taken care of."

The letter from Beneš's Military Office continued:

It is not readily apparent from your letter the kind of expenses you had or for what activity in Shanghai was that money spent. You are requesting a partial reimbursement of 250 pounds sterling. Military office of the President of the Republic judges that your request for money from the Ministry of Defence is not warranted due to the fact that you did not convincingly

LONDON, ENGLAND
15 OCTOBER 1942

support it. This situation needs a better clarification so it could be accepted and if possible concluded by the Ministry of Defence.

Head of the Military Office
of the President of the Republic
General A. Nizborsky

The Ministry of Defence officials wrote one another that not only did they not wish to pay me for my activities in Shanghai, but also that my claims about recruitment activities in Shanghai needed to be analysed: "From those that Taussig selected in Shanghai and provided transportation... to either England or the Middle East only a small part—a few individuals—were capable of serving in the military. It looks like that, by saying they wanted to join the army, they mostly took an advantage of the situation so they could get, often with their family, to Palestine or directly to England."

In late March I received a further letter from General Nizborsky stating that it was the opinion of the Military Office of the President of the Republic that I never should have been called to active duty, "due to [my] age and [the] surplus of officers," and that, instead, "immediately after arrival in England" I "should have been handed over to the Ministry of Social Welfare for support and care." Nizborsky criticized the Czechoslovak Brigade for putting me on "a leave of undetermined duration" and for paying me to do nothing since my arrival in London.

"The use of military leave is totally irregular," Nizborsky wrote, "and should not have been used even if the military commanders had the best of intentions. This includes the denial of pay and gives real reason for complaint that he was without civilian documents, without a ration card, without any money and no way to find a suitable employment. The Military Office of the President of the Republic also in the interest of the military authorities recommends that the Ministry of Defence changes its procedures so that such an event can not happen [again]."

I was finished. And I was no nearer to being usefully employed in war work, nor was I any closer to my aim of getting over to Francy in the States. The situation was unspeakably frustrating. Meanwhile, the bombing raids on London were becoming a nuisance, owing to the shrapnel from the new AA rocket guns, which sent jagged fragments flying each time they fired.

I wrote to Francy in April: "I was just walking from the bus station when they let loose. Those blinking bits of shrapnel came down like rain drops. You should have seen me removing my valuable body into the nearest pub. That blasted air raid cost me ten bob, which I originally did not intend to spend on liquor."

I added, "I shall probably apply to the British War Office for an army job." I wrote, "I shall be much happier in the army as long as it is not our army. Conditions there are pretty grim, one would sooner think that one has to deal with representatives of the Nurnberg laws and not with a supposed-to-be democratic army."

TEREZÍN, OCCUPIED CZECHOSLOVAKIA
Tuesday, 29 June 1943

*"...Taussig Marie, transport number AAe 463
is attending the funeral of Taussig Julie..."*
—Terezín Pass

THE RABBI recited the well-practiced mourner's kaddish for Julie. Jaromír and Marietta stood mutely by.

After the rabbi finished, Jaromír said, "This year in Terezín was one of the longest of her life. Now she is finally with Father."

Marietta nodded. "As she so often said she wanted to be."

The rabbi looked at the siblings. "If you would like to say a few brief words..." He emphasized "brief." It was just past nine o'clock and already that day the central mortuary had performed similar rites for Christian families. Then they had begun the Jewish funerals, which would last well into the afternoon.

Stoically, Jaromír said, "Mamicka was a dear woman. Her greatest joy was her family. We shall never forget her tireless letter writing, her clutching at photographs, her visits to see Father in the cemetery. We will continue the prayers she said each day—that Francy remain in good health, that Jiří stay safe from the war, and that Vlada will be kept from harm."

Marietta cut his speech short: "And that they all decide to begin sending parcels to us, post haste, so that we might avoid such starvation as our dear mother suffered."

The rabbi nodded and the pallbearers, who had seen this scene thousands of times—each time different and yet, each time

THE SUITCASE

also the same—lifted the coffin that held Julie Taussigová's frail body.

The Taussigs watched as the assemblage of boards, held together with paper nails, was carried from the room. Coffins in Terezín had been nicer prior to the "great dying" of the previous summer, 1942. That summer, each day, about one hundred of the forty thousand prisoners died, the elderly, especially, dropping dead like flies. Sometimes they lay on the floor all day before their corpses could be removed to the mortuary.

Having only just been transported in June '42, Julie had survived the "great dying." She had also survived the winter of 1942-'43, surely the coldest winter of her life, as she slept on excelsior on the cold stone floor in the blacked-out Dresden barracks. That winter, even minor illnesses weakened the half-starved populace. Many contracted pneumonia. Many died. A typhoid epidemic had stricken the camp in January '43 when a sewage pipe had burst. This, too, Julie had survived.

Perhaps most importantly, owing to Jara's privileged status, Julie had survived transports "East," especially the Elder Transports at the end of 1942. Back in February '42, after the Wannsee Conference, SS-Obersturmbannführer Adolf Eichmann had told Jewish representatives in Prague that Terezín was to be a ghetto for the elderly—and Terezín's population had indeed become quite elderly. By October, ninety percent of Terezín's inhabitants were over the age of sixty-five.

Despite the fact that the Nazis presented Terezín as a destination, not a waystation, transports frequently left Terezín for "the East." Late in 1942, an order was given to dispatch ten special transports, totalling eighteen thousand people—the "Elder Transports." These transports were purportedly destined for a privileged ghetto, but instead, deportees found themselves in Treblinka. By the end of 1942, only one third of Terezín's

TEREZÍN, OCCUPIED CZECHOSLOVAKIA
29 JUNE 1943

population was over the age of sixty-five.

Although Jaromír's status as a privileged Aufbaukommando worker extended protection to Julie and Marietta, there was still a tense feeling when the car from Prague was seen on the road carrying Adolf Eichmann or his aides. The Nazi official would visit the Central Office, and Terezín's Judenrat council would be instructed on the number and type of people to be included in the transport, whether it be elderly inmates, families, or workers. The Judenrat would create a transport list, omitting the indispensable workers and protected inmates. In this way, Julie had survived twenty-four transports, including both the "Elder transports" and regular transports.

But the miserable diet that the elderly received, combined with horrible conditions that surrounded Julie and the other prisoners, had led to cardiac degeneration and complications. Just over a month after her seventieth birthday, Julie's heart had stopped beating.

Jara and Marietta followed the pallbearers, passing other rooms in the central mortuary where other rabbis prayed over other families.

They exited the central mortuary near the railroad siding constructed by prisoners beginning in August '42. It had taken three hundred prisoners, almost two hundred tons of iron, five thousand tons of gravel, and fifty-five hundred metres of rails — all were materials that had been diverted from the war effort — to create this railroad siding. Becoming operational in early June '43, the camp's trains could bypass the town of Bohušovice, and hide arrivals, and, most importantly, departures, from sight.

Between July and October '42, and again in January and February '43, prisoners had left for the "East," one thousand or two thousand people at a time. No transports had departed since February, and Terezín's population was swelling to dangerous levels again. New arrivals would enter Terezín that very day.

Unless something changed soon, Jaromír was certain there would be another "great dying."

To their left was the ghetto itself. Nearest to them was a small park, and Marietta's barracks. The barracks, once called C III, had been renamed "Hamburg" in anticipation of Himmler's visit—a visit which never came to fruition, owing to the prevalence of epidemics. From where they stood, "Hannover," a men's barracks, was also visible. The nearby bakery and food store in the fortress town's wall emitted cruelly tempting smells for the chronically undernourished and overworked prisoners.

To the Taussigs' right was Südstrasse, South Street, which led to the cemetery and crematory.

Julie's coffin was loaded onto a flat, horseless cart laden with other coffins. It was the same cart that was used for the daily bread deliveries from the ghetto bakery to the various barracks' kitchens. Jara and Marietta followed the cart that carried their mother's body as far as the Bohušovice gate. From there, they watched the cart sway slowly off towards the crematorium.

"When I built that crematory, I never imagined that my own mother would someday be consumed by it," Jaromír said. "About a year ago, there were only watery graves. All the new arrivals had to dig graves. But the graves tended to flood. There were more bodies to bury than solid land to bury them in. So we were ordered to construct the crematory. And still, when the ovens become overtaxed, they put the bodies into the watery graves and toss chlorinated lime on them for the stench. At least Mamicka will be burned instead. Like Father."

Marietta scoffed. "At least she will be burned, like Father," she repeated. Marietta thought about her mother's body being engulfed in flames, her flesh melting away to reveal her bones. At one time, her mother had been horrified by the thought of

TEREZÍN, OCCUPIED CZECHOSLOVAKIA
29 JUNE 1943

cremation. Now Julie was beyond caring.

Jara said, "Someday, when the war is over, we'll bring Mamicka's ashes back to Prague, and put her in the cemetery with Father. I'll visit her the way she and Molinka used to visit him."

"Yes, before restrictions. Before deportations." Mitcka said with bitterness.

Jara envisioned his mother's frail body being removed from its coffin and being placed on the boards of the coffin's lid. The coffin itself would be returned to Terezín on the same bread cart and would be disinfected for reuse.

He sighed. "I have done so much to keep the two of you alive and away from the truly awful work. You are lucky you are not assigned to 'glimmer' detail, splitting mica like the others. You should be happy to be in the fields, with fresh air and access to extra food—and no sexual blackmail by male supervisors. And Mamicka was lucky to have her wash guard position. It helped time pass. It put her in contact with a variety of people. It provided her with free-time opportunities."

"I hate the fields, and you know it," Marietta said. "Roasting with burns in the sun and freezing with frostbite in the winter." She held up her hands to examine them. "My hands will never be the same again. Never. And from the fields, we can see what they do in the Little Fortress." The Little Fortress was Terezín's prison just across the Ohře. Since 1940, the Nazis had used it for special imprisonments and for executions.

"You would complain and be contrary about any manner of work."

"And Mamicka hated being a wash guard. Spending day in and day out in the lavatories."

"Being a wash guard classified her as a worker, so that she received larger food portions than the other elderly inmates."

Non-workers received the smallest and least-diversified rations and had the worst accommodations, owing to the Nazis' purposeful plan of starvation and malnutrition. "It kept her out of the potato peel piles and prevented her from begging for soup like the other elderly inmates. Our mother never had to scavenge or beg."

"And look where it's gotten her," Marietta scowled. "She is dead just the same." Jaromír had noticed that confinement in Terezín tended to magnify personalities. If someone was mean, the meanness was intensified. If someone was already unhappy, as Julie had been, this, too, was intensified. She continued, "The potato peels only give people enteritis. There's no nutrition in them, and she knew it. Mamicka would never have scrounged from trash piles behind the kitchen. She was too proud. "And, she told me not to sneak food from the fields for her. She said it wasn't worth taking the chance of being shot or taken to the Small Fortress." The fields were called the "Šance" — the chance. Yields were intended solely for the SS.

As Jara and Marietta talked, bustling began on the railroad siding. A transport was arriving. Three small transports would arrive that day: one hundred people from Berlin, thirty-three from Muenster, and five from Karlovy Vary. Jaromír's attention was drawn to the movement. Marietta was still talking — something about how knowing Francy and Vlada had not forgotten about them might have saved their mother.

Jaromír did not want to engage in such thinking. Their siblings abroad likely had no idea that he and Mitcka were in Terezín. And whatever might have saved Julie in the past, was irrelevant now. Her body was probably already being consigned to the flames. What did it matter what might have been?

"You are not even listening," Marietta was saying. "I've got to be off anyway. We are harvesting the 'early' potatoes. I will see

TEREZÍN, OCCUPIED CZECHOSLOVAKIA
29 JUNE 1943

you tonight."

"Okay, Mitcka." Jaromír sighed. "See you tonight."

Marietta moved to show her pass to a Czech Ghetto Guard. She would then be escorted to work.

Jara watched as his sister walked away. Marietta passed gardens, where teenage girls worked in and around Terezín's moats, cultivating herbs and vegetables—parsley, beans, leeks, celery, spinach, cauliflower, carrots. She passed livestock—horses, cattle, sheep, pigs, hens, geese, ducks, turkeys, beehives, silkworms. She passed fruit trees—apple, pear, plum, cherry, apricot, peach. None was for the prisoners; all was for their captors.

While his sister was escorted out into the fields, Jaromír turned back toward the walled town. He had work to do that day, too. The Aufbaukommando was constantly busy with repairs and improvements as they attempted to prevent the overtaxed infrastructure from failing and descending the overpopulated ghetto into chaos and disease. The water and waste systems alone required enormous attention to prevent the spread of epidemics. After the previous summer's typhoid epidemic, when it was found that Terezín's wells had been contaminated, the Aufbaukommando had dug new wells further from town, and had run long pipes to reconnect the water supply.

Jaromír walked down Bahnhofstrasse, Train Station Street, where the new transports would soon be arriving. The buildings Sudberg and Jäger were on his left. There, the new arrivals would be searched for contraband and submerged in a lice-killing chemical while their clothing was disinfected with hot steam.

He then walked onto Seestrasse, Lake Street. The name was a great joke—there was no lake in Terezín. Jara passed the Sudeten barracks on his left—his own barrack. When the Aufbaukommando had arrived, the building had been a weapons storehouse. It was mostly storerooms, with concrete floors and barred windows. Where space was available, the Aufbaukommando had constructed three-tiered bunks. Where there was no room for bunks, excelsior-filled mattresses covered the floors. The building now had a total capacity of six thousand men.

If Jara had continued on Seestrasse, he would have passed the police headquarters, some workshops, and a large park, before arriving at the schleuse in Aussig barracks, where new arrivals were processed, and where they were separated from their luggage. As Jaromír set to work, he could hear the recently-arrived transport members making their way there.

When Jaromír was deported to Terezín, there hadn't been a schleuse. By the time Julie and Marietta arrived some months later, they had been whisked into the machinery of the schleuse. They had spent the night on the excelsior-covered stone floor. They had been joined by a transport of one thousand people from Vienna that arrived the following day, and by transports from here and there of fifty from Berlin and fifty from Munich; they had been relieved of most of their belongings, deloused, and disinfected.

Some died of shock in the schleuse. Especially those from Berlin, who were uniquely confused as to why their contracts for "accommodations in the spa for old persons" would not be fulfilled. They had no idea that "Theresienbad, the health spa," where they expected to live comfortably in hotels overlooking parks and lakes, was, in actuality, a ghetto fortress town amid the grass-topped brick bulwarks.

In the schleuse, everything they had so carefully packed, guarded, and carried, was confiscated, sorted, and placed on the shelves that Jara and the Aufbaukommando had built, and had then reinforced when they began to sag with the weight of stolen

TEREZÍN, OCCUPIED CZECHOSLOVAKIA
29 JUNE 1943

possessions: beds, blankets, quilts, foods, herbs, spices, soaps, slippers, clothing, even undergarments. The SS took the best items for themselves and sent anything else that was useful to the bombed-out German citizens who lacked necessities. "Third-choice" items, like candle stubs, mostly-used tubes of toothpaste, torches without batteries, resurfaced in Terezín's "second-hand" shop.

Jaromír turned towards the main square, moving past the seat of the ghetto guard. A high fence separated Terezín's prisoners from the SS and their barracks, cafés, restaurants, cinema, and clubrooms. All had been constructed or renovated by Jaromír and the others of the Aufbaukommando. This same wooden fencing also isolated Terezín's central main square.

Around the square were buildings that contained Terezín's town hall, post office, bank, shop, café, and some that housed infants and children. The basements and rooms of some of the children's buildings also hosted concert practices, art lessons, theatrical performances, and contained a children's library. Once the Nazis knew they wanted to put the ghetto on display, the formerly-forbidden artistic life of the ghetto had been encouraged.

In the middle of the square was a two-masted circus-like tent, erected earlier in the month. Inside, hammering and banging was constant as one thousand inmates constructed crates. They nailed together the crates' sides and packed them with "winter equipment for motor vehicles," before securing the crates' lids. Their work would continue "throughout the summer and into the fall."

Also on the main square, the "glimmer" detail was busy splitting mica, which was in high demand for the war effort, for its electronic and mechanical uses. The working day had been increased from eight-hour days to ten-hour days. The work, which had been taking place since September '42, was awful. Prisoners "stripp[ed] the mica core of its worthless surface layer" and split "mica into thin slices."

Elsewhere in Terezín, beyond the main square, were other barracks buildings. There was a hospital, with a large staff of excellent doctors and nurses who dealt with enteritis, typhoid, scarlet fever, diphtheria, encephalitis, starvation, pregnancies, and other conditions and afflictions. There was a shower and laundry room that made use of the hot steam from the kitchens.

In the eastern corner of the town was the Magdeburg building, home to the Judenrat. The Magdeburg building was also where, in the building's loft, rehearsals were underway for the famous Bedřich Smetana opera, *The Kiss*. The opera would have no curtains or costumes, and only a piano to accompany the ensemble, but the familiar music and moving songs were a comfort to the Czechs in Terezín just the same.

Jara found his work detail and began the day's labour.

*****

After the workday, at around six o'clock, Terezín's streets filled with people going either "home" from work, to visit loved ones, or to enjoy some cultural immersion. Jaromír remembered when evening free time was not yet permitted. When Julie and Mitcka had arrived in June of '42, families had not been allowed to reunite in the evenings. It had only been in July, when the townspeople were gone and the ghetto "opened," that evening free time had been instituted.

Some went to the café on the main square, which had been open since the previous winter. The Ghetto Swingers in the coffee house played American jazz by artists like Count Basie and Duke Ellington. Their signature number was Gershwin's "I

TEREZÍN, OCCUPIED CZECHOSLOVAKIA
29 JUNE 1943

Got Rhythm." Neither jazz, nor songs by Jewish composers, were heard anywhere else in Nazi-occupied lands. Since the "bank" had opened, the café was charging a fee for "patrons" to sit for the allowable two hours, listening to the band and drinking ersatz coffee, a vile substance made from chicory, roasted acorns, or other organic materials.

Jaromír joined the crowds and made his way towards "Hamburg" to visit Mitcka. There, the ceilings were too low to accommodate the usual three-tiered bunks that the Aufbaukommando had installed in many of the other buildings. Marietta and the other working women slept on excelsior-filled mattresses on the floor, where they fought constantly against dirt, fleas, and bedbugs.

Marietta's "bed" was easy to spot—it was graced by the robe fashioned from Julie's Soochow blanket, frayed and faded as it was. Jaromír saw his sister standing in line near the stove, waiting to warm her unsweetened ersatz. The "coffee" helped curb hunger, for a time. Marietta had received a half-loaf of black bread at both lunch and dinner, and a grey soup made from ground lentil pods at both meals. At lunch she had also received a potato. Once a week she received a sliver of margarine and, every two weeks, a yeast dumpling. She was always hungry. Everyone was.

As Marietta waited to warm her ersatz, the lights in the barracks began to flicker. Some inmates possessed hidden hot plates, a necessity for doing any real "cooking," like making ghetto cake from breadcrumbs, "coffee" grounds, and carefully-saved sugar or margarine. They had made such a cake for Julie's seventieth birthday. When the hot plates were in use, the power plant intended to serve seven- or eight-thousand inhabitants became grossly overtaxed. Moments after the flickering light, Block Elders would come in searching for the forbidden hot plates.

With warmed ersatz in hand, Marietta made her way to her bed area and sat. She and Jara watched the Elders' fruitless search for the contraband hot plates.

"I wish she was here," Marietta said. "It's strange, not having her here."

"What a selfish thing to say. I assure you she is infinitely happier where she is," Jara replied.

"With Father," Marietta said. She took a sip of the ersatz. "But at least we were together. Even if she was miserable. We were always together."

Across the room, Marietta noticed a familiar figure, a frail and greyer version of Cousin Olga—Julie's niece. Just as Marietta took notice of the woman, someone was pointing the Taussigs' location to her. Olga began to advance.

Marietta put her cup to her mouth to hide her words as she warned Jara: "Don't look now—here comes Mamicka's favourite person."

Jaromír turned to follow his sister's gaze. "This ought to be interesting," he quipped. "And it seems she's brought food."

Indeed, Olga was carrying some semblance of a "salad," made from foraged dandelion and ribwort, along with a ration of lentil soup. "How are you, my dears?" the woman asked, standing over the seated siblings. "I have heard the news, and I organised a halfway decent seudat havara'ah."

"No one wants your old soup, Cousin Olga," Marietta muttered.

"Nonsense," Jaromír said. "Come, sit here by me, Olga Katzová. How thoughtful of you."

"Everyone hates the soup here, I know," Olga said, glancing at Marietta, "But it's only proper. Besides, I had them scoop from the bottom, on account." The top of the pot was only broth.

TEREZÍN, OCCUPIED CZECHOSLOVAKIA
29 JUNE 1943

As Olga lowered her soon-to-be-fifty-two-year-old bones onto the mattress, Marietta said, below her breath, "Mamicka would die all over again."

Jara said, through gritted teeth, "What does an old grudge matter now?" To Olga, he said, "I shall never forget how your mother brought soup and eggs for our family when Father died."

Olga nodded. "And Julie brought them for me when my father died, and again when Mother passed."

"When your mother passed, Marietta met her beau. Surely she is grateful for that," Jara said, giving Marietta a wide-eyed look to tease her.

"Yes, I am glad," Mitcka said with flushed cheeks. "I am grateful he was able to help with our dear aunt's estate, and that I made his acquaintance."

Olga busied herself preparing the "soup" and "salad" for their consumption. "Are you able to partake?" Olga asked Jaromír. "Is your diet limited by your diabetes?"

"Not at all," Jara said. "I have found that the starvation, and the hard labour, have quite cleared my symptoms."

"I'm glad to hear it," Olga said.

Marietta scoffed. "Yes, the silver lining to starvation and labour."

Olga said calmly, "Good health is a precious thing."

Jara glared at his sister. "You are our only family here, Olga" Jaromír said. "Our Father's brother, Artur, and his family passed through Terezín briefly, but they were transported again before Mamicka and Mitcka ever arrived. I never even saw them. My friend in the administration tells me their transport arrived on 24 April and that they were sent East on the twenty-eighth. I doubt they ever even left the schleuse." Arthur, his wife Mariana, their daughter Hana, her husband Rudolf, and their five-year-old son, Arnošt, had all been taken to Zamość.

THE SUITCASE

"I hope they are all well in the East. I suppose it is just us, then," Olga said. "I have been here, in Terezín, since last May. But I knew how your mother felt about me." She sighed. "May I ask how she died?"

Jaromír said, "She lasted longer than many of the elderly here, but in the end, her heart seems to have given out."

"Oh, like the starving ones," Olga said. "I'm sorry to hear it. I wish we had resolved our differences long ago. She was quite a woman, your mother."

Marietta cleared her throat and shifted on the bed but remained wordless.

"Didn't her birthday just pass? I shall never forget the occasion of your father's seventieth—your villa, the guests, the flowers, the food, the cakes from Berger."

"Yes," Marietta said finally. "Mother's seventieth was spent right here, eating 'ghetto cake' with 'poor man's cream' after a long day of work as a wash guard."

Olga nodded. "An important position. Did you help her attain that employment, Jaromír? How wise."

Jaromír shot his sister a look. Marietta folded her arms. Wasn't it clear to her brother that Olga was just trying to win a place on the protection list?

"Come, let's have some of that salad you brought," Jaromír said. "Where did you find such leaves?"

"On the bulwarks," Olga said with a smile.

"How resourceful," Jaromír said.

Marietta declined the "salad" at first, then begrudgingly took a bite. They all chewed on the bitter leaves for a few moments before Olga asked, "Do Vlada and Francy know you are here?"

Jaromír said, after a pause, "We have attempted to contact Francy in New York, but there has been no response. Who knows whether she ever received our message."

TEREZÍN, OCCUPIED CZECHOSLOVAKIA
29 JUNE 1943

"Surely if she had, she could be sending parcels," Olga said. She offered the soup to the Taussig siblings, who sipped it politely. "And Vladimír?" Olga asked. "Still in China?"

"As far as we know," Jara said.

"I hope he and Francy are well, God keep them." Olga said.

Before they could speak much further, the announcement was made: "Quarter to nine, ladies and gentlemen. Time to go home."

Olga rose and straightened her shabby dress. Jaromír stood and helped his sister from the floor. Olga drew them both into an embrace. Marietta made an unpleasant face. "I shan't be a stranger any longer," Olga said. "Your mother would have wanted you to stick with your own people. Whatever passed between us is water under the bridge now."

"Thank you for your visit," Jaromír said.

Marietta nodded, her face still unpleasantly scrunched up.

Olga took her leave. Jaromír looked at his sister and said, "All right, little sister. Don't let it give you indigestion. Chin chin," he said, echoing the Chinese toast of "please please" that had become popular with their brother, and also with the Italians.

"Chin chin," Marietta grumbled as she turned back to her mattress on the floor. She settled down and laid on her side, her bones jabbing painfully into the stone floor through the mattress and sawdust.

Excelsior scraps scratched at her, bugs nibbled, nearby humans stirred. She closed her eyes and imagined herself at the family's favourite restaurant in Stromovka park, a short stroll from their villa, where the scenery was beautiful, the food was delectable, and her family was together — even Vladimír, who had been away for so many years.

In the darkening barrack she repeated the prayers that Julie had always said — that Francy continue on in good health, that

Jiří remain safe from the war, that Vlada be out of harm's way. Then Marietta added her own—that her beau be faithful, that he send parcels, and that the war, and their imprisonment, end soon.

*****

Within a fortnight, another of Julie's less-than-favourite faces would appear in Terezín, when, in July of '43, the last of Prague's Jews were deported. Vlada's friend Karoline Fischerová—or Karly, or Fischerka—and her husband and their six-year-old son, Petr, arrived in the ghetto town.

When Marietta noticed the Fischers in Terezín, she asked her brother, "Did you see? Karly Fischerová's here now."

"Fischerka?" Jaromír asked. "Mamicka did nothing but gossip about her. Have you spoken with her?"

Marietta shook her head. "Certainly not."

Jaromír looked over his sister's shoulder at the approaching woman. "Well, you are about to now."

Marietta paled. She heard Karoline Fischerová exclaim, "Jaromír Taussig!" Marietta turned to look. "And Marietta! How nice to see you both."

Marietta grumbled.

Jaromír smiled. "Karly Fischerová, you look well."

Marietta muttered, "Yes, well she's only just arrived. Give her some time and she'll look as lousy as the rest of us."

Karoline said, "Otto and Petr and I are all here now—and hopefully we won't be staying long."

Jaromír understood what the woman meant. Just days before, they had heard news that the British and American attack on Europe had begun in Italy. The Russians had also been repelling the Nazis following the June '41 surprise attack by their former

TEREZÍN, OCCUPIED CZECHOSLOVAKIA
29 JUNE 1943

ally. Months previously, in February '42, they had prevented the Nazi seizure of Stalingrad. Hopes were high with the feeling that the war was winding down.

Karoline asked the Taussigs, "Is it just the two of you?"

Marietta hid her emotions behind her stoicism and allowed her brother to answer. Jaromír said, "Mother was with us, but like so many of the elderly here, she died. Quite recently."

"Oh!" Karoline exclaimed. "I'm so sorry to hear it."

Marietta bit her tongue. She wanted to say something about how their mother had never possessed any love for "that Fischer woman," as Julie had called Karoline. But Marietta's heart softened somewhat when Karoline spoke again: "Your mother was such a good, respectable woman, with a wonderful character," she said earnestly.

Jaromír said, "That's kind, thank you."

Marietta said simply, "Yes."

Karoline said brightly, "I have just seen the children's artwork exhibition. Have you been? It was reassuring to see it and to think that little Petr will be among such talented children while we are here."

Marietta said, "No, I have not seen it."

Jaromír quickly added, "But I have heard it's excellent. Pictures, sculptures, many modes of expression. Petr will be in good hands with Fredy Hirsch. They take good care of the children here."

Like Jara, Hirsch had arrived in Terezín in December '41. Hirsch had seen that special rooms were created for children, who lived apart from their parents. These rooms were later transformed into heims—children's homes, with teachers and caretakers. The children exercised daily, and attention was paid to their hygiene and the maintenance of their physical and psychological health. They were given lessons and participated in artistic endeavours. After all, weren't the children the ones who had the best chance of surviving the war?

Karoline said, "What a relief to hear that Petr will be taken care of. I have been so fretful since we were separated, but they say it is better for the children not to be housed with us adults, who are working."

"And perhaps you are right," Jaromír said with false hopefulness, "Perhaps none of us will be here much longer."

*****

A month after Fischerka's arrival, in the midst of the intolerable late-August heat, a different sort of children arrived in Terezín. The ghetto town had never seen anything like it — an entire transport consisting solely of children from the East. Fifteen hundred of them arrived from Białystok on 24 August. They spoke Polish and Yiddish.

Terezín's prisoners were forbidden to interact with the newly-arrived children. The inmates were sent indoors and kept away from the windows while the SS themselves escorted the children to be disinfected. No other transport had consisted exclusively of children. No other transport had been so carefully kept away from Terezín's populace.

Those who did see the children could attest to their poor condition — the children were starving, barefooted, bedraggled, and dressed in rags. When they were taken to be disinfected in the showers, the children screamed in terror: "Gas! Gas!" They calmed when they realised that only water was pouring from the showerheads.

The children were kept in the western barracks, separated by barbed wire from the rest of the camp. The rest of Terezín was busy with numerous censuses and registrations. People of

TEREZÍN, OCCUPIED CZECHOSLOVAKIA
29 JUNE 1943

working age, fourteen to sixty, were registered. By late August, when the children arrived, even the Aufbaukommando had been made to register. Rumours circulated — were there going to be transports? Work transports, or transports "East"? If they were to go "East," would they encounter the same things the children from Białystok had come to dread? What did those children know about the East, and why was contact with them so forbidden?

And then, as feared, transports were announced.

In early September, Prague's Office for the Settlement of the Jewish Question passed instructions to Terezín Commandant Anton Berger, who gave orders to Terezín's Judenrat. The Judenrat's Daily Orders announced the transport. Select Terezín inmates then received written notice of their assignment to a "work transport," ordering them to assemble at the schleuse, which, by then, had moved to "Hamburg" barracks. There were told to carry only a limited amount of luggage.

That transport would be composed of young families previously deported from the Protectorate, as well as a number of specifically-named people. These included one hundred and fifty ghetto policemen and members of Terezín's administration, including former elder Jakob Edelstein, and the head of the ghetto police, Kurt Frey. Also specially named for inclusion in the transport was Fredy Hirsch, who had been jailed in the Small Fortress for talking to the mysterious children from Białystok.

No transports had left Terezín since February. Now that transports were departing again, and prominent people were being included, no one was safe.

BRISTOL, ENGLAND
Monday Morning, 20 December 1943

"Czechoslovaks Get Around"
— M.O.I. Presentation by Vladimír Taussig
Speaking as Captain Vlado Jiří

I SCANNED the University of Bristol's Willis Hall, locking eyes with a man here and there. My voice was the only sound in the residence hall's oak-panelled dining room. As a travelling speaker for the British Ministry of Information, or M.O.I., I used several different aliases, particularly Captain Vlado Jiří and Captain X. That day, I was speaking to officers, instructors, and the University's Vice Chancellor at the Regional Committee on Education for His Majesty's Forces.

I had delivered my "From Prague to London via Japanese-Occupied China" speech the previous evening before supper. That day, Monday, I concluded the presentation of my topic, "Our Enemy Japan," with a final speech, entitled "Report from the Pacific."

For that particular function, I had been introduced as Captain X, "a former head of the Czecho-slovakian Propaganda Department in the Far East." I told the audience how I had been sent out to the Far East to help my countrymen who were escaping to China after the German occupation. The Japanese invasion of December 1941 — a full two years before my speech! — had ended all that. For the benefit of the British crowds, and especially for the officers in attendance that day, I emphasized my recounting

BRISTOL, ENGLAND
20 DECEMBER 1943

of the final moments of the *Peterel*, and of Polkinghorn's response to the Japanese command that he surrender: "His Majesty's ships do not carry white flags."

I certainly knew, by that time, what audiences liked to hear; I had been "on tour" for several months and had made speeches all over the United Kingdom. Based on the assignment, the audience, and the duration of the discourse, I focused on different aspects of my time in China, and also borrowed from those of Francy, who had witnessed the Nazi occupation of Prague, as well as those of my Boy, Cheng, and of my business partner, Ed Kann, who both had been brutalized inside Bridge House.

Because I was addressing officers at that particular event in Bristol, I shared a few details I would have refrained from telling, say, to a women's club meeting. For a more mixed crowd I would describe a typical cell in Bridge House, saying: "The cell contained twenty-three other people, including two women, in a space so small that, when some wanted to lie down blanket-less on the stone floor, others were left to lean against the walls. Once a day, prisoners are given one small bowl of filthy rice. Once a day, the waste bucket in the corner, shared by all, is emptied." For the audience at the University of Bristol event, who needed to know the nature of the enemy, I also included something of the treatment and tortures that were commonplace in those Japanese interrogation centres and prisons.

Those who had heard my talks tended to react with one of two feelings. On one hand, some felt a disregard for the seemingly-distant Japanese threat. On the other, some felt a hatred for all Japanese people. Both were erroneous modes of thought. Months prior to my appearance in Bristol, I had begun adding a statement to my talks to address both parties. Borrowing from Carroll Alcott's 1943 book, *My War with Japan*, I said: "If the Japanese were to succeed and 'unite all Asians, one billion people, under their flag, the political, military and economic consequences would be unimaginable... [U]nconditional surrender is inadequate; we must also suppress their ambition. They want to rule the world...'"

I borrowed from John Morris, Sandy Tittman's husband, and his comments in his 1943 work, *Traveler from Tokyo,* when I said: "The ever-increasing military and economic might of Japan is evidently beginning to worry her Axis partners who consider there may be no limit to Japan's expansion." Unbeknownst to most of my audiences, the Germans and the Japanese hated one another, neither group making any attempt to disguise their contempt for the other. The Nazis were known to refer to the Japanese as "accursed yellow apes." Japan called their counterparts "Nazi dogs" and allowed the Soviets to broadcast anti-Nazi propaganda in Shanghai. "Japan," I explained to audiences, "has only one ambition—'Asia for Asians.'"

The Japanese public rarely heard of the atrocities their troops committed—the "brutality of the empire's troops, how they reconcile the bayoneting of nurses and unarmed men and the murder of soldiers who have surrendered." The Japanese people "were the identical people they had been yesterday, and the day before that, and a week ago. The stolid, complacent creatures were willing to accept the crumbs a war-hungry government gave them. But to me, they have become the enemies whose ignorance had made such a war possible." This I borrowed from Max Hill, who had also been part of the diplomatic exchange, and who had written 1942's *Exchange Ship* to recount the experience.

"You will find the Japanese Gendarmerie, the Kempeitai, is about the most ruthless and rotten force at the disposal of their military. The Gendarmerie is responsible for running Bridge House and other dreaded interrogation centres. The Japanese Army is pompous and stupid," I continued. "There are at least

BRISTOL, ENGLAND
20 DECEMBER 1943

ten thousand Imperial Japanese Army soldiers in Shanghai." Their headquarters were located a few kilometres down the Bund from the Cathay. The Japanese Marines are no better. There are about six thousand in Shanghai. The Navy is perhaps the best of a bad bunch." The Navy had established themselves at Jardine's on the Bund.

I continued: "The only decent Japanese people I have met are the civilians, and only in interactions where they are sure they are not being watched by the government or military spies that have permeated Far Eastern society." The businessmen, the artists, the socialites, are guilty only of ignorance and misplaced nationalism. The military, however, needs to be stopped at any cost, and this will only be possible through the combined effort of Allied forces."

I was nearing the conclusion of my speech. "The job out there will have to be done as well as the job over here," I said, arriving at my final point. "It is not a question only of Great Britain and the U.S.A., but of all the United Nations. The job will be a difficult one, but I feel that somehow it might not take as long as many people think." I ended with one of my M.O.I.-prescribed talking points: "It was not the Russian stand at Stalingrad which turned the tide of the war, but the combined effort of the Western Allied Armies," and that it had been the same combined effort "which resulted in the ousting of the Germans from Africa, with its subsequent elimination of Italy as an Axis war potential. Imagine what the combination of forces could do to Japan," I said.

After letting my last comment sit for a moment, I thanked my audience, rekindling eye contact with various audience members around the dining room. I then returned to my seat on the stage while the presentation was concluded, and the officers were invited to luncheon. I, in turn, was thanked, and then the meeting was adjourned.

THE SUITCASE

While the others tucked into their lunch, I quietly departed the dining hall, and the University. I was headed back to London.

Outside was a typical English winter day, with the wind dropping the temperature to near-freezing. Though it was midday, the sun was nowhere to be seen.

The clock tower at Bristol's train station had been damaged by bombs in 1941. At the station, groups of servicemen dozed beneath lists of towns that travellers were forbidden to visit, and posters that read: "The time has come for every person to search his conscience before making a railway journey. It is more than ever vital to ask yourself: 'Is my journey really necessary?'" Others stood waiting, suitcases and packages piled about, policewomen checking papers here and there.

When the train arrived, there was a great surge of passengers struggling to get a spot. People climbed through windows to get inside, squeezing in beneath placards that read: "Food, shells and fuel must come first. If your train is late or crowded—*do you mind?*"

I had certainly suffered worse accommodations, but the situation was far from the first-class style of travel I usually insisted upon. But it was wartime England—no one would have stomached my complaints. I stood in the dimly-lit train car amid dozing and farting men as the car lurched and swayed back towards London.

There was always the chance of an air raid, since, as had been the situation in Shanghai, trains and stations were favourite targets for bombers. The in-car air raid instructions to the sitting-duck passengers humorously read:

BRISTOL, ENGLAND
20 DECEMBER 1943

1. Do not attempt to leave the train... You are safer where you are.
2. Pull the blinds down... as a protection against flying glass.
3. If room is available, lie down on the floor.

As if any such thing would have been remotely possible. British trains were more crowded than Japanese prison cells!

In spite of the blackout material on the windows, and the train stations we passed without identifying signs, I knew fairly well when we should arrive back in London, as I had made that particular trip before.

Eventually, the sardines emerged from the darkened train, stiff and stretching. I was "home."

*****

Back in March, I had moved from Prokock's — that awful flat in Priory Road. My new flat was a far sight better. It was in Kensington, near the embassies, where the Japanese diplomats, whose paths I had crossed in Lourenço Marques, had lived before repatriation. My own flat was in Courtfield Gardens. The flat was heated; it had a telephone; the bathroom wasn't two floors below; it had views of the garden in the square, instead of the Priory Road view of a few sparse trees between the endless rows of townhouses.

When I had relocated in the spring, bushes had been in full bloom. The houses' stairs lead directly to the gardens, with benches next to the front doors. It all looked so peaceful. There were hardly any people around. One would not believe that there was a war on, and that Nazi planes have only about a hundred miles to fly to pay a visit. Now it was late December, and the

THE SUITCASE

gardens looked sad and grey.

The house manager of my flat thought I was quite a character. "Have my accolades been pouring in?" I asked her as I collected my mail.

"Not pouring, just trickling," she said. "And will you be having breakfast for one or for two in the morning?" She thought it was frightfully fun if I only asked for one breakfast.

"Not yet sure," I said.

"Oh? And why not? Have your girls gone on a sit-down strike?"

I laughed. "Nothing of the sort. But I am expecting company this afternoon. Won't you show him up when he arrives?"

"Naturally, naturally. You just let me know about that breakfast. If it'll be for four, I'll need extra ration coupons from you."

I gave her a wink and headed up to my flat, tossing my mail onto the desk over which I had affixed various mementos, including a photograph of Betty Wragge with her family and a dachshund. They were visiting Camp Upton in Yaphank, New York, on the occasion of her brother Edward joining up. Another photo showed Betty at the World's Fair, standing and smiling in front of the deserted Czechoslovak pavilion, which never opened for the spring season.

There was also a London Symphony programme from late-March. I had been present when Moiseiwitsch was playing Rachmaninoff's Second Concerto and the news of Rachmaninoff's death was announced. Moiseiwitsch requested the audience refrain from applause. After the conclusion of the concerto, he played Chopin's funeral march. Everybody got up and remained standing in tribute to Rachmaninoff. So did I, sincerely. Whenever I was fed up and in a tight spot, a dose of Rachmaninoff's C Minor made me feel again that the whole world could go on.

BRISTOL, ENGLAND
20 DECEMBER 1943

Most pertinent of these over-the-desk mementos was a note from Desmond O'Neill, whose company I was expecting. It was owing to his introduction that I had taken the M.O.I. position, and it had been for his district that I had given my very first M.O.I. speech several months previously, in May. We had visited, and had gone to view *The Gentle Sex*, the A.T.S. film, before I had had to dash off to my next speaking engagement. The A.T.S., or Auxiliary Territorial Service, was the women's branch of the British Army.

Above my desk, Desmond's official Alton and District National Savings Committee letterhead bore his thanks for my "extremely interesting and useful talk," saying, "I have no doubt whatever that [your speech] is exactly what is very much needed, and I only hope that we can arrange another meeting in the near future. I know that a large number of people would like to hear you."

Even as I read his words, I heard a noise in the hall and grinned. It was a happy occasion that his business had brought him to London when I was also present. The house manager showed him up to my room. The door opened on Des, who was already dressed for an evening out.

Desmond greeted me with a big smile and an enthusiastic handshake. "How was Bristol?" he asked.

"Good. The syndicates are still meeting now, but I took my graceful leave."

Des looked me over. "You look well. A little dingy perhaps. Have you only just arrived?"

"Yes. I haven't even sat down. Allow me to go wash up and put on something more appropriate."

He laughed, "Yes, you certainly can't be seen at the Dorch wearing that." He gestured to my travelling suit.

I left him in the other room while I prepared for our evening.

THE SUITCASE

I fetched my best suit, one of my Fifth Avenue purchases from New York City, though after years of shortages and rationing, the tailoring was no longer what it had been. Nevertheless, I wanted to look my best. It was going to be an expensive outing. Neither Desmond nor I possessed the same sort of disposable income to which we were once accustomed. I had been saving for some time in anticipation of his visit and was prepared to spend almost a month's wages that evening in order to entertain him in high style—and still, owing to the wartime conditions, it would be merely a shadow of the extravagant life we had led in Shanghai.

"I like your flat," Des called.

"It's no Cathay Mansions," I said. He gave a single laugh in reply. "But I have certainly had worse," I added. "I quite enjoy the gardens outside, and I can hear the bells of Big Ching—"

"Big Ben," he corrected. Though the tower's clock face remained dark, Big Ben didn't stop ringing during the war.

"...Big Ben, chiming on the Thames. It's comforting." I began to dress. There was a lull. I could hear him shuffling papers around out in the main room and wondered what he was looking at. "I apologize for taking so long," I said as I fiddled with my collar stays and cufflinks. "Where is my Boy when I need him? I miss him all the time. You know, he was the only one who could keep a time table without conflicts."

"Oh, not to worry, I'm in no great hurry." He sounded distracted. He must have discovered my England scrapbook, left on seemingly-casual display on a tabletop, to impress women visitors. It had apparently been a magnet for Desmond as well. "The same Boy I met in Shanghai? What was his name, Cheng?"

"None other."

"What became of him?"

I paused, then said, "I honestly don't know. I hope he's escaped to Free China. The Japs did quite a number on him. I

BRISTOL, ENGLAND
20 DECEMBER 1943

used some of my last money on his medical treatments. It took a fortnight before he even resembled a human again."

"My God. You never told me that," Des said from the other room.

I sighed. "At least he shall have no further trouble on my account."

I heard him turn a page in the scrapbook. "What did they want with him—or with you?"

"Banking matters. At the very outset of the occupation they went straight for the banks. They did quite a job on my business partner, too. And he had just been through cancer treatments."

"Despicable. You shall have to tell me every dreadful detail over our drinks this evening." I heard another page turn.

"What have you found in there?" I called. "My M.O.I. scrapbook?"

"It seems so, yes. I didn't know you had visited the H.M.S. *Collingwood.*"

"Oh yes, for a group of Wrens," I said, referring to the Women's Royal Naval Service—WRNS.

"You devil, you." He turned another page. "Your book makes me wish I had kept mementos of my own." Desmond had been a regular speaker for the M.O.I. since late '41, giving weekly War Commentary talks at Portsmouth and Fareham and smaller coastal cities near Alton. And of course, he also worked for the Alton and District National Savings Committee, the same group that had invited me to give my own first M.O.I. lecture. He began speaking like a radio or newsreel announcer: "Ministry of Information War Commentary will be given by Mr. Desmond O'Neill, staff speaker, on Wednesday, the second of January, 1942, at half past six in the evening, in the Town Hall, Berkshire." He sighed. "Too late to start a scrapbook now, I suppose."

"You shall just have to gaze wistfully on my mementos

THE SUITCASE

instead," I said with a chuckle. "After I left you in May, I did Alton's R.A.F. station, a concert in Winchester, and then the Wrens on the *Collingwood*." I was fiddling with the cuffs on my trousers. "In June I did another Wrens speech, and another National Savings Movement lecture."

"I see that. Vera Ackland?" he asked.

"Vera Ackland. A fan of mine," I smiled. I could recite her note of thanks from memory:

Ministry of Information
9 Normandy Street
East Hampshire Local Committee
Alton, Hampshire

Chairman: Mrs. Vera Ackland, M.B.E.
1st July, 1943

Dear Captain Taussig,
I feel I cannot let this opportunity go by without expressing to you my most grateful thanks for having come to Alton, on behalf of all those who were privileged to hear your talk on Tuesday evening. The impression of sincerity and the knowledge that has left you so unembittered has made, I know, a great impression upon everyone. In fact I don't quite know how to really express my thanks to you in every way.

I hope that one day we may have the privilege of a return visit from you to Alton.

Believe me with all the best wishes,
Yours sincerely,
Vera Ackland

BRISTOL, ENGLAND
20 DECEMBER 1943

"Oh, I'm sure there are plenty of ways she might show her appreciation," Desmond chuckled. As I debated between hats, I heard Des unfold a poster. "Inside a Jap Prison," he read aloud. "Were you really?"

"I was taken in for questioning several times," I said, "but to be perfectly honest, probably half of that lecture is drawn from what my Boy and my business partner later related to me." He refolded the poster. "Where else was I sent during the summer? Let's see... Stella Lamp Company's factory—I spoke as 'Captain X.' You would have liked it."

"Ah, à la *Sergeant X*. Quite so!" He turned a page in the scrapbook then began reading aloud from a press clipping: "'Last Night's Guildhall Concert'—what's this, 'a Czech flying officer?'"

I laughed. "I just give the lecture. What the reporters glean from it, is not up to me."

"'A Czech flying officer who... at one time had been in enemy hands. This monocled officer, speaking excellent English'—they are not wrong—'had been in China, where everything was all right until the Japanese joined the party....'" Desmond chuckled. "Quite the journalist. '...And came in with far superior forces and equipment... He spoke of the devastation caused by the Japanese aircraft in Chinese cities, and although it might take some time, the Japanese must be blasted and smashed out of their territory by bombers.'"

He flipped a few more pages, reading lines here and there. "R.A.F. Station, Lasham. 'I feel that everybody should know the truth about the situation in the Far East and the habits of that objectionable breed, the Japanese.' Goodness—what have you been telling them?" he laughed.

"Oh, don't worry. I do tell them that the ordinary Japanese aren't all bad. The military, however..." I trailed off.

THE SUITCASE

Desmond continued. "Savings Office, Winchester. 'Your speech was excellent and appreciated by all. It just gave that Allied touch, and everybody was keenly interested.' Very impressive, Taussig. I don't receive letters like this, you know."

I emerged from the other room fully dressed. "Dashing as ever, Captain X." He lifted the scrapbook in his lap, gesturing, saying, "This really is something. In many ways I suppose my job is easier. As you know, fundraising is no fun, but I talk to people who already hate the Nazis. You, on the other hand, have the task of making them care about the Japanese, half a world away."

"You are right," I said to Desmond. "Now my main task is usually to inform people about the Japanese, and to make them realise that Nazi Germany is only one piece of the puzzle. If they do not care about the situation in the Pacific, the entire world is at stake. The common Britisher has no idea..."

"They really don't," Desmond agreed. "And, I suppose, why should they? It is far outside their realm of worries to even consider how the Imperial Japanese and her designing superpatriots hate the white race. Nor do they have any idea about Japan's intent to conquer all of Asia, and then..." he trailed off. I knew — if the Japanese could conquer all of Asia, and its resources and peoples, then little would be able to stop her from wreaking havoc on the rest of the world.

"No one here has any idea about these things," I said. "It's amazing."

He chuckled, "Yes, but you have been living in China. They have been living here, trying to survive. Worrying about bombings and rations and —"

"And all the same things we had been living with in Shanghai," I laughed.

"You know what I mean, though." He thought for a moment,

BRISTOL, ENGLAND
20 DECEMBER 1943

then added. "The morale is different here. The enemy isn't as near as he was in Shanghai, but his attacks are more certain. And these are just common Londoners. It takes a special sort to live in Shanghai. An adventurous sort."

I grinned. "And I'm happy to have met a fellow adventurer such as yourself." There was a comfortable pause.

"Now," I gestured at the scrapbook, "In July you will see a break in speaking engagements, because I was told I was approved for immigration to the States. My application was supported by several important Americans living in Washington—Judge Milton Helmick, attorney Joseph McCloy, Senator Carl Hatch. The Czechoslovak Ministry of Defence gave their blessing for my departure; the U.S. Embassy set an appointment to come present my case and obtain my visa. The Vice Consul gave me a letter stating that I shall get the visa immediately, as soon as I could prove that I secured my passage and my British exit permit. I wrote my sister and borrowed funds to book passage."

"Clearly something went wrong," Desmond said, "For here you still are."

"Indeed, I am," I said. "I was quite irate when it all fell through. During the first week of August, I went to the American Embassy to get the visa in my passport as I had been directed. When I arrived at the embassy in Grosvenor Square, the acting Consul, Winfield Harrison Scott, didn't rise to greet me. He didn't offer me a chair. He looked at me as if I could be Hitler's and Hirohito's first cousin in one. He then informed me that the Department of State had instructed him not to issue my visa after all."

"And why not?" Desmond asked.

"He said, 'After all, there is a war on,' and 'people change.' You can imagine my discontent."

"I'm sure 'discontent' is putting it mildly," Desmond said.

THE SUITCASE

I nodded. It was difficult to recount the situation without becoming upset all over again. "I can't imagine what reason the U.S. State Department could have not to give me the visa. I feel like a real blasted fool. I'm certain the trouble can be traced back to baseless rumours that began in Shanghai." I sighed. "I did point out to Scott that, while speaking for the M.O.I., I have been taken to all the vital war production factories and received thanks from Admirals and Air Marshalls; I have spoken on cruisers, in secret aerodromes, and what have you — and in recognition of all that, somebody feels I am not trustworthy enough to be allowed into America."

"It would be laughable if it wasn't so infuriating. You would think that after your initial interrogation in Liverpool, and then through your work with the M.O.I., that the authorities would have discovered anything nefarious about you. It's absurd."

"I can't think of any other reason for the attitude of the State Department, than the vague possibility that, while making inquiries, someone shot his or her mouth off, either to make themselves important, or out of sheer stupidity, or low meanness," I said.

"I wonder who."

"I do have my suspicions, but nothing concrete. I wish I could lay my lily white hands on that someone. But I am afraid that whichever way the State Department shall decide, I will never be told who was responsible for the cancellation."

"Likely not."

"So, on August ninth, I was summoned again to the Embassy for further discussion of my case, and had an interview at the American Consulate General with two officers of the United States Navy. There, I gained the most regrettable impression that the United States Immigration Authorities are regarding my activities as a representative of the Czechoslovak Army in China

BRISTOL, ENGLAND
20 DECEMBER 1943

with a certain suspicion."

"The activities you were ordered to carry out by Ingr? The duties you were sent back to Shanghai to fulfil?"

"The very same," I said.

There had also been the matter of a banking transaction I had performed for Willy Wltzek back in Shanghai in September of 1941. It had been unimportant at the time. In fact, I had been grateful for the business. But the funds had never come through at their destination. Wltzek eventually contacted the authorities to accuse me in the matter—never mind that the Far Eastern banking systems as we knew them had collapsed, and that a lost transaction was not anything for which I myself might be held responsible.

I decided that the best course of action was to admit that a debt existed and to make arrangements to repay him in instalments—though the money was missing through no fault of my own. I had no access to the records for the transaction with the Chartered Bank of India, Australia, and China. Like the situation with Maglič so many years before, it was my word against Wltzek's.

Wltzek was one of the non-Jewish Czech refugees who had arrived in Shanghai. He had been the managing director of three of Czechoslovakia's leading newspapers in Brno, the German-language *Tagesbote*, the *Morgenpost*, and the *Neues Volksblatt*. The Nazis' treatment of journalists had scared him all the way to Shanghai, where he had been active in the community and had even joined my company in the S.V.C. Why his accusation was delivered years after the fact was beyond me. Perhaps his wallet was as thin as my own, and it was an act of desperation. Or perhaps he was attempting to tarnish my reputation.

I felt no need to mention the incident to Desmond, but it had certainly eroded my credibility.

THE SUITCASE

I realised my fists were clenched. I flattened my palms and took a breath. "Pravda vítězí," I said. "The truth prevails. Or at least, I hope it will. I should very much like to go to New York with my sister. I can only hope that the G-men will soon discover that somebody was barking up the wrong tree. I would not be at all surprised if the army leaders did not have a hand in it—particularly those who have not realised yet that this war is fought for democracy and not the fascistic principles they would like to apply after their return to Czechoslovakia. Perhaps they feel that a bit of straight information about their real mentality might not improve their chances for getting fat jobs and large country estates after their return."

"Good heavens," he said. I knew I had been ranting, but how could I not be upset? And, as time would reveal, I wasn't at all wrong about my suspicions that the supposedly-democratic Czechs had indeed fallen into fascistic thinking.

By the end of 1943 the world would know that the Jewish population of Protectorate of Bohemia and Moravia had been relocated. I had no idea where my family had been sent. I would see in the press that the Czechs were grateful to the Germans for cleansing the Protectorate of its Jewry. That the public support Czechs had once displayed for the Jews had only been a method of conveying anti-German sentiments. Once the Protectorate had been rid of its Jewry, and once it had become apparent that the Czechs would not be the next group targeted by the Nazis, opinions apparently changed.

A 1943 report from the Prague Resistance to the London Government-in-Exile would state: "Anti-Semitism will probably be the only thing we shall partially adopt from Nazi ideology. Our people do not agree with the bestial methods of the Germans; nevertheless, they are of the opinion that most of the Jews deserve just what is happening to them now."

BRISTOL, ENGLAND
20 DECEMBER 1943

Desmond was quiet for a moment, thoughtfully letting my fire dwindle. "Have you had word from your family in Prague?" he finally asked.

"None," I said. "Nothing since sometime in 1941 when they told my sister and me not to expect more letters."

"I see."

"And I fear that making inquiries will only cause trouble for them."

"That may be." He, too, had seen reports in the news regarding the deportation of Jews from the so-called Protectorate.

"So, it seems we will all be stuck for the duration. Anyhow," I said with a sigh, "some people over here are pleased that I shall be around for a little longer — those are the girlfriends."

Desmond grinned. "So what did you do after your plans for the States fell through? Continued speaking, I suppose?" He placed the remaining scrapbook pages in hand, feeling the weight of them.

"Well, after I received the letter that I shall be given the visa, I naturally cancelled all speaking engagements with the M.O.I."

"Naturally."

"And so my assignments were given to other speakers."

"I see," he said.

"The M.O.I. was certainly surprised to hear that I may be here for quite some time yet, since I had shown them the letter from the American Embassy about my visa. And so I started all over again to secure some lectures. In September they sent me to Birmingham."

"Ah, manufacturing..." Birmingham produced vehicles, aeroplanes, engines, arms, shells, and explosives. The whole area had been heavily bombed through that spring on account.

"Yes. 'Vlado Jiří' quite enjoyed doing his 'From Prague to London via Occupied China' routine. I was then sent to Leeds

THE SUITCASE

to begin a tour of the northeast region. I was there when Italy surrendered." I had been at my room at the Great Northern Hotel when I heard the news. "Let's see. I spoke to the Linthwaite Youth Club, the Leeds National Fire Service," or N.F.S., "personnel, the Barnsley and Bradford Civil Defence Services — and at more factories."

Desmond pointed to the scrapbook. "This says Messrs. Joseph May and Sons."

I gave a nod, "The clothing company. They asked me to two locations, giving two separate addresses at each."

"The Prague-to-London programme?"

I gave a shake of my head. "'Europe Under Hitler.' I spoke three times at Messrs. George Bray & Company."

"Ah," he nodded, "Brays." The lighting company was quite well-known.

"Then there was a textile mill, John Crowther & Sons. And a tank works, W.P. Butterfield, in Shipley."

"Impressive," Des said, turning the page.

"Then it was back to the southern regions, to the Bristol Channel, where 'Captain X' spoke at the Council School in Portway for the Westbury Parish Hall's local M.O.I. meeting. In October..." I waited for him to turn the page.

"Ah! There I am!" Desmond said when he saw the photos from that day. The race course had been filled with lorries and tanks and JEEPs. A large tent had been set up with examples of weapons and other battle-related paraphernalia inside. As "Captain X," I had spoken from five o'clock until quarter-past six doing my "Lectures on Eastern Europe." "Cheltenham," Desmond mused. "Lovely spa town, if there wasn't a war on."

I laughed. "Not compared to the spas where I'm from. And it's not owing to the war." I sighed, trying not to think about the spas of Europe, which would lead to thoughts of Karlovy

BRISTOL, ENGLAND
20 DECEMBER 1943

Vary, which would in turn make me think of my sister, and of the forces preventing me from joining her in New York. "After Cheltenham, I was sent to Liverpool. I was there when Italy declared war on Germany." By that time, 13 October 1943, I had been in England for about a year.

"What was the topic in Liverpool?" Desmond asked.

"'The Japs in Peace and War.'"

Desmond was looking at a thank-you note from the scrapbook. "Oh! Crispen!"

"None other," I grinned. Desmond knew the name from Shanghai. I recalled the Rotary Club's lively meetings at the Metropole.

Crispen's letter read:

The Round Table
Table No. 8   Liverpool

14th October, 1943

Capt. V. Jiri,
c/o Ministry of Information,
14, Castle Street
L I V E R P O O L, 2.

Dear Captain Jiri,
On behalf of the Speakers' Committee may I express our sincere thanks to you for the most interesting "Report from the Pacific" which you gave to the Table at lunch yesterday.

Your subject was a most appropriate one for a Liverpool audience – we have of course so many business interests in the Far East – and everyone

393

THE SUITCASE

thoroughly enjoyed listening to you.
Once again, very many thanks.

Yours sincerely,
C.A. Crispen
Chairman,
Speakers' Committee

Desmond turned to a page that held an itinerary, a hotel menu, and a business card.

"I stayed in the Stork Hotel, just across the River Mersey from Liverpool proper. The head of the Birkenhead Conservative Association was quite pleased with my speech — you see her card there," I nodded towards the scrapbook:

BIRKENHEAD CONSERVATIVE ASSOCIATION

With Miss de Jonghe's Compliments

46 HAMILTON SQUARE
BIRKENHEAD

Desmond gave me a look, then chuckled. I neither affirmed nor denied his suspicions about my relationship with Miss de Jonghe.

"Then," I sighed — we were nearing the end of the scrapbook — "I travelled overnight to Glasgow and checked into the North Bristol Hotel, the home base from which 'Captain Vlado Jiří' relayed his 'Report from the Pacific' to the surrounding region. They had me giving about three talks a day. I then did a large public meeting at La Scala Cinema in Hamilton. I spoke to the shipbuilders at Harland & Wolff in Finnieston and in Scoutston. I

BRISTOL, ENGLAND
20 DECEMBER 1943

went to Abbotsford to speak to the N.F.S. there. In Stonehouse and in Killbride I addressed the E.M.S. Hospital staff and patients."

Desmond had been turning pages, following along.

"Let me think. The Argus Foundry in Thornliebank. The Mond Nickel Company. One day I walked from my hotel over to the Ca' D'Oro Restaurant on Union Street to address the Glasgow City Business Club. That was a good one. The Rotary Club in Hamilton. Shipbuilders A&J Inglis in Pointhouse. N.F.S. personnel in Greenock. A public meeting at the Olympia Cinema in Bridgeton."

Desmond said, "It looks like they sent you back to London."

"Yes, 'home' to London to give more lectures. A long, long train trip that was."

"Public meetings?" Des asked, turning the page. "Captain Jiri" was printed on page after page of the newspaper: 26, 27, 28, and 29 October, all the same. The headline: "Japan Can Be Beaten Quickly."

"After London, they sent me back to Scotland."

"You are joking."

"I wish. Just after my birthday."

"Forty-four years old," Desmond said, shaking his head. "Tsk tsk."

"I think I arrived in Edinburgh on the seventh."

Desmond skimmed the page for a moment, then let out a hearty laugh. He read aloud from the *Edinburgh Evening News* article entitled, "The Not So Pacific": "'Captain Vlado Jiri, who is speaking at an M.O.I. meeting in the Dominion Cinema tomorrow, has been a riding instructor with the Czechoslovakian Army, garage mechanic in Shanghai,'" he erupted in laughter, "'and foreman on a plantation in Dutch Borneo'"? Desmond wiped a tear from the corner of his eye as he read: "'He later became a foreman leader in a tin mine near Bangkok, Siam.'"

THE SUITCASE

His laughter cooled as he resumed reading: "'In 1934 he moved to Shanghai, whence he worked as a garage mechanic and an insurance salesman.'"

I gave an exaggerated shrug. "As I said, I can't help what the newspapermen take away from my lectures." I laughed a little, then said, "The last bit's half-true, anyway. When I first got to Shanghai, before I met you, I did sell life insurance."

"I believe you could sell anything," Desmond said. He continued to read from the article: "'He was captured by the Japanese when fighting in a Czech Rifle Company alongside the Allies, and made several unsuccessful attempts to escape from the camp where he was held with British and American citizens.'"

"Well, something like that," I grinned.

"'Having entered the Czechoslovakian Diplomatic Service at the outbreak of war, he was eventually repatriated. His 'Report on the Pacific' is based on experience of the Far East in peace and war,'" he finished. "Well."

"Maybe after a few drinks I'll tell you the long and short of my escape attempts. Not since the Great War had I experienced such excitement."

"Even Bloody Saturday?" he asked.

"Even Bloody Saturday. Now," I gestured for him to turn the final page, "after Scotland—Wales. The King's Head Hotel in Newport. The local Information Committee's War Commentary Meeting. From Newport to Cardiff. The Royal Hotel. A big meeting at the Ely Racecourse with the 166th Mixed Regiment troops and the A.T.S."

"I bet you enjoyed the ladies of the A.T.S."

I gave him a wink. "After the A.T.S. talk, later that same evening, I did another war commentary meeting, at the Reardon Smith Lecture Theatre in the National Museum of Wales."

BRISTOL, ENGLAND
20 DECEMBER 1943

"Impressive."

"It was. Then the following day, the Baldwin Steel Employees Club meeting in Griffithstown, then an Overseas Club meeting in Cardiff. Then they asked me to tour the prison there—with the governor."

"Really!"

"Then more of the usual: a war commentary meeting in Pontypridd, a Home Guard meeting at Cardiff University, a Rotary Club luncheon meeting in Penarth. That one was in a little café. I gave them the watered-down version—'Czechoslovaks Get Around.'"

"That they surely do!" Desmond exclaimed. "So," he said, shutting the scrapbook, "What has been your favourite part of your 'Grand Tour'?"

With not a moment's hesitation I blurted out—"The women!" to give Des a laugh.

Big Ben began chiming to announce the hour. "Well," I said, "shall we venture out?"

"Yes. And we'll start with a drink, to celebrate," Desmond said as he placed the scrapbook on the nearby table.

"What are we celebrating?" I asked.

"Alton has exceeded their fundraising goals yet again."

In May '42, before my repatriation, Alton had raised enough money to purchase a destroyer. Their themed fundraising drives, like December '42's "Tanks for Attack" week and June '43's "Wings for Victory" week, traditionally surpassed targets and raised more than other districts, owing much to Desmond. He had also been recognized for his efforts a few months previously, in August.

A piano began to play as we donned our overcoats, the sound coming clear as day through the wall I shared with my neighbours. The discordant notes and improperly-struck keys

THE SUITCASE

caused me to grimace. "We are leaving just in time, then," I said. "Some days those women do nothing but play the piano until well nigh ten o'clock at night. By then, their drunken boyfriends arrive for a visit, and then I get to hear the details of quite a different sort of performance."

He laughed again. "I see. I'm sure that if you yourself were one of the said boyfriends—a cast member and not an avid listener—you would have no complaints."

"I would never lend my talents to such women," I said. "And if they would actually play the piano I would not mind, but they are murdering the strings the whole blooming day—and often with Grieg's Peer Gynt suite, and you know how I love Edvard Grieg."

"I do indeed."

"Most days I am in the mood to march in and break their lazy bones. One day I probably shall."

"Why aren't they engaged in war work?" The noisy piano music continued; even Des was flinching at the noise.

"It is a mystery to me."

"The 'prevailing disease'?"

"They don't look pregnant, but who knows. It's rather trying to prepare an hour's speech, meanwhile a couple of bitches are hammering 'Ase's Death' and 'Solveig's Song' continuously in your ears."

"Well, come, let's go hear some real music," he said.

"If it was warmer then I would suggest we walk through the park. As it is, why don't we take the tube down to Hyde Park Corner?"

"Whatever you think best. Although," he said, glancing down at his figure, "I do feel I could use the exercise. I sorely miss riding every day."

"You and I both! To say nothing of how much I miss tennis.

BRISTOL, ENGLAND
20 DECEMBER 1943

What I wouldn't do to play on a nice sunny court at the French Club again."

We headed out into the cold. Outside, men in teams of three were busy laying poisoned meats to kill the rats in Kensington. It was believed that a million London rats had already been murdered in recent weeks. The annihilation was to such an extent that even I, who had seen human lives wasted on such great scales, had begun to feel bad for the rodents, who stood little chance against such coordinated attacks of gas and poison.

Desmond chose to ignore the death squads and continued pleasant conversation on the way to the tube station. "Have you been to the Dorchester?" he asked.

"I haven't been anywhere, really. When I am in London I'm working." I said, as if money wasn't also an enormous factor.

"I hope 'Les Girls,' the Dorchester Follies, are still performing, though I vaguely remember reading that Maurice Winnick took them on tour."

"Oh, any girls will do," I smiled.

"I'm sure there'll be plenty. The Dorch has reinforced concrete and is one of the safest buildings in London, and the food and entertainment make it one of the most popular. Valet parking out front, prostitutes out back. You are going to love it." He continued, "I wonder if Law Stone's dance band is there. And there's a grill room, and an oriental restaurant. We won't worry with the basement—the homosexuals tend to meet there."

"I'm most looking forward to the food. I couldn't tell you how long it's been since I have had a truly decent meal."

"There's some disdain for the 'Ritzkrieg,' but I think it's well worth fielding the ire of the occasional malcontent. Besides," he added, "they are only allowed to serve three courses."

I could understand their frustrations—why should most people straggle along with their ration coupons, while the wealthy elites, who could afford the cover charge of seven shillings and six pence, and the five-shilling three-course meal, feasted almost as if there wasn't a war on? In addition to those costs, we also paid two shillings and six pence for the privilege of dancing that night.

"If we bring any girls back to your flat, we should show them your Shanghai scrapbooks—the ones where I figure highly," Desmond said.

"I will say, the scrapbooks have not failed me yet. Women love them." We had made the short walk and were entering the Gloucester Road tube station. The other nearby tube station, at Earl's Court Road, had been closed since before my arrival in the country. "We had high times in Shanghai, didn't we?" I mused.

"Have you kept in contact with Lucien Ovadia?" Desmond asked as we waited.

"He's well enough, I suppose. He says I should write my memoirs."

"So you should," Desmond said. "Others are."

"He's been in India about a year and hopes to leave soon and come to England. He says Viva's been driving an ambulance. Has a uniform and everything."

"Is that so? I can't picture it—I have only ever seen her in evening gowns or leisure wear. Quite the athletic figure, as I recall." He added, "I don't blame Ovadia for wanting to leave, what with the Indian struggles to gain independence from the Empire. I can't imagine it's a pleasant place to be. Is he still working for Sassoon?"

"Oh, always. And Sir Victor is still Sir Victor. Did you see him in the news? He was spotted at the Mocambo in Hollywood with Merle Oberon, Charlie Chaplin, and Chaplin's new wife Oona."

"Oona? What happened to Goddard? I'll never forget when they arrived in the *Coolidge* and stayed at the Cathay, dodging

BRISTOL, ENGLAND
20 DECEMBER 1943

questions about their relationship when the reporters asked. Danced at the Paramount, then left the next day. You and I saw *Modern Times* not long after. Remember?"

"How could I forget? He and Goddard divorced last summer—shortly before he married Oona. Very shortly. He is fifty-four and she was freshly eighteen. At the Mocambo he was heard whispering to Oona—his fourth wife—'Look around at those old bags. Every one of them's jealous of you.'"

Desmond laughed so heartily he drew the attention of people passing nearby. "I'm sure it's just the opposite—everyone's jealous of Charlie!"

I waved my hand, "Oona's too young for my tastes. Oberon, though... If I had been at the Mocambo, my sights would have been on her."

"Her husband is a producer. Alexander Korda. You know, *The Private Life of Henry VIII*. And *The Scarlet Pimpernel*, your favourite."

"I didn't realise the connection." I didn't tell Desmond that the *Scarlet Pimpernel* had only been so popular with our friends because of the Nine-Fifteen Club and their involvement with sneaking soldiers out of Shanghai. He was still going on about Goddard and her husband.

"Korda's been knighted, so Goddard is Lady Korda now. She's lovely as ever. Did you catch *Forever and a Day*? They showed it in Portsmouth in October."

"I wouldn't have missed it. So many stars in one film!"

The train arrived and we settled in for the short ride to the Dorchester. "Who else do you have gossips about?"

I thought for a moment. "Did you hear Tony George has been knighted?"

"Has he?" Desmond asked.

"Around the time I saw you in May. He's being sent to

diplomatic posts in the States now." After I pause, I added, "He was never the same after his release from Bridge House." The party-going, speech-giving, pony-racing, tennis-playing Tony that Shanghai had known and loved, was gone. In his place was a man irrevocably damaged physically and mentally by his captivity and the untold tortures he had suffered at the hands of the Japanese. The following month, January 1944, Tony George would jump from his hotel window in Baltimore. After his death, the *Shanghai Evening Post and Mercury* would print: "There can be no doubt his [final] act was a direct result of depression arising from his experiences in Shanghai."

"Poor Tony George. Anything cheerier?" Desmond asked, laughing.

"David Innes-Ker's sister has had a daughter. Remember Jean?"

"How could I forget her?" He paused for a moment, then said, "What a shame. Her, the Chieri sisters, the Lucas sisters—all the nice young socialites chose nice young men and nice young soldiers when they might have had slightly-older ruffians like us,"

"Gentlemen," I corrected him with a grin.

"Bachelors... Veterans, like us, who are sitting this one out."

"C'est la vie," I said, shrugging. "I suppose the Dorchester will be filled with the same ilk as Innes-Kers and Chieris and Lucases. Too bad the nice young men are all at war..."

London, England
Monday Evening, 20 December 1943

> *Hell is empty and all the devils are here.*
> – William Shakespeare, *The Tempest*, I. ii

"We should do this more often," Desmond said. We sat with our drinks and watched the people around us as we chatted. The band played Gershwin's "I Got Rhythm."

"Yes, we should," I said, clinking my drink against his. "If those Dorchester Follies were performing, I think I would insist that we do this all the time," I said. We had been disappointed to learn that Desmond was right—the Follies had gone on tour performing for troops and factory workers and other vital wartime personnel.

"So," Desmond said, "you have alluded to tantalizing stories of interrogation and torture, for yourself, for your business partner, for your Boy. I have waited long enough!" he finished dramatically. "Now, divulge." He took a sip of his drink and then looked at me expectantly.

"Well," I said, taking a swig of my own drink before I began, "I was one of the first people taken in for questioning when the Japs occupied Shanghai, but many men did not survive their interrogations. You have heard a little about Bridge House. Leroy Healey, of XMHA, was treated so badly that he went insane and died in his filthy Bridge House cell. Edward Elias was also among the first to be taken in. Surely he had been participating in espionage—and surely he had no training in withstanding such pressure. Neither he nor Ellis Hayim," I said pointedly. "I can only imagine the tortures they endured at the hands of the Japanese."

"I shudder to think of it," Des said.

"So," I continued, "The very morning of the takeover, I was brought in. Financial institutions were the first to fall to the Japanese. Once they began to review transaction records, my name shot to the top of their list. Now, the preceding night had been spent out on the town, naturally," I said.

"Naturally," Desmond parroted with a smile.

"I had been out with the American commander of the U.S.S. *Wake* and other friends. When I arrived home in the wee hours, I saw the events of the Japanese takeover and her attack on the *Peterel*. After the fireworks show out on the river, I shut my eyes for a few hours, all the while leaving my door unlocked in anticipation of a visit from the Japanese. Cue sunrise over the Metropole," I said theatrically. "Taussig is awakened by a terrible pounding and banging on his unlocked door. Enter the Japanese Gendarmerie, stomping in their heavy boots, holding bayonets and pistols." I laughed, "They got me out of bed a damn sight quicker than my Boy ever managed."

Desmond chuckled. "I'll say."

"So they summon me down to their Big Cheese. We go out into the cold. It's practically snowing with ash from people incinerating papers in the business district and at the consulates. Across from the Metropole, at the American Consulate, the Japanese are taking books from the American Club's library and creating a burning pile. Aeroplanes are flying overhead, dropping leaflets to inform everyone of the takeover. News dissemination lorries are running up and down Nanking Road with loudspeakers, announcing that a state of war has arisen between Japan and the United States and the British Empire, and that detachments of the Japanese Army and Navy would

LONDON, ENGLAND
20 DECEMBER 1943

be dispatched in the International Settlement. Light tanks and armoured cars roll right down the Bund."

"Quite the scene," Desmond said.

"The Gendarmes delivered me to the Cathay, of all places, and escorted me upstairs, directly to Sir Victor Sassoon's desk. There sat none other than Japanese Naval Captain Koreshige Inuzuka. This was a man whose name I knew well from his position as head of the Imperial Japanese Navy's Advisory Bureau on Jewish Affairs. He had tried to work with Shanghai's Jewish community many times in the past, and had often been unsatisfied with the result."

"Where was Sassoon during the December takeover?" Desmond asked.

"Bombay," I said.

"Ah." He made a gesture with his hand. "Please, continue."

"So I was taken before Inuzuka. As I said, I had been out all night, and had eaten no breakfast. You can imagine that my mood was not the best. Now, I naturally assumed that the reason I had been summoned somehow pertained to my activities for the Czechoslovak Government-in-Exile here in London. My training and movement of troops. My pro-Allied propaganda broadcasts. My transfers of money to the Czech Ambassador in Tokyo. Instead, Inuzuka asked me about the banking transactions for my bill at the Metropole."

Desmond laughed. "He what?"

I nodded. "Inuzuka had begun to look through Sassoon's books. He asked what transactions I had performed for Sassoon on Saturday, December sixth. I told the truth, as there was nothing to hide. I calmly explained that the general manager of Sassoon's hotels had paid me my due commission," from our 1935 Copper Trick, "and had wiped out my Metropole bill for the month of November and the first half of December. He knew I had no money to pay, and that I had maintained friendly relations with the Sassoons."

I paused to draw a cigarette from my case and light it. Desmond waited intently.

"The meeting with Inuzuka threw my escape plans into action," I said. "I already had some vague ideas about getting to Free China in the event of a Japanese takeover. I had some Chungking friends who were located about ten miles from Shanghai with the Chinese partisans. The Japanese had created a hundred-mile zone separating occupied China from Free China. The zone would be impossible to cross unaided. One needed help from the Chinese Nationalists to sneak through perimeters and bribe police and soldiers. First, I would need to secure a pass that would enable me to leave the Japanese-occupied zone. For the declared enemies of Japan, this pass had to be approved by the Swiss embassy. For the citizens of Axis and neutral countries, approval by a country's own diplomatic representatives would suffice."

"And for occupied countries like Czechoslovakia?" Desmond asked.

"I went to the Japanese police and, on the basis of my Czechoslovak passport, I asked for permission to cross the border. I was informed that the Czechoslovak government was not recognized by Japan, that Czechoslovakia did not exist as a country, and that I would need to visit the German consulate and obtain proper documentation."

Desmond laughed. "Slim chance."

"I explained to the Japanese officer that we Czechoslovaks did not recognise the occupation of our country. 'I would rather have no pass at all, than go to the German consulate for permission.'"

"What did they say?" Desmond asked.

"The officer in charge said he would consult with his superior. They took my address and telephone number and dismissed me."

LONDON, ENGLAND
20 DECEMBER 1943

"Did they call you?"

I nodded. "They called the very next day and told me to come pick up a special travelling pass that would be issued on the basis of my Czechoslovak passport. When I returned to my hotel with the new pass, I discovered a Japanese Naval Corporal waiting for me. He transported me to the Naval command post for another interrogation. This time, they wanted to know about the money I had been receiving from London. After four hours of questioning, I finally convinced them that this money was nothing more than common bank transactions. In actuality, this was the money I had been receiving from the Government-in-Exile and transferring to Ambassador Havlíček in Tokyo. Havlíček and I had pre-arranged an explanation for the money transfers — that I had borrowed to pay for my Exchange Broker's Association seat and was repaying him in instalments — and this I repeated to the Japanese until it was finally met with satisfaction. However," I said, putting my cigarette out, "soon after, they took an interest in my business partner, Eduard Kann, the former head of the American Asian Bank."

"I see," Desmond said.

"Around Christmastime I went to our office to collect some belongings. I was alone there when Jap Gendarmes came in and asked for Kann. But he was not in. Our business, by then, was nothing more than a building with a phone bank. We had been effectively shut down by the new Japanese banking regulations. On that occasion, the difficulty was in convincing the Gendarmes that I myself was not Kann. Even with my paperwork in hand, it took me ringing up Kann's wife, Margaret, to convince them that Kann was indeed ill at home, where he had been convalescing after receiving cancer treatments."

"Did they go fetch him from his home?" Desmond asked.

"That didn't happen until March," I said. "One day, around

THE SUITCASE

the beginning of March, I went to the office to pay the telephone bills. After the December encounter I just mentioned, I had stopped visiting the office but once a month, in hopes of avoiding any further run-ins. I arrived at the office around ten o'clock and sat down at my desk, when suddenly one of the seventy-two telephones rang. It was Margaret Kann, and she was very excited. I could hardly blame the old girl—the Gendarmes had come at four in the morning and arrested her husband."

"In the middle of the night?"

I nodded. "Terror tactic. So Mrs. Kann was hoping that, since I had such experience with being questioned, I could help Kann. I was just telling her to start at the beginning and tell me everything, when the office door flew open, and in marched three Jap Gendarmes. They presented a mighty fine military parade, complete with pistols, swords, gas masks, and haversacks. They looked ready to go into battle at any moment and were certainly overdressed for searching a supposedly empty office. When they entered I put on my most innocent face and said that I was just there waiting.

"'For whom are you waiting?' they asked.

"'Well, I am waiting for Mr. Kann,' I said.

"'Who are you?'

"'Well, I want to sell him a stamp. Mr. Kann is a philatelist.'"

Desmond asked, "Did you have a stamp on you? To supposedly sell to him?"

"No. But it didn't matter. They said, 'Vrrr, come here.' I had to park myself between two of those monkeys while the third one started ransacking the office. They collected every little bit of exchange quotations Kann had, going back to 1910, and then we went for a ride. At the station, I made myself comfortable in what had become, by then, my usual chair, and I waited. After about three hours I had a glimpse of Kann being led into

LONDON, ENGLAND
20 DECEMBER 1943

the inquisition office. The poor old chap was only four months after his cancer operation and looked like concentrated death in person. I could not talk to him and he was quickly led away. I continued to wait. By five in the afternoon I would have eaten tinned sausages, including the tin, I was so hungry. I was finally taken to the examiner. He seemed very friendly: 'Please smoke a cigarette,' he said.

"'Thank you, no, but a steak would do me fine.'

"Verrrrry sorrrry. Please, do you know Mr. Sze?'

"'Yes, I know about two hundred and forty-seven Mr. Szes — which one do you mean?'

"'Please, Mr. Sze, he, he, he Chungking agent.'

"'Sorry, I don't know Mr. Sze who is a Chungking agent.' And so it went until about seven o'clock.

"During those two hours I realised that the Japanese suspected Kann of connection with the Chinese Chungking government. He was an advisor to the Chinese Central Bank, similar to my own position with the Bank of Canton." For Desmond's benefit I added, "This was not an active function but an advisory role."

O'Neill nodded.

"But Kann was never interested in politics. He had lived in the Far East for forty years and is known for his expertise on Chinese currencies. After two hours of questioning I was brought back to the waiting room, and at about nine o'clock I was told to go home. This time there was no motorcycle ride, no sirens, no escort. I simply had to take a bus. I was very hurt."

Desmond gave a chuckle.

"The next day, they took my Boy, who knew little to nothing of my banking or other activities, as had been my intent. They tried to refresh his memory for a solid week, using all the mediums of persuasion. Bamboo sticks. Electric shocks. Water suffocation. He would not confess anything to them because he did not know

THE SUITCASE

anything."

"Hence the fortnight he spent in the hospital regaining his humanity," Desmond said.

"As for my partner, he was released after five days, after many kicks in the stomach and below. He was a complete wreck. Months later, when the repatriation ship left Shanghai, he still had not recovered. He told me that he slept on the bare floor in a small room with seven other prisoners. There was an iron barrel in the corner of the room for necessities of nature and it was emptied but once every twenty-four hours. Food consisted of a handful of rice at ten in the morning each day, and it was full of dirt and bugs. Everything was filthy. People were diseased. And then there were the abuses…" I trailed off for effect and took a sip of my drink. "When I was taken in for questioning I always managed to get out within thirty-six hours. They seldom questioned me about the things I thought I ought to be questioned about. My success involved a great deal of quick thinking and a whole lot of self-control." I sighed. "If I may give you my honest assessment?"

Desmond nodded. "Please do."

"The trouble with the Japs is that one department does not know what the other is doing, and the Army, Navy, and Gendarmerie do not think too much about the efficiency of the others' investigative qualities. That's the reason why I would hardly be back from a visit to the Army, when the Gendarmerie began to feel that an Imperial ride across town on a motorbike would do me a power of good. I shall never forget the atmosphere of fear that permeated Shanghai. People waited sleeplessly, sweating in their beds at the thought of hearing footsteps approaching in the night."

"I imagine so," he said.

"In mid-February I left instructions that, in the event of my disappearance or death, my Exchange Broker's Association

LONDON, ENGLAND
20 DECEMBER 1943

seat should pass to my brother, and I nominated him for membership. Since I could no longer stay at the Metropole, I stashed some furnishings at our Kiukiang Road banking office as a contingency, then I began staying with friends of mine — Czechoslovak refugees who had built a home in the French Concession." This was the Voticky/Kanturek family. "It was safe there because Vichy was cooperating with the Nazis, so the French in Shanghai were left alone by the Japanese."

"Clearly you had but one place to go."

I smiled. "To be granted entry into the French Concession, I fooled the Gendarmes using an official-looking hundred-dollar debenture certificate issued by the Swiss Club. The English-illiterate patrolmen saw 'Swiss Club' written in large letters and were proud that they could make out the word 'Swiss.' They didn't bother with the rest of the document."

"So you are hiding out with a family in Frenchtown. What next?" Desmond asked.

"I was soon alerted, by the Chief of the French police — whose sympathies lay with de Gaulle — that Japanese police had requested that I be followed by Chinese detectives who were working with the French police. By then, I thought it was about time to scram, and scram fast. It took a few months, but by April I decided I would try to get to Chungking through occupied China."

"All the way to Chungking?" O'Neill asked with wonder. He knew that the city in question was about fifteen hundred kilometres into the Chinese interior.

"I established contact with my guerrilla friends and we organised a party of mostly journalists. There were two Belgians, one Free French, three Britons, a Pole, and myself."

"Anyone I know?" Desmond asked.

"I don't think so," I said. "It was Pierard of the French

Independent Agency; Lebas, a French student; Verune, a teacher. There were Skepper and Waller, and Corinne Bernfeld, all from the English propaganda station. And then Kittay, of the Polish Propaganda Service. We were also joined by four American soldiers who had escaped from the Prisoner of War camp in Woosung. We were divided into three groups. The Free Frenchman and myself formed the last group. The arrangement was to leave Shanghai in intervals of three days, with each group being led out by another guerrilla. We were to meet about thirty miles west of Shanghai, in Soochow, in a Buddhist monastery near a railway line—the seat of Chungking's partisans."

"Clearly that did not pan out..." Desmond said.

"We received a message from one of the Chinese guides that the first two groups had reached the meeting point safely. At dusk, around quarter past six, the Frenchman and I went on our way, following our guide and marching in the darkness for hours. We had nearly reached our destination when Chinese peasants stopped us. A Chinese guide had been apprehended by a company of Jap Infantry, and he had been tortured into betraying the hiding place of the first two groups."

Desmond listened with rapt attention.

"I told my partner, 'It is obvious that, when our companions are questioned, they will tell the Japs that you and I were in the final group. When the Japs come looking for us, we had better be asleep in our beds. It is the only way we might prove that their allegations are false—that perhaps we had been asked to join the escape party, but that we preferred to stay in Shanghai and are clearly not serious parties to any escape attempt.' I had no way of knowing when the Japanese would come to look for us, but the Frenchman and I had sufficient motivation to race the entire way back to Shanghai. It was a marathon effort—a twenty-five mile race against daylight, and against the Japanese lorries. After

LONDON, ENGLAND
20 DECEMBER 1943

many hours of running, I reached Shanghai just before six in the morning, when dawn was breaking. At the Kiukiang Road flat it actually took a few more hours before the Japanese came to visit. During that time, I burned my knapsack, had a bath, and ate a hearty snack before finally being summoned for the usual ride for questioning."

"Hm," Desmond said. "Damned lucky."

"The Gendarmerie major could not believe his eyes when he saw me. He had been entirely convinced that my bed would be found empty and I would be located somewhere along the road to Free China. I was released after two hours and took a bus back to my office. Once there, I slept for eighteen hours without waking. For days after, my body ached as if I had been thrown from a pony, trampled and savaged."

Desmond asked, "What happened to the people who were caught?"

"Oh, they had a hell of a time with the Japanese. They all received heavy prison sentences. The English woman, Corinne Bernfeld, who had been part of the second group, suffered so badly in the hands of the Japanese soldiers that she committed suicide two days after she was released. I shudder to think of the ways she was mistreated."

Des's eyebrows were raised.

"If the Chinese peasants had not stopped us and warned me and the Frenchman and our guide, I would have shared their fate." Many of my fellow almost-escapees would spend two and a half years in Bridge House before being taken to Ward Road Jail. After a pause, I said, "I tried to escape again the following month, in May."

"Are you mad? Even after what happened to the others?"

I nodded. "The British director of the British American Tobacco Company, Frank Geldart, was my companion for that particular attempt. Geldart and I had a Chinese guide lead us through the no-man's land that separated Shanghai from Free China. We made it quite far and were climbing under the very last barbed wire fence that separated us from our freedom — when a Japanese patrol heard us. They opened fire on us with their machine guns. Immediately our Chinese guide was hit in the shoulder. He fell limply onto the barbed wire fence. We had known that taking fire would be a possibility, and had stationed two more Chinese guides further along the makeshift border, about fifty yards away. They began making a commotion, which drew the fire away from us long enough to tear our guide off the barbed wire and run with him back to relative safety. Once again, it was a sprint back to Shanghai. Then there was the matter of finding a discreet doctor to assist the man."

"And to think that after all that, just a few months later, you would be repatriated anyway," he said.

"Even that took a great deal of effort," I said. I then recounted how I had wangled my way onto the repatriation ship.

By the time I finished that little tale, the band had heated up and I felt ready for a dance. We quickly found a pair of ladies who were up to it.

*****

The following day, I showed Desmond the local M.O.I. offices on Wardour Street. Wardour Street was a part of "Film Row," so-called because about a hundred film companies occupied the area. Lucien Ovadia, the risk assessor, would have explained this positioning in simple terms: large quantities of highly-flammable film meant that film companies tended to occupy low-rent buildings far from the business districts. In London, this was the theatre district, which included Wardour Street, as well as the nearby Shaftesbury

LONDON, ENGLAND
20 DECEMBER 1943

Avenue, Gerrard Street, and Charring Cross Road.

After visiting the M.O.I. offices, Des and I walked over to Brewer Street to lunch at Isow's famous "Yiddish Restaurant," once recommended by Lady Luisa. I hoped we would glimpse some film and theatre stars, who were known to frequent the place. I encountered Brewster Morgan, a radio producer who worked for C.B.S. in New York. He was the producer of Edwin Jerome's radio programmes *Aunt Jenny's Real Life Stories* and *When a Girl Marries*, as well as Elizabeth Reller's show, *Doc Barclay's Daughters*.

I knew that Morgan would remember me, and reintroducing myself to him in front of Desmond was a way to impress my old friend. I didn't know that I was laying the groundwork for a future opportunity.

Back at my flat, as Desmond collected his valise, the house manager rapped at my door. "The post has just arrived, Captain," she said. "This one looks to be of importance."

I reached for the message and instantly saw that it had been sent by the Czech Embassy. Inside was a summons to report to 8 Grosvenor Place.

"Thank you," I said.

"That does look important," said Desmond. "Captain Taussig, famous speaker of the M.O.I. Always in high demand. I shall leave you to it."

"Yes, I suppose duty calls," I said with a grin, though I was unsure whether my directive to visit the Government-in-Exile would have a positive outcome.

"See that the M.O.I. sends you back to Alton soon. We would love to have you speak again and come for a visit. Maybe the Savings Movement will request your presence."

"I should enjoy that very much," I said. "They have got me booked solid until February, but hopefully after that…"

THE SUITCASE

"I shall see what I can arrange," said Desmond.

We moved to the door and went out into the street. "I'm off this way," I said.

"Safe travels," said Desmond.

"Same to you," I said.

Not long after Desmond's visit, I received a very special sort of holiday card in the post, one drawn by Desmond O'Neill himself. The card featured me, wearing my monocle and grinning like the Cheshire Cat, standing in the midst of three patriotic pinup girls he had drawn—a blonde W.A.A.F., a redheaded W.A.A.C., and a blonde "Wren." They wore suspenders and stockings, but no skirts; the jackets of their uniforms gave way to frilly white panties in place of the usual government-issued knickers.

*****

But on that day, upon arrival at 8 Grosvenor, I received a very unexpected telegram regarding Liza Kanturková and the family's friend, Professor Pribram:

WHI395   ZEURICH   37   22   1815
ELT   TAUSSIG   CARE   MASARYK   8 GROSVENOR PLACE   LN
AM INFORMED BY REDCROSS GENEVA PROFESSOR PRIBRAM AND LISA WISH PRESS EVACUATION PROFESSOR PRIBRAM PLEASE INSIST AND BEWARE OF STEPAN DONT FORGET IN FUTURE CABLE   ANSWER THROUGH REDCROSS — JOSEF HENGGELER
WHI395   8

"I don't see why they are asking you for assistance," Lieutenant

LONDON, ENGLAND
20 DECEMBER 1943

Colonel Kalla, the Czechoslovak Military Attaché, said. I didn't know that Kalla had been party to the grapevine of letters and telegrams that had been exchanged between London and Shanghai regarding my untrustworthiness.

"Why shouldn't they ask for assistance?" Something had clearly changed with the situation in Shanghai, and my old friends were exploring every possible channel in an attempt to escape the Japanese. "I am their friend and military delegate," I said.

Kalla scoffed. "What do you know of Pribram?" Kalla asked. I also didn't know that Kalla's daughter had died on Pribram's operating table just a few years previously.

Kalla was the guardian of a sixteen-year-old girl, Zora Bartiková. In May of 1940, Zora had gone to have her tonsils removed. While she was on the operating table, her blood pressure took a plunge and she died. Though it was ruled an accidental death, surely Kalla continued to blame Pribram for his loss.

"What do I know of Pribram?" I asked. "I know he didn't go for repatriation when I did. Clearly the situation in Shanghai has deteriorated if he's seeking evacuation now."

"Pribram is asking because there has been talk of another exchange, but now it doesn't seem as if that will come to fruition," Kalla said. "The war has spread, and a British-Japanese exchange agreement isn't possible at this time. And who is this Lisa?" he asked.

"Liza," I said. "Eliska. A friend. An educated and trained social worker."

"Why do they say to beware of Stepan?" Kalla asked.

"Clearly Major Stepan is refusing to recognize Pribram and include him in the evacuation list—the evacuation which, you say, will not go through. Does Shanghai know that there will be no exchange?"

Kalla did not answer.

What Kalla omitted was that Stepan's reports to the Government-in-Exile had told of an increasingly divided Czechoslovak community in Shanghai, where "old-timers" were pitted against the Jewish refugees.

The refugees, Stepan had secretly written, "were good Czechoslovaks only when our Czechoslovak interests coincided with Jewish ones." When interests did not align, the Czech refugees allegedly "promot[ed] their interests at the expense of Czechoslovak interests... This group of people has never been Czech or Slovak... They will never make state-forming citizens of our republic and are not able to work for the benefit of the Czechoslovak state." Stepan said that the "Jews" had "unproven national reliability." The Czech Circle "became an immigrant organisation."

What did Stepan, and other "old-timers," who had been in the Far East for so long, know of the real problems faced by those who had more recently fled Europe? What did they care what those refugees did in order to survive in a strange and Japanese-occupied city where, as of February 1943, it had been decreed that anyone who had arrived more recently than 1937 would be forced to live in a designated Sector for Stateless Refugees in Hongkew.

Instead of supporting the Jewish refugees, the "old-timer" Czechs like Stepan adopted a hostile attitude and furnished a "blacklist" to both the Exile Government in England and to Japanese authorities in Shanghai.

Among those in the "blacklist" were names of my Czech troops—names like Ervin Singer, the man who had participated in propaganda activities under the name Tomáš Pravda or "Thomas Truth"; Private Miroslav Loewy; Private Ota Lustig;

LONDON, ENGLAND
20 DECEMBER 1943

Lance Corporal Jan Lux; Private Julius Fried; Private Max Schneider; and Private Erich Stransky. Other names on the list included attorneys, businessmen, and others whom Stepan had had no business denouncing for national, religious, social, or any other reason.

It was lucky I then knew nothing of these developments, aside from the vague warning in the telegram to "beware of Stepan." My frustration with the situation in Shanghai, and my inability to rectify it, might have given me a heart attack.

After the war, Stepan and the Circle would say of these blacklisted men that, "at a time when the Czechoslovak Circle in Shanghai was a resistance organisation," they had "stood in the ranks of our enemies." And, after the war, Stepan would be given honours "for resistance" by the Ministry of Defence.

At that time, I knew only that Pribram and Liza wanted to get out of Shanghai, and that another exchange was not going to happen.

"Who else was included in the list for possible exchange? Can you say?" I asked.

Kalla glanced at a folder and casually read: "Lilling. Kanturková family. Julius Steiner. Albert Sax. Otto Lustig. Pribram." How I would have liked to have seen any of those people!

Kalla shuffled some sheets of paper then said, "Stepan has recently written to us that he reported Pribram's non-Czechoslovakian affiliation last year. Stepan wrote: 'Despite my report, the name of Pribram was given to our evacuation list in London.' Stepan says Pribram has been to the Swiss Consulate General asking for assistance in evacuation: 'Although I told Pribram that he is not a Czechoslovak national, he did not abandon his intention to join, at any cost, the Shanghai quota. Now he offers some Czechoslovaks considerable amounts to advance his place on the evacuation list,'" Kalla finished.

"Why does Stepan say Pribram has no Czech affiliation?" I asked. "His German nationality was annulled by the Nazi Regime. He was born in Prague..." I trailed off. I wondered whether there were other avenues for my friends to get out of Shanghai. Back in April, the Soviet Foreign Ministry had refused to give Czechs in Shanghai a permit to enter Soviet territory. However, on 12 December, just prior to my being summoned regarding the telegram from Shanghai, a Czechoslovak-Soviet Treaty of Friendship and Military Alliance had been signed. Perhaps the situation would change and my friends would be able to evacuate with Soviet assistance.

But that was not to come to pass. Unfortunately, I was in no position to help Liza and Pribram, and had no authority with the Czechs in London. And the reasons for my lack of authority were all too similar to the reasons why the Czechs back in Shanghai had been so divided — because of their respective religions, and because of relentless gossip by people who hoped for commendations after the war.

OSVĚTIM, OCCUPIED POLAND
Wednesday, 8 March 1944

"Your hour has come."
—Oberscharführer Peter Voss

ALL OF AUSCHWITZ II-Birkenau sat under a strict curfew. Extra guards with dogs were stationed at each of the subcamps, at the railroad tracks, at the guard towers, at the warehouses filled with confiscated property.

The prisoners sat crammed in the barracks—all except the members of the Czech Family Camp, who had been transported to Auschwitz-Birkenau from Terezín in September and December of 1943. In the Czech Family Camp, Marietta Taussigová and the others had lived a relatively privileged life for the past six months in the converted horse stables with their wooden bunks. But recently, the September arrivals had been relegated to a quarantine camp, supposedly pending another transport.

In anticipation of relocation, the September Czechs had packed their bags with the entirety of their possessions and with the extra food rations they'd been provided for their journey. They expected to move to the nearby camp, Heydebreck, a part of the Auschwitz III-Monowitz complex—an I.G. Farben workcamp on the Soła, a few kilometres from Auschwitz-Birkenau. Heydebreck was real. However, the September Czechs' relocation to the camp was not.

"I never thought I would miss Terezín, and Jara," Marietta said. She adjusted her scant luggage.

THE SUITCASE

Olga Katzová sighed. "You have been saying that for six months."

"And I have never meant it more than I do today," said Marietta. "After over a year in Terezín, with all the hardships and deprivations, surviving twenty-four transports, I somehow thought I was capable of handling any privation — but living here changed all that." Back in September, the old and young, from infants to elderly, had been crammed into train cars so tightly it was impossible to move. There had been "no air, no light, no water, and one bucket."

The train had passed through Dresden, then Wrocław, then Katowice, before arriving at Osvětim — Auschwitz-Birkenau. The place had a pungent, offensive, roasting stench. When the train doors were opened, bony, "wild-looking creatures in striped prison clothes boarded the wagons and flung [the Czechs] and [their] bundles out onto the platform." SS men with dogs and whips were there to separate the Czechs into columns — men in one, women and children in another — and march them through the camp's gate, over which appeared the now-infamous phrase, ARBEIT MACHT FREI, or WORK SETS YOU FREE. The Czechs from Terezín "had been told [they] were going to a labour camp, and knew nothing of extermination camps or gas chambers."

As they had been marched past the long guardhouse at the main entrance, an orchestra had been playing songs like "Glow Little Glowworm" and "You Are My Lucky Star." After they passed the camp's gates they found an immense open space, and had realised — "This must be a concentration camp!"

"There was no grass, there were no trees, no chirping birds, no comforting sight of the distant [mountains]. There were only mud and barracks." Hundreds of the pre-fabricated barracks buildings sat in rows in the mud, separated at intervals by electrified barbed wire. A charred corpse clung to the fence here

OSVĚTIM, OCCUPIED POLAND
8 MARCH 1944

and there, awaiting removal by prisoners. Tall guard towers overlooked the entire scene—the wires, the concrete fence posts, the machine-gun nests.

Beyond the rows of barracks buildings, distant chimneys belched flames and smoke. Beyond the chimneys was a birch forest.

The Czechs from Terezín had been marched to one of twelve subcamps. The "area... had not yet been built up and had no other inmates." It was called B-2-b and would become synonymous with the "Czech Family Camp." The subcamp was only "one hundred fifty metres wide, seven hundred fifty metres long" and was "divided into two sections of parallel streets. [I]n each section [were] sixteen wooden barracks, each barrack nine metres wide and forty metres long." Each "barrack" was a prefabricated horse barn with a pointed roof in the middle, the only windows being beneath the roofline. The building was divided into sixty-two bays, each bay with a three-tiered bunk. The floor was mud. Everywhere was mud, to slip and fall in, to lose one's shoes in.

All five thousand and seven of the September Czechs were housed in B-2-b. It was the first time in Auschwitz's history that men and women were housed together in the same compound, with men on one side and women on the other. On the other side of B-2-b were railroad tracks, and, across those, B-1, which housed the regular women prisoners.

The Czechs were anything but "regular" prisoners. On their arrival, Obersturmführer Schwarzhuber, a tall man of about forty, and Hauptsturmführer Mengele, a doctor in his early thirties, had made an announcement informing them of their privileged status.

The captors told the inmates they were under the protection of Himmler and would enjoy special benefits. As in Terezín, they would have autonomy. Their block elders, work foremen, and kapos would be appointed from their own ranks. They would not be subjected to hard labour outside the camp in industrial plants, agricultural work, or mining operations, and would instead perform construction and maintenance within Auschwitz. The aged would be exempt from work. The sick would be treated by inmates who were physicians—"noted university professors and doctors." The few pregnant women and few hundred children would receive extra butter rations. The Czechs would be permitted to write one postcard each month and receive one package.

How else had the Terezín Czechs been treated differently than regular Auschwitz prisoners? On their arrival, they had been allowed to keep their civilian clothing and were not issued striped prisoner uniforms, nor was their hair shorn. They had been registered and tattooed in their own barracks, by inmate clerks. At the end of every Czech Family Camp inmate's prisoner number was "6SB"—meaning Sonderbehandlung or "special treatment" after six months of imprisonment. For regular Auschwitz prisoners, tattoos meant survival. The Nazis wouldn't waste tattoos on people they only intended to gas.

The Czechs spent six months in Auschwitz-Birkenau sleeping in the barracks' bunks. Six months of the whistle blowing at four in the morning, of going out into the mud to be counted—in the cold, or heat, or frost, or rain. Six months of working in that same weather, doing jobs around the camp—levelling the ground, pouring concrete foundations, digging hundreds of fence holes, placing fence posts, digging drainage ditches, erecting new buildings, performing maintenance, building a new camp road, improving the landscape, and on and on. The women performed nursing chores for the aged and infirm, worked in the camp kitchens and administrative offices, and mended and altered

OSVĚTIM, OCCUPIED POLAND
8 MARCH 1944

clothing. They paused throughout the day for counts.

Back in Terezín, various room elders in the barracks buildings had compiled daily rosters and reported to the Judenrat, who reported to the SS.

In Auschwitz-Birkenau, the Czechs stood and were counted.

Now, in March, six months had passed since their September arrival, and the Czechs were soon to discover what "special treatment" entailed.

A few days previously, on 5 March, preparations for the transport to Heydebreck had begun. The September Czechs had been separated and placed in quarantine from the other group of Czechs who had arrived from Terezín in December. They had been instructed to write postcards and to date them for three weeks out. This was, the Nazis said, to allow for the postcards' censoring in Berlin.

Now their departure for Heydebreck was imminent.

Karly Fischerová said, "I hope the next camp will be better."

Olga Katzová said, "At least we are all going together."

Marietta scoffed. "Do you really thing we are going to a 'next camp'? In spite of all the rumours?"

There had been warnings that the Czechs were not heading for Heydebreck at all, but were instead to be murdered en masse.

Karly covered her son Petr's ears. "Those are unreliable and ugly rumours, Marietta Taussigová, and I choose not to believe a word."

Olga offered, "I heard the rumours are 'a deliberate attempt to cause panic, with the aim of getting [us] involved in a hazardous attempt to escape.'"

"Besides," Karly added, stroking her son's hair, "They said the same thing when we were taken for disinfecting. All those warnings, and how tense we were, marching to the bathhouse, where we were actually disinfected, and sent back to camp with clean underwear, wrapped in blankets so we wouldn't catch cold. Is that not how we would be treated before a real transfer?"

"I suppose we shall soon see," said Marietta glumly. "Thank God I have no children for whom I must feign positivity."

Olga asked, "What does Petr think about the move?" She turned her attention to the boy. "Are you frightened to go to the new camp?"

Petr shook his head. His mother said, "He is braver than me. All that time with Fredy Hirsch has been a blessing. And knowing that Hirsch is also coming to the new camp has been a great comfort to Petr." She didn't know that, even as she spoke, Fredy Hirsch had been found unconscious, overdosed on tranquilizers.

Towards the end of February 1944, members of the camp's resistance movement had contacted Fredy Hirsch, a potential leader of a planned uprising. It would be an opportunity to kill several members of the SS, and, possibly, a chance for a handful of prisoners to escape. For the rest of the camp, such a revolt would result in punishment, if not certain death.

When, earlier that 8 March morning, Hirsch had been told that there was no doubt the Terezín Czechs were headed for the gas, Hirsh requested an hour to decide whether he would take part in the planned uprising. One hour later, Hirsch had been found unconscious.

Prior to all this, Fredy Hirsch had convinced the SS to dedicate one of the wooden barrack buildings, Block 31, as the "children's block," of which Hirsch was the head. Instead of three-tiered bunks, Block 31 contained little tables. Just recently, in February, an inmate artist named Dina Gottliebová had painted the walls with flowers, Eskimos, and scenes from *Snow White*. During the day, the children had lessons in secret, which turned into German songs when the lookout saw the SS approaching the

OSVĚTIM, OCCUPIED POLAND
8 MARCH 1944

Block. The children never stood outdoors for count. They were sometimes given parcels of food and other goods that had been sent to prisoners long-dead, which helped alleviate their hunger and malnutrition. At night, they were returned to their families. When, in December, another five hundred Czech children had arrived from Terezín, adding to September's three hundred, Hirsch had secured a second barracks building for the children.

Karly went on, smiling at her son, "The music has been especially nice, and the *Snow White* performance," she said. "They have kept his spirits high." In late '43 and early '44, the children had rehearsed and performed a production of *Snow White and the Seven Dwarfs*. The children's play was "supplemented by melodies of Czech folksongs with new German lyrics... Due to the unavailability of a piano accompaniment, a mouth harmonica had to suffice." The performance had been attended by men of the SS, including Doctor Mengele, who had applauded the children enthusiastically. The children had also learned to sing "Ode to Joy" by Friedrich Schiller, set to the melody of Beethoven's 9th Symphony. The Czech Family Camp also included adult orchestra members and vocal musicians, including members of Raphael Schächter's choir who so beautifully and fiercely sang Verdi's "Requiem." Because Terezín had been home to so many prominent and talented artists, on occasion, various musicians of the Family Camp had been asked to perform before the SS.

"I doubt there will be such music in Heydebreck," Marietta said. "If Heydebreck even exists."

There was an uneasy lull in the women's conversation.

Lorries rumbled past the subcamps, past the extra guards and dogs at the entrances. When they reached the quarantine camp where the Czechs waited, the lorries backed in with their tailgates open to receive the prisoners. Of the initial five thousand and seven September deportees from Terezín, over three thousand

THE SUITCASE

seven hundred Czechs were still alive that March day.

"Los!" came the command. Marietta, Olga, Karly, Petr, and the other women and children exited the wooden quarantine barracks and emerged into the cold evening rain. Nearby, the men were also being loaded into the lorries. All were clutching their belongings, heads down and shoulders hunched in the downpour.

Once loaded, the lorries moved out of the quarantine camp and onto the road, but instead of moving towards the main road and Heydebreck, the lorries turned back into the camp and down a side road — headed for the chimneys.

"This isn't the way to the main road."

"Where are we going?"

Before they had much time to express their confusion, the lorries had already arrived at their destination — the courtyard of Crematorium 3. How many trainloads of people had the Czechs seen disappear into the crematoria within the past six months? Why had they been loaded into the lorries, just to be driven a walkable distance within the camp? Why had they been given privileges for the past six months, if they were only to be brought to the crematorium?

Crematorium 3 was a T-shaped building with a large chimney. The crematorium itself was located on the ground level. It contained five retorts, each with three openings, each opening capable of holding up to three bodies at a time. The crematorium room "rumbled and trembled" with heat as the furnace fires roared, the fans hummed, the kapos shouted, the stokers brandished the iron forks they used to move bodies in and out of the retorts and reposition bodies at intervals throughout the cremation process.

In the courtyard, the lorries' tailboards were lowered. The confused prisoners were blinded by floodlights and beaten by

OSVĚTIM, OCCUPIED POLAND
8 MARCH 1944

truncheons as they climbed down into the mud. They ran the gauntlet, struck by blows from both sides as they were driven down into the building's lower level, into the subterranean undressing room. The old, the sick, the children, all were "beat[en] and clubb[ed]... without mercy."

Once inside the undressing room, the Czechs found the exit blocked by dozens of SS guards and their barking Alsatians. The dogs were excited by the battered and bloodied people who stumbled past. Around the room were the fake signs for showers that the Czechs had heard rumours of. Certainty grew. They were destined for the gas.

Families clung to one another, tearfully embracing. Karly and Otto Fischer held one another, and their son. Marietta had no one to comfort her. Several hundred Czechs stood in the changing room, waiting to be joined by the rest of the Family Camp members. As they waited, panic mounted.

When SS leaders, among them Lagerführer Schwarzhuber and Doctor Mengele, appeared in the doorway of the changing room, those standing nearby flew into a rage. Suffering and sorrow gave way to unrestrained hatred for those men who had made such false promises. Those same men who had smiled and applauded as their children sang "Ode to Joy," had become harbingers of their deaths.

As the SS men looked with satisfaction at the way things had gone thus far, people shouted, "We want to live! We want to work!" as if they might still escape from the anteroom of death. The SS leaders gave them no response. Some of the Czechs rushed towards the door, and were shot by the armed SS guards, who numbered at least fifty. The SS men flung themselves upon the crowd in the changing room, beating the prisoners about the head with their truncheons, allowing their snarling dogs to tear into flesh. They drove the prisoners into the back of the room, then they erected machine-guns in front of them.

The Czechs crowded together, bloodied, shaking with terror, with anger. Marietta was crushed in among them.

One of the higher-ranking Nazis, knowing the second "lot of victims" was due, stepped in front of the crowd. Oberscharführer Peter Voss, commander of the crematoria, raised his hands and called for silence. Those within earshot heard his speech: "Now what is the meaning of all this, you Jews? Your hour has come. There is nothing in the world which can reverse your fate. It is entirely up to you. If you are sensible, you can spare yourselves and your children a great deal of distress. A great deal... Everything will be much easier if you get undressed quickly and then move on into the next room. Or do you want to make your children's last moments needlessly distressing?"

Some who had heard his words began to undress; others did not. Before many could make themselves follow the command, the SS began pushing the crowd into the gas chamber.

Where were the Czechs to run? Straight into the waiting machine guns? The armed SS men? The snarling dogs? There was chaos: crying, shouting, wailing, barking.

Suddenly, above the din, a voice began to sing. Another voice joined in, and another. The voice swelled to a mighty choir, filling the dimly-lit gas chamber, echoing in the undressing anteroom, swelling from the underground, competing with the roaring furnace, masking the idling engine of the Red Cross-painted lorry that delivered the Zyklon B that would murder three thousand seven hundred and ninety-two Czechs that evening.

The voices united in song:

OSVĚTIM, OCCUPIED POLAND
8 MARCH 1944

Kde domov můj,
kde domov můj,
voda hučí po lučinách,
bory šumí po skalinách,
v sadě skví se jara květ,
zemský ráj to na pohled!
A to je ta krásná země,
země česká domov můj,
země česká domov můj!

In English:

Where is my home?
Where is my homeland?
Water roars across the meadows,
Pinewoods rustle among crags,
The garden is glorious with spring blossom,
Paradise on earth it is to see.
And this is that beautiful land,
The Czech land, my home,
The Czech land, my home!

HERTFORDSHIRE, ENGLAND
Tuesday, 23 May 1944

> *"The sun shines alike on the rich and poor,*
> *on the black man and the white.*
> *And wars, son, are because men forget these things."*
> — Anton Walbrook as Karel in
> *The Man from Morocco*

THE ACTORS AND extras stood in their places and waited patiently for the racket from the adjacent railway to quiet down. Welwyn Garden City in Hertfordshire was not ideal for filming talkies, owing to noise pollution like the railroad. When the film set was quiet once more, and the director and crew were ready, the "rain" resumed on the set. We were filming *The Man from Morocco*, a B.B.C. adaptation of the novel written by the prolific Edgar Wallace.

The rainy courtyard was filled with film extras standing quietly around a ration supply cart — soldiers and refugees alike waited for Mutz Greenbaum's shout: "Action!" The camera on its crane then began to move, capturing the uniformed men who had, on cue, begun passing rations into the crowd of displaced people. The camera then panned away from them and up to a building. On the other side of the rain-spattered window, a man at a desk looked in desperation at the scene below as he spoke into a telephone.

I stood near the man on the telephone, French actor Paul Bonifas, and waited to deliver my line. Because it is raining

HERTFORDSHIRE, ENGLAND
23 MAY 1944

in our scene, in the film I am wearing a light-coloured belted mackintosh. I hold my hat and gloves in front of me.

"But something must be done!" Bonifas, playing the French mayor, exclaims into the telephone. "I tell you, it is a nightmare!" He pauses to listen to the voice on the other end of the telephone line, then says, "Well, I demand to speak to the Minister himself!" —not realising he is already on the phone with the man. "Oh! Monsieur Minister…"

As he delivers these lines I am standing in the background, making small, carefully-planned movements that I had intended to convey that I am listening intently to the Mayor, and am concerned that he is delivering the appropriate information to the authority on the telephone. I shift my weight from one foot to the other; I move my hat from waist-level down to my side; I fiddle with the belt of my trench coat; I move my hand to my pocket, then back to waist-level where it meets my hat-holding hand.

"Monsieur Minister," Bonifas pleads into the telephone, "I beg of you, the situation has gotten quite beyond our control. At least four thousand refugees have come—"

This was my cue. I step from stage right and move towards the Mayor. Lifting my free hand, I deliver my line: "Five thousand."

I then take a few steps back and turn, putting myself in shadow and slipping out of the frame as the camera moves to Bonifas for a close-up. He says, with emphasis, "Five thousand have crossed the frontier. …Yes, women and children. It is terrible! Monsieur Minister, will you please arrange that tomorrow, relief planes come for refugees? And please, we must have food and medical supplies! …You will do your best? You do what you can. Oh, thank you, Monsieur Minister, thank you."

"Cut!" came the shout from Greenbaum. I was thrilled to be working under him—he had directed 1937's *Return of the Scarlet*

THE SUITCASE

Pimpernel. If only the members of the Nine-Fifteen Club could have seen me then, working with a director of the highest calibre.

The Man from Morocco tells the story of a Czech officer named Karel who leads a group of multi-national volunteers in the fight against fascism. The film takes place in 1936, when the Spanish Civil War was only beginning. Karel's volunteers are detained and sent to Morocco, where they are imprisoned in "Camp Vernon" and spend their days constructing the Saharan railway for the Germans. The wire fences enclosing rows of narrow barracks buildings looked very much like the images of some Nazi concentration camps I would later see. Inside the barrack buildings, three-tiered wooden bunks — another soon-to-become familiar sight — held the prisoners after their long days of labour in the desert. Karel manages to escape from Morocco with important information to carry to the Allies...

I had had no direct interactions with the film's star, Anton Walbrook, but still boasted of my involvement in the project where he was the lead actor. I loved his films, like *Gaslight, Dangerous Moonlight, The Life and Death of Colonel Blimp,* and *Viktor und Viktoria* — which had been produced by none other than Alfred Zeisler, whom I'd met in New York City. In the mid-1930s, the homosexual and half-Jewish Walbrook had left Vienna for more tolerant realms. In *The Man from Morocco*, Walbrook delivers a line I particularly liked: "The sun shines alike on the rich and poor, on the black man and the white. And wars, son, are because men forget these things."

Bonifas, with whom I had shared my scene, was an artillery lieutenant who had been wounded at Dunkirk and evacuated to London. Once there, he joined the Free French and made radio broadcasts into occupied France. In mid-December 1943, about the time Desmond had come for his visit, Bonifas's "Moliere Players" had performed in London. The troupe appeared in a

HERTFORDSHIRE, ENGLAND
23 MAY 1944

short film shot by Alfred Hitchcock, which was based on a troupe member's illegal radio station in Vichy-controlled Madagascar. I was fascinated by the Frenchman.

I couldn't wait to tell Desmond O'Neill, in person, about my experiences. He was busy that month with his War Savings Assembly work. He had just launched a new Savings Centre on East Street in Havant and had given a speech on post-war savings for "Salute the Soldier" week. Their fundraising target? One million pounds! He had declared that the Savings Movement was not going to "fold up" when the war ended, and stressed the importance of post-war savings.

It would be nine months before *The Man from Morocco*'s late-March 1945 premiere at London's Warner Theatre. And it would be another month beyond that before the film played in Hampshire, enabling Desmond to see my big-screen debut.

Much had happened between the time of Desmond's December 1943 visit and the *Morocco* filming in late May. I had received a new M.O.I. itinerary in January of '44. I was in Cornwall when the Luftwaffe visited London and the bombs fell; the period from January to May was later referred to as the "Baby Blitz." In late-January, I visited Cornwall's Trevol Rifle Range, and the Plymouth Museum and Art Gallery.

In early February, I reported to Bristol and checked in to the Whiteoaks Hotel. I spoke in nearby Keynsham and at the canteen at J.S. Fry & Sons, a chocolate factory. When I rose to speak, within two minutes the canteen noise had completely stopped. My audience listened in dead quiet and applauded at the end. I went on to Highbridge for the United Youth Club's Sunday Evening Club and canteen, before doing a public meeting in Taunton. After that, it was back to London, where the incendiary bombs were still falling, and the AA guns were doing substantial damage of their own.

THE SUITCASE

It was in March that I resigned on good terms from the M.O.I. Miss Harling, Assistant Specialist in the Public Meetings and Speakers Section wrote: "I hope you will find the work you are taking up to your liking. You will, in any case, I expect, be glad to be relieved of the constant uncomfortable travelling that speaking work entails."

In April, I began working for the O.W.I. — the American Office of War Information — in the transcription department. The O.W.I.'s London office was located in the American Embassy in Grosvenor Square at Carlos Place, near the Connaught. At the Connaught, I had again encountered Brewster Morgan.

After some gossip about New York City — mainly how, in April, Elizabeth Reller had married a Lieutenant in the U.S. Naval Reserve's Medical Corps — Brewster Morgan offered to introduce me to a higher-up at the B.B.C., with whom he had formed a relationship the previous summer when Morgan had helped launch AFN, the American Forces Network. Through Morgan's B.B.C. contact, I had gained my role in the *Morocco* film.

After filming, I returned to my position with the O.W.I. There, trouble arose.

About a week prior to my approval for film work, I had been called to the Viscountess Tarbat's office, decorated, in part, by a framed Ponds advertisement featuring the American woman's lovely face.

The Viscountess told me, "You have been requested," and presented me with the following memorandum:

HERTFORDSHIRE, ENGLAND
23 MAY 1944

INTER-OFFICE MEMO.
OFFICE OF WAR INFORMATION
Date: 17th May, 1944
To: Mr. Taussig, c/o Lady Tarbat.
From: Mr. W.H. Kennedy.

Will you kindly complete the attached form and return it to my office at your early convenience. We are requesting your employment on full time basis for the German Desk and the attached form completed is necessary for our files. Thank you very much indeed.

I assumed my employment was a foregone conclusion and completed the form in question. It was to be signed by the Security Department at the American Embassy. It should have occurred to me that some complication would arise when my name touched the American Embassy — which was exactly what happened.

The Embassy's Security Department was to sign the form in a fortnight to three weeks. Two weeks went by and I heard nothing.

Three weeks passed. D-Day came and went without my knowledge that my only nephew, Corporal Kühnreich, had climbed Pointe du Hoc with the US Army Rangers and, in taking that cliff, "began to seize back the continent of Europe." Jiří had enlisted in mid-January 1943 and had shipped out to England in September.

Another week passed. V1 bombs had begun buzzing into London. It was then, a full month after I had been requested for the German desk, that I received a letter at my personal address, dated 16 June and signed by someone from the Personnel Office at the American Embassy, informing me that "the vacancy for which [I] applied" was "no longer available." I hadn't applied for any vacancy—I had been specially requested, pending the submission of certain paperwork. I was furious.

In the month between my employment being requested, and the decision that the "vacancy" was "no longer available," I had repeatedly interviewed with my superiors at the O.W.I., during which time I was told that my services had been accepted, and that only the approval of the Security Department was awaited in order for me to resume working. There was no doubt left whatsoever that the Intelligence Department of the American Embassy rejected my application on security grounds, and that the American Embassy's letter of 16 June was only a polite excuse to cover up the real reason.

I wrote to Brewster Morgan in hopes he might be able to shed some light on the situation, owing to his contacts and connections:

> I dare say that the gentleman, or gentlemen, of the Intelligence may feel very pleased with themselves for having reached a decision which to prove their watchfulness, but it is me on who they have put a stigma of the greatest consequences. I wonder whether the gentlemen realise that even many years after the war is over, people might point their fingers at me and say, *That is a man who could not be trusted by the Democracies.*
>
> To reach their verdict, these officials had to make their enquiries either from me or my friends, which they did not do; or they accepted statements made by common informers. Under the heading 'Common Informers' I include anybody, disregarding their nationality or possible official rank, who makes

HERTFORDSHIRE, ENGLAND
23 MAY 1944

derogatory statements about somebody else and who will hide behind their official position, having full knowledge that their names will never be disclosed to the investigating authorities. Such informers may have various motives, which might be an ambitious desire to earn admiration, or personal spite, or just stupidity and inefficiency. In any case, I cannot refrain from stating that, war or no war, the investigating American officials, before making up their minds, might have given me a decent chance to speak for myself, which in a Democracy is the right of anybody, whether rightly or wrongly suspected.

For the last year I have travelled all over Britain on behalf of the British Ministry of Information and with the approval of the Czechoslovak Ministry of Foreign Affairs. During that time, I visited hundreds of secret production centres, aerodromes, naval stations, invasion ports, and was also taken on board one of His Majesty's ships while minesweeping the channel of a very important naval port. I addressed during that time tens of thousands of people about the importance of the war in the Pacific; and it strikes me as extremely odd that the British security authorities were unable, within that year, to discover things about me, which took the U.S. security only three weeks to find out. I wonder whether the British Security Police are so utterly inefficient, or whether it is that their American colleagues have slipped up somewhere.

There is no need to tell you that I am extremely concerned, to say the least, about the inexplicable attitude of the U.S. F.B.I. or whichever authority is responsible for this gross injustice.

THE SUITCASE

I put the same sentiments I had shared with Brewster Morgan into a letter to the American Consul-General in London, to the American State Department, to the British Ministry of Home Security, and to the Czechoslovak Foreign Office.

At the same time, I also wrote to one of the most influential Americans I knew, my old friend Judge Milton Helmick. Francy and Zikmund had actually met Helmick while vacationing that summer, and it seemed as appropriate a time as any to reach out to him. When I wrote in August 1944, I didn't know that his niece Sandy's husband, John Morris, had just died in mid-July. He had left this world via a window in his twelfth-storey office. Sandy was out to lunch at the time. John had been on his first visit home since December 1941. Surely the Helmicks were in shock following John's death.

I wrote to Helmick both to save face, and to fish for information. In my letter I apologized for not having written sooner, but explained I had honestly thought I would have gotten my visa and would have seen Helmick in Washington by that time:

> I was informed by [the] American Consul here that I shall not get the visa until the war is over. When I asked him which war, the one in Europe or the Far East as well, he gave me an evasive answer. So that's that. However hard I try to think back to find a reason for the attitude of the authorities in Washington, I am quite unable to find even the slightest argument which could justify their action.
>
> Only quite recently I remembered a casual remark made by a friend of mine, whom you also knew very well and who is now in Washington, Mr. G. Boissevain, Netherlands Consul General in Shanghai. On arrival in Britain, I was asked to have cocktails with him

HERTFORDSHIRE, ENGLAND
23 MAY 1944

and Mrs. Boissevain and, while talking about some of our mutual friends, they remarked: 'Some people in Shanghai were talking quite some rubbish about you.' They did not, or possibly did not wish to, satisfy my curiosity, all that they did remember was that somebody — they thought it might have been an American official — was spreading stories that I was a Nazi spy or some similar nonsense to that effect.

Now I am wondering whether that gossip has anything to do with my difficulties.... I have written to my sister the names of two American Consuls who had some purely personal but otherwise more unimportant reasons to possibly dislike me, but somehow I can't see that a Federal Official would be so stupid or so base to allow his personal antipathies to overrule his better judgment. So that puts me right back from where I started, and I still haven't got the faintest idea what it's all about.

I sent these letters, and I waited. The war in Europe was ending. The "boys" would soon be coming home to London — and where would that leave me? The same old troubles that had caused me to be arrested at bayonet-point, had apparently also cost me my position with the O.W.I., and were also preventing me from immigrating to the States to be with Francy.

I was stuck in London, and I needed to find myself a new position — and find it quickly.

Terezín, Occupied Czechoslovakia
Tuesday, 26 September 1944

> *"...We found in the ghetto a town which is living a nearly normal life... This Jewish town is remarkable."*
> —Red Cross Report on Terezín

JAROMÍR TAUSSIG sat on his suitcase, his arms folded beneath the overcoat he wore like a blanket. The men had been instructed to bring light luggage and a day's provisions when they reported to the schleuse for transport. Until that time, these men had been considered indispensable workers and had enjoyed their protected status. But the protection had come to an end. Nearby were other men who had arrived with Jara on transport J in December of 1941, and who were preparing to leave Terezín with Jara on transport Ek.

For the purposes of transport Ek, Jaromír was number 209; Jiří Katz, who was no relation to Olga Katzová, was number 213; Jindřich Wallerstein, the composer's son who was Vlada's age and who, like Vladimír, had fought in the Battles of Isonzo, was number 216.

The transport had been announced five days previously, on the evening of Thursday 21 September. A work transport of five thousand men was to be "dispatched within the shortest period." The men would return after six weeks, "upon completion of their required duties"—establishing a new ghetto near Dresden, or so they thought.

TEREZÍN, OCCUPIED CZECHOSLOVAKIA
26 SEPTEMBER 1944

"The selection will... include all men, regardless of any important position they hold. Maintain discipline. This has to be," they had been told at the announcement of the transport. There would be no reklamace — only the most extreme situations would warrant exclusion from the transport.

No large transports had left Terezín since May. Did it occur to the men that perhaps there was some reason why all of the "indispensable" "healthy" workers of a fighting age were being sent away?

Jara scanned the Hamburg barracks and sighed. The men had been waiting in the schleuse since the previous day. They had reported for their transport and had waited all day, and all night, but the train had never arrived. "Do you suppose we'll ever board this transport?" Jara asked. He looked out the window. Outside, Ghetto Guards stood in the afternoon rain, surrounding the building.

Jara sighed again.

Jiří scoffed. "Are you in a hurry, Taussig?"

"In a hurry to get back to Terezín," Jara replied. "I don't want to go a hundred kilometres further from Prague, and I don't want to build a new ghetto."

It was rumoured that "the invasion" — the invasion of Normandy — was underway and that the Nazis' days were numbered. Air raid sirens had become increasingly frequent. The prisoners had seen "planes soar[ing] overhead... like a flock of storks. The engines roar[ed]... [b]elow, the big noise [became] a mere growling. [Was]... freedom under their grey wings?"

Jindřich Wallerstein said, "I worry about my family — my wife, father, and step-mother's safety in my absence." He sighed. "I suppose we did such a splendid job of building Terezín, they want only the best for this new ghetto in Dresden."

Jara laughed at the idea of building the "best" possible ghetto.

THE SUITCASE

"Yes," Jara said wryly, "We did such a good job that we fooled both the Red Cross and the movie cameras."

The plan to use Terezín as a Potemkin village to trick the rest of the world had begun almost a year previously, in October 1943, when a transport of Danes had arrived. The Danish King and Danish Red Cross insisted that delegates be allowed to visit the ghetto and observe the conditions under which the Danish subjects were living.

The Nazis assented to the Danes' request and, in December '43, efforts to improve the ghetto began. Under Commandant Burger, the streets had been renamed, the cafés had been improved, and some of the worst attic bunks had been removed. When, in February '44, Commandant Rahm replaced Burger, the real Beautification had commenced. Jara and the men of the Aufbaukommando saw to an endless list of improvements.

The first official visitor had been Karl Hermann Frank, who had succeeded the assassinated Reinhard Heydrich as the Nazi Protector of Bohemia and Moravia. Frank's name was one that Jaromír had been familiar with since the '30s when he had encountered the Sudeten Deutsche Partei in Ústí nad Labem.

Then, on 23 June, Red Cross delegates visited and were taken on a tour using a planned route, with Terezín's inmates acting on cue. The ruse worked. The Red Cross had been convinced that Terezín was a Jewish-administered settlement town, flourishing with cultural and spiritual opportunities — and that it was definitely not a transit camp, contrary to reports from the East made by people like Auschwitz escapees Rudolf Vrba, Alfréd Wetzler, and Siegfried Lederer.

Lederer had actually returned to Terezín to bring warning. After being sent East from Terezín in December of '43, he had escaped from the Czech Family Camp at Auschwitz-Birkenau in April '44 with the assistance of a staunchly-Catholic member

TEREZÍN, OCCUPIED CZECHOSLOVAKIA
26 SEPTEMBER 1944

of the SS who had provided Lederer with a guard's uniform, an escort out of the camp, and a train ride to freedom. Lederer then snuck back into Terezín to warn the Jewish administration that the September deportees had been murdered en masse on 8 March. "If you are to be deported from Terezín," Lederer advised, "resist."

But the Jewish leaders to whom Lederer had given the warning decided to not to share the news with Terezín's thirty-five thousand inmates, lest chaos and "catastrophe" befall them. By that time, rumours about Auschwitz had already spread through Terezín, but many refused to believe them, and none could really comprehend that gas and certain death awaited them in the East, or that those who had been sent East before them had faced that fate.

The beautified Terezín had fooled the Red Cross delegates into believing that the "Jewish settlement town" was quite a pleasant place to live, and a destination, certainly not a waystation to the East. Here, food was available like nowhere else in the Reich; here, music was allowed that, in other places, would have been banned. Look at how much latitude the Nazis were giving the Jews in this idyllic Jewish-run town!

Inside the town itself, the streets and buildings looked welcoming enough, with their fresh paint and newly-installed curtains. The fence that had long separated the inmates from the Nazi barracks and meeting rooms had been removed. The large manufacturing tents in the square had been replaced by park benches and rose bushes. For the big show, the benches were filled with people who listened to the violin orchestra playing on the newly-constructed wooden pavilion there. "Every afternoon at 5:00 an orchestra plays in the town square," the Red Cross report had later stated.

Around the square was the post office, with Red Cross parcels being doled out, and the bank, where Moses-emblazoned "Ghetto Kronen" currency was distributed to workers. The shops and food stores held sugar, margarine, and vegetables. The "butcher shop" displayed sausages and canned meats, when the prisoners had not actually eaten a decent meal in years. The café on the square overflowed with people listening to the Ghetto Swingers playing their signature tune—Gershwin's "I Got Rhythm."

In the dining hall, which was only used for the Red Cross visit, tables were adorned with white linens, flowers, and real plates, and were attended by white-aproned staff. As far as the visitors knew, no one suffered from malnutrition in Terezín—although in reality, many whose ashes rested in a mouldy bulwark, or in the for-show columbarium, had starved to death in Terezín. A faux graveyard had also been added outside the town's walls, to give the impression that a reasonable number of deaths had taken place, and had been handled with dignity. The mortuary was staged with Hebrew signs, and the flat bread cart that had always carried Terezín's dead was replaced with a real refurbished hearse.

The Aufbaukommando had transformed the former encephalitis hospital into a Sokol sporting hall and community centre. There, a soccer match was staged, with a well-timed goal made for the benefit of the visitors. The sporting hall held a library with two hundred thousand volumes—all confiscated from prisoners—along with a stage where the children's opera *Brundibár* was performed.

A playground had been constructed, with sandboxes and swings, and a pavilion with big wooden animals. The children were only allowed to enter on the day of the Red Cross visit. A former hospital had been furnished like a school, with a "Boys' School" sign placed over the entry by Commandant Rahm. On the blackboards in the "classrooms," "Closed for the Holidays"

TEREZÍN, OCCUPIED CZECHOSLOVAKIA
26 SEPTEMBER 1944

had been written in chalk. In an infants' home, a dozen cribs were visible on a glass-enclosed veranda — in a town where abortions were, at that time, strictly enforced by the Nazi captors.

The visiting Red Cross delegates had concluded that a productive and fulfilling life was being had in the "Jewish-run settlement" — especially compared to the conditions the rest of the Reich and Protectorate faced.

So convincing had the Red Cross charade been, the Nazis decided to showcase Terezín in a propaganda film. In this way, they could further combat rumours emerging from the East. The famous actor and film director, Kurt Gerron, was key to the production's success. He had been deported from the Netherlands to Terezín in February '44. The Berliner had moved to Amsterdam after the Nazis consolidated power in 1933, but even so, he had not remained safe from the Nazis' reach.

Filming had begun in August and had only concluded a fortnight previously, on 11 September. What the prisoners of Terezín had been ordered to perform for the cameras was not dissimilar to their presentation for the Red Cross visit.

It would be March 1945 before the film was edited and completed, and *The Führer Gives a City to the Jews* would be screened a handful of times. By then, most of the film's cast, and its director, had been murdered.

Jara and his companions in the schleuse discussed the film. Jara said, "My brother loves movies and newsreels. When he hears I worked with Kurt Gerron, he's going to be quite jealous."

Jiří scoffed. "I would hardly say we 'worked with' Gerron."

Jara ignored him.

Jindřich Wallerstein mused, "The Great Kurt Gerron." He began humming the tune of "Mack the Knife," or the "Mackie Messer" song, Gerron's signature melody from *The Threepenny Opera*. It had been sixteen years since Gerron first appeared as the play's Tiger Brown on the Berlin stage, but Gerron had recently featured the song in the Terezín cabaret show he had been asked to mount — *The Carousel* — performed during the summer of '44. During the filming of the movie, Gerron took to the stage and "recited" his song again for an audience of two thousand of his fellow prisoners, and for the cameras.

The irony of the lyrics, about a killer named Mack the Knife who hid his weapon and feigned innocence of his crimes, was not lost on Terezín's inmates.

Jara said with amusement, "You shouldn't have such reverence for Gerron, Jindřich. You who had Ullmann give private concerts in your parlour. I wish I had known you back then!"

After the Nazi occupation of Czechoslovakia and the increasing restrictions that followed, Jewish cultural life had to be enjoyed in secret. Recitals and private concerts had been held in villas and apartments. Viktor Ullman's work had sometimes been presented in Professor Konrad Wallerstein's apartment.

Jindřich Wallerstein sighed and said, "Ullman, Strauss, Stravinsky, Suk... We were friends with so many wonderful composers."

Jiří muttered, "And now Ullmann is here with us in Terezín." Ullmann had been in Terezín for two years, since September of '42. He, and others like Raphael Schächter, had organised concerts, including Smetana's operas and Verdi's *Requiem*. Wallerstein continued humming.

"I would be careful humming those German songs," Katz said with a hint of venom. "I never attended any of the German-language productions..." He trailed off, leaving his companions with the implication that any decent Czech would have boycotted the German productions too.

Jara ignored him. Wallerstein said simply, "Music has no language. Only mathematics. And heart." Wallerstein began

TEREZÍN, OCCUPIED CZECHOSLOVAKIA
26 SEPTEMBER 1944

humming a different tune from *The Carousel* cabaret, the "Viennese Song" about meeting a sweetheart in a park in Vienna every night in dreams—when in reality, the singer is in Terezín and his lover is "somewhere in the East."

"Speaking of 'somewhere in the East,'" Wallerstein began, "have you heard anything more from your sister?" he asked Jara.

Jaromír shook his head. "Only the postcard." Many of Terezín's inmates had received postcards dated 25 March 1944 — more than two weeks after the Czechs' "special treatment." He continued, "I'm glad she wasn't here for the Red Cross visit. I don't know if she would have kept her mouth shut. She's almost as contrarian as our friend Jiří Katz."

Katz waved a hand at Jara. "Certainly she would have gone along with it. We all did."

Wallerstein said, "I do wish they had deviated from the planned route, even once, to see the real Terezín and not what the Nazis wanted them to see."

The only people who'd had the opportunity to show Terezín through the lens of truth was a group of artists. During the day, their job was to make drawings for the Nazi administration. During their free time, they secretly composed scenes of real life in the ghetto: the bread cart stacked high with shoddy caskets; the gaunt, hollow-eyed inmates crowded into dim attics; the fence in the square separating the great crowds of prisoners from the tree-lined central square; the hungry children searching the bread cart for crumbs while the elderly inmates scoured the potato peel pile for any edible scrap; the luggage-carrying deportees headed for transports to the East.

Some of the pictures were smuggled out of the camp. A few weeks after the Red Cross visit, the artists were punished. The men who had been drawing in secret were Ferdinand Block, Bedrich Fritta, Otto Ungar, and Leo Haas. The men, and their wives and children, were imprisoned in the Small Fortress. Bloch was beaten to death. Fritta, Ungar, and Haas were transported to Auschwitz, where Fritta died of dysentery. Ungar died of typhus in Buchenwald shortly after liberation. Haas was transferred to various camps until he was liberated, becoming the only surviving artist from what became known as "The Painters' Affair."

As Jindřich Wallerstein continued to hum, he, Jara, and Jiří Katz were approached by other men of the transport, musicians Pavel Weisskopf and Adolf Strauss. Both men had also been on transport J, back in December '41.

"They are calling off the transport," Pavel Weisskopf said.

"For good, or for now?" Wallerstein asked.

"Yes," Jara said, "dissolved, or just delayed?"

Weisskopf and Strauss exchanged unsure glances. Weisskopf said, "I don't know."

Jara said, "There have been an awful lot of rumours these past couple of days — a lack of trains, broken tracks, labour strikes…"

"If the rumours are true, then I'm sure there will be an announcement," said Adolf Strauss.

Around them, men were standing, straightening their clothing, collecting their bags.

With a yawn, Jiří said, "If they are just going to wake us in the middle of the night and again summon us back to the schleuse, then I think I would just as soon stay put, gentlemen." He nestled further down into his luggage. "No one to say goodbye to anyway," he muttered. His wife and child had been sent East in April.

"But you are not sure it's official?" Jindřich Wallerstein asked.

"Official or not," Jiří said from beneath his overcoat, "it's highly unorthodox." Once collected, no transport had ever left the schleuse and re-entered Terezín.

TEREZÍN, OCCUPIED CZECHOSLOVAKIA
26 SEPTEMBER 1944

"Maybe they are rewriting the list again and changing the requirements once more," Pavel Weisskopf joked. The list for transport Ek had originally included only men aged eighteen to fifty, but had been expanded to include ages sixteen to fifty-five. But the administration would never remake a list once the transport members were already in the schleuse.

"Changing the requirement?" Jara asked. "Sure. This time they'll include boys of twelve and men of seventy," he joked.

"Well, gentlemen," Jindřich Wallerstein said, "once they officially call off the transport, don't expect to see me. I plan to visit my family in their barracks and organise more supplies in case we do get called back."

Jaromír said, "If it is official, and we are not leaving Terezín just yet, then I have some more goodbyes I could be saying, if you catch my drift, gentlemen." He gave his companions an exaggerated wink.

"Lucky you," Jiří Katz grumbled. Jaromír smiled. Katz was almost as disagreeable as Marietta. Almost.

A voice rose over the din. "Gentlemen, quiet please. There is to be an announcement..."

*****

After days in the schleuse facing the uncertainty of an impending transport. The men returned to their "homes." As the sun set that evening, the observant Jews burned candles for Yom Kippur.

Because of his privileged status, Jaromír had been afforded some measures of privacy. As a protected worker, he had his own private kumbal, a space he had carved out of an attic, where he spent nights with a woman. And as a protected worker who had been, to that time, unconcerned with transports, he'd possessed the energy necessary to have a relationship with a female

THE SUITCASE

prisoner.

As the light from the half-moon fell onto Terezín, Jaromír rested next to the woman beneath his mother's Soochow blanket, left for him by Marietta, so recently unpacked from his luggage. His mind wandered.

Would they be called back to the schleuse for transport? When? Had he organised enough provisions to see himself through another day of delays if that should come to pass? Was the transport really bound for Dresden? Would their new location be a target for Allied bombing raids? If the war ended when he was in Germany, how would he get home? Then again, if the war was ending so soon, why would the Nazis be building another camp?

He did not want to go on the transport, but he had no choice. Jara had once fantasized about escape. Jaromír thought back to December of 1941, back to his first night in Terezín, when the hundreds of men of transport J had arrived and had been directed by just two SS men. He had spent the entire first night, and many subsequent nights, laying sleeplessly on the floor of building "B V," which the men had later turned into the "Magdeburg" barracks, daydreaming of freedom and of returning to the woman he had left behind.

He had tempered these thoughts with what he then supposed were more "realistic" fantasies—about the things he planned to do with his girlfriend on his weekend visits. How naïve he had been. There had never been any visits home to Prague, as promised. The only communication he had managed to have with the girlfriend in all those years were "postcards with thirty words that passed the censor… [T]heir content was meaningless and unimportant."

He rolled over, feeling the warmth of the woman by his side. What if she, too, was deported within the six weeks' time that he

TEREZÍN, OCCUPIED CZECHOSLOVAKIA
26 SEPTEMBER 1944

was away building the new camp? They had always said they would meet in Prague if they were ever separated, but then, his Prague girlfriend was in Prague — if she even still cared for him. Better to worry about that if the time came, he decided.

The woman scratched at something in her sleep, some bedbug or other pest.

It occurred to Jaromír that he could refuse to report, if and when the transport was resumed. Back in October of '42, some one hundred and eighty people had delayed a transport by refusing to report to the schleuse. The entire ghetto had been punished with an early curfew and lights-out. There'd been no evening free time after work. The Ghetto Guard had been given truncheons to carry from that time onward. The one hundred and eighty prisoners who had refused to report were imprisoned in Terezín's Small Fortress, starved for three days, given twenty-five lashes — and were likely included on the very next train East when transports resumed in January of '43. Their resistance had only delayed the inevitable, and the rest of the ghetto had been punished in the interval.

Jara sighed. He thought about another opportunity when he might have snuck away — after the Burger count. If only he'd had the strength to wander off on his own after the infamous census, Terezín's authorities might have mistaken him for dead. Who would have missed him? His mother was already dead then; his sister had been deported — and good thing, too, because Jaromír doubted very much that either of them would have survived the brutal count.

During the Burger count, all thirty-eight thousand of Terezín's inmates, the oldest and youngest included, were marched out of the town into an enormous flat space within a basin. When Terezín was originally established as a garrison town, the basin space had been the troops' parade grounds. On 11 November

1943, during the Burger count, the empty space was used to count Terezín's prisoners, "as if [they] were cattle or sheep." The prisoners had stood all day, in the freezing rain, from seven in the morning until eleven o'clock at night, while they were counted and recounted. There had been no food, and no restroom. They had "reliev[ed] themselves as animals" as machine guns stood watch on the basin's rim and aeroplanes buzzed overhead. After the count, they were abandoned there without instructions.

Those who hadn't died during the count eventually found their way down the dark and muddy road back to Terezín proper. On their arrival, they found the gates locked. The prisoners were eventually allowed back into the ghetto, where they collapsed into their bunks and onto their floors, frozen, more starved than usual, and exhausted. The hundreds of deaths during and after the ordeal had disrupted Terezín's essential operations for days. Who would have noticed then if Jara hadn't made it back to the ghetto?

Jara knew that, if he timed it correctly, he might have made it out of Terezín and into Litoměřice, just a few kilometres away across the Labe. A vast forest sat between Litoměřice and Ústí nad Labem. Though he was a city boy, Jaromír had once felt confident that he would be able to survive in the forest, foraging for food, sheltering for warmth, keeping quiet, waiting out the war.

He had visited Litoměřice once—a lifetime ago, it seemed—when Vladimír had been married to the Maglič girl. Jara had visited them at Nový Berštejn and had accompanied Vlada on his "rounds" of collecting monies and making payments. They had gone to Litoměřice, where Vladimír's father-in-law, Tomáš Maglič, had opened his sawmill.

As Jara lay in his kumbal on that late-September night in 1944, Maglič's youngest daughter, Vladimír's ex-wife, Ann, had

TEREZÍN, OCCUPIED CZECHOSLOVAKIA
26 SEPTEMBER 1944

long since been remarried. In fact, she would die that year—1944. Maglič's wife Adéla, who had been born Jewish before marrying the Lutheran Maglič, had passed through Terezín and had been sent East to Maly Trostenets straight from the schleuse. She became one of the thousands of bodies rotting in the Blagovschina forest near Minsk.

Now, escape had become impossible. The end of the war was his only hope...

After the war, he would return to Prague. Free Prague. He would reclaim the villa and the apartment that he would have inherited, had the Nazis not interceded. Maybe he could secure Julie's ashes and inter them with his father's.

When Marietta returned from the East she could wed her beau. Maybe Vlada would return from his Far Eastern adventures. Perhaps they would all move to the States with Francy and Zikmund and Jiří. Julie and Karel would have liked that. They were family and belonged together, not spread over continents.

As he began to doze restlessly, vague thoughts of Shanghai passed through Jara's mind, accompanied by gratitude that his planned trip hadn't gone through. Had Jara gone to Shanghai, his mother and Mitcka would have been left to navigate Terezín on their own. At least they had been together in Terezín. Even if, in the end, he hadn't been able to protect his mother from starvation and death, he hadn't been able to protect his sister from transport, and now he was unable to protect himself—at least, for a time, he hadn't had to wonder where or how they were.

Jaromír's final thought before he fell asleep was that of the old tale of the Knights of Blaník. He imagined the knights emerging from their mountain and surging through Prague to liberate the city. In Jara's fantasies, Vlada on his warhorse was one of the knights. After freeing Prague, they rode to Terezín to free Jara and the others. From there, they would head East, to reclaim any Czechs who had been deported. They would all converge on Free Prague, where the bells would be ringing—never mind that the Nazis had collected Prague's bells two years before and had melted them for their war effort.

*****

The following evening, Wednesday, 27 September, it was announced that the transport's railroad cars would be arriving on Thursday morning. At 06.00 on the morning of the twenty-eighth, the transport would finally be loading.

At the appointed time, Jaromír returned to "Hamburg" barracks, his Terezín girlfriend accompanying him as far as she was able. The building was surrounded by a mass of people saying another, final goodbye. Ghetto Guards and Gendarmes stood shoulder-to-shoulder to shield the building from the weeping women, children, and elderly whose loved ones disappeared inside.

He gave the woman a kiss, turned his back and walked towards the barracks. She took steps to follow him but was stopped by a guard.

Once Jara was inside the building, it was impossible to look out from the crowded window to glimpse the woman one last time. So much the better, he supposed. He returned to his spot on his luggage near Wallerstein and Katz.

A train of about thirty freight cars arrived at the railroad extension. The men were called up according to transport number. Transport Ek, numbers 201 to 250. Number 201: Pavel Weisskopf. Number 209: Jaromír Taussig. Number 213: Jiří Katz. Number 216: Jindřich Wallerstein. Once they had been crammed into the train, they waited for two thousand four hundred ninety-

TEREZÍN, OCCUPIED CZECHOSLOVAKIA
26 SEPTEMBER 1944

five other men to be squeezed in.

Jaromír survived over a thousand days in Terezín. He had survived fifty-five transports East.

It was beyond belief to find himself crammed into a freight car as so many thousands before him had been. As his sister had been.

There was shock all around. Even after the train had been filled, until the moment the wheels slowly rolled into motion, there was talk that the train wouldn't depart.

These rumours were wrong.

At first, the train travelled northwards, towards Dresden, as expected. Near Dresden, the men were asked to write postcards to their loved ones in Terezín, saying that they had arrived safely and had found the accommodations and the work agreeable — that the loved ones should join them in the new work camp when possible.

Did this alert anyone to the impending danger? Did they know that the Nazis only instructed prisoners to compose postcards boasting about good treatment, just before meting out very ill treatment? Had they known, what could possibly have been done about it?

Two hours later, the train was moving again.

The train passed Dresden at night and began travelling towards the East.

A warning was shouted over the clatter of the moving train: "You are going to Birkenau!" But the prisoners did not equate "Birkenau" with Osvětim or "Auschwitz." Auschwitz they had heard of. Auschwitz, they knew, meant death.

The passengers on the train were unaware that the "Reich was in its death throes" and "the Nazis were taking advantage of their last chance to liquidate Terezín's prisoners." Jara's transport was the first in a month-long mass deportation of eighteen thousand

THE SUITCASE

four hundred and two prisoners.
The train moved eastward.

London, England
Tuesday, 8 May 1945

> *Land of Hope and Glory, Mother of the Free,*
> *How shall we extol thee, who are born of thee?*
> *Wider still and wider shall thy bounds be set;*
> *God, who made thee mighty, make thee mightier yet,*
> *God, who made thee mighty, make thee mightier yet.*
> — A.C. Benson, "Land of Hope and Glory"

I EXITED THE tube at the Gloucester Road station and enjoyed the short walk home. I was glad to be away from the crowds, the loudspeakers, the victory bells, the floodlights. London had gradually lifted lighting restrictions, from blackout, to dimout, to full-on "lighting up." Buildings that had been shrouded in protective darkness for so many years were now spectacularly lit for all to see: Saint Paul's Cathedral, Big Ben, The Houses of Parliament, Buckingham Palace.

Many people were living in ruins, exposed to the cold, the heat, the damp. Over a million houses had been damaged by Nazi V rockets. The bombings had only stopped in March. But Kensington had been spared. In my neighbourhood, fairy lights had been strung in the park. I could smell the smoke from bonfires as I approached my flat at 13 Bramham Gardens.

Inside, my girlfriend was in a jolly mood.

"There you are, darling," she said, rising to kiss me on the cheek. She was warm and giggly. "It must have been an awfully long day at the Troc." I was then working at The Trocadero, an entertainment complex on Coventry Street near the West End theatres and Piccadilly Circus. It was something like the "Great World" of Shanghai.

"It was a long day, yes," I said as I removed my jacket and shoes, unbuttoned my collar and sleeves, and rolled the latter up to my elbows. I had not wanted to work at the Troc, necessarily. When, in September, the "Second Blitz" began and the V2 rockets fell on London, I had requested a transfer to the British Army for the duration. None other than Colonel Oldřich Španiel approved my request. Nothing had come of it.

I had also applied with the Intelligence Corps at Hobart House in Grosvenor Place, and had been selected for a language test before they discontinued their interest. A similar situation occurred with the Ministry of Social Care's Repatriation Committee. In both instances, I assumed it had been discovered how "unreliable" I was rumoured to be.

Unbeknownst to me, the Czechoslovak Embassy had vouched for my bona fides while, at the same time, the Czechoslovak Ministry of Defence had contradicted them. The Ministry of Defence wrote to the Ministry of the Interior: "Vladimír Taussig is not in the active service and was not an official military deputy in Shanghai. He did not work in Shanghai as an official army deputy but as an individual banker and broker."

The British authorities had written: "Mr. Vladimír Taussig did not work in Shanghai with a position of an official army deputy, but instead was only given a task of recruitment and evacuation of the Czechoslovak volunteers. Based on the statements of the repatriated people in Shanghai he is a cordial man who helped a lot of the Czechoslovaks, he organised and financed community life and other activities. In England, he tried to get into the army, and when he did not succeed, he tried to get back payment from the Czechoslovak government offices for the expenses he had

LONDON, ENGLAND
8 MAY 1945

with the Czechoslovak people in Shanghai. He survived from support of the Ministry of Social Care but got into poverty... Since he was not accepted back to the army here and he could not find a good job, he wanted to move out to America. He is an adventurous man, in the stage of nervous exhaustion, but a soft-hearted person." Nervous exhaustion was right. The struggles of recent years had begun to take a toll on me, both physically and emotionally.

My girlfriend brought me a much-needed whiskey. "So, how was it?" she asked.

"Tiring," I said. "They did special VE Day menus. Even after the food was gone, people came in for drinks. We had extra supplies of lagers and spirits, but we ran out of glasses." I took a swig of the whiskey, welcoming the warmth that radiated through my chest and belly. She sat down next to me. "And how are you?" I asked her.

"The slightest bit sloshed," she giggled.

After a moment's quiet, I said, "It was nearly impossible to get home. The crowds are incredible. I'm surprised you aren't out with the revellers."

"There was celebration enough here. They did a little parade. People made costumes from everything — even blackout material. Everyone shared food they had stored up. There was music."

I gave a short laugh. "I heard music all day. At the Monico," the restaurant across Shaftesbury Avenue from the Troc, "there was a band playing on the balcony. They played 'Land of Hope and Glory' and 'There'll Always Be an England.' People looked like sardines in the streets, and climbed all over posts and statues and fountains."

"Would you like to go out?" she asked. We both liked to go "out." I had met her while I was "out," in late September '44, at a performance of *The Merry Widow* at the Coliseum Theatre near Wardour Street. I had gone the night after opening night and had sat in the stalls near the orchestra. So had she. We had both enjoyed watching that famous married duo, Madge Elliott and Cyril Richard.

"If we were going to go out, we should have bought tickets to a VE Day dance. Everything is going to be quite full, I'm sure." I took the last swig.

"I'll pour you another," she said as she stood.

"Bring the bottle," I called after her. She returned and filled my glass. I sighed. "I don't mean to spoil such a gay mood, but…"

"What is it?"

"I know Britain has had a long go of it, and you have lost a lot. And you deserve your celebration…"

"But?"

"But I suddenly feel as if I have nothing to celebrate. There has been no news of my family yet. I have had no word from Shanghai. The war with Japan certainly isn't over."

"Churchill said the same thing. Didn't you hear?"

I had not been present to catch his speech from Number 10 Downing. But I later heard his message:

> A terrible foe has been cast on the ground and awaits our judgment and our mercy… But there is another foe who occupies large portions of the British Empire, a foe stained with cruelty and greed — the Japanese. I rejoice we can all take a night off today and another day tomorrow… and after that we must begin the task of rebuilding our hearth and homes… and we must turn ourselves to fulfil our duty to our own countrymen, and to our gallant allies of the United States who were so foully and treacherously attacked by Japan. We will go hand and hand with them. Even if it is a hard

LONDON, ENGLAND
8 MAY 1945

struggle we will not be the ones who will fall...
We may allow ourselves a brief period of rejoicing, but let us not forget for a moment the toil and the effort that lie ahead. Japan, with all her treachery and greed, remains unsubdued. The injury she has inflicted on Great Britain, the United States and other countries and her detestable cruelties call for justice and retribution. We must now devote all our strength and resources to the completion of our task both at home and abroad.

While the rest of London was springing back to life, just across the river from my flat, in and around Battersea, the bombed-out areas were being used to train men bound for the Far East. Instructors carried Japanese weapons and schooled soldiers in street-fighting.

"I don't think most people care about Japan," I said.

"You might be right," she said. "Most everyone is talking about the end of the war, and about the general election. Not about Japan."

"Meanwhile, my friends back in Shanghai are still rotting away in internment camps — or worse."

At the end of that summer, in August 1945, war-ending atomic bombs would be dropped on Hiroshima and Nagasaki. I felt horror, thinking of my visits to Nagasaki, and to nearby Miyajima — of the torii gate, the temples, the deer in the park, the colourful kimonos, the maple pastries; of the businessmen I had befriended, the beautiful women I'd seen, the shop clerks and hotel staffs and restaurant workers. I had no sense of the scale of the blast. Of the radiation sickness that would linger.

VJ Day would come and go. I would initiate attempts to have my property in Shanghai restored to me. The Votickys

THE SUITCASE

would return to Prague. Pribram would arrive in England in mid-December. I would finally learn how Jewish friends in Shanghai had been restricted to the ghetto for Stateless Persons in Hongkew, while non-Jewish friends had been imprisoned at one of several civilian internment centres.

"What about your family?" my girlfriend asked. "Have you heard anything? Are they in camps?"

"I can't help but hope. But every bit of news I hear is more and more troubling."

Men who had escaped from Auschwitz made reports. These reports had been combined into the "Auschwitz Protocols," which had been published in November '44. They were discussed in detail by presses like the *New York Times*. The camp itself had been liberated in January of 1945. But I was not aware that this camp in Poland, "Auschwitz," had anything to do with my family.

In April '45 when the Bergen Belsen newsreels were shown in London, crowds, having seen that "warning to future generations," left theatres silent with horror. Burned into my mind were the bodies being crushed beneath the bulldozer as it moved more corpses into the pit, and the piles of bodies that waited to be shovelled into the earth. Even I, who had seen death—soldiers starving and freezing in Europe, and beggars doing the same in China; I who had witnessed blood and gore on the battlefields and in the streets, whose grand- and great-grandfathers had been butchers, and who had death in my very blood—even my stomach was turned by the Bergen Belsen newsreels, by the endless heaps of dead, the skeletons in mass graves. Tossed into lorries, dropped into pits. Naked. "There are fifty SS here to bury seventeen thousand dead," the narrator said, "and they have another half as many yet to go." Who were these nameless, skeletal dead? These mothers, fathers, sisters, brothers, aunts, uncles, loved ones?

LONDON, ENGLAND
8 MAY 1945

In May '45, when the Prague Uprising broke and the Russian Liberation Army and Soviet Red Army came to the Czechs' aid, my family was not there. During the same early-May days, when the Soviet soldiers entered Terezín, my family was not among the seventeen and a half thousand remaining prisoners.

There was a United Kingdom Search Bureau for German, Austrian, and Stateless Persons from Central Europe. I scanned lists and listened to radio announcements that named survivors. In the States, Francy worked with the Search Bureau for Missing Relatives. What were the odds than an elderly widow, a lovestruck diabetic, and an anxious spinster had survived the camps to which Prague's Jews had been taken? What had the supposedly-Christian Germans done with our family? Eventually our worst fears would be confirmed.

In March of '46 Francy would receive a letter from our former housekeeper:

> I found the address that Madame your mother gave me to have contact with you before she had to go. I don't know whether you have any information and whether at least your brother returned.
>
> I wish I could write something nice to you, but unfortunately I only have very sad news for you. I hope that Dr Funk, who was your sister's beau, has already made everything known to you...
>
> I had often visited the old lady. She was so unhappy. Then they lived in such a small room and the landlady made her life so difficult. She wept so much. This was when she had still been getting letters from you. The young lady was full of expectations for the future. I have no words to express how sorry I feel for all these people.

Madame, write to me where Herr Director's grave is. I would bring him flowers from time to time. Your mother used to go there all the time and now it must be abandoned...

Madame, you would make me very happy if you wrote to me. My sincere regards to everybody and I kiss your hand,
   Your Ružena

In April '46 we would initiate the process to reclaim the villa, and in July we would receive a letter informing us that "the last owner of the house... is... [the] Deutsches Reich" and that it was therefore "under the national management." We were told, "In order to be able to reclaim the house you must submit to this office an application for the restitution of the house. You also have to supply a testimonial about national trustworthiness or a certificate about participation in a foreign army together with a document from the archive of the Ministry of Interior attesting that at the time of the last census in 1930 you were registered as having the Czech nationality."

The latter requirement would be easy. The former, not so easy. I had been serving the Czech Army, but then they had later denied my status. I had tried the British and American armies, with little success.

In October, Francy would separately make her own claim. It would be August '47 before she was told to appoint an attorney in Czechoslovakia with whom a settlement could be negotiated. The Communist Coup would occur in February '48.

"Will you be going home, to Prague?" my girlfriend had asked on that VE evening in London.

"Even if my family is alive and well there, they'll be wanting to go to the States." Czechoslovakia did not want Jews, or any

LONDON, ENGLAND
8 MAY 1945

minorities.

"And what will you do now that the war is over?" I asked her.

"Oh, I'll stay in the A.T.S., I suppose. Unless I can find some other position right away. The workforce will be different, with our boys coming back." For most troops, demobilization was coming, we all knew.

I was lost in thought, thinking that, yes, the "boys" could be coming home — shell shocked and war-weary. Those "boys" would never be the same. And they would need jobs, and girlfriends, and flats.

In September '45, I moved to a flat in a rowhouse, 32 Earls Court Road. The month I moved was also the month I left the Lyons-owned Trocadero to take a position as a trainee with the J. Lyons Company. Lyons was an English empire of goods and services, known for their innovation, for their attention to trends, and for their "Nippy" serving girls. The Lyons Corner Houses featured deli counters, cases of chocolates and cakes, fruits and flowers, food halls and restaurants.

I started as a backdoor checker for one of the Corner Houses, and achieved two rapid promotions — from backdoor checker to backdoor clerk, then to backdoor office clerk, whose role it was to assist the backdoor chief clerk.

During the long and cold winter of 1946-47 I was promoted to linen, cutlery, and china clerk. The weather produced snowdrifts the size of houses, and, with snow blocking the roads, coal supplies were soon depleted. Television was suspended, radio was limited, magazines were discontinued, newspapers were cut in size, domestic electricity was reduced to nineteen hours per day.

By the time the winter ended, and everything thawed, and the flooding began, I was advanced to chief clerk. I assessed costing, evaluated rationing, approved food purchases, hired and fired all backdoor personnel, maintained the stockrooms, and even arranged the menus.

In the midst of a heatwave, in July '48, during the summer Olympics — the first such event since the Berlin Olympics — I was again promoted, to Inspector of Standards and Costing. I was excellent at locating the departments, goods, and menu items not operating at maximum potential and adjusting their anticipated returns. Finally, the sort of job at which I could really excel. I constantly checked competitors and trends. I answered only to the boards of directors, under managing director Mr. Isidore Montague Gluckstein.

I mediated the various and oft-conflicting interests present within the Lyons Empire, which, by that time, I knew intimately. The Front of House Managers wanted more waiters, more flowers, better furnishings, fancier food, bigger portions, but no price increases for the guests or wage increases for the staff. The Head Chefs wanted more sous chefs and cooks, new equipment, smaller portions, trendier menus, but no price increases for guests or wage increases for staff. The Back of House Managers objected to both the Front of House and Kitchen demands, but had at least seen the figures and knew what was and was not fiscally possible. Meanwhile, one also had to think of consistency — no Corner House could serve larger portions than the others, or have more attractive china, or nicer uniforms, or fresher ingredients than the others, so an improvement for one had to be an improvement for all.

I was delighted to navigate the position, convincing the Lyons bank to give credit in certain cases, arguing over the costing figures as if I were the head chef himself, delivering the causes of the lowly backdoor clerks to the mighty managers. I was a tactful diplomat, aligning all interests and finding compromises that maximized profitability and satisfaction for all involved —

LONDON, ENGLAND
8 MAY 1945

to say nothing of navigating rationing restrictions, price control, cover charge restrictions, liquor allocations, cigarette shortages, and union troubles.

And then, news.

In February'48 our Czech democracy, the last of its kind in Eastern Europe, fell to the Communists, and Czechoslovakia came under Communist Party leader Clement Gottwald's control. A few weeks after the coup, former Foreign Minister Jan Masaryk was found dead in his pyjamas in the courtyard beneath his bathroom window—a "suicide." In June, Beneš died following an illness.

I considered myself stateless. After the communist usurping of power in Czechoslovakia, I did not ask for an extension of my passport, which lost its validity, and I did not sign a declaration of loyalty. I would not be the only one who wished to escape the new regime, and I grew concerned that the new wave of Czech refugees would displace me in the American immigration quota.

Two years before the Communist Coup, in February '46, the American Vice-Consul, W.J. Ford, had written to inform me that I "appear[ed] to be inadmissible to the United States under the war-time regulations still in effect. Under these regulations the reasons for this refusal may not be divulged. It is therefore regretted that no further action may be taken on [my] case."

It was clear that whatever rubbish people from Shanghai had been talking about me was keeping me from leaving for the States, where my only surviving relatives had become citizens. I waited several months, then responded:

THE SUITCASE

To The American Consul
Immigration Section
United States Embassy
London.

Sir,
Should you be kind enough to inspect the files pertaining to my case, you will find that I am endeavouring for more than three years to obtain an immigration visa to the United States. My case has been put off under the heading "War regulation," although I have never been told what the unfortunate reason might be, which bars me from entering the U.S.

I should like to stress that I never belonged to any political organisation, nor have I been engaged in any active or passive support of such. The fact is that because of the proximity of Soviet ideologies, I have not gone back to Czechoslovakia, not even for a visit.

On the other hand, if there was any doubt with regard to my activities in Shanghai, where I spent 10 years before coming to England in 1942, surely the authorities concerned had all the opportunity since the termination of the war in the Far East, to corroborate their suspicion, if any. I am positive had they done so, they would have had to report that their former statements were the result of special care, which they had to exercise for the duration of the war, but which they have found unsubstantiated.

I therefore wonder, whether it could be arranged to have me questioned about anything they wish to know, by expert interrogators.

    I HEREWITH DECLARE THAT I AM

LONDON, ENGLAND
8 MAY 1945

PREPARED TO SUBMIT VOLUNTARILY TO SUCH INTERROGATION AND THAT I WOULD WELCOME THE USE OF LIE DETECTORS, TRUTH DRUG OR ANY OTHER SCIENTIFIC METHOD.

My mother, brother and sister died during the war in concentration camps and I have only one sister left, who is a naturalized American citizen, living with her husband and son in New York. I am a single man and greatly attached to all of them, but none of us is getting any younger.

If the suggested interrogation could take place, I am sure it not only would help me to obtain my visa, but it also would enable me to prove myself innocent of some wrong of which I know nothing, as there does not seem to be any authority interested enough to prove me guilty.

I never heard a single word from the U.S. Consul General in London. I even sent a copy of the letter six months later, in April '47, saying: "I beg to refer to my last letter, dated 17 October 1946. I very much regret that I had no answer whatsoever, so I presume that my letter must have been lost in the mail.

"I therefore take the liberty to submit a copy and I shall be very grateful if given the earliest opportunity to clear up that unfortunate matter."

In May of '47, American Consul Eldred Kuppinger had responded: "...no useful purpose will be served by continuing your application for an immigration visa.... Your attention is invited to the Embassy's letter of 15 February 1946. The circumstances indicated in that letter have not altered and therefore it will be seen that the Embassy still cannot initiate action on your application."

THE SUITCASE

It is needless to say that this response was deeply unsatisfactory.

In July 1948, during the heatwave and the Olympics, I sent Francy an entire kilogram of letters, reports, certificates, and photographs, with a long cover letter detailing my time in Shanghai and my present situation, in hopes she could be of assistance.

Years earlier, in the winter of 1940, when Francy had been suffering from her usual bronchitis, she had retreated to the Greenbrier resort in White Sulphur Springs, West Virginia. Famed for its natural mineral springs and beautiful scenery, the Greenbrier was nestled between the Greenbrier River and the Virginia state border.

After America entered the war in December '41, the Greenbrier was one of the luxury hotels that became a relocation centre for Axis diplomats. In the summer of '42, those diplomats were part of the exchange at Lourenço Marques, Mozambique, and were returned to their respective homes.

The Greenbrier had then been used as an Army hospital for the duration.

Upon its reopening in April of 1948, my sister and Zik were in attendance, as was Colonel Orren Lee Jones of West Virginia. Jones had served the Army Air Corps during the war and was a special assistant to the Joint Chiefs of Staff. He also served as a consultant to the U.S. Senate Subcommittee on Immigration, which resulted in the creation of the Displaced Persons Act in June 1948.

It seems I had not been the only one with concerns that the latest Eastern European refugees, those fleeing Communism, would replace me in the quota. At Zikmund's request, Orren Jones had agreed to speak with West Virginia Senator William Chapman Revercomb of the Immigration Committee. Jones

LONDON, ENGLAND
8 MAY 1945

wrote:

"I have discussed this matter today with the Immigration Committee (friends of mine) and one of the staff will correspond directly with you, requesting additional information. I am with the staff every day, and we'll keep you informed of any developments. Cases of this type are more than difficult, and the Committee has thousands of requests on file. However, we will find out the facts, and you may be assured of my personal attention in this case."

In February of '49 my number for the Czech quota became available—if I qualified for a visa. I was told to call at the Visa Section of the Embassy or my "quota number may become void." I was to bring my passport, and the visa fee, between 15 and 18 February.

My passport for stateless persons was stamped "U.S. Immigration Visa, Quota Number 950" on 16 February 1949, and was signed by the American Consul.

There were few goodbyes to say. The girlfriend I had been seeing at the end of the war had long since left me for greener pastures. Desmond O'Neill had left in January 1948 for Germany, as part of the British Army of the Rhine. There was Edward Gerald Smith-Wright, whom I had known for some fifteen years by that time, and Errol Shorrock Barraclough. My employers at J. Lyons. My landlady.

Leaving was easy. It was the waiting that had been difficult.

*****

I stood next to the Captain of the S.S. *American Planter* as the camera snapped. We posed again, one of us on either side of a life preserver bearing the ship's name. I smiled, having already been invited to his table for dinner that evening.

THE SUITCASE

I held a cabin-class ticket, but the *Planter* was not exactly one of the luxury cruise liners to which I had grown accustomed. The ship began its life as an attack transport for troops and cargo. She had been part of the Fifth Amphibious Force in the Pacific Fleet before being decommissioned in 1946, transferred to commercial service in '47, and renamed *American Planter*.

I stood on her decks as we left port. No one had come to the Royal Victoria Docks to see me off. I gazed at Spiller's Millennium Mills, which was under construction. It had been bombed during the war — reduced to rubble and skeleton-like beams.

A man who stood nearby me followed my gaze. He said, "They rebuilt it after the Great War too. Sat there looking like rubbish until the '30s, then someone restored it. Now they'll rebuild it again, until she's destroyed the next time."

I looked at him and said, "I sincerely hope there is no next time." I left the deck and returned to my cabin. My trunk had been stowed away, but the stewards had left my suitcase. In it were my camera and film, my scrapbooks, my letters and papers and photographs, menus and programmes and ticket stubs, calling cards and business cards, my silver cigarette case, an A.T.S. ring, the Czech roundel patches from my S.V.C. uniform, some Chinese coins, my brass knuckles, and a thousand other artefacts of the lives I had led.

It was mid-March 1949, and I was headed across the Atlantic to New York City, to my only surviving family, and my new life in America. Finally.

Epilogue

Tuxedo Park, New York
June 1964

The movers are scheduled to arrive this morning.

It is nearly dawn. Joan is asleep.

I sit in a halo of lamplight in my family's Tuxedo Park apartment. My whiskey glass is empty. My ashtray, nearly full. An ended Dvořák record makes a light scratching noise as it spins in the Stromberg Carlson machine. I move a hand to lift the needle.

Sitting in front of me is one more envelope, a large manila affair with a metal fastener, its tabs long since broken. I remove the contents, revealing bits of my life after arriving in the United States: reminders of my first job as a travelling salesman, a job that taught me American selling techniques; copies of a collection of stock market trade orders from my employment with a number of Wall Street brokerage firms; relics from my matches at the Forest Hills Tennis Club; a membership card from New York's Shanghai Tiffin Club, where I had been able to reconnect with other Shanghailanders.

My hand grazes over another stack of remembrances, once wrapped by a thick rubber band that had long since disintegrated. This contains my marriage certificate to Joan, the sweetest and noblest girl I have ever met—and I was certainly no saint in the fifty-four years before I fell in love; my U.S. naturalisation certificate that officially changed my name to George; the birth announcements and locks of hair from my two daughters,

THE SUITCASE

Deborah Joan and Marietta Julie. How I wish to always be near to my girls and their mother, as to protect them from all trouble.

The rest of the contents of the suitcase lay fanned out around me, singly and in stacks, contents I had not examined in years, yet which I still knew like my own shoes: photographs of my conscription during the Great War; my mother's heart-wrenchingly familiar Czech script on fragile onionskin paper; my typewritten military reports from Shanghai; clippings from the society and sporting pages of the *North-China Daily News*; portraits of young starlets; theatre tickets; steamship tickets; posters from my speaking tour in England; the letter from my family's former housekeeper confirming my most horrible fears...

In the intervening years I have come to terms, as much as possible, with my family's fate. I will tell my daughters, matter-of-factly, "They were ruthlessly murdered." We light a candle for them on Yom Kippur. Save holiday celebrations for the girls, it is my only religious habit.

I think of my father, and his views on organised religion, and I hope that I have done enough to impart his views, and my own, onto my daughters. In 1961, just before my sixty-second birthday, I wrote a letter for them, to be given to both daughters when they turned fifteen.

I wrote: "Your mother and I believe in God, but we do not care for religious dogmas and find that most of all religious fanatics are usually self-centred dictators who believe in their own rights but nobody else's. Your grandfather Karel as well as I believe that God is everywhere, not only in churches or synagogues, and that the best religion is to live by the principles of courage, decency, honesty, and tolerance."

In conclusion, I had written, "If I am around after some time, I shall add to this letter. If not, then remember, my darlings, that

EPILOGUE - TUXEDO PARK, NEW YORK - JUNE 1964

I loved you more than any words can express right to my last breath and that you are a Taussig and God bless you all your life."

When my daughters ask why the Allies won the war, I tell them, "Because truth and good always win." And I hope I am right.

I replace the suitcase's contents, and return the letters to and from my family, marked by postmen and censors on four continents, to their stack on one side of the suitcase. The other keepsakes, I pack in neatly, filling the suitcase's space with remembrances of my lives in Prague, in Shanghai, in New York City, and in London.

I fold the suitcase's lid back onto the frame and secure the snap locks. The once-fine leather veneer is dull and scratched. The cardboard beneath the leather is softened and frayed. My finger traces my initials, printed in white in the centre of the case. My eyes locate the faded but familiar logos of exotic hotels, and the steamships that had carried me there.

My old suitcase. This, I am not trusting to the care of the moving company. I set it on the dining room table along with several other precious items that we will carry in our car.

I stand and move to the doorway, turn out the light, and pause for a moment in the mostly-empty room. Light has begun to seep in from the now-curtainless window.

One day, when I retire—if I can ever afford to retire—I will take my old friend Lucien's advice and write my story. It is all here, in my old suitcase, waiting to be pieced together.

But not now. The movers will be arriving in a few hours.

Epilogue for Marietta and Jaromír Taussig and others of transports Dl and Ek

THE AUTHORS do not know exactly what became of Marietta and Jaromír Taussig—only which transports from Terezín they were on, and that they did not survive being transported East.

It is possible that Marietta Taussigová died during transport Dl to Osvětim. It is possible that she perished at some point during her six-month imprisonment in Auschwitz-Birkenau's Czech Family Camp that was created expressly to fool any potential Red Cross inspectors. It is equally as possible that she survived until the day of the infamous 8 March mass murder.

Even today, as of this writing in 2022, Czechs know that 3,792 September transportees from Terezín, prisoners of the Czech Family Camp at Auschwitz-Birkenau, were murdered en masse in March 1944, and that they sang the Czech national anthem, the "Hatikvah," and "L'Internationale" before their deaths.

Of those September deportees on transport Dl, only thirty-eight people survived the war.

In September 1944, the Red Cross did in fact decide to tour a labour camp. They were shown a group of British Prisoners of War in Auschwitz. The very same Maurice Rossel who had previously toured Terezín had one main goal during his visit to Auschwitz—to determine whether packages sent to the prisoners by the Red Cross were being properly distributed. During his limited tour, Rossel failed to notice that the "shower rooms" were gas chambers. He mentioned that the fixtures needed updating, then moved on. This visit took place on 29 September.

EPILOGUE FOR MARIETTA AND JAROMÍR TAUSSIG

Jaromír Taussig's train, transport Ek from Terezín, arrived at Auschwitz-Birkenau on the same day as the Red Cross visit. On the selection ramp, Otto Zucker—the supposed head of the new work camp "near Dresden"—and one thousand others, including Zucker's hand-picked staff, were selected to be gassed immediately. And to think that that particular transport had supposedly been carefully chosen based on members' construction skills and their ability to quickly build the "new camp." In reality, the Nazis were removing any able-bodied men from Terezín who were capable of resistance, and who had borne witness to the staged Red Cross tour and subsequent movie filming.

On 29 September 1944, after the initial selection of Ek on the ramp at Auschwitz-Birkenau, 1,499 men were left—less however many died during transport. It is possible that Jaromír died on the train and never made it as far as the selection ramp. If Jara was not gassed, then he certainly met the fate of "liquidation by work."

"Some [men of transport Ek] were sent to work within the Auschwitz branch camps and perished in the Monowitz factory of the I.G. Farben complex, [others] in the cement works of Golesow near Ciesyn, [still others] in the coal mines Furstengrube or Mismarckhutte." Many "were sent to Kaufering and Landesberg where the prisoners of eleven branch camps of Dachau were... working on the large-scale construction of one of the factories of the aircraft industry."

After Jaromír's transport departed Terezín on 28 September, a dozen more transports followed, all destined for Auschwitz. Director Kurt Gerron was included. Of these autumn 1944 transports from Terezín, containing 18,042 men, women, and children, only 1,474 people survived. The transports ended on 28 October, which was, ironically, the same day Czechoslovaks had celebrated independence each year since 1918.

After these transports, Terezín was left with "only" 11,068 prisoners, none of whom had much ability to resist. During that time, 17,000 boxes of ashes were dumped into the Ohře. The remainder of the ashes were buried in a pit near Litoměřice. Julie's remains were never placed near Karel's in the Prague cemetery.

The Soviet Red Army arrived in Terezín in May 1945 to liberate the prisoners. "Within days... the original Christian residents of the Habsburg fortress town began to drift back — as if nothing at all had occurred in [the previous] four years."

For those who remained in Auschwitz-Birkenau, Lagerführer Schwarzhuber had been replaced by SS Obersturmführer Joseph Kramer, "a brutal creature." Killings reached their peak. Prisoners were continually fed into the camp. Transports came from Hungary, Slovakia, Subcarpathian Ruthenia, and Transylvania. Gassing selections took place on the ramp day and night, and in full view of the earlier arrivals. The crematories were so overtaxed that the Sonderkommando resorted to burning bodies in ditches.

The Sonderkommando revolted in October 1944. On 29 October, Himmler gave the order to close the gas chambers. In November, as Soviet troops approached, the SS ordered the destruction of the crematoria. In mid-January 1945, prisoners who might have lived to tell about the Nazis' atrocities were led on a death march. Thousands died from cold, exposure, or starvation during the thirty-plus mile trudge to the west in the fierce winter weather. Those who lagged behind were shot. The few who did survive the march were taken to concentration camps in Germany.

Left behind to die in Auschwitz were those already too weak to march, and who were expected not to survive much longer regardless. Some seven thousand living skeletons were discovered by the Allied forces when Auschwitz-Birkenau was liberated

EPILOGUE FOR MARIETTA AND JAROMÍR TAUSSIG

in late-January 1945, almost exactly four months after Jaromír's transport.

Whatever his fate, Jaromír Taussig did not survive.

Epilogue for the Others

Abrahams, Luisa Raudnitz. The Czech woman with whom Vladimír connected during his first days in London continued to be a "prominent personality in the English golf scene after the war." There is a room named after her in the Royal Golf Club in Mariánské Lázně. She died in 2006.

Andrews, Lewis and Hope. Following their time in a Japanese internment camp, the noted Shanghai couple Lou and Hope Andrews moved to the States and purchased "Tulip Hill," an 18th-century estate in Maryland, where they lived until Hope's death in 1984. Lou died in 1990. Hope, who had spent her years in the internment camp dreaming of food, created a "thoroughly researched regional cookbook," *Maryland's Sway*, in 1963.

Boissevain, Gideon Walrave. The Dutch diplomat married his second wife, Maria — granddaughter of Grigori Rasputin — in 1947, and his third wife, Emma, in 1978. He died in 1985.

Cathay Hotel. The Cathay Hotel, and the majority of the Sassoon House, became the Peace Hotel in 1956. In 1965, the Peace Hotel annexed the neighbouring Palace Hotel. The 2010 Shanghai world's fair, "Expo 2010," saw the hotels re-emerge as the Fairmont Peace Hotel and the Swatch Art Peace Hotel, respectively.

Culbertson, Chuck. One of the partners of Swan, Culbertson and Fritz, Shanghai sportsman Chuck Culbertson was repatriated to the United States in the *Gripsholm* in 1943.

Freeman, Helene. The New York City radio star of *Meet Miss*

EPILOGUE FOR THE OTHERS

Julia married Edwin Jerome in 1943. The couple ended up in Hollywood, where Freeman met a tragic end: she was murdered in 1958. Edwin, who "never recovered from the shock of the unsolved murder of his wife," died in 1959.

Fritz, Chester. Vladimír's former boss, sportsman Chester Fritz, separated from Bernardine in 1944; they divorced in '46. Chester remarried in 1954, and he and his new wife, Vera Kachalina, went to live abroad. Fritz died in 1983; Vera in 2005. Bernardine Szold died in 1982.

Grant-Jones, Penrhyn and Sylvia. Judge Penrhyn Grant-Jones of H.B.M. Supreme Court for China was interned by the Japanese for five months before being repatriated to England. He was receiving treatments at Ticehurst House in Sussex at the time of his death in the summer of 1945. Sylvia remarried as a Stewart.

Hahn, Emily "Mickey." The American writer was repatriated from China in 1943. In 1945 she married Charles Boxer, a British Army intelligence officer in Hong Kong. They had two children. When Hahn died in 1997 she left behind hundreds of published works, including 1941's *The Soong Sisters*, and 1944's *China to Me: A Partial Autobiography*.

Havlíček, Frantisek. The Czechoslovak diplomat in Japan to whom Vladimír had funnelled money from the Czechoslovak Government-in-Exile, was repatriated to England in 1942 on the MS *Gripsholm*. Havlíček returned to Czechoslovakia after the war.

Helmick, Milton John. The American judge was repatriated to the States in 1942. He returned to China in 1944 and worked in Shanghai until 1951. He retired in 1954 and died in San Francisco that same year.

Innes-Ker, Major David Charles. Innes-Ker, of the Royal Artillery, married Crista Irene Valentine de Paravicini. They had a daughter in 1941. David Innes-Ker died in 1957.

Kann, Eduard. Taussig's one-time business partner, Eduard Kann, was interned by the Japanese. Following his release, he continued his Shanghai brokerage business until 1949's Communist Revolution. Kann and his wife Margaret then moved to America. Kann died in 1962. The American Numismatic Society is in possession of part, or all, that remains of Kann's Chinese coin, banknote, and ingot collection.

Kanturková, Liza. Liza married Franta Vilim, a childhood friend and tennis companion. Vilim had served the Government-in-Exile in England before being selected to fight on the Eastern Front, in General Svoboda's army. He served in the unit that liberated Auschwitz. The couple had a daughter, born in Prague. In 1948, after Jan Masaryk "fell" out of a window and the Communists took control of Czechoslovakia, the Kantureks (including Ernst and Vilda), the Votickys (Anka and her husband and their children), and the Vilims (Liza and Franta) made their way to Canada. Liza died in 2004.

Kühnreich, Francy and Zikmund. Francy was involved in philanthropic efforts for the Jewish community. Zikmund died in Chicago in 1961. Francy died in New York in 1970.

Kühnreich, Jiří ("George"). After climbing Pointe du Hoc on D-Day, Vladimír's nephew Jiří was transferred to the 63d Infantry Division, whose motto was "Blood and Fire." Jiří was injured as the 63d prepared to cross the Saar River and the German lines. On his return to the States, Jiří completed college and worked on the New York Stock Exchange and, later, became an attorney for the Tandy Corporation in Texas. He died in 1991.

LeRougetel, John Helier. Vladimír's detractor was awarded the Order of St. Michael and St. George in 1943. He was appointed to various ambassador positions, traveling to

EPILOGUE FOR THE OTHERS

Romania, Tehran, Belgium, and South Africa. He retired in 1955, having been made a Knight Commander of the Order. He died in 1975.

Nový Berštejn. In 1935, well before Tomáš Maglič's death, the estate was sold to the Kabát family. During the war, the estate was occupied by a German, Baron Ludolf von Wedel-Parlow. Under Communist control, the estate was divided into multiple parcels. The "castle" itself was used for many purposes, including a clinic and a boarding school. It fell into such a state of disrepair that demolition was contemplated. In 1991, a multi-year renovation began; it is now an award-winning hotel and golf resort.

O'Neill, Desmond. O'Neill's fate is unknown as of this writing.

Ovadia, Lucien and Viva. After writing his 1948 letter to Taussig from India, Lucien returned to Shanghai. He became stuck there after the People's Republic of China was created in October 1949. He managed Sassoon's hotels, apartments, and other holdings under increasingly difficult conditions. It was 1952 before he was allowed to leave China, at which time he flew to London to tender his resignation to Sir Victor. He retired to Jersey, in the Channel Islands off the coast of France. He died in the fall of 1969. As of this writing, Viva's fate is unknown.

Pribram, Bruno Oskar. The doctor from Shanghai did eventually make it to England, arriving in Southampton in mid-December, 1945.

Reimannová, Anna Magličová. Taussig's ex-wife, Ann Magličová remarried a man named Reimann in 1933. Her new husband worked for the German film industry. She died in her thirties in 1944 and is buried in Prague.

Reller, Elizabeth. The young radio starlet from Young Doctor Malone, Betty and Bob, and other serials, as well as the

THE SUITCASE

Broadway production A Day in the Sun, married a naval officer, Doctor Frances Bewley Warrick. She died in Indiana in 1974. Her husband died in 2003.

Sassoon, Sir Ellice Victor, 3rd Baronet, GBE. Sir Victor remained a fixture in business, social, and horse-racing spheres in England, Bombay, and Shanghai. India became independent from the British Empire in 1947, the same year Sir Victor received the Knight Grand Cross of the Order of the British Empire. At the time of the Communist revolution in China, Sir Victor packed a single suitcase and discreetly left Shanghai for the Bahamas. There, he would eventually marry his nurse, Evelyn Barnes. Sassoon died in 1961. His widow established the Sir Victor Sassoon Heart Foundation to assist Bahamians afflicted with heart disease in obtaining quality cardiac care. The foundation is still operating as of this writing.

Schicht, Franz, Georg, and Heinrich. The last Schicht shareholder in the Unilever Corporation left the board after the war. Heinrich returned to Ústí nad Labem. He was arrested when a letter to Göring was discovered that professed that Schicht had always been a German company and had never employed any Czechs. He was expelled, with 2.4 million other Sudeten Germans, to the Russian Zone in Germany. From there, Heinrich fled to Switzerland, where he died in 1959. Franz moved from London to Berlin shortly before the outbreak of war in Europe. He became a leading businessman in Germany. In 1972 he died in Argentina, a place where many Nazis migrated after the war. Georg moved to London in 1931 and became a British national, which spared him from being removed from Unilever's board of directors. He died in London in 1961.

Smith, Captain Columbus Darwin. Smith, the man with whom Taussig spent his last dinner party in Shanghai, escaped

EPILOGUE FOR THE OTHERS

from Japanese imprisonment on multiple occasions, risking beheading each time. He walked several hundred miles to Chungking. He is the subject of World War II correspondent Quentin Reynolds's 1945 book, *Officially Dead: The Story of Commander C. D. Smith*.

Španiel, Oldřich. The man to whom Taussig reported in New York City—and to whom only one other Czech stepped forward in 1940—became, after the war, the first commander of the corps in Prague. In 1949 he became the head of the military history institute. He died in 1963.

Štembera, Emil Jan. The Czech leader in Shanghai's fate is unknown as of this writing, but research suggests that he denounced Czech nationalists to Japanese authorities in Shanghai and was later awarded honours "for resistance" by the Czech Ministry of Defence.

Stepan, Jaroslav. The Czech leader in Shanghai's fate is unknown as of this writing, but research suggests that the leader of the Czechoslovak National Committee in Shanghai did deliberately sow seeds of division in the Czech expat community.

Swan, Joseph Edwards Corson. The partner of Swan, Culbertson and Fritz moved to New York and became President of the China Society of America, director of the Far East-America Council of Commerce and Industry. From 1945, he worked with Hayden, Stone and Company, becoming the senior partner. Swan died in 1960.

Toeg, Edmund. In 1948 Toeg married Lorraine Murray, also of Shanghai, in Middlesex. Toeg died in London in 1974.

Voticky Family. The family returned to Czechoslovakia until 1948's Communist coup, whereupon they relocated to Canada. Their eldest son, Milan, or "Lou," knew Vladimír Taussig in Shanghai. Lou later became an officer in the Canadian Air

THE SUITCASE

Force and a commercial pilot. His book, *Dreamers Refuse to be Victims*, was published in 2019. After several interviews with Vladimír's daughter Deborah, Anka died in 2014 at the age of 100. Anka's 2010 book, *Knocking on Every Door*, mentions Vladimír Taussig.

Wiesner, Bedrich. The Ministry of Defence official who interrogated Vladimír on his arrival in Britain was, himself, arrested after the war as the Communists searched for enemies within their own ranks. Along with many men of the Ministry of the Interior under the new Communist regime, Wiesner was killed in 1949, dying from injuries received during interrogation.

Wragge, Elizabeth "Betty." Betty's most famous radio show, *Pepper Young's Family*, continued to air intermittently until 1959. She enjoyed a long career, not only in radio but also acting on Broadway and other theatrical venues, dubbing foreign films into English, acting in television commercials, and lending her talents to training videos. She died in 2002.

Deborah Taussig-Boehner's Acknowledgments

The Suitcase took yet another trip to the Far East when **Graham Earnshaw** of Earnshaw Books decided that it was worthy of publication. Instead of steamships, the internet has made this part of the voyage much more efficient. During initial conversations, Graham expressed his joy and satisfaction in his ability to work with the author to bring the manuscript to the point of publication; a process that is challenging, painstaking, and at the same time, gratifying. I am indebted to Graham for his guidance, wisdom and encouragement.

It has taken over a decade for *The Suitcase* to be written. It is a story that was created and documented from the contents of Vladimír's suitcase but would not have been possible without the interest and support of countless individuals and agencies worldwide. Every single person has been so very willing to add their assistance and knowledge along with their encouragement to pursue the eventual creation of this book. In the late 1970's my sister, **Marietta Boon** located and hired a graduate student to translate numerous letters that had been written by Julie and Karel and sent to Vladimír while he lived in Shanghai. All of them were handwritten and on terribly fragile onion-skin paper and many were subjected to censorship and had pieces cut from the content. It is from those letters that we were able to reconstruct the fate of the family. The letters went into much more detail regarding family dynamics, and some of those dramas were originally included in *The Suitcase*. As the book evolved, the history overshadowed the drama, and much was omitted.

A number of years ago, I began researching family trees on both sides of my family thanks to **Keira Murphy's** encouragement. Subsequently, Keira established her company, **Jumpstart Genealogy** and is well regarded in her beloved second profession. A master teacher, Keira has incorporated the use of genealogy in numerous curricula spanning multiple disciplines. Prior to embarking on my father's history, I had already completed comprehensive histories of my mother's family and my husband's family and had given them to my four children as Christmas gifts. *The Suitcase* is based on the same genealogical research afforded to the rest of the family, but with the added advantage of firsthand memoirs, documents, photographs, and family documentation. In addition to the letters, I was fortunate to have a copy of an employment application and accompanying detailed resume from the year 1955. I had just been born, and my father was applying for a management position at the soon to be opened Disneyland. This one document described his life from his WWI conscription through the year 1955. It was the jumping off place for an incredible journey to come.

I met with several local authors, including **Marti Healy** and **Dacre Stoker**, and university English professor **Lynne Rhodes**, all who offered their encouragement, recognizing what a huge task lay in front of me.

I then discovered that Vladimír was included in a book by the late **Anka Voticky** called *Knocking on Every Door*, her memoir of her family's escape to Shanghai. The publisher was the **Azrieli Foundation** in Toronto, and their editor, **Arielle Berger** introduced me to Anka's son **Milan "Lou" Voticky**. After several emails and phone conversations, I had the opportunity to visit Anka in Montreal. She was in her late nineties at the time and sharp as a tack. She vividly remembered Vladimír; identified a

DEBORAH TAUSSIG-BOEHNER'S ACKNOWLEDGMENTS

photo that I had brought as being her sister, Liza, who Vladimír dated; and translated several documents from Czech into English. Such a remarkable lady.

The next step in the puzzle was to visit the archival collection at **DeGolyer Library at Southern Methodist University** in Dallas, Texas. It is there that Sir Victor Sassoon's diaries and photo albums are preserved. My sister joined me for this adventure, and we scoured page after page of the diaries and albums and found our father mentioned and photographed on numerous occasions. **Pamalla Anderson,** Head of Public Services and **Anne Peterson,** Curator of Photographs took particular interest in our research and introduced us to **Evelyn Cox,** whose father was the sister of Nurse Barnes, who Sassoon eventually married.

I also spent several days in the **New York Public Library,** whose staff was incredibly helpful.

I renewed my relationship with the **University of South Carolina-Aiken** and thanks to **Jane Tuten, Brigette Smith, Kelsey Crump** and the **inter-library loan staff,** I have been able to access countless volumes of documents that otherwise would have been much more difficult to obtain.

I then contacted the **National Archives in Prague** as well as the **State Regional Archives in Prague and Litoměřice** and was able to obtain volumes of information related to the Taussig family, the Maglič family, as well as lengthy transcripts of court depositions. Because they were in Czech, I needed to locate someone who could translate them for me. Thanks to a recommendation from a family friend, I was introduced to the late **Steve Zemko.** He was retired and very willingly took on the challenge. He translated hundreds of pages and got to the point where he was engrossed in the story! After he passed away, his daughter told me that he really looked forward to getting the next installment. I'd like to think that this project kept him engaged during his declining years.

Several documents were written in German and my brother-in-law, **Dave Boon** came to the rescue. I also received help from **Julius Schml**, a German exchange student at Aiken Preparatory School.

Over 30 years ago I worked with **Val Lumans**, then Professor, now Professor Emeritus of European History at the University of South Carolina-Aiken. At that time, I told him that I had a book to write...one day... and asked him if he would ensure historical accuracy. When I began my research he offered advice as I was about to embark on my first trip to Prague, and yes, he did, in fact read the manuscript for accuracy.

It was in Prague that my sister and I engaged the services of **P.A.T.H. Finders**, owned by **Marie and Tom Zahn**. They assisted in taking us to all the houses that were owned by Vladimír's family, and sadly, the addresses where his mother, sister, and brother were relegated prior to their transports and murders. They also assisted in genealogical research. Also, while in The Czech Republic, we stayed at **Nový Berštejn** and experienced firsthand what it might have been like to live in the grand house. Even though they were about to close for the season, the owners, **Markéta and Miroslav Slezák** were proud to show us their restoration efforts and Miroslav proved to be a first class host providing a delicious evening meal and hearty breakfast. After leaving, we made the short trip to **Terezín**. It was a grey and damp day, and it was not difficult to imagine the horrors that were encountered there. The railroad tracks, the barracks, the crematorium, the fort still stand for all to witness along with the ironic and hopeful artwork of the children. Also, while in Prague, I met with **Tomáš Jakl** and **Jiří Plachý** at the **Vojenský Historický Ústav Praha** and shared Vladimír's story. Since my visit, Plachý has published an article titled "In the Far East Under Czechoslovak Flag" in *Paměť a*

DEBORAH TAUSSIG-BOEHNER'S ACKNOWLEDGMENTS

Dějiny Journal using information and photos that I had provided.

After leaving Prague, my next step was to visit the British **National Archives in Kew**. It was during this visit that various documents and telegrams were unearthed that shed light on the British's distrust of Vladimír.

Shanghai was my next stop, and thanks to the efforts of my son **Chris Boehner**, I was introduced to **William Patrick Cranley**, whose knowledge of pre-war Shanghai was incredible. I was able to bring a number of photos that he put into context and then we enjoyed a day of travel around the city where he brought me to all of the locations of Vladimír's work, home, and play. At every step, he recounted historical events that had occurred at each location. I also had the pleasure to meet and work with **Irene Fang**, who served as my guide and translator during my stay. We visited the library housing the *North China Daily News* archives and she assisted in my search of articles. She also arranged for a visit to the Center of Jewish Studies on the campus of the Shanghai Academy of Social Sciences with **Professor Pan Guang** and his graduate student, **Xu Tao** whose thesis and research was the Shanghai Volunteer Corps. Finally, we visited the Jewish Museum and the park dedicated to the stateless residents of Shanghai. Irene made navigating in Shanghai easy, especially in rush hour metro stations!

Having never attempted to write such a story, my next step was to enroll in a distance taught introduction to writing course by **Ginger Moran**. Her simple breakdown of the "rules" helped clarify and organize the task at hand. Through her expertise, I began to dabble in using the first-person as the most comfortable method to tell the story. My goal has always been to tell the history using engaging scenes and dialogue, rather than simply recounting events. I wanted the reader to be able to envision and insert themselves into Vladimír's world, yet maintain the

THE SUITCASE

accurate historical context in which they existed.

It just so happened that **Lauren Housman**, the daughter of a colleague, had recently completed her master's degree in creative nonfiction. She and I have had a wonderfully collaborative relationship for the past eight years, and she has taken the level of research to depths much beyond my original attempts. We have passed the manuscript back and forth more times than I can count as we mutually edited to our satisfaction.

Almost four years ago, we began to share the manuscript with several Beta Readers. **Jim Garvey, Cody McNeill, Luuki Pekkala, Cynthia Ritt, Debbie Kasper, Nancy Marks, Jan Collova, Marsy McFerrin, Mary leBlanc, Denise Housman, Karen Lehrhaupt Kolosek, Karen Matthews, Marietta Boon, Dave Boon, Brian Boon, Andrew Boon, Chris Boehner and Val Lumans.** Thank you all for your time and suggestions.

Throughout this journey, I could not help but notice numerous coincidences… important dates, hobbies, careers etc. of the Taussig family that have paralleled the lives of my four children: **Christopher**, the world traveler and entrepreneur. **Jaime**, the artist and creator. **Philip**, the analytical scientist. And **Megan**, the seeker of fairness and justice. Vladimír would have been proud of his grandchildren. Finally, I thank my husband, **Jim**. He has patiently and quietly encouraged this labor of love. Without his support, the story hidden within the suitcase would not have emerged.

Deborah Taussig-Boehner, 2022

Lauren Housman's Acknowledgments

I WOULD like to thank those who acknowledged and encouraged my love of reading and research, those who shared their stories with me, and those who made me feel I was capable of telling a story of this magnitude. Those people include my mother, **Denise Housman**, who never said "no" to buying me books and who shares my love of a Good Story; teachers at Schofield Middle School, including **Sally Jenkins**, who was so creative in her methods of literary analysis and immersion; **Frau Margaret Jilani**, who shared her own story with her German classes each Friday; and whoever arranged for Elie Wiesel to come speak to the students.

The late **Joseph Laorenza**, who taught so many students at Aiken High School to communicate with their hearts, and during whose band trips to Washington DC and New Orleans we were able to visit the World War II Museum and Holocaust Museum, which left a lasting impression.

USCA English department professors, including **Carla Coleman** for her comments on how I "quilted" together a paper about a Romantic English poem, making scholars' voices speak to one another while completely omitting my own opinions. I thought of "quilting" so often during this project as I researched, organized, wrote, and re-wrote this book; **Dr. Tom Mack** for preparing me for graduate studies, and for this book, without my realizing it at the time, and for showing so many students how to "instruct and delight"; **Dr. Lynne Rhodes** for making all students feel their stories and essays were significant and could find literary homes; **Dr. Doug Higbee** for his courses on contemporary British literature and on war, and for his encouragement.

Graduate school mentors **Dan Wakefield** for his advice on "telling it straight," and for his unwavering belief in me and my work; **Richard Tillinghast** for his travel writing and fascination with details of period dress; **Robert Olmstead** for always knowing where a story actually begins, how a story might end, and what does and doesn't belong on the page; **Susan Tekulve** for her work on novels-in-stories; the other faculty of the Converse College Low-Residency MFA program; the Creative Nonfiction "**MaFiA of Love**" and other students who gave me a wonderful place to escape when I was so unhappy and so far from home, and who taught me so much about writing and rewriting.

The late **Nancy Bennett**, who enjoyed travel, Prague, and Art Nouveau, and who lent me architectural books early in the project; and the late **Dr. Liam Brockington**, who so loved studying history, war, and PTSD, and who would surely have devoured this story in a single sitting with Shadow in his lap. **Shadow**, who became my own "shadow" after Dr. B's passing, and who worked on this manuscript with me for fourteen months before his passing. Their memories are a blessing.

My many thanks go, of course, to **Debbie Taussig-Boehner** for the priceless opportunity, and for her excellent collaboration. What a gift our friendship, and this experience, have been for someone who loves to read, to research and to write. Her travels, translations, and initial research became the scale upon which the notes of this proverbial symphony were written. She has been conductor, and audience, through countless rehearsals until we felt the work ready for its final performance—publication.

And to **Graham Earnshaw**, for ping-ponging with Debbie

LAUREN HOUSMAN'S ACKNOWLEDGMENTS

and me as we prepared *The Suitcase* for publication. I am so glad that he has been able to give this work its proper home.

Finally, and most importantly, **Meir**, my boyfriend and my "person" since 2014. I began this project shortly before meeting him. All he has ever known is "The Book" and the stresses, and joys, that it has brought. His support, both emotionally and tangibly, has been invaluable.

I would work at the same level for another eight years if it meant I could find answers and connect the dots all over again. To be able to tell just one family's story has meant a tremendous amount to me.

Thank you all for enabling me to reach this occasion.

Lauren Housman, 2022

Selected Bibliography

Adler, H.G. *Theresienstadt 1941-1945: The Face of a Coerced Community.* Translated by Belinda Cooper. Cambridge UP, 2017.

Albright, Madeleine. *Prague Winter: A Personal Story of Remembrance and War, 1937-1948.* 2012. Harper Perennial, 2013.

Aldrich, Richard J. "Britain's Secret Intelligence Service in Asia During the Second World War." *Modern Asian Studies*, 32, 1, Cambridge UP, 1998.

Alcott, Carroll Duard. *My War with Japan.* H. Holt and Company, 1943.

Allman, Norwood. *Shanghai Lawyer.* Whittlesey House, 1943.

Ardent, Hannah. *Eichmann in Jerusalem: A Report on the Banality of Evil.* Penguin Books. 1977.

Aristophanes. *Lysistrata.* Translated by The Athenian Society. Digireads.com Publishing, 2018.

Bacon, Ursula. *Shanghai Diary: A Young Girl's Journey from Hitler's Hate to War-Torn China.* M Press, 2004.

Baenninger, Ron. *In the Eye of the Wind: A Travel Memoir of Prewar Japan.* McGill, Queen's UP, 2009.

Baennings, Rob. "Getting Out." *Headwaters: The Faculty Journal of the College of Saint Benedict and Saint John's University.* Vol. 25, 2008, pp. 122-130. *Digital Commons.*

Balfour, Michael, editor. *Theatre and War 1933-1945: Performance in Extremis.* Berghahn Books, 2001.

Baxter, Ian. *Auschwitz and Birkenau: Rare Photographs from Wartime*

SELECTED BIBLIOGRAPHY

Archives. Pen and Sword, 2016.

Bird, Peter. *The First Food Empire: A History of J. Lyons & Co.* Phillimore, 2000.

Black, Robert W. *Rangers in World War II*. Random House, 2010.

Blodig, Vojtěch, Miroslava Langhamerová and Jan Vajskebr. *Terezín Small Fortress 1940-1945: A Guide to the Permanent Exhibition in Terezín Small Fortress Museum*. Jitka Kejřová, V RÁJI Publishers, 2009.

Booker, Edna Lee. *Flight from China*. CreateSpace Independent Publishing Platform, 2012.

Bright, Frank. "Nazi Restrictions on the Jews of Prague and The Role of the Jewish Community Council." Holocaust Education & Archive Research Team, 2008. HolocaustResearchProject.org

"British Pathé: Newsreels, Video, Archive, Film, Footage, Stills." www.britishpathe.com

Brown, Alan. "'The Army of Lords': The Independent Czechoslovak Brigade 1940-45." *Exile Armies*. Bennett, M., and P. Latawski, editors. Palgrave Macmillan, 2005, pp. 7-17.

Brown, Alan. *The Czechoslovak Air Force in Britain, 1940-45*. 1998. University of Southampton, PhD dissertation.

Brown, Ian, ed. *The Economies of Africa & Asia in the Inter-War Depression*. Routledge, 2014.

Brown, Mendel. "The Jews of Modern China." *Jewish Monthly*, 3, 3, June 1949, pp. 158-163.

Brugioni, Dino A. and Robert G. Poirier. *The Holocaust Revisited: A Retrospective Analysis of the Auschwitz-Birkenau Extermination Complex*. Studies Archive Index, vol. 44, no. 4. pp. 11-29. CIA.gov.

Burg, David F., and L. Edward Purcell. *Almanac of World War I*. University Press of Kentucky, 2004.

Bush, Lawrence. "Jews in the Soviet-Polish War." Jewish

Currents, 24 August 2017.

Čapek, Thomas. *The Čechs (Bohemians) in America: A Study of Their National, Cultural, Political, Social, Economic and Religious Life*. 1920. Forgotten Books, 2012.

Chang, Iris. *The Rape of Nanking: The Forgotten Holocaust of World War II*. Basic Books, 1991.

Christina Warinner. "China 1934-1947." *Hennie Warinner: A Family History*. https://sites.google.com/site/henniewarinnerfamilyhistory/china-1934-1947

Clark, George B. *Treading Softly: U.S. Marines in China, 1819-1949*. Praeger, 2001.

Clinton, Fred. "Headquarters and Headquarters Company, 253d Infantry Regiment." 63rd Infantry Division. www.63rdinfdiv.com

Cohen, Gary. *The Politics of Ethnic Survival: Germans in Prague, 1861-1914*.

Collar, Hugh. *Captive in Shanghai: A Story of Internment in World War II*. Oxford UP, 1991.

Cooper, Nick. The Underground at War. *www.nickcooper.org.uk*

Cornwall, Mark. "'National Reparation'?: The Czech Land Reform and the Sudeten Germans, 1918-38." *The Slavonic and East European Review*. Vol. 75, No. 2 (April 1997), pp. 259-280.

Cox, Jim. *American Radio Networks: A History*. McFarland, 2009.

Cox, Jim. *The A to Z of American Radio Soap Operas*. Scarecrow Press, 2009.

Cox, Jim. *The Great Radio Soap Operas*. McFarland, 2008.

Crampton, Benjamin and Richard Crampton. *Atlas of Europe in the Twentieth Century*. Routledge, 1997.

Crichton, Tom. *1941: The Last Year of 'Our' East Asia*. River's Bend Press, 2013.

Danyan, Chen. *The Peace Hotel: A Non-fiction Novel*. Translated by Liu Hai Ming. Shanghai Press. 2015.

SELECTED BIBLIOGRAPHY

Davidson-Houston, J. V. *Yellow Creek: The Story of Shanghai.* Putnam, 1962, p.143.

Davis, Charles Noel. *A History of the Shanghai Paper Hunt Club, 1863-1930: With Complete Records of Hunts, Hunt Handicaps, Steeplechases and Point-to-Points.* Kelly and Walsh, 1930.

De Silva, Cara. *In Memory's Kitchen: A Legacy from the Women of Terezín.* Jason Aronson, Inc., 1996.

Denison, Edward and Guang Yu Ren. Building Shanghai: The Story of China's Gateway. Wiley, 2013. VirtualShanghai.net

"Der Fuhrer Schenkt Den Juden Eine Stadt." Archive.org, uploaded by Rhino White on 15 June 2014.

Dickson, Paul. *War Slang: American Fighting Words and Phrases Since the Civil War.* 3rd ed. Dover Publications, 2011.

Djordjevic, Nenad. *Old Shanghai Clubs and Associations: A Directory of the Rich Life of Foreigners in Shanghai from the 1840s to the 1950s.* Earnshaw Books, 2009.

Dong, Stella. *Shanghai: The Rise and Fall of a Decadent City, 1842-1949.* William Morrow Paperbacks, 2001.

Drubek, Natascha. 2016. "The Three Screenings of a Secret Documentary: *Theresienstadt* Revised." *Ghetto Films and their Afterlife.* Natascha Drubek, editor. *Apparatus. Film, Media and Digital Cultures in Central and Eastern Europe,* number 2-3, 2016. DOI: http://dx.doi.org/10.17892/app.2016.0003.51

Dunning, John. *On the Air: The Encyclopedia of Old-Time Radio.* Oxford UP, 1998.

Eber, Irene, ed. *Voices from Shanghai: Jewish Exiles in Wartime China.* University of Chicago Press, 2008.

Fantlova, Zdenka. *My Lucky Star.* Herodias, 2001.

Felton, Mark. *China Station: The British Military in the Middle Kingdom 1839-1997.* Pen and Sword Military, 2013.

Felton, Mark. *Japan's Gestapo: Murder, Mayhem and Torture in Wartime Asia.* Pen and Sword Military, 2012.

Field, Andrew David. *Shanghai's Dancing World: Cabaret Culture and Urban Politics, 1919-1954*. The Chinese University Press, 2010.

Flesch-Brunningen, Hans. "Die verfuhrte Zeit." Brandstatter, 1988. p. 15.

Frank, Benis M. "The Jewish Company of the Shanghai Volunteer Corps Compared with Other Jewish Diaspora Fighting Units." China and the Jewish Diaspora: A Comparative Historical Perspective on Acculturation, Economic Activity, Assimilation, Anti-Semitism, 1992.

Frank, Benis M. "The Shanghai Volunteer Corps: A Socio-Military History." Oral History Section, History and Museum Division, Headquarters U.S. Marine Corps.

French, Paul. *Bloody Saturday: Shanghai's Darkest Day*. Penguin China Specials, 2017.

French, Paul. "China Rhyming." www.chinarhyming.com

French, Paul. *Carl Crow – A Tough Old China Hand: The Life, Times, and Adventures of an American in Shanghai*. Hong Kong UP, 2006.

French, Paul. *Censoring Lady Chatterley in Shanghai: The Censorship of Western Culture and Entertainment in the Shanghai International Settlement, 1940/1941*. China Rhyming, 2017.

French, Paul. *The Old Shanghai A-Z*. Hong Kong UP, 2010.

Freyseisen, Astrid. *Shanghai und die Politik des Dritten Reiches*. Königshausen & Neumann, 2000.

Friedman, Herbert A. "The German-Japanese Propaganda Connection." Psywar.org, 2012.

Gellner, John. *Moonlight Flyer: Diary of a Second World War Navigator*. Fonthill Media, 2016.

Gilbert, Martin. *Atlas of the Holocaust*. William Morrow & Company, 1993.

Gillick, Muriel R. *Once They Had a Country: Two Teenage Refugees*

SELECTED BIBLIOGRAPHY

in the Second World War. University of Alabama Press. 2010.

Ginsbourg, Anna. "Shanghai: City of Refuge: Jewish Refugees in Shanghai." *China Weekly Review*, 1940, Shanghai, pp. 26-32.

Goldberg, Michelle. *The Goddess Pose: The Audacious Life of Indra Devi, the Woman Who Helped Bring Yoga to the West.* Vintage, 2016.

Goldstein, Jonathan and Benjamin I. Schwartz. *The Jews of China: v. 1: Historical and Comparative Perspectives.* Routledge, 1998.

Green, Gerald. *The Artists of Terezín: Illustrations by the Inmates of Terezín.* Shocken, 1978.

Grescoe, Taras. *Shanghai Grand.* St. Martin's Press, 2016.

Groom, Francis A. "A Review of Groom's 'Guide.'" Review of *With Boat and Gun in the Yangtze Valley* by Henling Thomas Wade. *The Sportsman's Diary for Shooting Trips in Northern China.* The North China Herald, 1873, pp. 132-134.

Haers, Jacquer, Bert Ingelaere, Stephan Parmentier, and Barbara Segaert, editors. *Genocide, Risk and Resilience: An Interdisciplinary Approach.* Palgrave Macmillan, 2013.

Hahn, Emily. *China to Me: A Partial Autobiography.* 1944. Open Road Media, 2014.

Hahn, Emily. *Miss Jill from Shanghai: A Novel.* Avon, 1950.

Hamerow, Theodore S. *Why We Watched: Europe, America, and the Holocaust.* W.W. Norton & Company, 2008.

Hasted, Nick. "London's Little Hollywood." *Empire*, January 1993, pp. 40-41.

Hauser, Ernest O. Shanghai: City for Sale. Harcourt, Brace and Company, 1940.

Henriot, Christian. "Virtual Shanghai." www.virtualshanghai.net

Henriot, Christian. "A Neighborhood Under the Storm: Zhabei and Shanghai Wars." *European Journal of East Asian Studies*, vol. 9, no. 2, 2010, pp.293-321.

Heppner, Ernest G. *Shanghai Refuge: A Memoir of the World War II Jewish Ghetto.* University of Nebraska Press, 1993.
Hibbard, Peter. *All About Shanghai and Environs: The 1945-35 Standard Guide Book.* Earnshaw Books, 2008.
Hibbard, Peter. *The Bund: China Faces West.* Airphoto International Ltd., 2007.
Hill, Max. *Exchange Ship.* Farrer and Rinehart, 1942.
Horakova, Pavla. "The History of the Cremation Movement in the Czech Lands." Radio Praha, 2005. Radio.cz
Horne, Gerald. *Race War: White Supremacy and the Japanese Attack on the British Empire.* NYU Press, 2005.
Hošková-Weissová, Helga. Translated by Neil Bermel. *Helga's Diary: A Young Girl's Account of Life in a Concentration Camp.* W.W. Norton & Company, 2014.
Ingelaere, Bert, Jacques Haers SJ, Stephan Parmentier, and Barbara Segaert, editors. *Genocide, Risk and Resilience: An Interdisciplinary Approach.* Rethinking Political Violence. Palgrave Macmillan. 2013.
"Intruder Kills Former Actress, August 28, 1958." The Daily Mirror: Los Angeles History. 28 August 2008. LATimesBlogs. LATimes.com
Isaksen, Kai. "Czechoslovak Exile Units of WWII." Military History Online. 2014. Militaryhistoryonline.com
Jackson, Isabella. *Shaping Modern Shanghai: Colonialism in China's Global City.* Cambridge UP, 2017.
Jackson, Stanley. *The Sassoons.* William Heinemann Ltd., 1968.
Jacobson & Cohen. *Terezín: The Daily Life, 1943-45.* London, 1946. Cjh.org
Jelavich, Peter. Berlin Cabaret. Studies in Cultural History. Harvard UP, 1996.
Jordan, Donald Allan. *China's Trial by Fire: The Shanghai War of 1932.* University of Michigan Press, 2001.

SELECTED BIBLIOGRAPHY

Karas, Joža. *Music in Terezín 1941-1945*. Beaufort Books, 1985.

Karns, Maurine and Pat Patterson. *Shanghai: High Lights, Low Lights, Tael Lights*. 1936. Earnshaw Books, 2010.

Karny, Miroslav. *Terezín Memorial Book. Jewish victims of Nazi deportations from Bohemia and Moravia, 1941-1945*. The Terezín Initiative Foundation, 1995.

Kieval, Hillel J. *The Making of Czech Jewry: National Conflict and Jewish Society in Bohemia, 1870-1918*. Studies in Jewish History. Oxford UP, 1988.

King, Frank H.H. *The Hongkong Bank Between the Wars and the Bank Interned, 1919-1945*. "Return from Grandeur," Volume III of The History of the Hongkong and Shanghai Banking Corporation. Cambridge UP, Cambridge, 1988.

Kludsky, Rudolf. *Könige der Manege*. Zsolnay, 1950.

Knyazeca, Katya. "Katya Knyazeva's Scrapbook: Shanghai History and Architecture." avezink.liverjournal.com

Korda, Alexander. Producer. *The Scarlet Pimpernel*. Directed by Harold Young, London Films, 23 Dec. 1934.

Kounin, I. I. *Eighty Five Years of the Shanghai Volunteer Corps*. Cosmopolitan Press, 1938.

Kranzler, David. *Japanese, Nazis and Jews: The Jewish refugee community of Shanghai, 1938-1945*. Yeshiva UP, 1976.

Krasno, Rena. *Strangers Always: A Jewish Family in Wartime Shanghai*. Pacific View Press, 1992.

Kuděla, Jiří. Českoslovenští židé v Šanghaji za druhé světové války. Časopisu Slezského muzea, Série B, Vědy historické, ročník 53, 2004, číslo 3, str. 247-278.

Kühnl, Karel and Juraj Lišja. *Vojenské osobnosti československého odboje 1939-1945*. Ministerstvo obrany České republiky— Agentura vojenských informací a služeb, 2005.

Kuklík, Jan. "The Recognition of the Czechoslovak Government in Exile and its International Status 1939-1942." *Prague Papers* on *History of International Relations*. Institute of World History, 1997, s. 173-205.

Kulka, Erich. "Escape from a Death Train." Review of the Society for the History of Czechoslovak Jews. Vol. 2, 1988-89.

Kulka, Erich. *Židé v Československém vojsku na západě*. Naše Vojsko, 1992.

Lake. Robert J. *A Social History of Tennis in Britain*. Routledge, 2016.

Lamont-Brown, Raymond. *Kempeitai: Japan's Dreaded Military Police*. Sutton Publishing, 1998.

Láníček, Jan and James Jordan, editors. *Governments-in-Exile and the Jews During the Second World War*. Vallentine Mitchell, 2013.

Láníček, Jan. *Czechs, Slovaks and the Jews, 1938-48: Beyond Idealisation and Condemnation*. Palgrave Macmillan, 2013.

Laska, Vera, compiler and editor. *The Czechs in America 1633-1977: A Chronology & Fact Book*. Oceana Publications, Inc., 1978.

Leck, Greg. *Captives of Empire: The Japanese Internment of Allied Civilians in China, 1941-1945*. Shandy Press, 2007.

Lederer, Zdenek. *Ghetto Theresienstadt*. 1953. Howard Fertig, 1983.

Levine, Hillel. *In Search of Sugihara: The Elusive Japanese Diplomat Who Risked His Life to Rescue 10,000 Jews from the Holocaust*. The Free Press, 1996.

Lewis, Helen. *A Time to Speak*. Da Capo Press, 1997.

Lewis, Rebecca. *The Formation of the Ministry of Information*. 2004, PhD dissertation extract. drbexl.co.uk

Lias, Godfrey. *Memories of Dr. Eduard Beneš from Munich to New War and New Victory*. 1954. George Allen & Ulan Press, 2012.

Lockhart, R.H. Bruce. *Jan Masaryk: A Personal Memoir*. Philosophical Library, 1951.

Lockhart, Robert Bruce. *Comes the Reckoning*. Putnam, 1947.

SELECTED BIBLIOGRAPHY

Longmate, Norman. *How We Lived Then: A History of Everyday Life During the Second World War.* Random House UK, 2002.

MacLellan, J. W. *The Story of Shanghai, from the Opening of the Port to Foreign Trade.* North-China Herald Office, 1889.

Margry, Karel. "A False Start. The Filming at Theresienstadt of January 20, 1944." *Ghetto Films and their Afterlife.* Natascha Drubek, editor. *Apparatus. Film, Media and Digital Cultures in Central and Eastern Europe*, number 2-3, 2016. DOI: http://dx.doi.org/10.17892.app.2016.0003.54

Martin, Hugues. "Shanghailander." shanghailander.net

Masaryk, Jan. *Speaking to My Country.* Lincolns-Prager, 1944.

Mastny, Vojtech. *Czechs Under Nazi Rule: The Failure of National Resistance, 1939-42.* Columbia UP, 1971.

McLaine, Ian. *Ministry of Morale: Home Front Morale and the Ministry of Information in World War II.* Allen & Unwin, 1979.

Meehan, John D. *Chasing the Dragon in Shanghai: Canada's Early Relations with China, 1858-1952.* UBC Press. 2011.

Meyer, Eliah, compiler. "The Most Secret List of SOE Agents." Archive.org, 2015. Meyer, Peter. *Czech Republic Jews in Soviet Satellites.* Syracuse, 1952.

Meyer, Maisie. *From the Rivers of Babylon to the Whangpoo: A Century of Sephardic Jewish Life in Shanghai.* University Press of America, 2003.

Meyer, Maisie. *The Sephardic Jewish Communities of Shanghai 1845-1939 and the Questions of Identity.* 1994. London School of Economics and Political Science, PhD dissertation.

Mingos, Howard, editor. *The Aircraft Year Book for 1943.* Aeronautical Chamber of Commerce of America, Inc., 1943.

Mones, Nicole. *Night in Shanghai.* Mariner Books, 2015.

Moor, Andrew. "Dangerous Limelight: Anton Walbrook and the Seduction of the English." *British Stars and Stardom — from Alma Taylor to Sean Connery.* Bruce Babington, editor.

Manchester UP, 2001, pp.80-93.
Morris, John. *Traveler from Tokyo.* The Cresset Press, 1943.
Mortimer, Roger, Richard Onglow, and Peter Willett. *Biographical Encyclopedia of British Flat Racing.* Macdonald and Jane's, 1978.
Muller, Filip. *Eyewitness Auschwitz: Three Years in the Gas Chambers.* Ivan R. Dee, 1999.
Münzel, Martin. "Expulsion—Plunder—Flight: Businessmen and Emigration from Nazi Germany." Universität zu Berlin, 2013. Immigrantentrepreneurship.org
Munzer, Zdenka and Jan. *We Were and We Shall Be: The Czechoslovak Spirit through the Centuries.* Frederick Ungar, 1941.
New, Christopher. *Shanghai: A Novel.* Summit Books, 1985.
"Newspaper SG." National Library Board, Singapore. https://eresources.nlb.gov.sg/newspapers/
"Newspapers.com." Ancestry. newspapers.com
Nish, Ian Hill. *Japanese Foreign Policy in the Interwar Period.* Praeger, 2002.
Norden, Albert. *The Thugs of Europe: The truth about the German people and its rulers.* German American League for Culture, 1942.
North-China Daily News online, Advisor: Professor Peter O'Connor (Musashino University, Japan), Leiden and Boston: Brill, 2016.
Nosková, Helena. "Festivities and Everyday Life of Russian 'White' Emigres in Prague Exile in Blending of History and Memories." Journal of Ethnology, 28:1, 2018, pp. 51-63.
Oakes, Vanya. *White Man's Folly.* Houghton Mifflin, 1943.
Paneth, Philip. *Czechs Against Germans.* Nicholson and Watson, 1939.
Parkinson, Joel. "The Circus Goes to War: Show Business and the Armed Forces of World War I." *World War History and Art Museum,* 2014.

SELECTED BIBLIOGRAPHY

Paul, Burton. *British Broadcasting: Radio and Television in the United Kingdom*. University of Minnesota Press, 1956.
Pečivová, Hana. *Historie Schichtovy Vily V Roztokách*. Diploma thesis. Univerzita Jana Evangelisty Purkyně, 2015.
Pollak, Oliver B. "Felix Bachmann's Medical Memoir of Terezín Concentration Camp." *Jewish Medical Resistance in the Holocaust*. Berghan Books, 2014, Chapter 17.
Powell, J.B. "Why U.S.S. Wake Surrendered to Japs." The Washington Post. September 1, 1942. ProQuest.
Powell, John B. *My Twenty-Five Years in China*. Macmillan, New York, 1945.
Pringle, Henry F. *Bridge House Survivor: Experiences of a Civilian Prisoner-of-War in Shanghai & Beijing 1942-1945*. Earnshaw Books, 2010.
"ProQuest Historical Newspapers." ProQuest. https://www.proquest.com/products-services/pq-hist-news.html
Quartier, Thomas and Eric Venbrux, eds. *Changing European Death Ways*. Nijmegen Studies in Thanatology, vol. 1. Lit Verlag, 2013.
"Radio Prague." www.radio.cz
"Raphael Schächter." *Music and the Holocaust*. World ORT. holocaustmusic.ort.org
Redlich, Gonda. *The Terezín Diary of Gonda Redlich*. UP of Kentucky, 1999.
Rees, Laurence. *Auschwitz: A New History*. Public Affairs, 2006.
Rees, Neil. *The Czech Connection: The Czechoslovak Government-in-Exile in London and Buckinghamshire during the Second World War*. 2005.
Reynolds, Quentin. *Officially Dead: The Story of Commander C.D. Smith*. Random House, 1945.
Ristaino, Marcia R. *The Jacquinot Safe Zone: Wartime Refugees in Shanghai*. Stanford UP, 2008.

Ristaino, Marcia Reynders. *Port of Last Resort: The Diaspore Communities of Shanghai.* Stanford UP, 2003.
Roberts, Frank. *Dealing with Dictators: The Destruction & Revival of Europe, 1930-70.* Weidenfeld & Nicolson, 1991.
Roberts, Robin. *Anne McCaffrey: A Life with Dragons.* University Press of Mississippi, 2007.
Robson, James. "Aristophanes, Gender & Sexuality." *Brill's Companion to the Reception of Aristophanes.* Publisher, 2016, pp. 44-66. DOI 10.1163/9789004324657_004
Rogers, Andrei. *But in My Case: An Immigrant's Life Story.* iUniverse, 2018.
Rosholt, Malcolm Collection. Historical Photographs of China. University of Bristol.
Ross, James R. *Escape to Shanghai: A Jewish Community in China.* Free Press, 1993.
Rothenberg, Gunther. *The Army of Francis Joseph.* Purdue UP, 1999.
Rottman, Gordon L. *FUBAR: Soldier Slang of World War II.* Chartwell Books, 2017.
Russo, Peter V. "Radio War in Shanghai." The News. 14 February 1942. Adelaide. Trove.
Sachar, Howard M. *A History of the Jews in America.* Knopf, 1992.
Sassoon, Sir Ellice Victor Elias Papers and Photographs, DeGolyer Library, Southern Methodist University.
Sayer, Derek. *The Coasts of Bohemia: A Czech History.* Translated by Alena Sayer. Princeton UP, 1998.
Schlaefrig, Friedrich. "David P. Boder Interviews Friedrich Schlaefrig; August 23,1946; Paris, France." *Voices of the Holocaust.* Translated by David Boder. Illinois Institute of Technology, 2009.
Schulhof, Joseph as told to Lewish Weiner. "From Prague to the Far East... The experiences of a Czech Jewish refugee in

SELECTED BIBLIOGRAPHY

Shanghai and Tianjin." *Review of the Society for the History of Czechoslovak Jews.* Vol 3, 1990. pp. 41-63.

Schumacker, Harris B. *The Evolution of Cardiac Surgery.* Indiana University Press, 1992.

Schumann, Coco. *The Ghetto Swinger: A Berlin Jazz-Legend Remembers.* DoppelHouse Press, 2016.

Schwertfeder, Ruth. *Women of Theresienstadt: Voices from a Concentration Camp.* Bloomsbury Academic, 1988.

Seldes, Gilbert. *Lysistrata: by Aristophanes.* 1934. The Heritage Press, 1962.

Sergeant, Harriet. *Shanghai.* John Murray Publishers, Ltd., 1999.

Shaw, Ralph. *Sin City.* 1976. Sphere, 1992.

Skřivan, Aleš, Jr. "Czechoslovak Companies in the Chinese Market between the World Wars (Škoda Works and Sellier & Bellot Cases)." *The Central European Journal of Social Sciences & Humanities.* 2014. cejsh.icm.edu.pl

Smetana, Vít. *In the Shadow of Munich: British policy towards Czechoslovakia from the Endorsement to the Renunciation of the Munich Agreement (1938-1942).* Karolinum Press, Charles University, 2008.

Smith, Andreas Whittam. "Bombs over Kensington." *The Kensington Society, 2014-2015,* pp. 53.55. kensingtonsociety.org

Solomon, Harvey. "When the Greenbrier and Other Appalachian Resorts Became Prisons for Axis Diplomats." *Smithsonian Magazine.* 21 February 2020.

Španiel, Oldřich. "Ceskoslovenska Armada Druheho Odboje." *News Flashes from Czechoslovakia Under Nazi Domination: The News Which Is Coming Through in Spite of Nazi Censorship,* no. 123. Czechoslovak National Council of America, 1942.

Spies, Gerty. *My Years in Theresienstadt: How One Woman Survived the Holocaust.* Translated by Jutta R. Tragnitz. Prometheus Books, 1997.

Springfield, Maurice. *Hunting Opium and Other Scents.* Norfolk and Suffolk Publicity, 1966.

Spurná, Helena. *Divadelní režisér a člověk Oldřich Stibor (1901–1943).* Univerzita Palackého v Olomouci, 2015.

Stone, Peter. *The Lady and the President: The Life and Loss of the S.S. President Coolidge.* Oceans Enterprises, 1997.

Strobin, Debora and Ilie Wacs. *An Uncommon Journey: From Vienna to Shanghai to America: A Brother and Sister Escape the Nazis.* Barricade Books, 2011.

Sugarman, Martin. "Hagedud Ha-Sini: The Jewish Company of the Shanghai Volunteer Corps, 1932-42." *Jewish Historical Studies,* vol. 41, 2007, pp. 183–208.

Sweet, Matthew. The West End Front: The Wartime Secrets of London's Grand Hotels. Faber & Faber, 2011.

Swett, Pamela E. *Selling Under the Swastika. Advertising and Commercial Culture in Nazi Germany.* Stanford UP, 2013.

Taussig, Vladimír George. The Suitcase Collection. Owned by Deborah Taussig-Boehner, Aiken, SC.

"The Men of Shanghai: Budget for a Taipan." *Fortune,* vol. XI, no. I, Time-Fortune, January 1935, p. 120.

The Port of Last Resort. Joan Grossman and Paul Rosdy. National Center for Jewish Film, 2000.

Thomson, Ruth. *Terezín: Voices from the Holocaust.* Candlewick, 2013.

Thompson, Leroy. *The World's First SWAT Team: W.E. Fairbairn and the Shanghai Municipal Police Reserve Unit.* Frontline Books, 2012.

"TimesMachine." The New York Times. timesmachine.nytimes.com

Topol, Tom. "A Remarkable Czechoslovak Diplomatic Passport and Its Bearer's Destiny." *Passport Collector.com,* 27 October 2016.

SELECTED BIBLIOGRAPHY

"Transports To and From Terezín." The Terezín Initiative. www.porges.net/Terezín/TransportsToFromTerezín.html

Troller, Norbert. *Theresienstadt: Hitler's Gift to the Jews.* Edited by Joel Shatzky. Translated by Susan E. Cernyak-Spatz. UNC Press, 1991.

Tsuan, Victor T. H., editor. *For World Peace, Freedom and Justice: 60 Years: Shanghai Tiffin Perspective.* 2nd ed. Adams Press, 1988.

"Two Poems." Translated by Stephen Jolly from *The Death Factory* by Otta Kraus and Erich Kulka. *Jewish Quarterly*, 13:2, 33, 1965. DOI: 10.1080/0449010X.1965.10706436.

Ullrich, Volker. *Hitler: Ascent, 1889-1939.* Knopf, 2016.

"United States Holocaust Memorial Museum." www.ushmm.org

Vierling, Birgit. "Kommunikation als Mittel politischer Mobilisierung: Die Sudetendeutsche Partei (SDP) auf ihrem Weg zur Einheitsbewegung in der Ersten Tschechoslowakischen Republik (1933-1938)." *Studien zur Ostmitteleuropaforschung*, no. 27. Herder Institut, Marburg, 2014.

Voticky, Anka. *Knocking on Every Door.* E-book. The Azrieli Series of Holocaust Survivor Memoirs, 2010.

Wakeman, Frederic and Wen-hsin Yeh, editors. *Shanghai Sojourners.* Berkeley: Institute of East Asian Studies, University of California, 1992, pp. 5-7.

War Refugee Board. The Auschwitz Protocols: A Report by the War Refugee Board, November 1944.

Ward, Warwick. Producer. *The Man from Morocco.* Directed by Mutz Greenbaum, Associated British Picture Corporation, 9 April 1945.

Wasserstein, Bernard. *On the Eve: The Jews of Europe Before the Second World War.* Simon & Schuster, 2012.

Wasserstein, Bernard. *Secret War in Shanghai: Treachery, Subversion*

& *Collaboration in the Second World War*. Profile Books, 1998.
Watson, Milton H. *Flagships of the Line: A Celebration of the World's Three-Funnel Liners*. HarperCollins, 1988.
Wein, Martin. *History of Jews in the Bohemian Lands*. Koninklijke-Brill, 2016.
Wein, Martin J. "The Czechoslovak Exile in London and the Jews 1938-1945." *Governments-in-Exile and the Jews During World War II*. Edited by James Jordan and Jan Láníček. Vallentine Mitchell & Co Ltd., 2013.
Weiner, Pavel. *A Boy in Terezín: The Private Diary of Pavel Weiner, April 1944-April 1945*. Northwestern UP, 2011.
Weinzierl, Erika. (2003). The Jewish Middle Class in Vienna in the Late Nineteenth and Early Twentieth Centuries. University of Minnesota, Center for Austrian Studies.
West, Nigel. *Historical Dictionary of British Intelligence*. 2nd ed., Scarecrow Press. 2014.
White, Lewis, editor. *On All Fronts: Czechs and Slovaks in World War II*. East European Monographs. Columbia UP, 1991.
Who Was Who 1941-1950. Adam & Charles Black, 1967.
Williams, David. *Lifeline Across the Sea: Mercy Ships of the Second World War and Their Repatriation Missions*. The History Press, 2015.
Wingfield, Nancy M. *Flag Wars and Stone Saints: How the Bohemian Lands Became Czech*. Harvard UP, 2007.
Wiskemann, Elizabeth. *Czechs & Germans: A Study of the Struggle In the Historic Provinces of Bohemia and Moravia*. 2nd ed. Macmillan, 1967.
Wubs, Ben. International Business and National War Interests: Unilever Between Reich and Empire, 1939-1945 Routledge International Studies in Business History. Routledge, 2008.
"Yad Vashem: The World Holocaust Remembrance Center." www.yadvashem.org

SELECTED BIBLIOGRAPHY

Yeh, Wen-hsin. *Shanghai Splendor: A Cultural History, 1843-1949*. University of California Press, 2008.

Yokota-Murakami, Takayuki. "The Sexual Body in Exile: The Somatic Politics of the (White) Russian and Russian Jews in Manchuria and Japan." New Zealand Slavonic Journal, vol. 44, 2010, pp. 13-25. JSTOR.

Zeitin, Joseph. "The Shanghai Jewish Community: An Historical Sketch." *Jewish Life*, 12, 4, Oct. 1973, pp 54-68.

Zhaojin, Ji. *A History of Modern Shanghai Banking: The Rice and Decline of China's Finance Capitalism*. Routledge, 2002.

Ziegler, Philip. *London at War*. Alfred A. Knopf, 1995.

About The Authors

Deborah Taussig-Boehner is the owner of her father's suitcase and its contents. She began to seriously piece together the suitcase's story in 2012 and, after many years of research, she is now able to reveal the suitcase's fascinating stories to the world. Debbie is a graduate of Syracuse University with BS and MA degrees, and a retired educational administrator.

Lauren Housman is an emerging writer from South Carolina. She received her BA in Language Arts and Literature from the University of South Carolina Aiken in 2010 and her MFA in Creative Nonfiction from Converse College in 2014. Immediately after earning her MFA, she seized the opportunity to work on *The Suitcase*, her first book-length work.

Vladimir George Taussig (1899-1966), whose writings and memoirs are the basis for *The Suitcase*, and without which there would be no story to tell.

www.ingramcontent.com/pod-product-compliance
Lightning Source LLC
LaVergne TN
LVHW030054090526
838199LV00127B/6454